CUBISM

Authors: Guillaume Apollinaire, Dorothea Eimert, Anatoli Podoksik

Layout:
Baseline Co. Ltd
61A-63A Vo Van Tan Street
4th Floor
District 3, Ho Chi Minh City
Vietnam

ISBN : 978-1-84484-749-5

Printed in India

Guillaume Apollinaire, Dorothea Eimert, Anatoli Podoksik

CUBISM

PARKSTONE
INTERNATIONAL

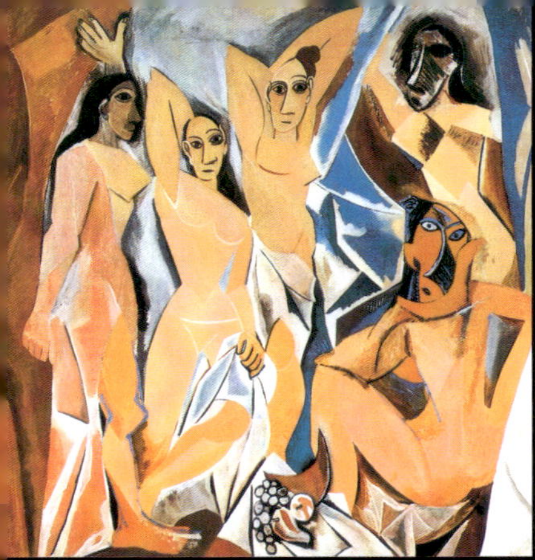

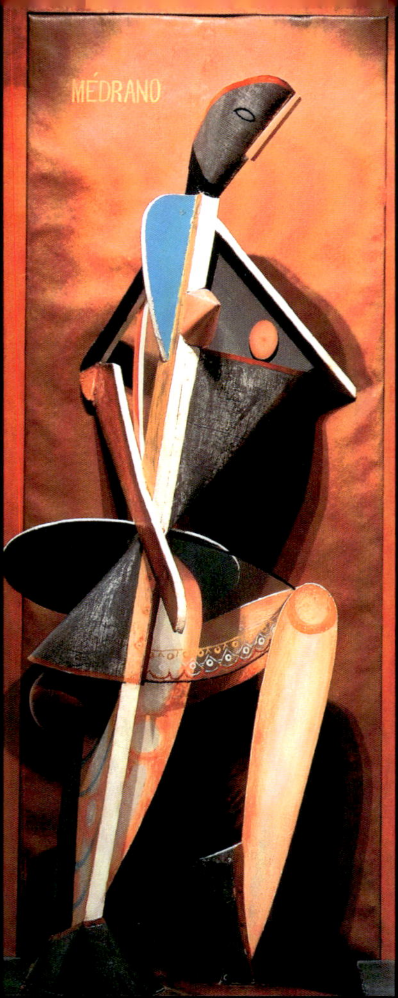
MÉDRANO

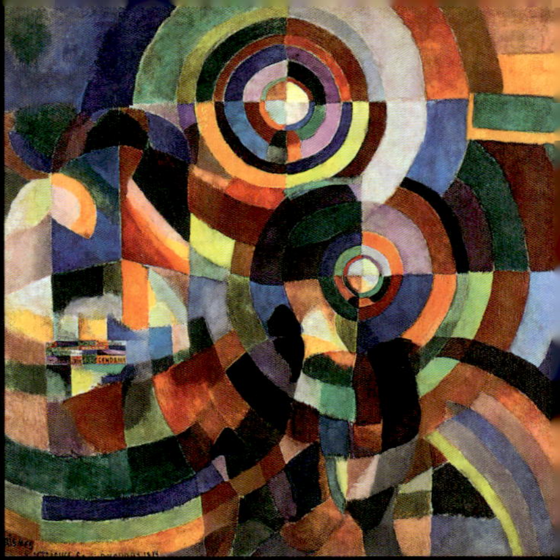

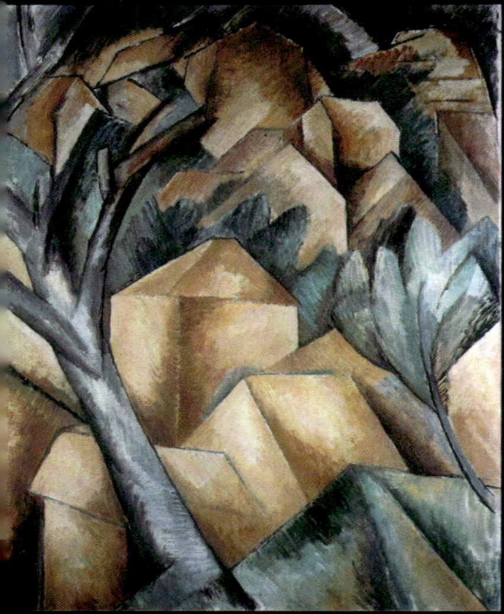

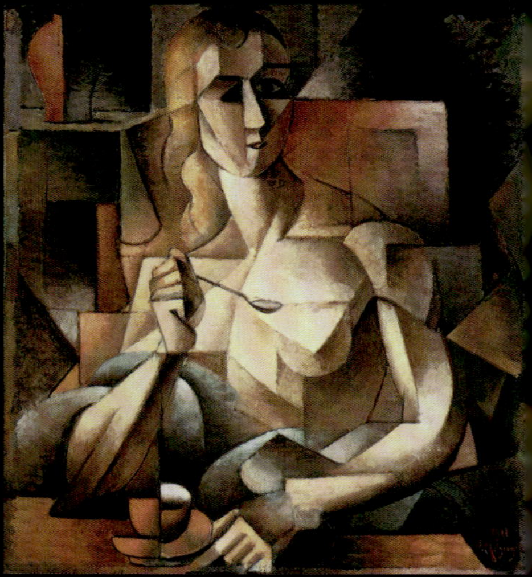

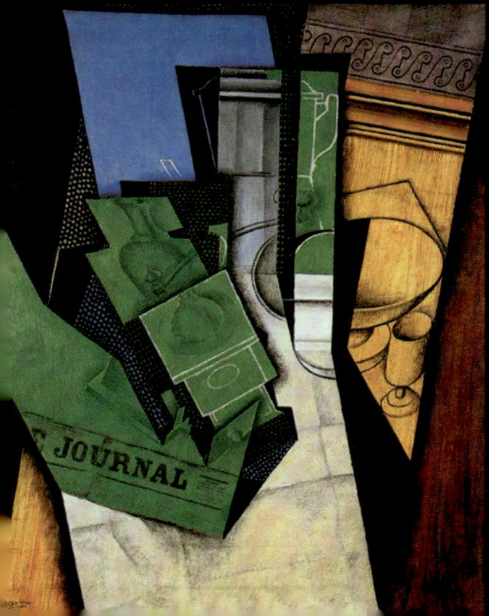
JOURNAL

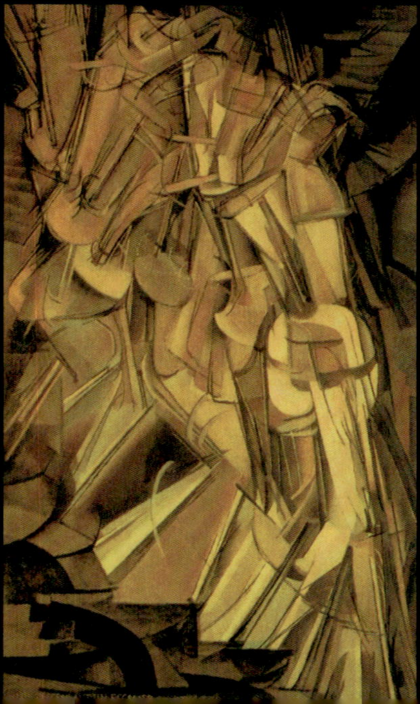

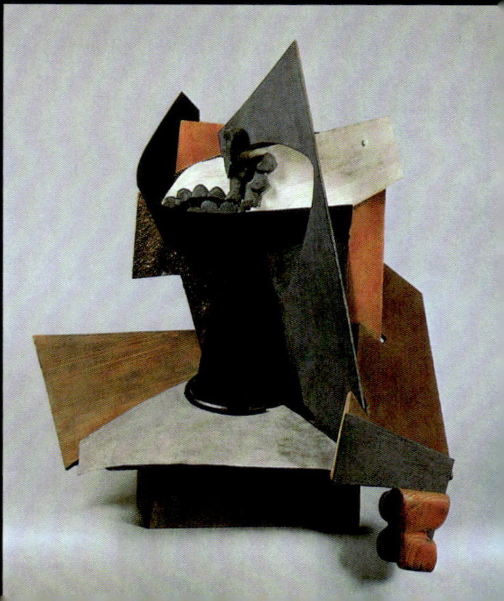

Contents

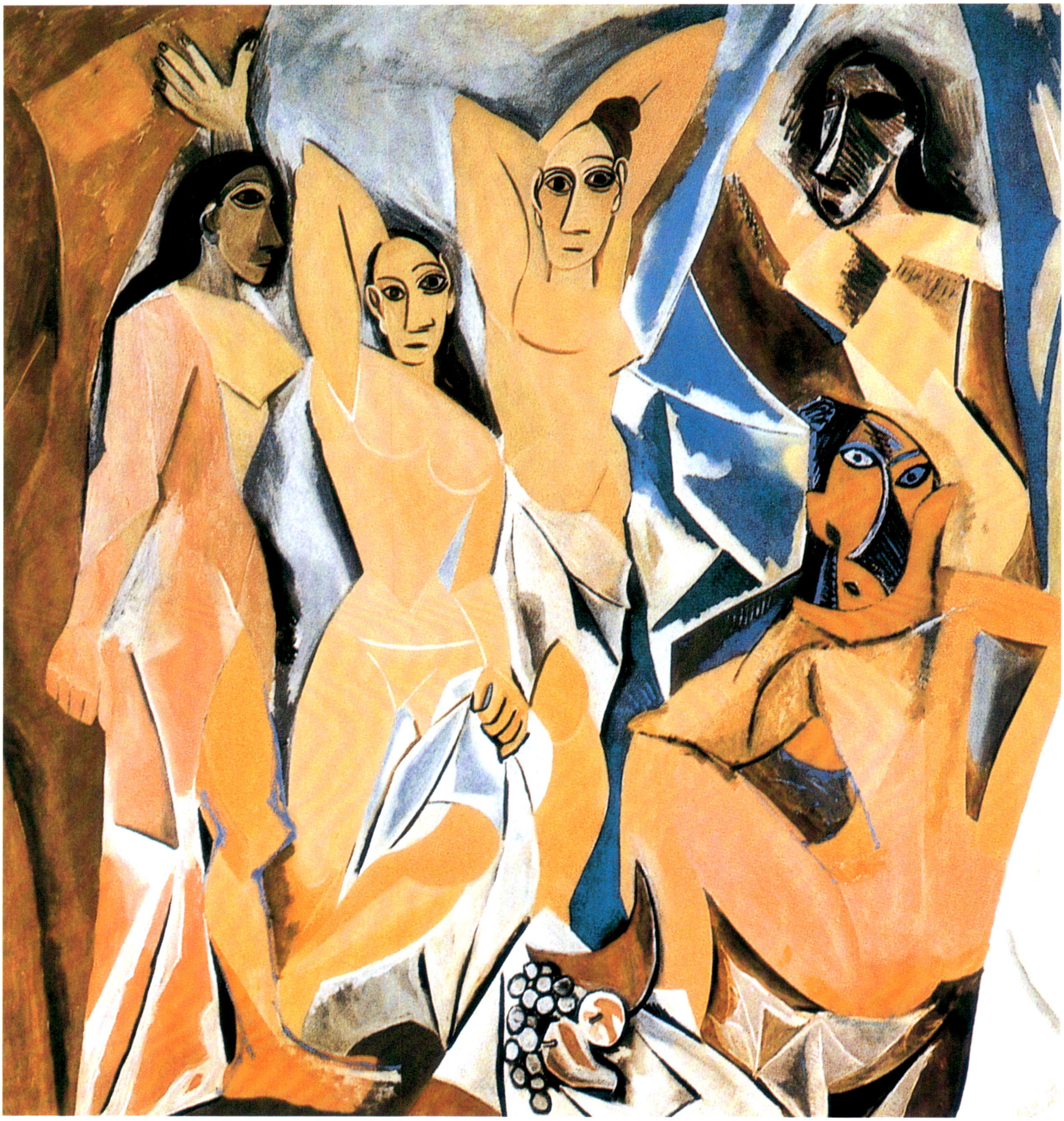

I. *Aesthetic Meditations on Painting: The Cubist Painters* by Guillaume Apollinaire

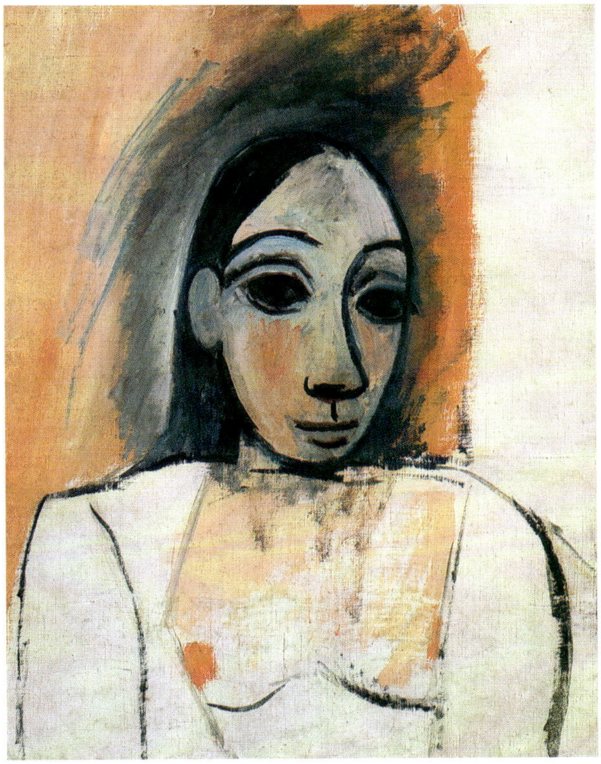

I

The plastic virtues, purity, unity and truth, hold nature down beneath their feet. In vain the rainbow is bent, the seasons vibrate, the crowds rush on to death, science undoes and remakes that which already exists, whole worlds withdraw forever from our conception, our transitory images repeat themselves or revive their unconsciousness, and the colours, odours, sounds which follow astonish us, then disappear from nature.

This monster of beauty is not eternal.

We know that our breath has had no beginning, and will have no end, but we conceive first of all the creation and the end of the world.

Nevertheless, too many artists still adore plants, stones, waves, or men.

One quickly becomes accustomed to the bondage of the mysterious. And this servitude ends by creating soft leisure.

One allows the labourer to dominate the universe, and gardeners have less respect for nature than the artists.

It is time to be masters. Good will does not insure victory.

The mortal forms of love dance on this side of eternity, and the name of nature sums up their accursed discipline.

The flame is the symbol of painting, and the three plastic virtues radiate in burning.

The flame is of a purity which tolerates nothing alien, and cruelly transforms in its own image that which it touches.

The flame has a magic unity—if it is divided, each spark is like unto the single flame.

It has, finally, the sublime truth of its own light, which no one can deny.

In spite of natural forces, the virtuous artist painters of this occidental epoch contemplate their purity.

It is forgetfulness after study. And, if a pure artist should ever die it would be necessary that all those of the past ages should not have existed.

In the Occident, painting purifies itself with this ideal logic which the old painters have transmitted to the new as if they had given them life.

Pablo Picasso,
Les Demoiselles d'Avignon, 1907.
Oil on canvas, 243.9 x 233.7 cm.
The Museum of Modern Art, New York.

Pablo Picasso,
Bust of a Woman (study for *Les Demoiselles d'Avignon*), 1907.
Oil on canvas, 58.5 x 46 cm.
Musée Picasso, Paris.

And that is all.

No one can carry his father's body everywhere with him. He abandons it to the company of the other dead. And he remembers it, regrets it, speaks of it with admiration. And, if he becomes a father himself, he must not expect any of his children to multiply themselves for the life of his corpse.

But, it is in vain that our feet detach themselves from the soil that holds the dead.

To contemplate purity is to baptise instinct, to humanise art, and to deify personality.

The root, the stalk and the flower of the lily show the progress of purity to its symbolic bloom.

All bodies are equal before the light and their modifications come from this luminous power which moulds them according to its will.

We do not know all the colours, and each man invents new ones.

But the painter must, above all, become himself the spectator of his own divinity, and the pictures which he offers to the admiration of men will confer upon them also the glory of exercising for the moment their own divinity.

For this it is necessary to embrace at a glance the past, present and future.

The canvas should present that essential unity which alone can produce ecstasy.

Then, nothing transient will be dashed off at random. We will not suddenly be turning backwards. Free spectators, we will not give up our life because of our curiosity. The salt smugglers of appearances will not be able to pass our statues of salt before the custom house of reason.

We will not go astray in the unknown future, which, separated from eternity, is only a word designed to tempt man.

We will not exhaust ourselves seizing the too fugitive present, for fashion after all can only be for the artist the mask of death.

The picture will exist inevitably. The vision will be entire, complete, and its infinity, instead of marking an imperfection, will only bring out the relation between a new creature and a new creator, only this and nothing more. Otherwise there will be no unity, and the connection which the different points of the canvas have with different geniuses, with different objects, with different lights, will show only a multiplicity of inharmonious dissimilarities.

For, if there can be an infinite number of creatures, each one attesting to its creator, with no creation to block the extent of those coexistences, it is impossible to conceive of them at one and the same time, and death is the result of their juxtaposition, of their mingling, of their love.

Each divinity creates after his own image: so too, the painters. And it is only photographers who manufacture reproductions of nature.

Neither purity nor unity count without the truth, which cannot be compared to reality, since truth is always the same, outside all nature, which exerts itself to hold us within the fatal order of things wherein we are only animals.

Pablo Picasso,
Nude (Bust), 1907.
Oil on canvas, 61 x 46.5 cm.
The State Hermitage Museum,
St. Petersburg.

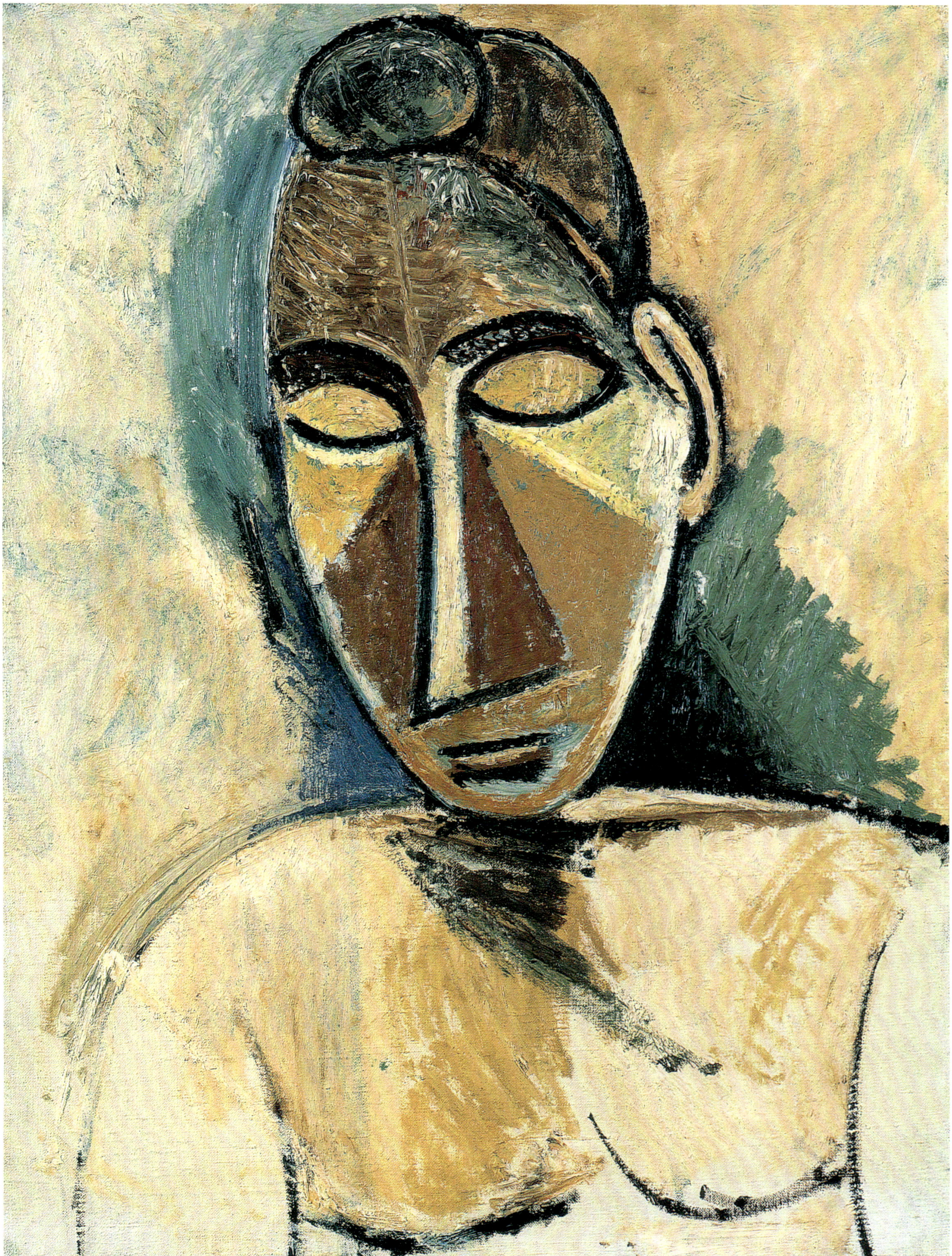

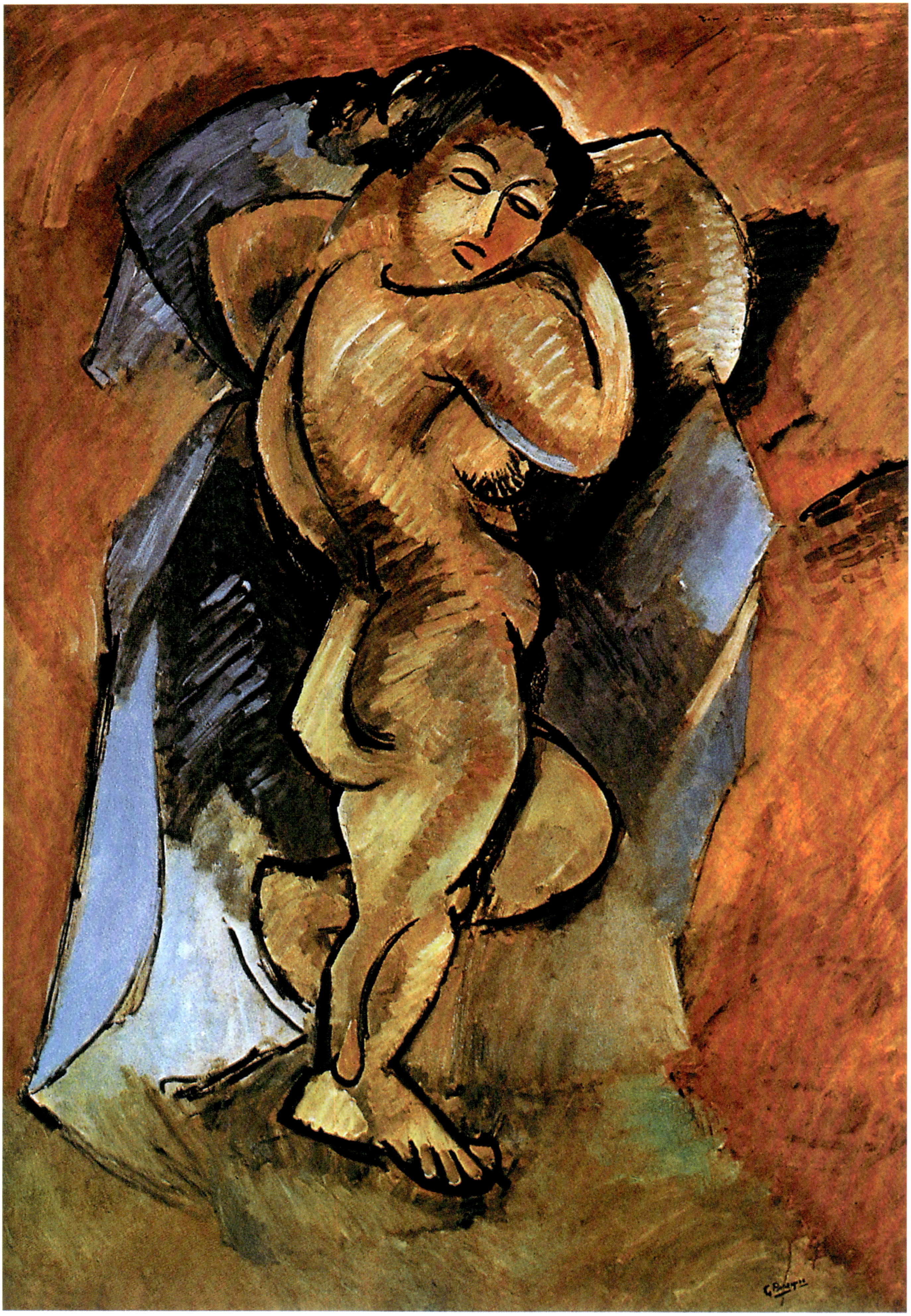

Above all, artists are men who wish to become inhuman. They seek painfully the traces of inhumanity, traces which are never found in nature. These are the real truths, and beyond them we know no reality.

But reality is never discovered once and for all. The truth will always be new. Otherwise, truth would be a system even more miserable than nature.

In this case, the deplorable truth, every day more distant, less distinct, less real, would reduce painting to a state of plastic writing destined simply to facilitate the relations between people of the same race.

In our day, a machine would quickly be invented which without our comprehension reproduced such signs.

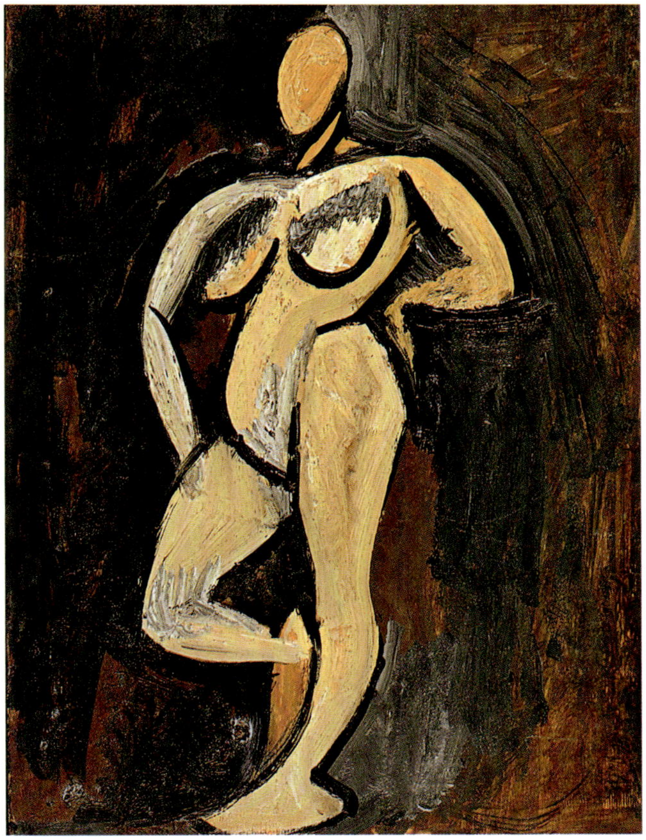

II

Many of the new painters paint only pictures which have no actual subject. And the titles which one finds in the catalogues play merely the role of the names that designate men without characterising them.

I have seen canvases entitled: *Solitude*, where there were several people, just as there are Mr. Stouts who are very thin, and Mr. Blonds who are very dark.

In the cases in question, the artists even condescend occasionally to make use of vaguely explicative terms, such as *portrait*, *landscape*, *still life*; many, however, of the young artists use only the general term, *painting*.

These painters, even if they still observe nature, no longer imitate her, and they carefully avoid the representation of natural scenes studiously observed and reconstructed.

Actual resemblance no longer has any importance because everything is sacrificed by the artists to the verities, to the necessities of a superior nature which he presupposes without exposing. The subject no longer counts, or if it counts at all, counts for very little.

Generally speaking, modern art repudiates most of the means of pleasing which were used by the great artists of past times.

Today, as formerly, the aim of painting is still the pleasure of the eye, but the demand henceforward made upon the amateur is to find a pleasure other than the one which the spectacle of natural things could just as well provide.

Thus one travels toward an entirely new art, which compared to painting as it has been looked upon heretofore, shall be what music is to literature.

It will be the essence of painting, just as music is the essence of literature.

The amateur of music experiences, in listening to a concert, joy of a different order from the joy he feels in listening to natural sounds, like the murmur of a stream, the roar of a waterfall, the whistling of the wind in a forest, or the harmonies of human language founded on reason and not on aesthetics.

Georges Braque,
Large Nude, 1907-1908.
Oil on canvas, 142 x 102 cm.
Private collection.

Pablo Picasso,
Standing Nude, 1908.
Oil on canvas, 27 x 21 cm.
Musée Picasso, Paris.

In the same way, the new painters will provide their admirers with artistic sensations due solely to the harmony of odd lights.

Everyone knows Pliny's anecdote of Apelles and Protogenes. It demonstrates clearly the aesthetic pleasure resulting solely from this odd combination of which I have spoken.

Apelles landed one day on the Isle of Rhodes to see the works of Protogenes, who lived there. Protogenes was not in his studio when Apelles arrived. An old woman was there guarding a large canvas ready to be painted. Instead of leaving his name, Apelles drew on the canvas a line so delicate that nothing subtler could be conceived.

On his return Protogenes, seeing the drawn line, recognised the hand of Apelles, and traced thereupon a line of another colour even more subtle, in such a way that there appeared to be three.

Apelles came back again the next day, without finding him whom he sought, and the subtlety of the line he drew that day reduced Protogenes to despair. This sketch was for a long time the admiration of connoisseurs who viewed it with as much pleasure as if gods and goddesses had been depicted instead of almost invisible tracings.

The secret aim of the young artists of the extreme schools is to produce pure painting. It is an entirely new art. It is still in its first stage, and is not yet as abstract as it would like to be. Most of the young painters work a great deal with mathematics without knowing it, but they have not yet abandoned nature whom they patiently question so that she may teach them the way of life. A Picasso studies an object as a surgeon dissects a body.

This art of pure painting, if it succeeds in disengaging itself entirely from the ancient school of painting, will not necessarily cause such painting to disappear, any more than the development of music has caused the disappearance of different kinds of literature, or than the acridity of tobacco has replaced the savour of food.

III

The new artists have been violently reproached for their geometric preoccupations. And yet, geometric figures are the essence of drawing. Geometry, the science which has for its scope space, its measurements and its relations, has been from time immemorial the rule even of painting.

Up to now, the three dimensions of the Euclidean geometry have sufficed for the solicitude which the sentiment of the infinite arouses in the soul of great artists.

The new painters do not propose, any more than did the old, to be geometricians. But, it may be said that geometry is to the plastic arts what grammar is to the art of the writer. Today scholars no longer hold to the three dimensions of the Euclidean geometries. The painters have been led quite naturally and, so to speak, by intuition, to preoccupy themselves with possible new measures of space, which in the language of modern studios has been designated briefly and altogether by the term the *fourth* dimension.

The fourth dimension as it is presented to the understanding from the plastic point of view would be engendered by the three known dimensions; it would show the immensity of space

Pablo Picasso,
Bread and Fruit Bowl on a Table,
1908-1909.
Oil on canvas, 164 x 132.5 cm.
Kunstmuseum, Basel.

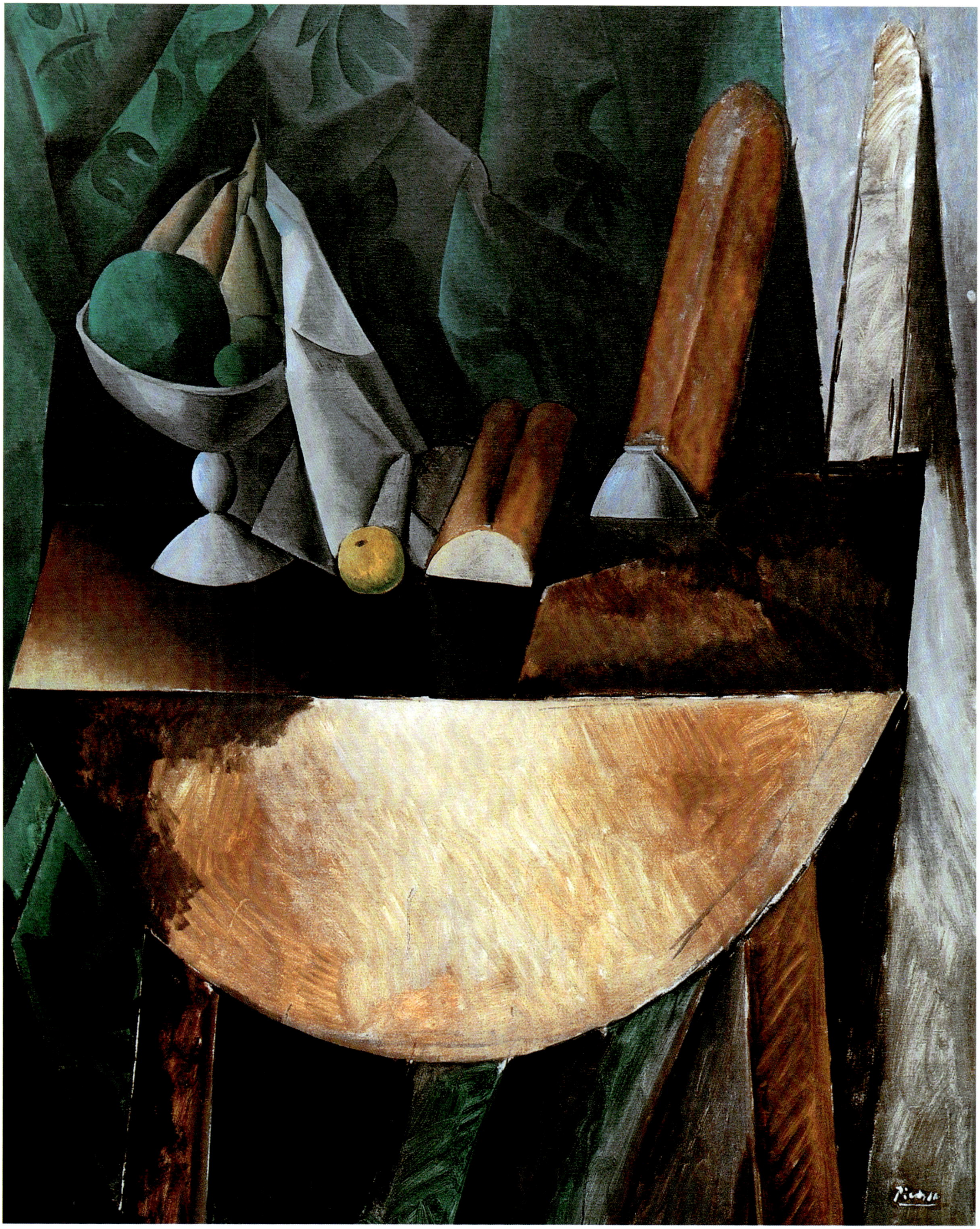

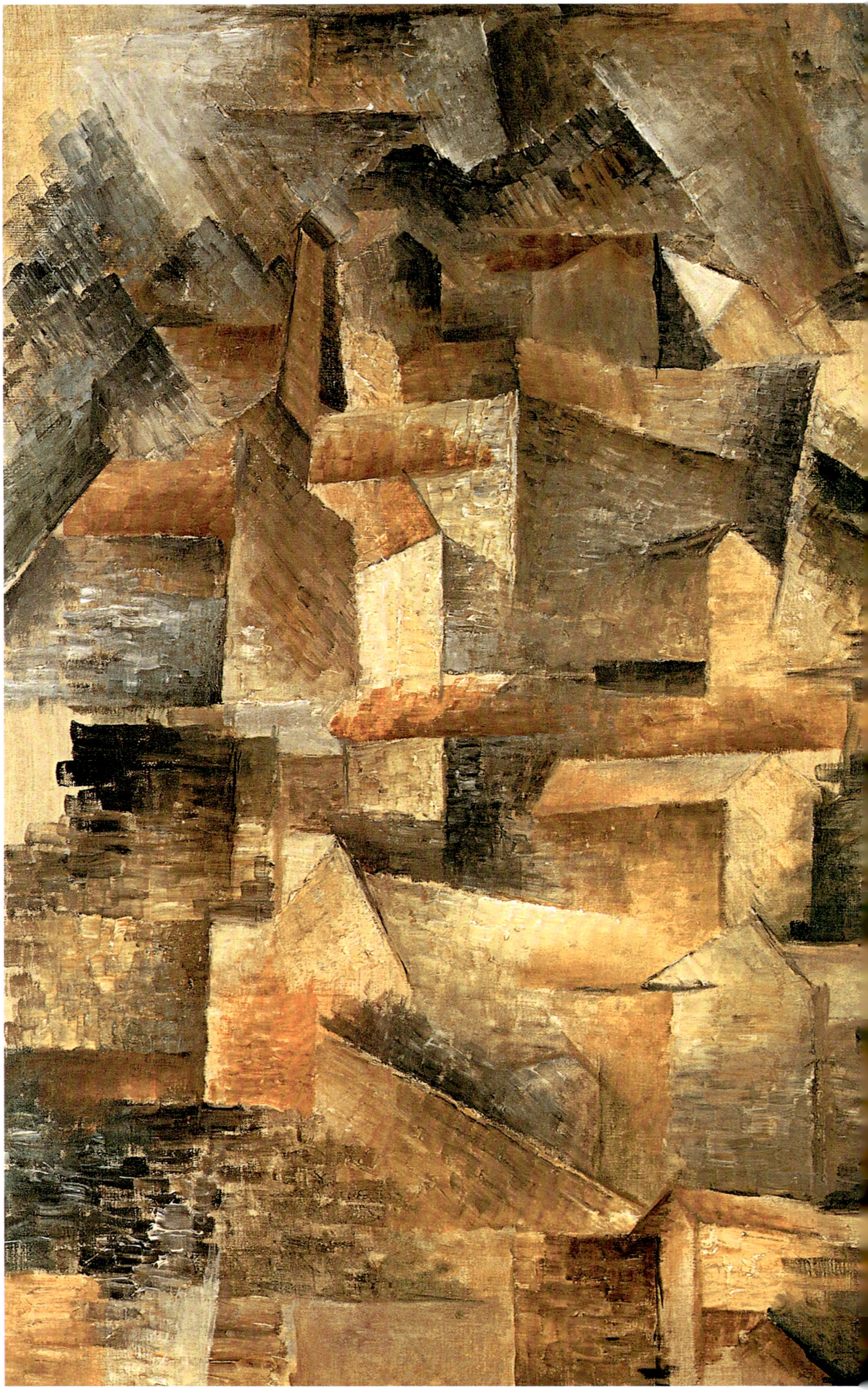

Georges Braque,
The Factories of Rio-Tinto in Estaque,
1910.
Oil on canvas, 65 x 54 cm.
Musée National d'Art Moderne,
Centre Georges-Pompidou, Paris.

Georges Braque,
Pitcher and Violin, 1909-1910.
Oil on canvas, 117 x 73.5 cm.
Kunstmuseum, Basel.

Pablo Picasso,
Nude Woman, 1910.
Oil on canvas, 187.3 x 61 cm.
National Gallery of Art, Washington, D.C.

Sonia Delaunay,
La Prose du Transsibérien et de la petite Jehanne de France (Prose of the Trans-Siberian and Little Jehanne of France),
1913.
Collaborative artists' book by
Blaise Cendrars, Copy 139.
Watercolour and text printed on
Japanese paper, open book:
199 x 36 cm; closed book: 18 x 11 cm.
Musée National d'Art Moderne,
Centre Georges-Pompidou, Paris.

Robert Delaunay,
Eiffel Tower, 1911.
Oil on canvas, 202 x 138.4 cm.
Solomon R. Guggenheim Museum,
New York.

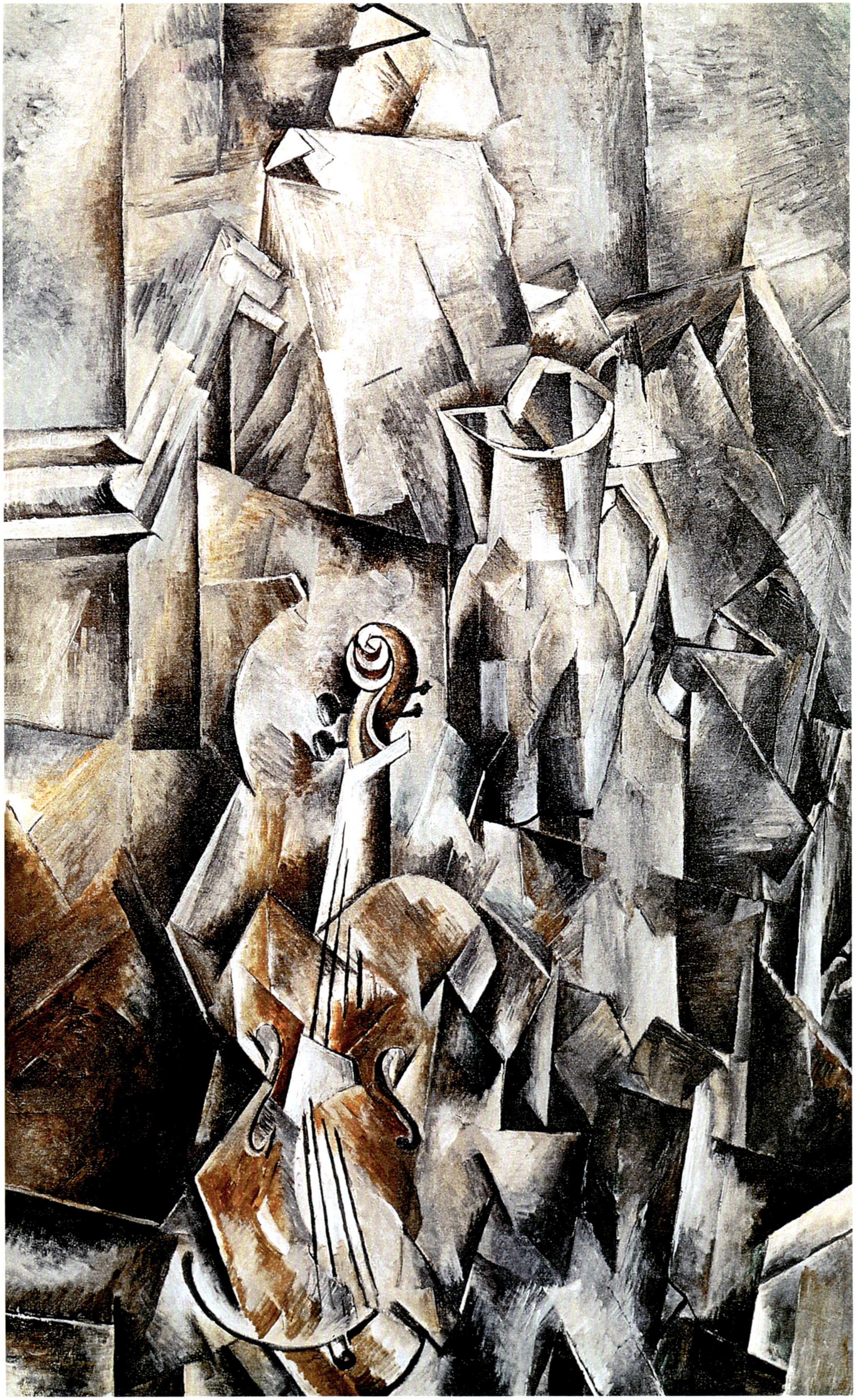

eternalised in every direction at a given moment. It is space itself, the dimension of the infinite: it is this which endows objects with their plasticity. It gives them the proportions which they merit as a part of the whole, whereas, in Greek art, for example, a somewhat mechanical rhythm unceasingly destroys the proportions.

Greek art had a purely human conception of beauty. It took man as the standard of perfection. The art of the new painters takes the infinite universe as the ideal, and it is this ideal that necessitates a new measure of perfection, which permits the artist to give to the object proportions which conform to the degree of plasticity to which he desires to bring it.

Nietzsche divined the possibility of such an art: "O divine Dionysius, why dost thou pull my ears?" Ariadne demands of her philosophical lover in one of the celebrated dialogues on *The Isle of Naxos*. "I find something pleasant and agreeable in thy ears, Ariadne. Why are they not still longer?"

Nietzsche, when he recalled this anecdote, put into the mouth of Dionysius the condemnation of Greek art.

Let us add, in order that today nothing more than an historical interest may attach to the utopian expression—the fourth dimension—which must be noted and explained, that it was only a manifestation of the aspirations and disquietudes of a large number of young artists contemplating the Egyptian and Oceanic sculptures, meditating on the works of science, and awaiting a sublime art.

IV

Wishing to attain the proportions of the idea, not limiting themselves to humanity, the young painters offer us works which are more cerebral than sensual. To express the grandeur of metaphysical forms, they withdraw further and further from the former art of optical illusions and local proportions. This is why the present art, even if it is not the direct emanation of determined religious beliefs, presents nevertheless several characteristics of religious art.

V

It is the social function of the great poets and the great painters to renew unceasingly the appearance which nature assumes in the eyes of men.

Without the poets, without the artists, men would quickly tire of the monotony of natural phenomena.

The sublime idea which they have of the universe would come tumbling down with a vertiginous rapidity.

The order which appears in nature and which is only an effect of art would immediately vanish. Everything would break up in chaos. No more seasons, no more civilisation, no more thought, no more humanity, no more of life itself; impotent obscurity would reign forever. By mutual consent the poets and the artists determine the features of their epoch and docilely the future falls in with their plan.

The general structure of an Egyptian mummy conforms to the figures outlined by the Egyptian artists, and yet the ancient Egyptians differed greatly from each other. They conformed to the art of their epoch.

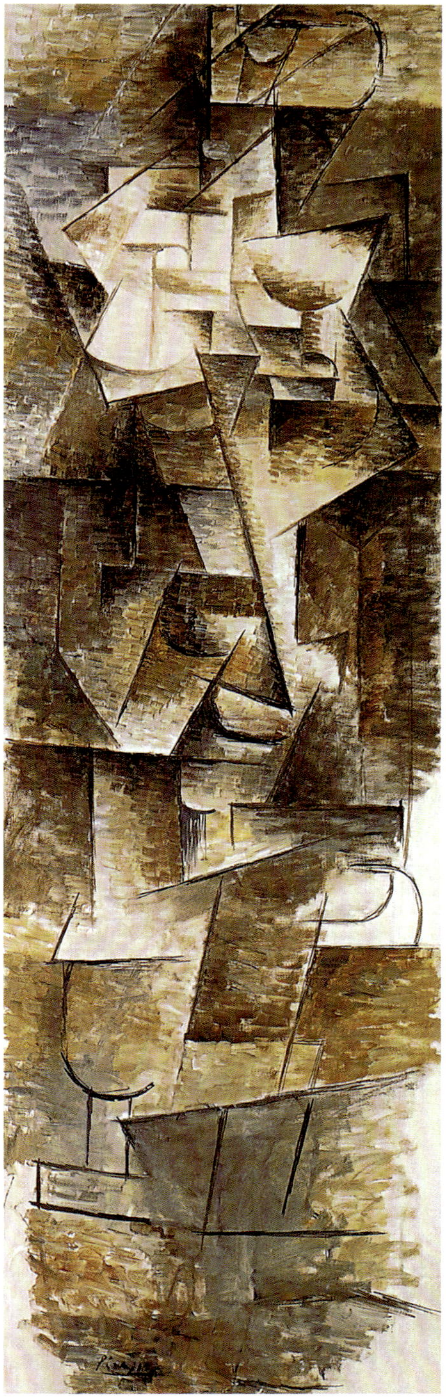

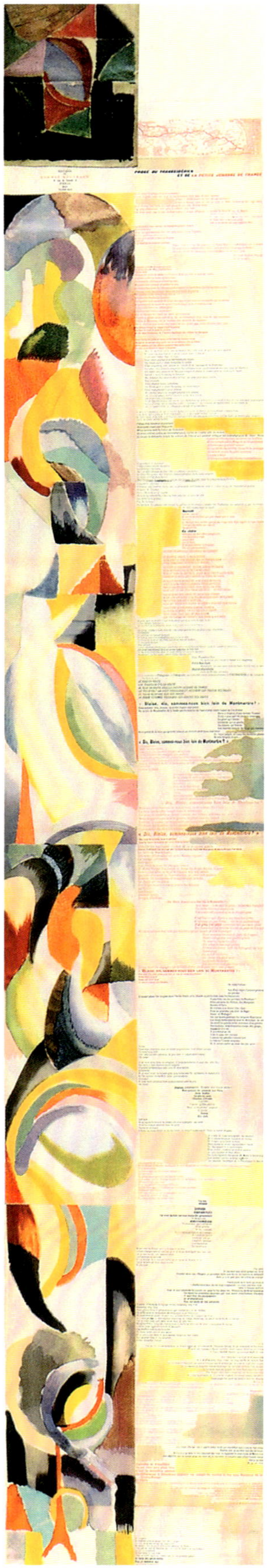

To create the illusion—the type—is the real quality of art, its social role. God knows how the pictures of Manet and Renoir were mocked! It sufficed to cast an eye upon the photographs of their epoch to see how the people and things conform to the pictures which these great artists have painted.

The works of art being, from the plastic point of view, the most energetic products of a period, this illusion appears to me quite natural. This energy imposes itself on men and is for them the plastic measure of an epoch. Thus, those who mock the new painters make fun of their own features, for the people of the future will imagine the human beings of today as they have been represented by the artists of the most vital, that is to say, the newest art. Do not say to me that there are today other artists who paint in such a way that mankind will recognise itself as portrayed in their image. All the works of art of an epoch end by resembling the most expressive and the most typical art of that period. Dolls are the outlet of a popular art; they seem always to be inspired by the great art of the same epoch. This is a truth easy to verify. And yet who would dare to say that the dolls which were sold in the bazaars of 1880 had been manufactured with a sentiment analogous to that of Renoir when he painted his portraits? Then, nobody noticed it. It signifies, nevertheless, that the art of Renoir was energetic enough and vital enough to impose itself on our senses, while to the great public at the time when he started his conceptions appeared to be mad absurdities.

VI

One has often, and notably in the case of the most recent painters, been confronted by the possibility of a mystification or of a collective error.

But no one knows, in all the history of art, of a single collective mystification any more than of a collective artistic error. There are isolated cases of mystification and error, but the conventional elements of which in part the works of art are composed assure us that errors would not know how to exist collectively.

If the new school of painting had presented us with one of these cases, it would be an event so extraordinary that it could be called a miracle. To conceive a case of this sort would be to conceive that suddenly in a nation all the children should be born without heads or with only one arm or leg, a conception evidently absurd. There are no collective errors or mystifications in art. There are only diverse epochs—diverse schools of art. If the end pursued by each one is not equally elevated, equally pure, all are equally respectable, and according to the ideas which each has of beauty, each school of art is successively admired, despised and again admired.

VII

The new school of painting bears the name of Cubism; it was so called in derision by Henri Matisse, who in the autumn of 1908 had just seen a picture representing houses, the cubic appearance of which had greatly impressed him.

These new aesthetics were first elaborated in the mind of André Derain, but the most important and audacious works which the movement at once produced were those of a great

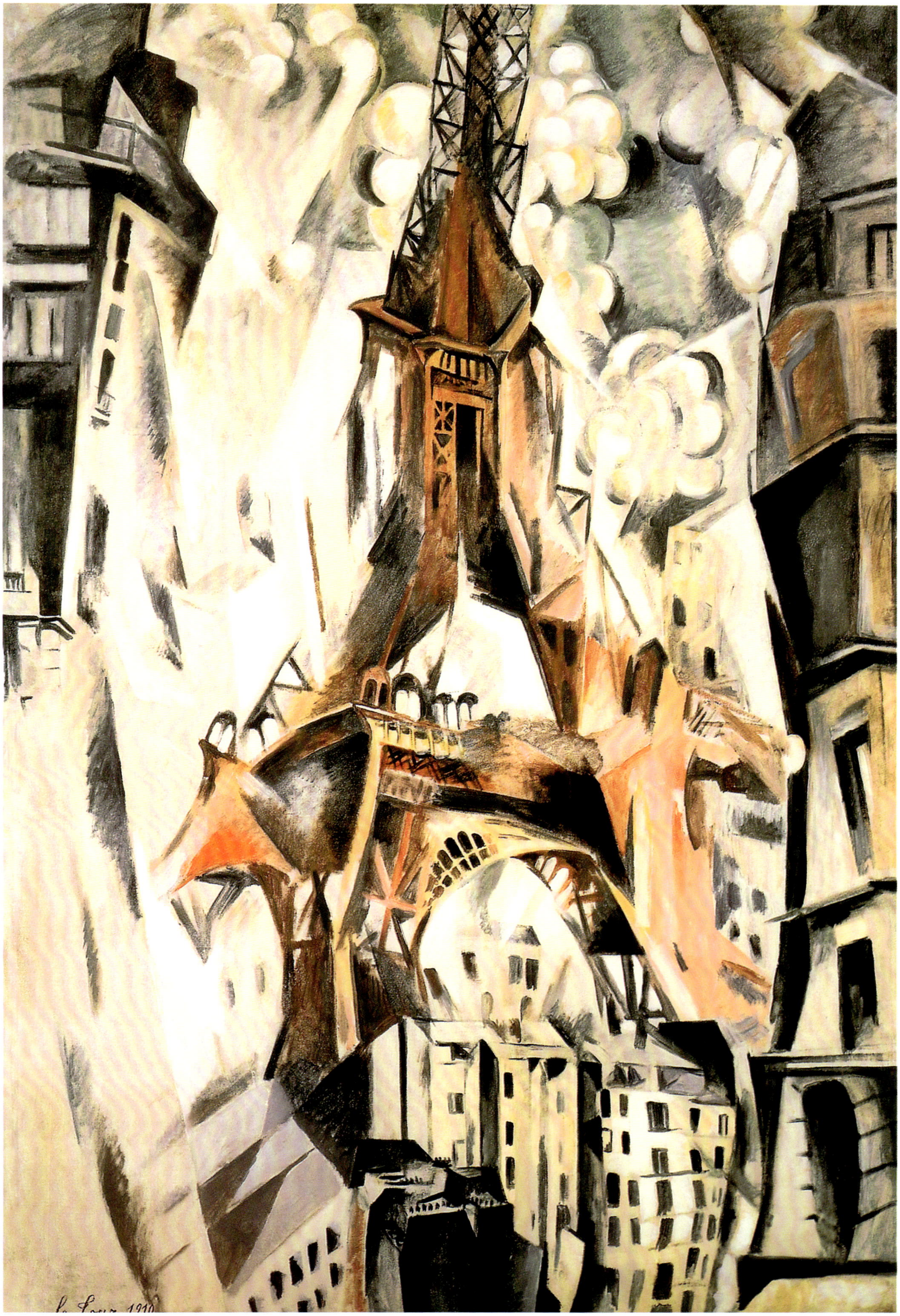

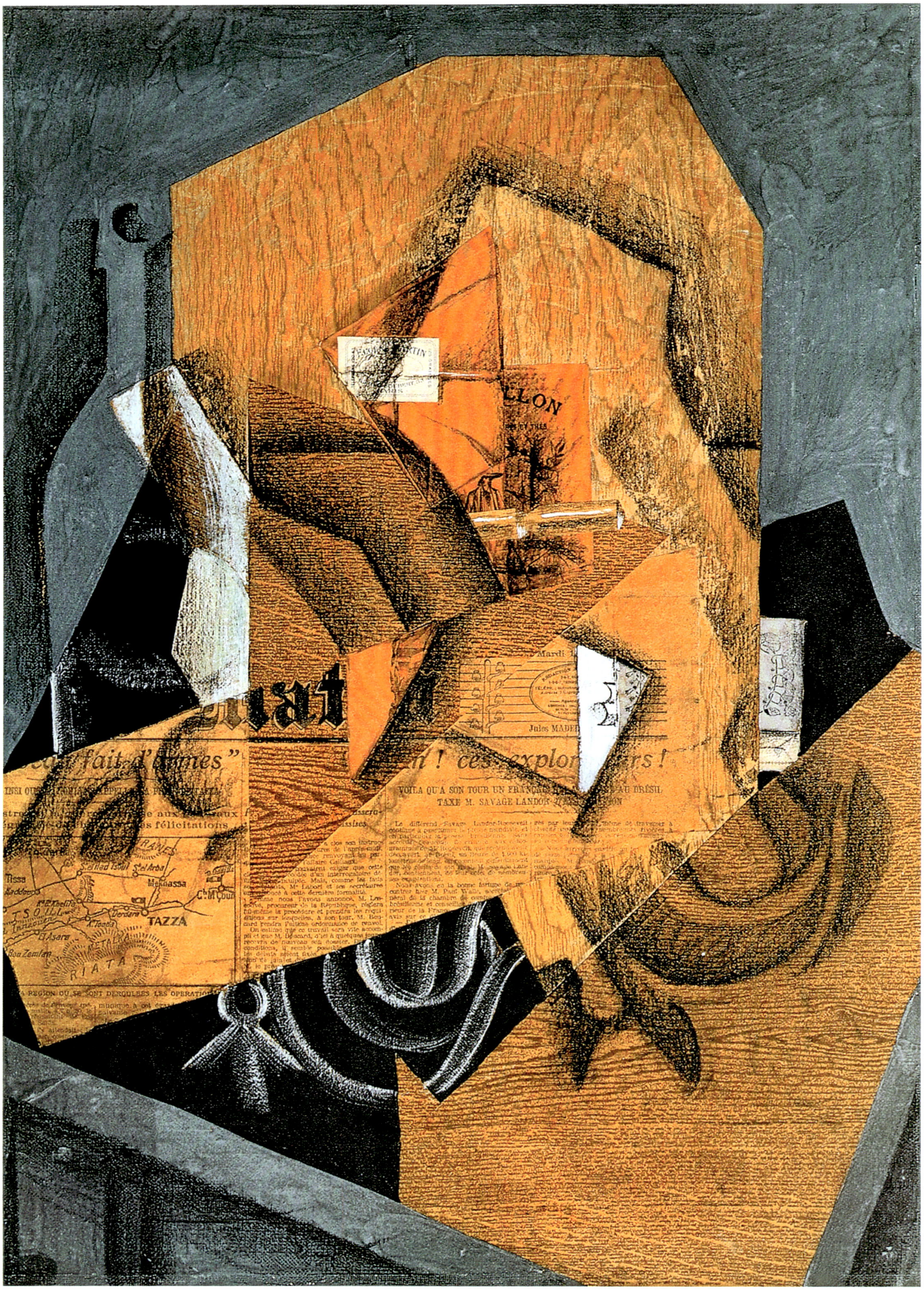
fait d'armes"
TAXE M. SAVAGE LANDOR
félicitations
TAZZA

artist, Pablo Picasso, who must also be considered as one of the founders: his inventions strengthened by the good sense of Georges Braque, who exhibited a Cubist picture in the Salon des Indépendants, as early as 1908, were formulated in the studies of Jean Metzinger, who exhibited the first Cubist portrait (it was mine) in the Salon des Indépendants of 1910. Cubist works were also admitted in the same year by the Jury for the Salon d'Autumne. It was also in 1910 that the pictures of Robert Delaunay, Marie Laurencin and Le Fauconnier, followers of the same school, were exhibited at the Indépendants.

The first general exhibition of Cubism, when its adepts had become more numerous, took place in 1911 at the Indépendants where Room 41, reserved for the Cubists, produced a profound impression. Here were seen the skilful and seductive works of Jean Metzinger; landscapes, *Male Nude* and the *Femme aux Phlox (Woman with Phlox)* by Albert Gleizes; *Portrait of Mme. Fernande X* and *Young Girls* by Mlle. Marie Laurencin; *Eiffel Tower* by Robert Delaunay, *L'Abondance* by Le Fauconnier, *Nudes in the Forest* by Fernand Léger.

The first foreign exhibition of the Cubists was held in Brussels in the same year, and in the preface of the catalogue to this exhibition I accepted, in the name of the exhibitors, the appellation Cubism, and Cubist.

At the close of the year 1911, the exhibition of Cubists at the Salon d'Autumne made a considerable noise; ridicule was spared neither Gleizes (*Hunting*, *Portrait of Jacques Nayral*) nor Metzinger (*Tea Time (Woman with a Teaspoon)*), nor Fernand Léger. A new painter, Marcel Duchamp, and a sculptor architect, Duchamp-Villon, were added to the group.

Other collective exhibitions took place in November of 1911, at the gallery of Contemporary Art, rue Tronchet, Paris; in 1912 the Salon des Indépendants was marked by the advent of Juan Gris. At Barcelona, in the month of May, Spain received the young Frenchman with enthusiasm. Finally in June, at Rouen, at an exhibition organised by the Society of Norman Artists, the advent of Francis Picabia was hailed by the new school.

That which differentiates Cubism from the old schools of painting is that it is not an art of painting, but an art of conception which tends to rise to that of creation.

In representing the concept of reality, or the created reality, the painter can give the appearance of three dimensions, he can, so to speak, *cube it*. He cannot do this in rendering simply the reality as seen, unless he makes use of an illusion either in perspective or foreshortening which deforms the quality of the form conceived or created.

In Cubism, as I have analysed it, four tendencies have manifested themselves, of which two are parallel and pure.

Scientific Cubism is one of the pure tendencies. It is the art of painting new ensembles with elements borrowed, not from the reality of vision, but from the reality of consciousness. Every man has the perception of this inner reality. It is not necessary, for example, to be a man of culture to conceive of a round form.

The geometrical aspect which so vividly impressed those who saw the first scientific canvases came from the fact that the essential reality was given with great purity and that the visual accidents and anecdotes had been eliminated.

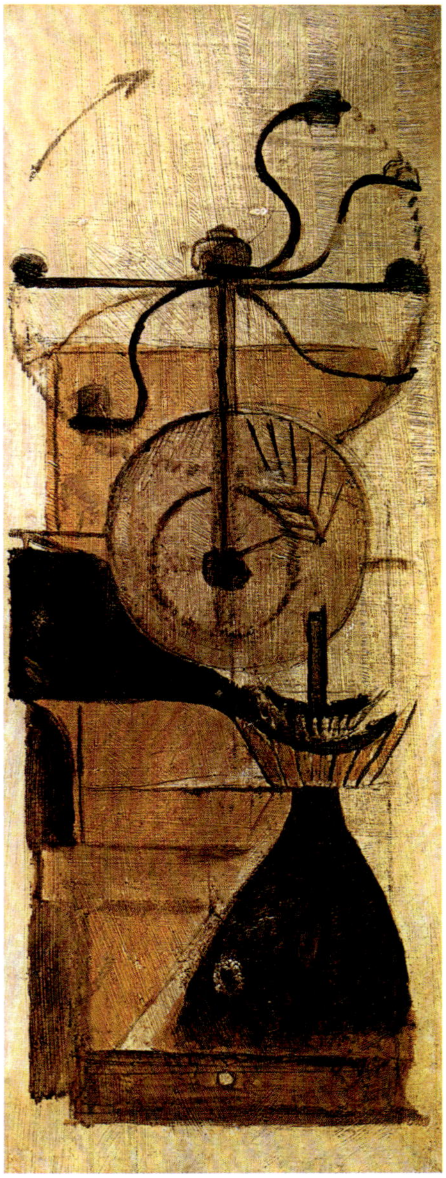

Juan Gris,
Pack of Coffee, 1914.
Gouache, 64.8 x 47 cm.
Ulmer Museum, Ulm.

Marcel Duchamp,
Coffee Mill, 1911.
Oil and pencil on cardboard,
33 x 12.7 cm.
Tate Modern, London.

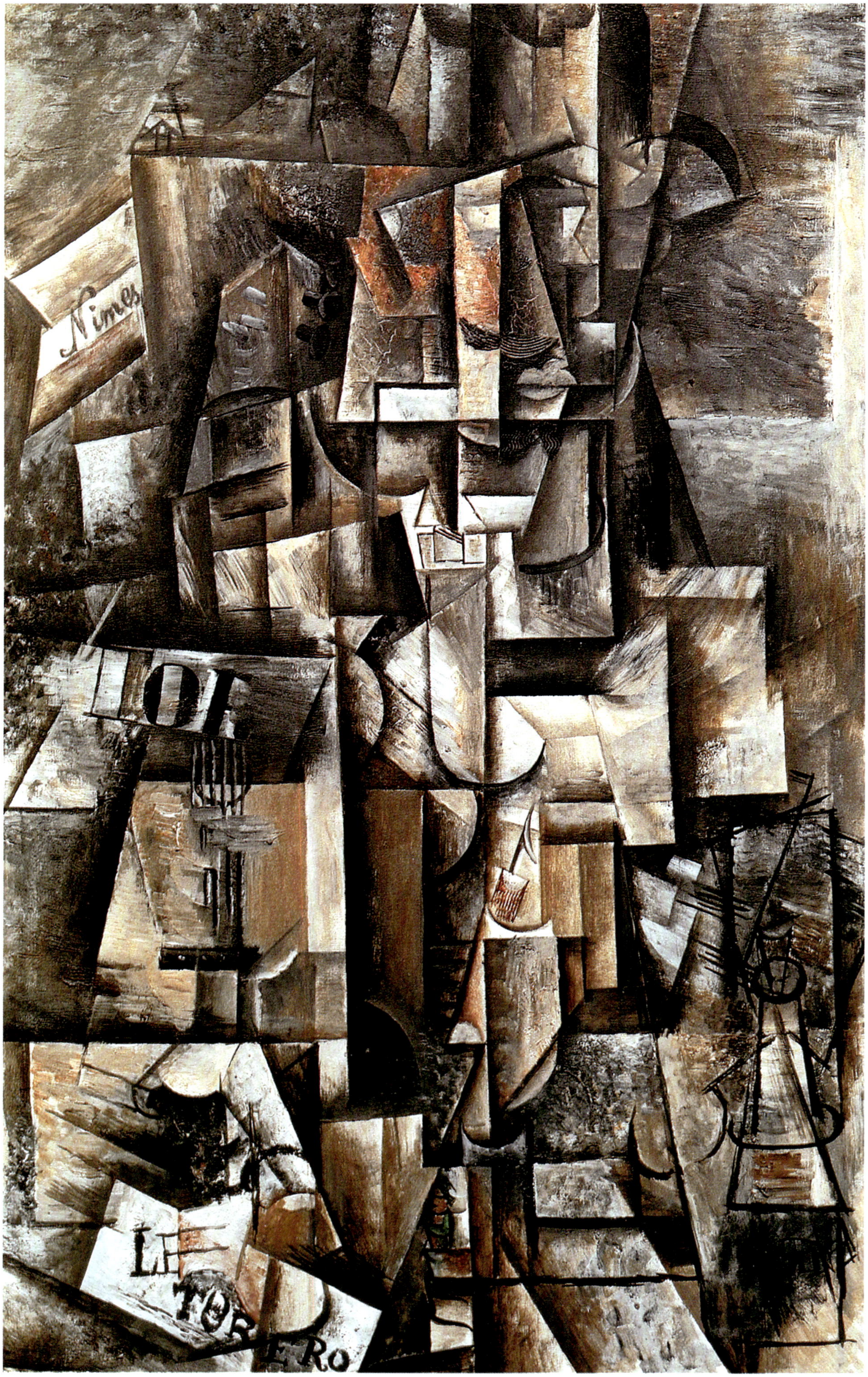
Nimes
LE
TORERO

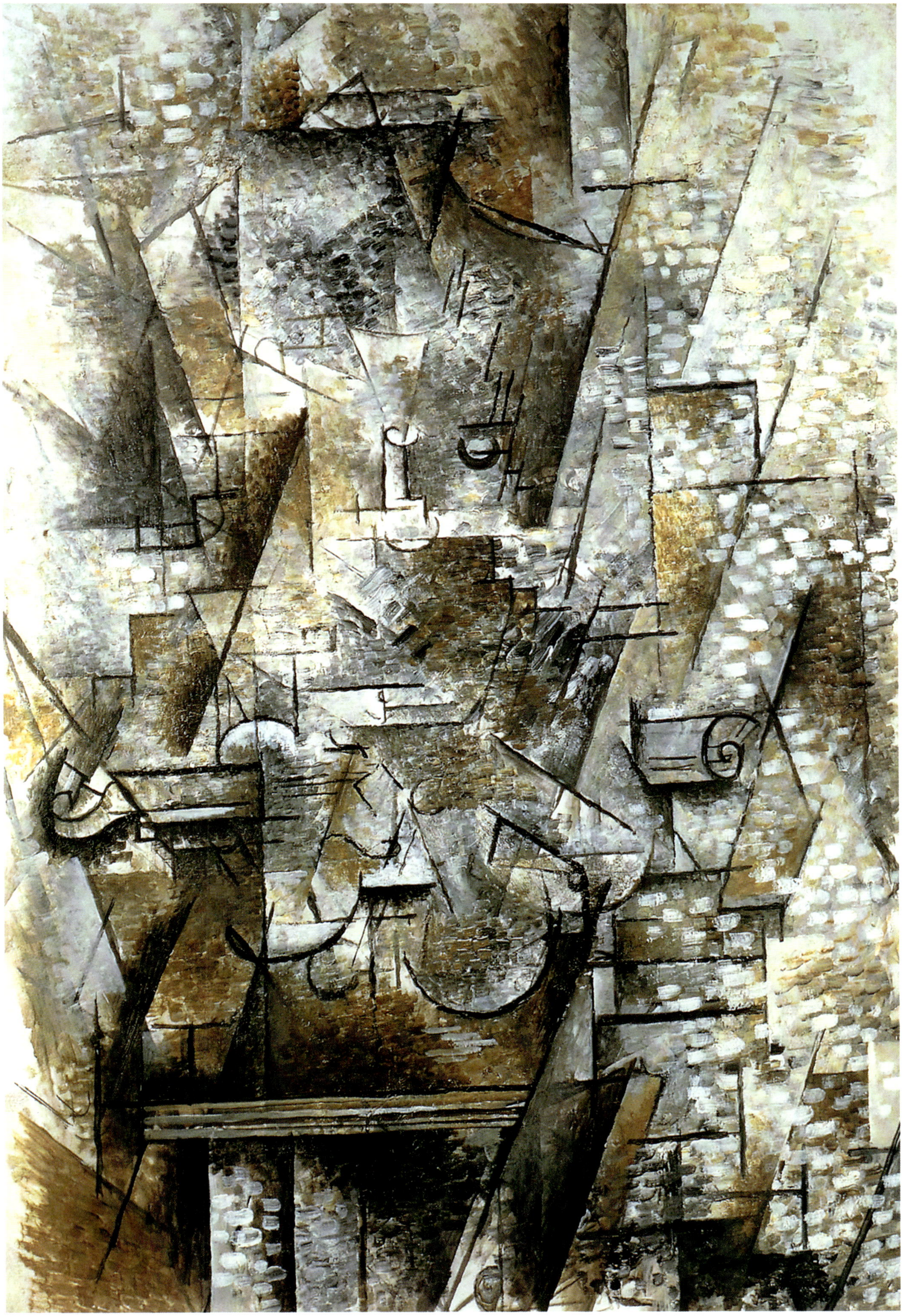

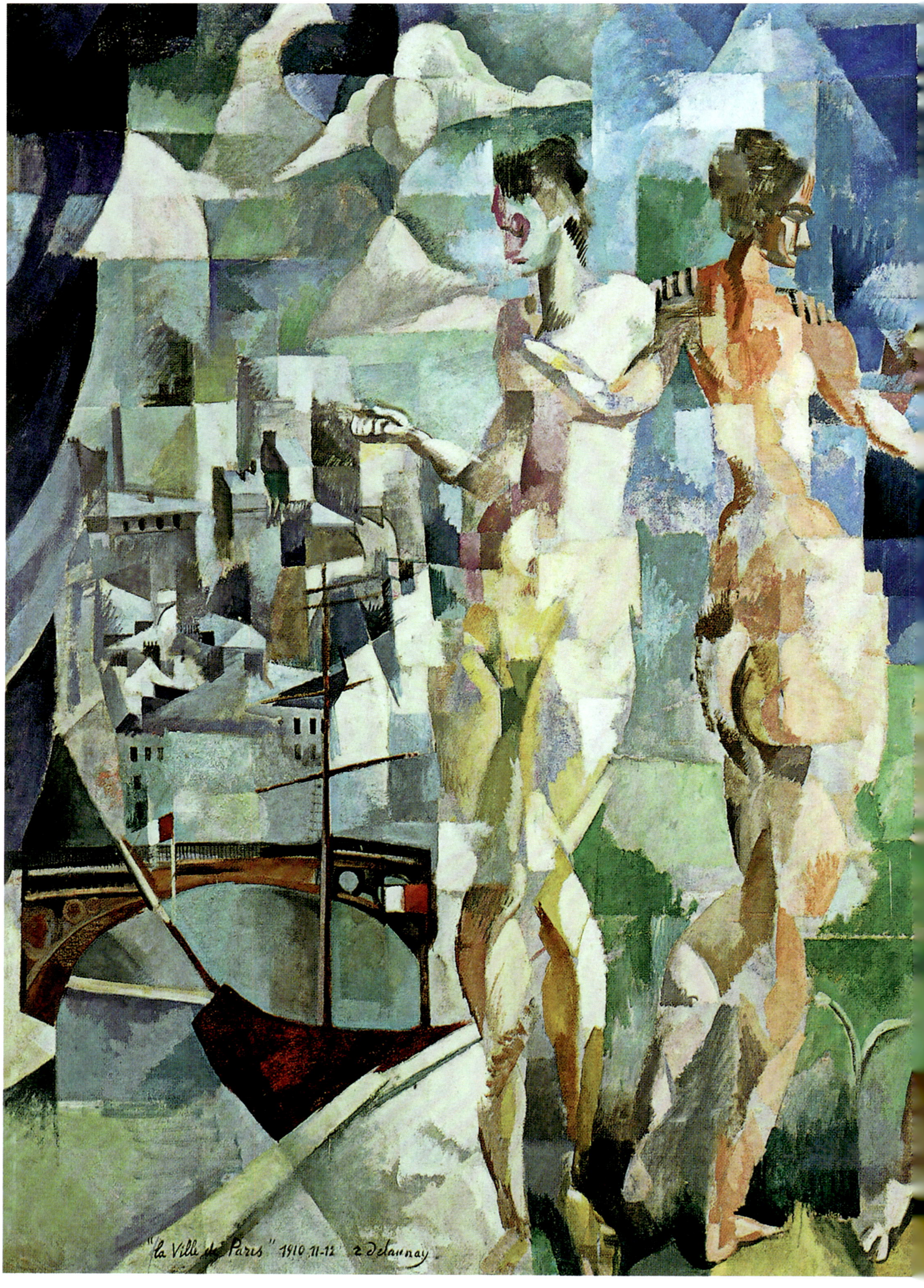
"la Ville de Paris" 1910-11-12 r delaunay

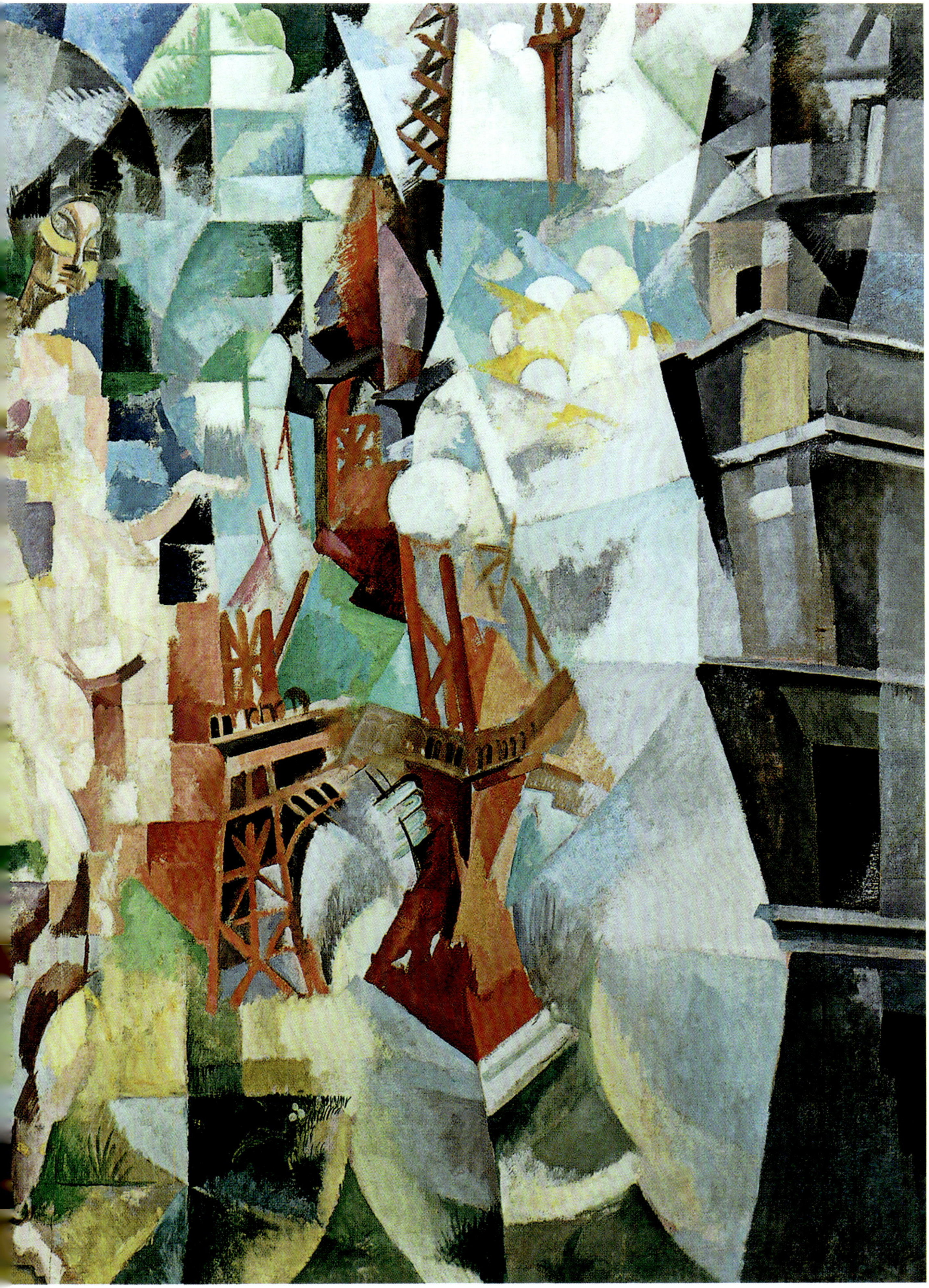

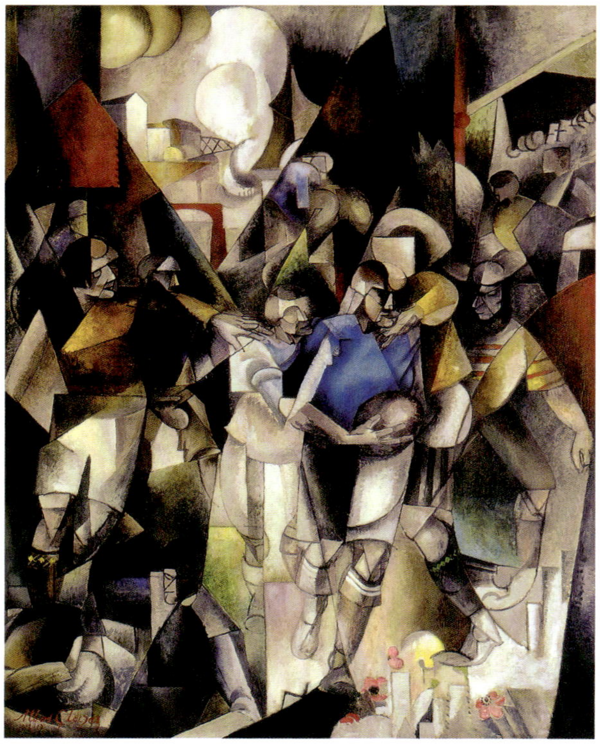

Pablo Picasso,
The Aficionado (The Bullfighter), 1912.
Oil on canvas, 135 x 82 cm.
Kunstmuseum, Basel.

Georges Braque,
Still-Life with a Violin, 1911.
Oil on canvas, 130 x 89 cm.
Musée National d'Art Moderne,
Centre Georges-Pompidou, Paris.

Robert Delaunay,
Paris, 1910-1912.
Oil on canvas, 267 x 406 cm.
Musée National d'Art Moderne,
Centre Georges-Pompidou, Paris.

Albert Gleizes,
The Soccer Players, 1912-1913.
Oil on canvas, 225.4 x 183 cm.
National Gallery of Art, Washington, D.C.

Jean Metzinger,
The Blue Bird, 1913.
Oil on canvas, 250 x 193 cm.
Musée d'Art Moderne de la
Ville de Paris, Paris.

The painters who follow this school are: Picasso (although his luminous art belongs also to the other pure tendency of Cubism), Georges Braque, Metzinger, Albert Gleizes, Mlle. Laurencin, and Juan Gris.

Physical Cubism is the art of painting new ensembles, with elements borrowed mostly from the reality of vision. This art is derived, nevertheless, from the constructive discipline of Cubism. It has a great future in the history of painting. Its social role is well marked, but it is not a pure art. It confuses the subject with its aspects. Le Fauconnier is the physical Cubist painter who created this tendency.

Orphic Cubism is the other great tendency of Modern Painting.

The last pictures and aquarelles of Cézanne belong to Cubism, but Courbet is the father of the new painters, and André Derain to whom I shall presently return, was the eldest of this best beloved sons, for he originated the movement of the *Fauves* who were a sort of prelude to the Cubists, and he also led the great subjective movement.

It would be too difficult however to write clearly today of a man who voluntarily holds himself aloof from everybody and everything.

The Modern School seems to me the most audacious that has ever been. It has put the question of beauty to itself. It wishes to visualise beauty disengaged from the pleasure that man causes man and, since the dawn of historic times, no European artist has dared to do that. The new artists must have an ideal beauty which will no longer be merely the proud expression of the species, but the expression of the universe, in so far as it has been humanised in the light. It is the art of painting new ensembles with elements not borrowed from visual realities, but created entirely by the artist and endowed by him with a powerful reality.

The works of the Orphic artists must present simultaneously a pure aesthetic charm, a construction which strikes beneath the surface and a sublime significance—that is to say, the subject. It is pure art.

The light from the works of Picasso contains this art, which Robert Delaunay invents on his side and for which Fernand Léger, Francis Picabia and Marcel Duchamp also strive.

Instinctive Cubism, the art of painting new ensembles borrowed not from visual reality but from suggestions made to the artist by instinct and intuition, has long tended to orphism. The instinctive artists lack lucidity and artistic faith. Instinctive Cubism includes a very great number of artists. It sprang from French Impressionism, and now this movement extends all over Europe.

The art of today clothes its creations with an imposing and monumental aspect, which surpasses in this respect everything that has been conceived by the artists of our age. Ardent in pursuit of beauty, it is noble, energetic, and the reality which it brings us is marvellously clear.

I love the art of today because above all else I love the light, and all men love light—above all else Man invented fire.

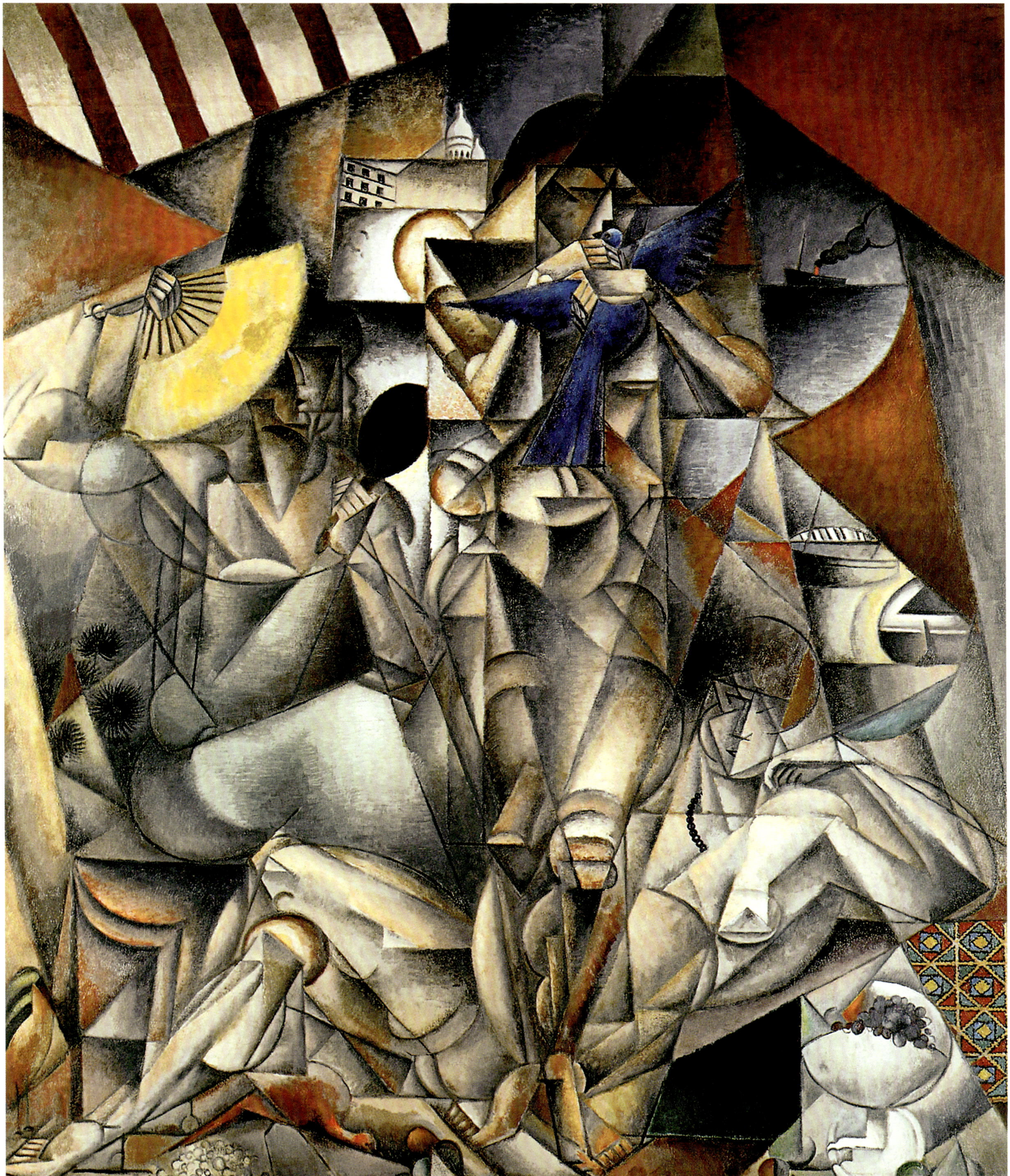

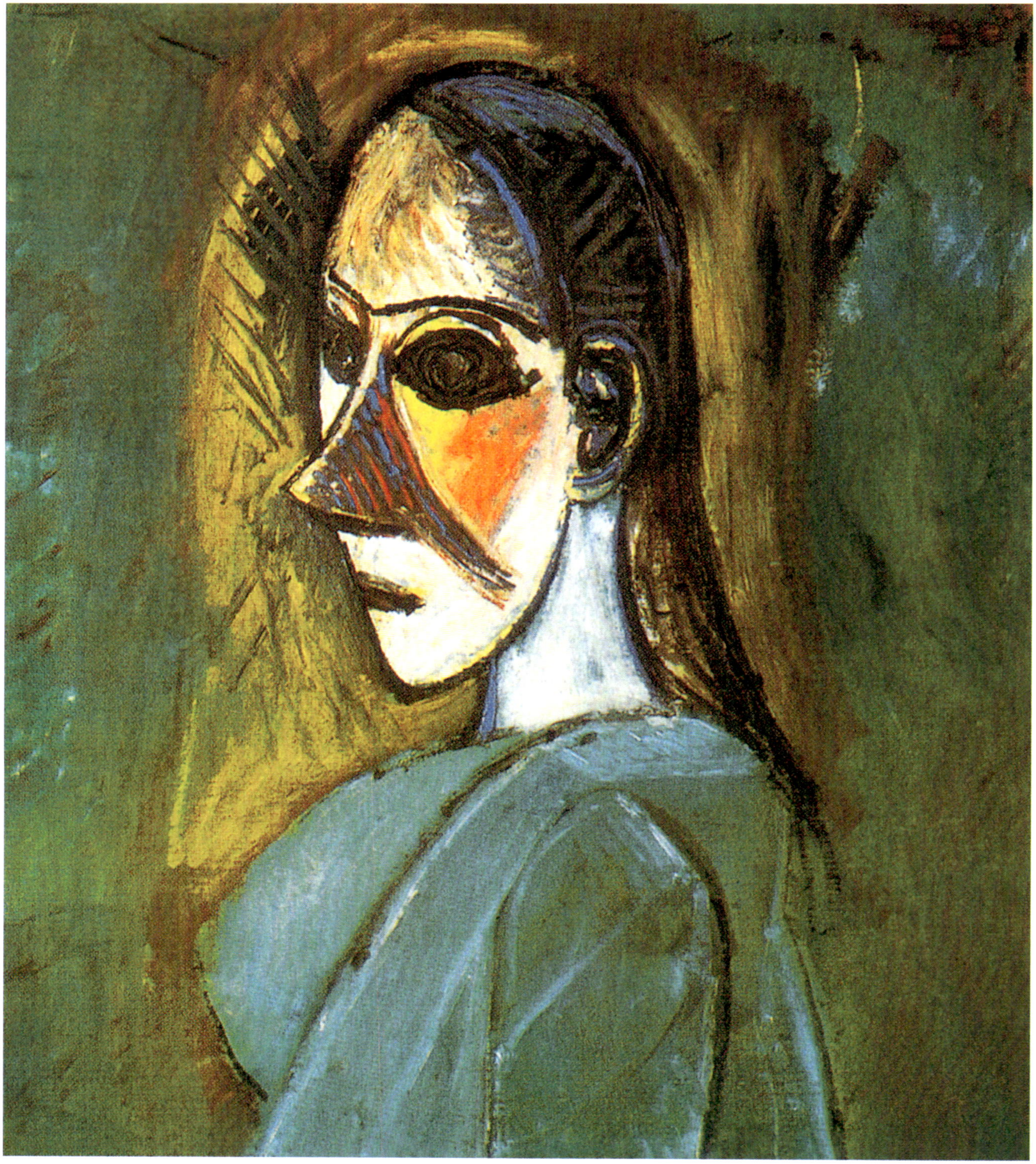

II. What Is Cubism?

The Analysis of Form

In 1907, one painting signalled the prelude to a change in painting: *Les Demoiselles d'Avignon* (p. 6). When Pablo Picasso first exhibited this bordello scene with five female figures, even the collector Sergei Shchukin and his friend Georges Braque considered the painting to be "a loss for French painting". However, the significance of this new view of reality was not lost on Braque. In this work, Picasso crafted for the first time a clear and rational lens without any aesthetic allusions. Taking Cézanne's analysis of shape further, Picasso fragmented the forms into small cubes. It was the task of the viewer, when standing before the canvas, to put this puzzle of various spatial views together into a whole. Moreover, the muted colours signalled another new direction for painting. However, most of the novelty lay in the independence of the painting from the preconditions given by nature. This was the artist's response to the changed preconditions of science regarding space and time, using Cézanne's demand that in nature one should seek out the sphere, the cone and the cylinder as the basis for his compositional ideas. At the 1909 Salon des Indépendants, the critic Louis de Vauxcelles spoke of cubes, and Cubism was born.

The movement underwent many evolutionary steps. Friends Georges Braque and Pablo Picasso said later: "We did not have the intention of creating Cubism. Moreover, we just wanted to express that which moved us. ... It almost seemed as if we were two mountain climbers who were hanging from a single rope." Between 1909 and 1912, they separated their art from everything real without turning completely to abstraction, in a phase called Analytical Cubism. In particular, the artists now painted figures and still lifes. They no longer painted an object viewed from one perspective, but rather layered views from many angles in order to capture the subject from all sides. They analysed the object and brought it to the canvas as a fragmented picture. Shape and space melted into one another in one composition of enmeshed, intersected and dissected surfaces. Instead of creating volume, the painters focused on revealing facets and constructing surfaces. The situation captured in the painting became far more indefinite. Some surfaces became transparent, weightless or suddenly transformed themselves into a book or an instrument, something recognisable. With regard to colours, the paintings were dominated by brown, grey and blue hues. Additionally, artists no longer painted in the open air, but rather kept to their studios, where the arsenal for their subjects was already at hand. Later, they no longer arranged their still lifes so that they could paint from reality; rather, they created them out of the imagination, adding numbers and word fragments to the compositions.

Braque and Picasso's artistic vision brought them to Synthetic Cubism, a movement in which they were joined by Juan Gris. Now, it was no longer about taking the objects apart;

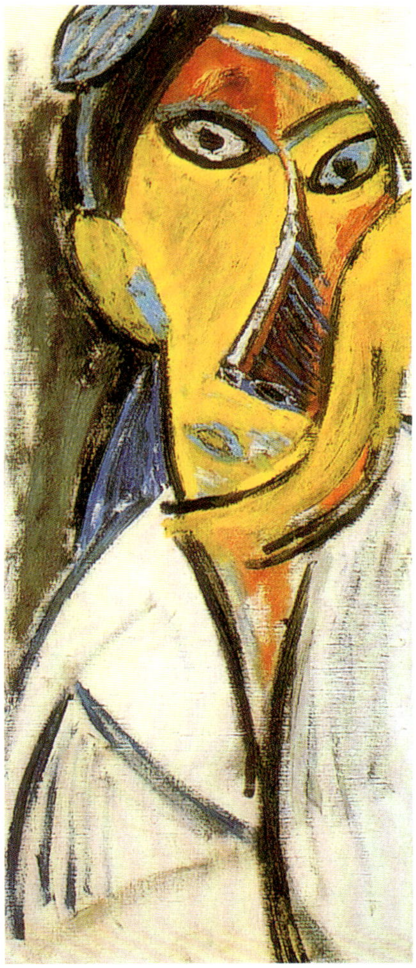

Pablo Picasso,
Bust of a Woman (study for *Les Demoiselles d'Avignon*), 1907.
Oil on canvas, 66 x 59 cm.
Musée National d'Art Moderne, Centre Georges-Pompidou, Paris.

Pablo Picasso,
Head (study for *Les Demoiselles d'Avignon*), 1907.
Oil on canvas.
Barnes Foundation, Lincoln University, Merion, Pennsylvania.

now artists set about creating new objects with new materials. One recognised new qualities for works of art, using the most varied materials, even items that were meant to be thrown away. During this period, the collage became a form of painting.

Picasso, Braque and the "Popular" Image

Georges Braque and Pablo Picasso invented a new type of painting, expressing daily life in the form of real materials. For this, they used fabrics, wax cloth, wallpaper scraps and newspaper shreds, using these items to create fine art. This was the birth of their so-called *papiers collés*. The interest of Picasso in the tactile and in unusual materials found its first visual realisation in May 1912 with his piece entitled *Still Life with Chair Caning* (pp. 36-37). This painting showcases Picasso's use of common materials in an unorthodox manner. The printed pattern on the wax cloth conveyed the illusion of chair caning. The pasted paper appears to be something else than what it truly is, while the rope framing it is a tangible object. Shortly thereafter, Braque found a roll of wallpaper with an oak pattern, which he then cut into pieces and integrated them into a drawing. These endeavours eventually led to pure surface textures being contrasted against one another and forming a coherent artwork.

Braque and Picasso considered their studio to be a place completely devoted to craftsmanship. Using everyday materials, they experimented with extending art into the realm of the ordinary. In 1912 and 1913, they chose paper as their primary medium. In order to develop their idea of a "popular iconography", they used cardboard, paper of many shades and patterns, sand, combs, sawdust, metal shavings, ripolin varnish, sheet metal stencils, razor blades and craft tools. Apollinaire and André Salmon compared the efforts of Braque and Picasso with those of the poet François de Malherbe; the painters sought readily comprehensible simplicity, just as the poet had studied the slang spoken by the dock workers in order to enrich his own language.

The *papiers collés* were preceded by paper sculptures, first by Braque and later on by Picasso. Already by 1911, Braque had created his first paper sculpture. Picasso, when viewing the construction scaffolding of these first Braque paper sculptures, was reminded of the Wright brothers' biplane.

Of all the artists of the 20th century, Pablo Picasso was a true genius. Like no other artist, he made important contributions and innovations to nearly all of the artistic movements of the 20th century. He journeyed to unexplored shores in the sea of the art world, and repeatedly produced surprising new masterpieces.

The Merit of Material

From ancient history until the end of the 18th century, artwork was evaluated according to its content. The material from which the artwork was made played a subordinate role. The premise was that an idea in its most complete and ideal state is

Pablo Picasso,
The Pont-Neuf, 1911.
Oil on canvas, 33 x 24 cm.
Private collection.

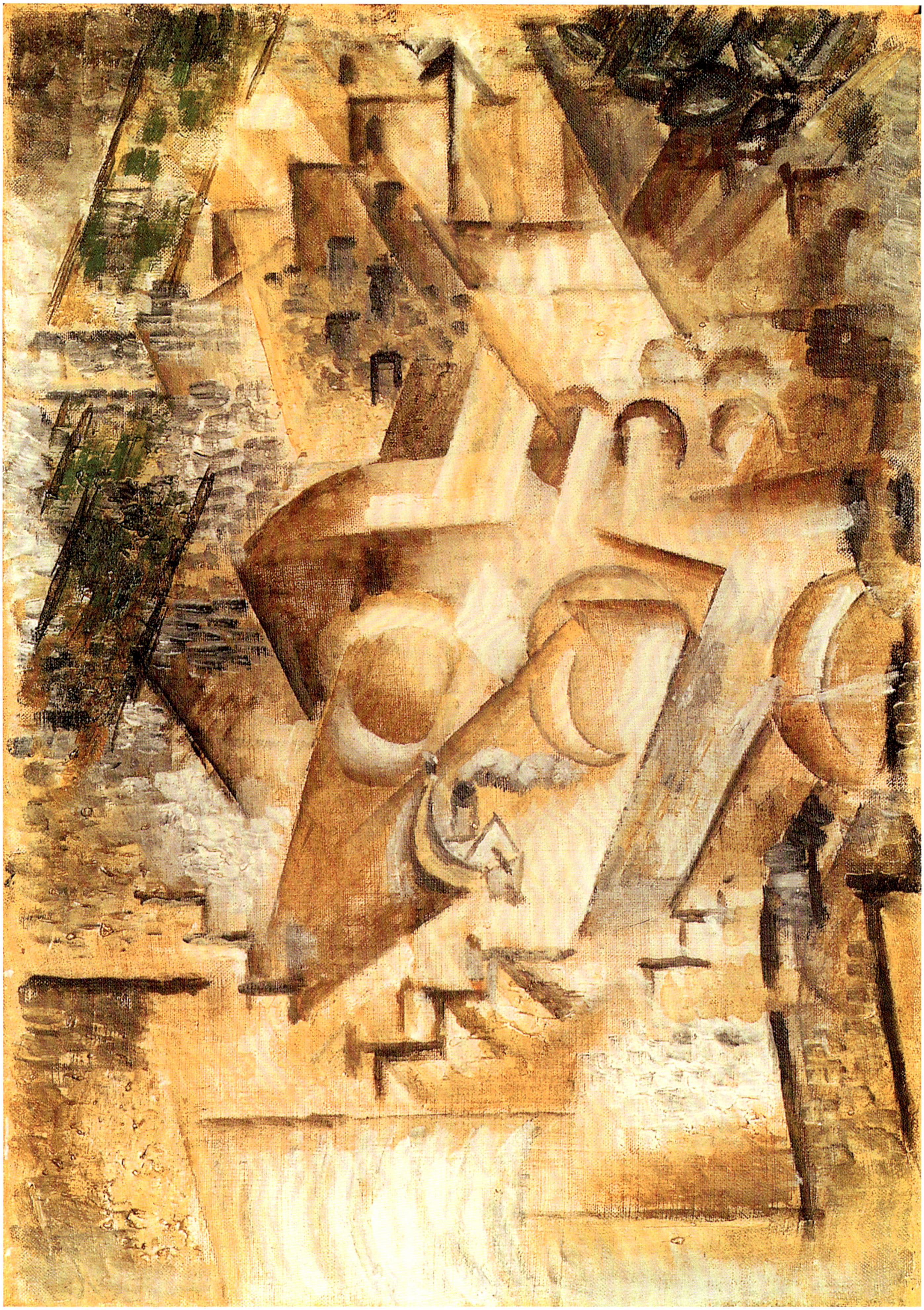

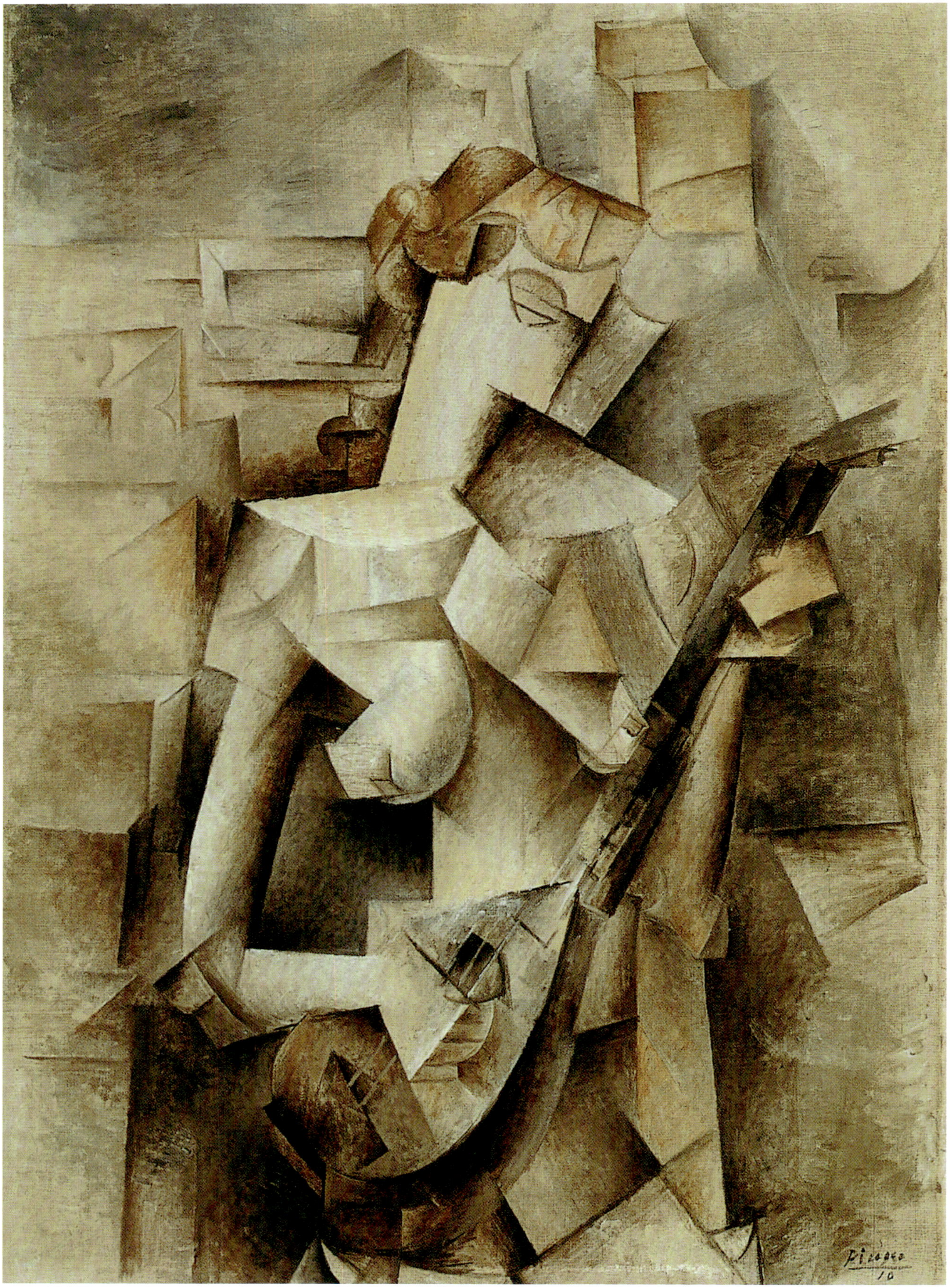

immaterial; thus, to a great extent, the material is secondary to the idea that it is helping the artist to express. Materials were placed in the hierarchical order that was determined by how little they would impinge upon the purity of the artistic premise. Only in the 20th century did the aesthetics relating to materials take hold. Material justice now became one of the criteria for a good work of art, as materials rose in esteem.

Edgar Degas was a forerunner for the appreciation of so-called "poor" materials. At the 1881 Impressionist exhibition of the Salon des Indépendants in Paris, he displayed the *Little Fourteen-Year-Old Dancer*, which he had completed between 1879 and 1880. The flesh-coloured wax figure, with her ponytail made of real red hair, clothed in real clothes-a flax bodice, a full white dress and ballerina shoes-shocked the art world. The critics called the figure a "young monster", and said that it evoked the idea of a specimen prepared for a zoological or physiological museum exhibit. However, the critic and poet Joris-Karl Huysmans vehemently defended Degas:

> All the ideas the public has about sculpture, about cold, lifeless, white apparitions, about these memorable and stereotypical works that have been repeated over the centuries will be toppled. The fact is that Monsieur Degas has knocked over the traditions of sculpture, just as he has for a long time now shaken the conventions of painting. [...] This statuette is the only really modern attempt that I am aware of in sculpture with her living flesh shaped throughout by working muscles.

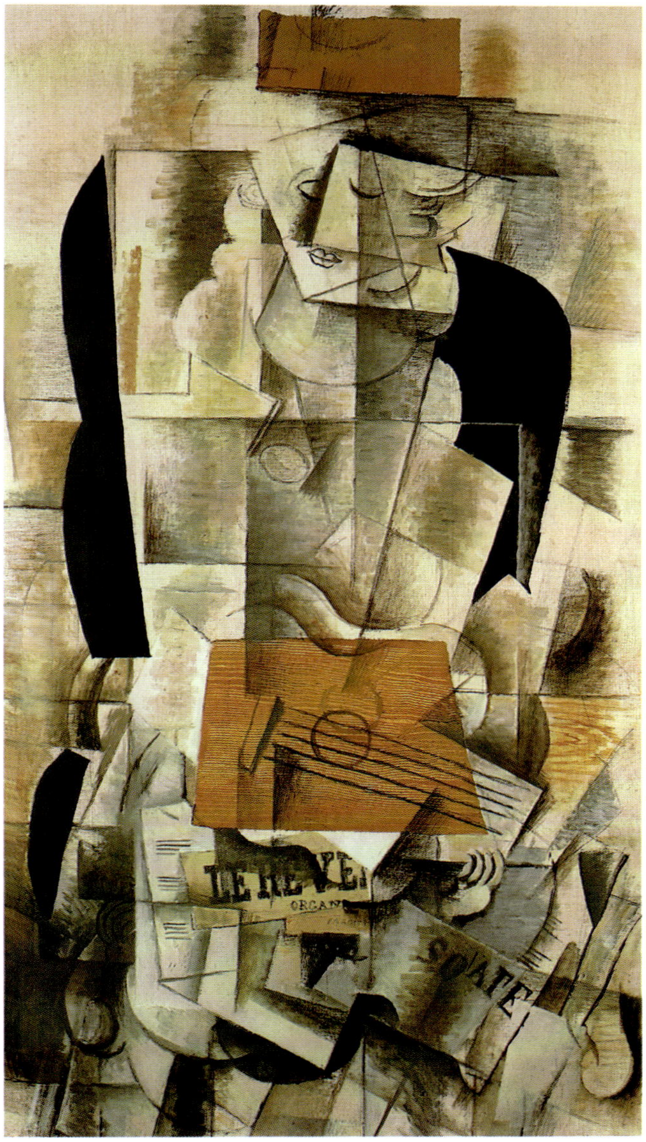

A similar view was expressed in the letter Vincent van Gogh wrote at the end of February or beginning of March in 1883 to his friend Van Rappard: "Tomorrow, I will get some interesting things from this rubbish dump." Like Degas, he would dream of the collection of discarded buckets, kettles, baskets, oil cans and wire, and would mould these materials into art in the following winter.

In 1890, Maurice Denis reflected on the materiality and substance of colour, space and technology: "A painting is essentially a tarpaulin surface covered by colours in a certain order." To support this statement, he cited one of the many works of Félix Vallotton, *Les Passants (Passers-By)*, dated 1897. The frame for the painting is a reddish brown cardboard box with fine fibre inserts. At certain strategic points in the canvas, the colour is lacking, baring the graphic structure. In doing so the artist revealed the beauty of the material.

In the later works of Paul Cézanne, large parts of the canvas also remain untouched. The level of sensitivity regarding the material quality of the painting is thus reflected. In his

Pablo Picasso,
Girl with a Mandolin (Fanny Tellier), 1910.
Oil on canvas, 100.3 x 73.6 cm.
The Museum of Modern Art, New York.

Georges Braque,
Woman with a Guitar, 1913.
Oil and charcoal on canvas, 130 x 73 cm.
Musée National d'Art Moderne,
Centre Georges-Pompidou, Paris.

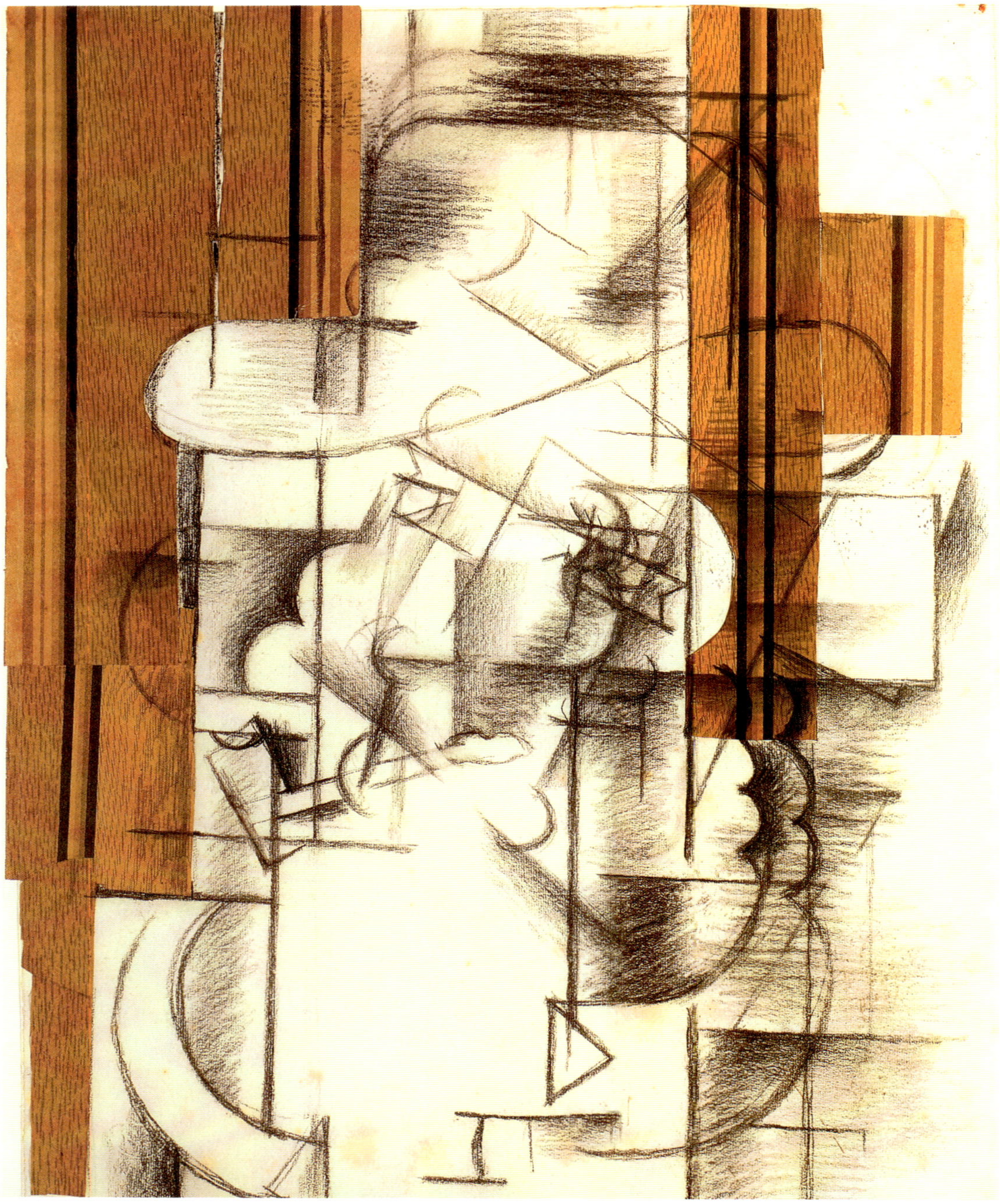

Georges Braque,
Man with a Pipe, 1912.
Glued paper on Ingres paper and charcoal, 62 x 48.6 cm.
Kunstmuseum, Basel.

Georges Braque,
Fruit Basket, Bottle and Glass, 1912.
Glued paper and charcoal, 62 x 46 cm.
Private collection.

Pablo Picasso,
Still-Life with Chair Caning, 1912.
Oil on polished canvas wrapped with rope, 29 x 37 cm.
Musée Picasso, Paris.

Marcel Duchamp,
The Bride, 1912.
Oil on canvas, 89.5 x 55.6 cm.
Philadelphia Museum of Art, Philadelphia.

Marcel Duchamp,
The Passage from the Virgin to the Bride, 1912.
Oil on canvas, 59.4 x 54 cm.
Museum of Modern Art, New York.

Blue and Rose Periods, Pablo Picasso gave the colours their independence. The *papiers collés* were the next logical step.

The themes and techniques of popular art influenced the development of modernist art. The avant-garde pioneers systematically acquired new sources of inspiration and the categorical separation between art, folk art and anti-art was lifted. Theodore Adorno specifically warned against comparing the insights of the modernist movement to similarities with older art. Only through the deliberate artistic use of techniques and material would the work become more than mere handicraft. He added that only when

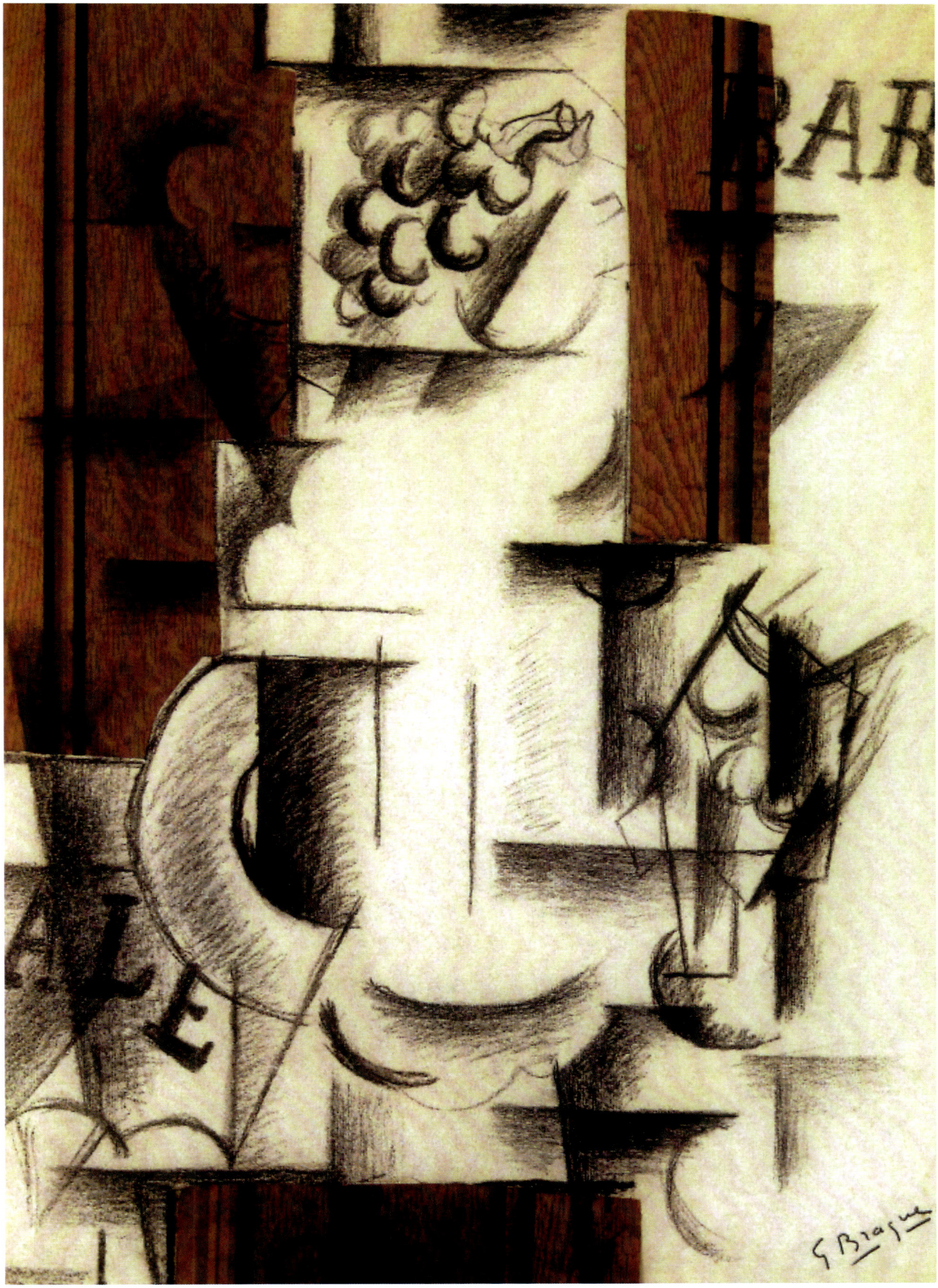
BAR
G Braque

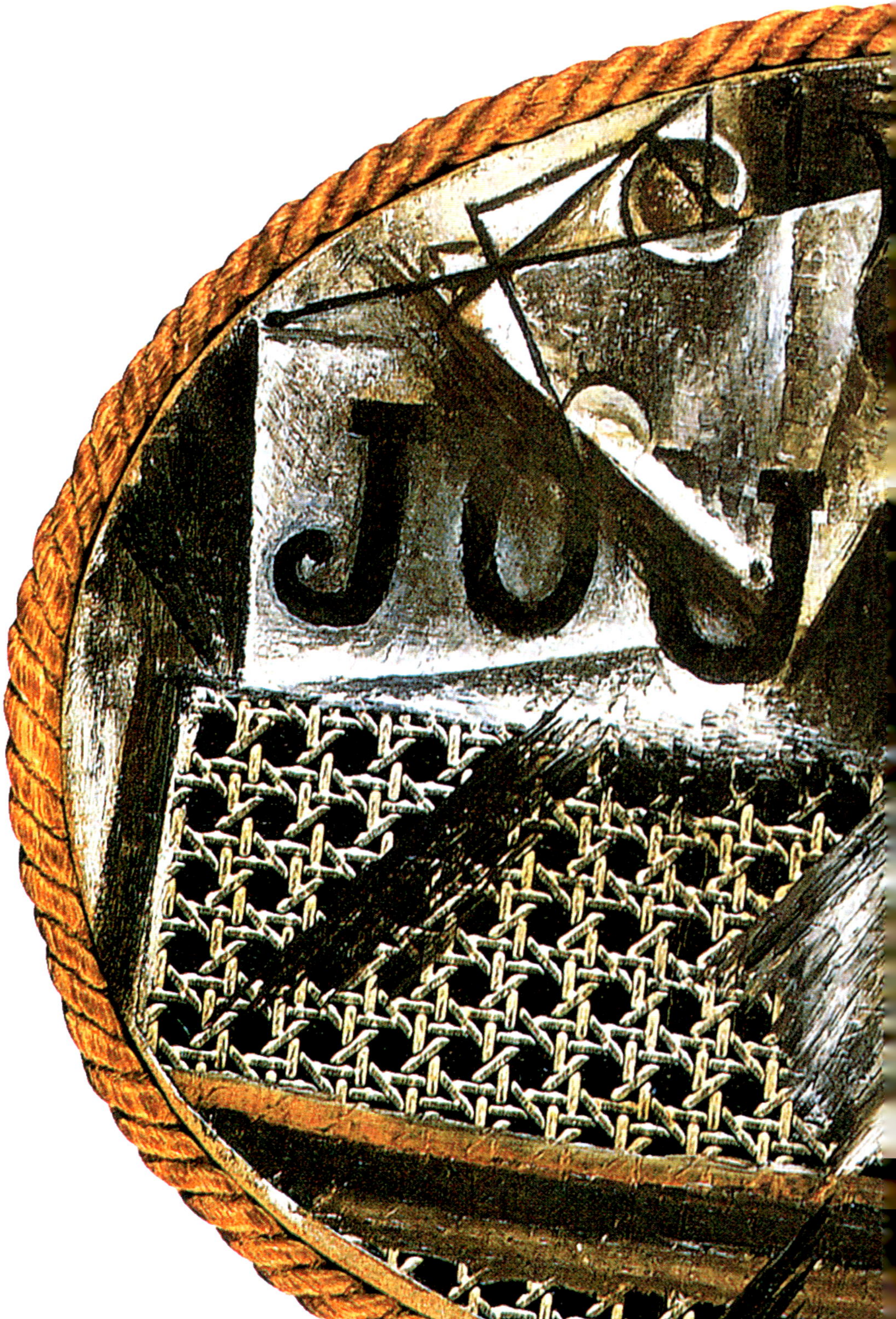
JOU

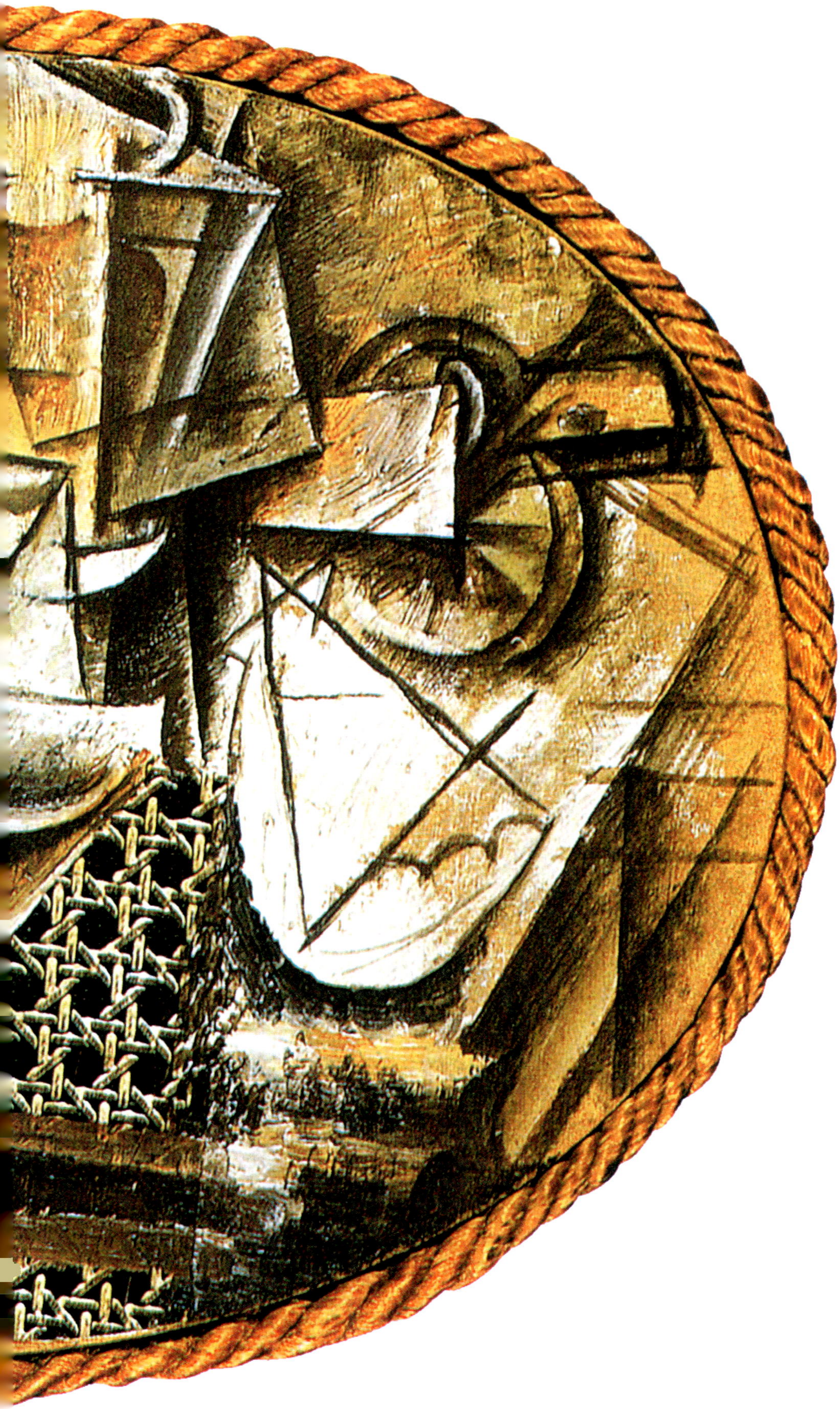

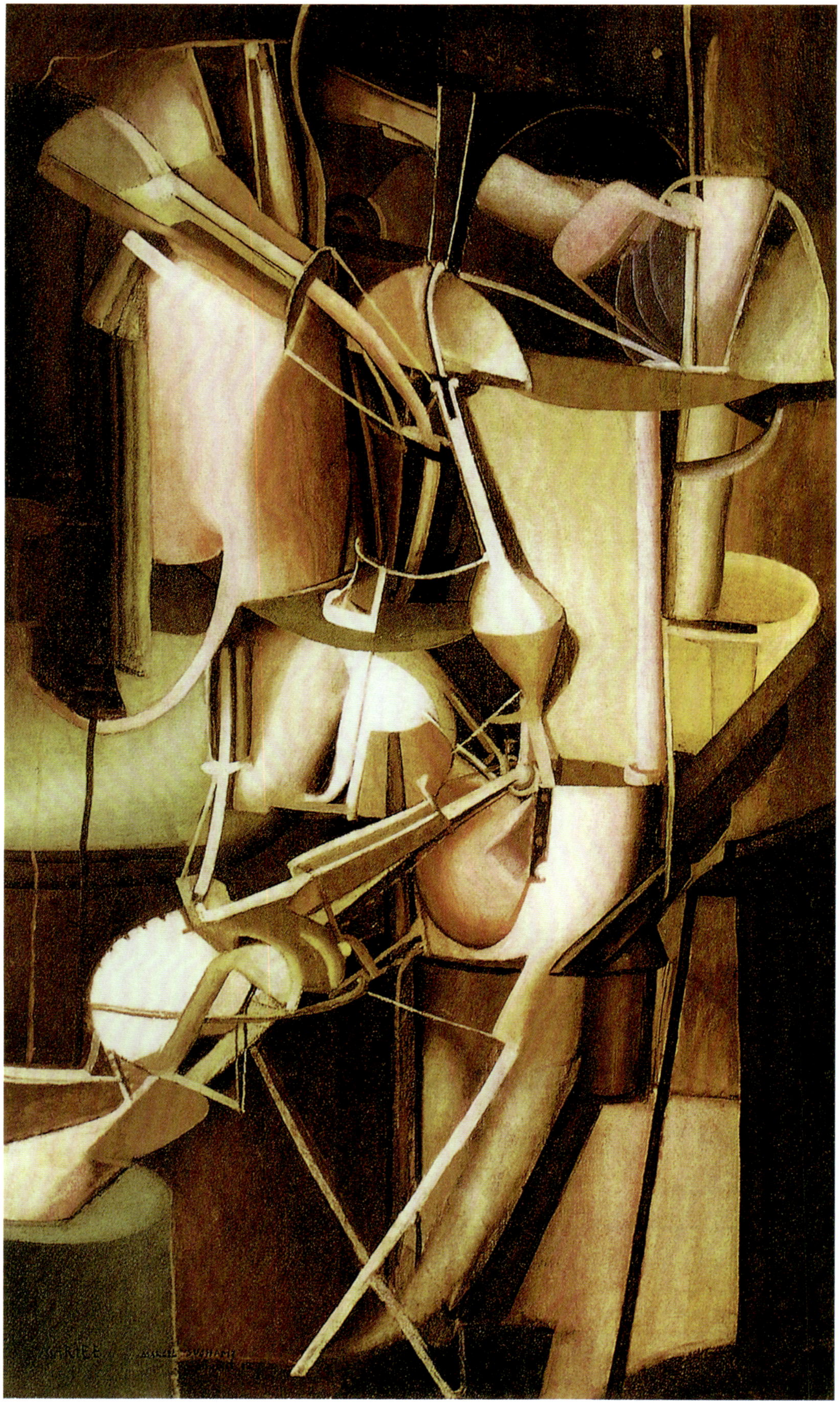

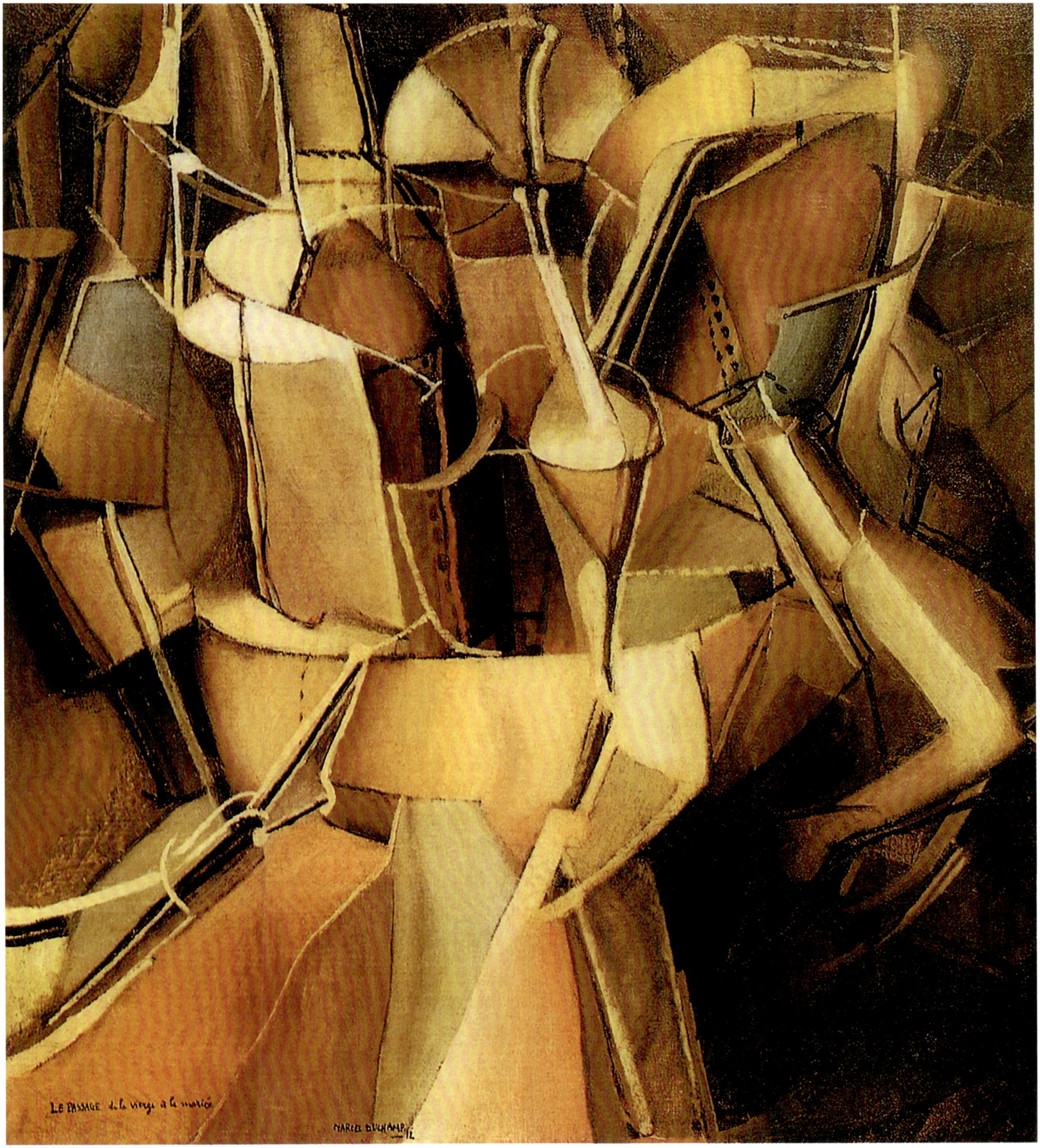
LE PASSAGE de la vierge à la mariée
MARCEL DUCHAMP 12

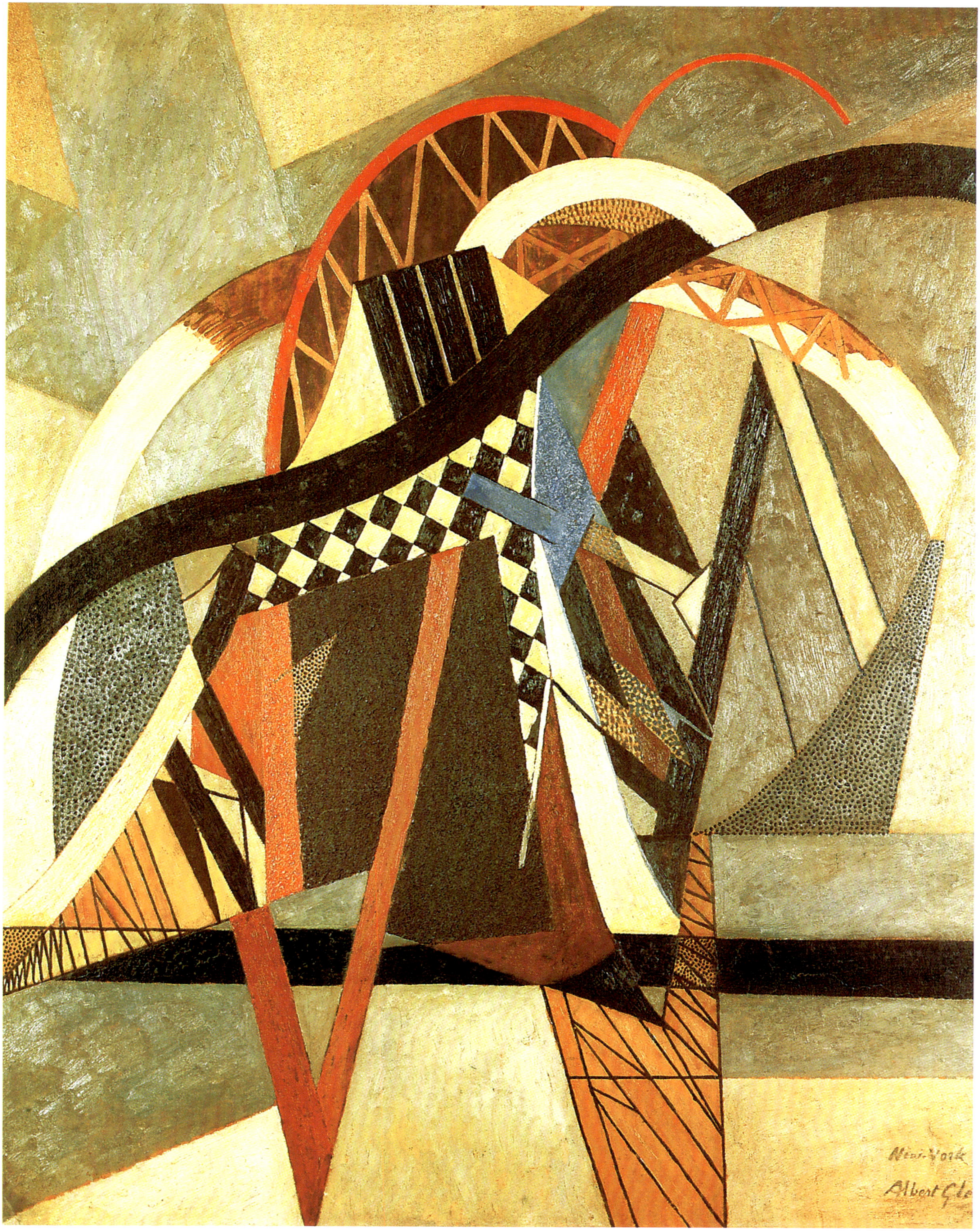
New-York
Albert Gle

Braque and Picasso first pasted pieces of paper in the *papiers collés* did this have the intellectual spark that surpassed the effect and dexterity of previous expressions.

Collage

Through the technique of collage, two-dimensional paper transformed itself into three-dimensional expression. Depending on colour, pattern or material, the paper surface appeared in the foreground or in the background, and the painting was transformed into a bas-relief. Picasso had experimented with this technique when he had cut up scraps of paper and used them to construct his guitar box sculptures (p. 130).

Futurism in 1911 and 1912 incorporated the flat surface of the *papiers collés* with rhythmic repetitions and the associated dynamic structure in a state of simultaneity. Futurism created a dynamic relief of the world in a state of unrest. The processes did not develop sequentially, but rather in a concurrence of the past, present and future.

Carlo Carrà created the prototype of a two-dimensional futurist paper collage using paper and newspaper cut-outs. The *Manifestazione Interventista* appeared on the 1st of August, in 1914, shortly before the outbreak of World War I, in the newspaper *Lacerba* in Paris. Evoking an explosion, printed strips of paper animated by an extraordinary dynamism rotate out from the central point in all directions. For the Futurists, the collage for the first time became a document of the period, using scraps of newspaper, advertising and musical scores. As if liberated, words and letters unfurled to symbolise sounds and noises, tumbling with an overflow of simultaneous information into the painting.

A short time later, this Futurist combination of text and sound further developed in the Dada movement. Printed fragments of paper that had their own separate meanings were combined to reveal new interpretations and send new messages. In reciprocal interaction, even unrelated levels of reality obtained unexpected new meanings.

Using already existing visual materials, collage created new possibilities in the total mutation of the original meaning of the material. Collage in the 20th century, as a way of thinking, opened unknown paths and unexpected possibilities.

Simultaneity in Cubist Circles

In 1913, the poet Guillaume Apollinaire dedicated his work *The Cubist Painters* to Cubism, thereby helping the movement attain broad renown. Painters like Jean Metzinger and Albert Gleizes made impressive contributions to the Cubist language of shapes. In 1912 one of the most famous paintings of the 20th century was created: the *Nude Descending a Staircase (No. 2)* (p. 156) by Marcel Duchamp. Aided by the Cubist vocabulary of shapes and his familiarity with Étienne-Jules Marey's photos depicting movement, Duchamp painted a picture that moved the world. Five moments of the movement of one person, descending a spiral staircase, are captured in time-lapsed

Albert Gleizes,
Brooklyn Bridge, 1915.
Oil on canvas.
Private collection.

Sonia Delaunay,
Contrastes Simultanés (Simultaneous Contrasts), 1912.
Oil on canvas, 46 x 35 cm.

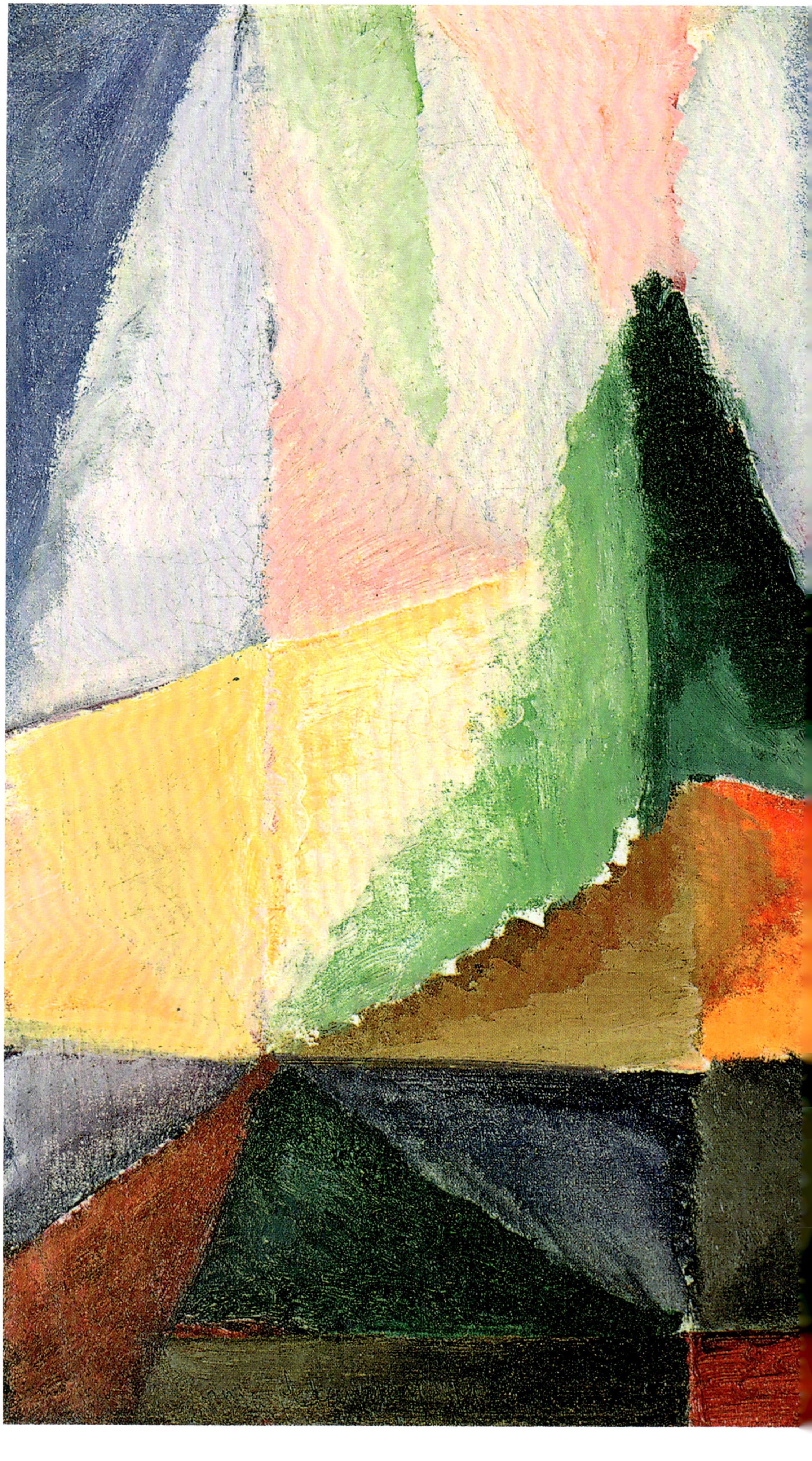

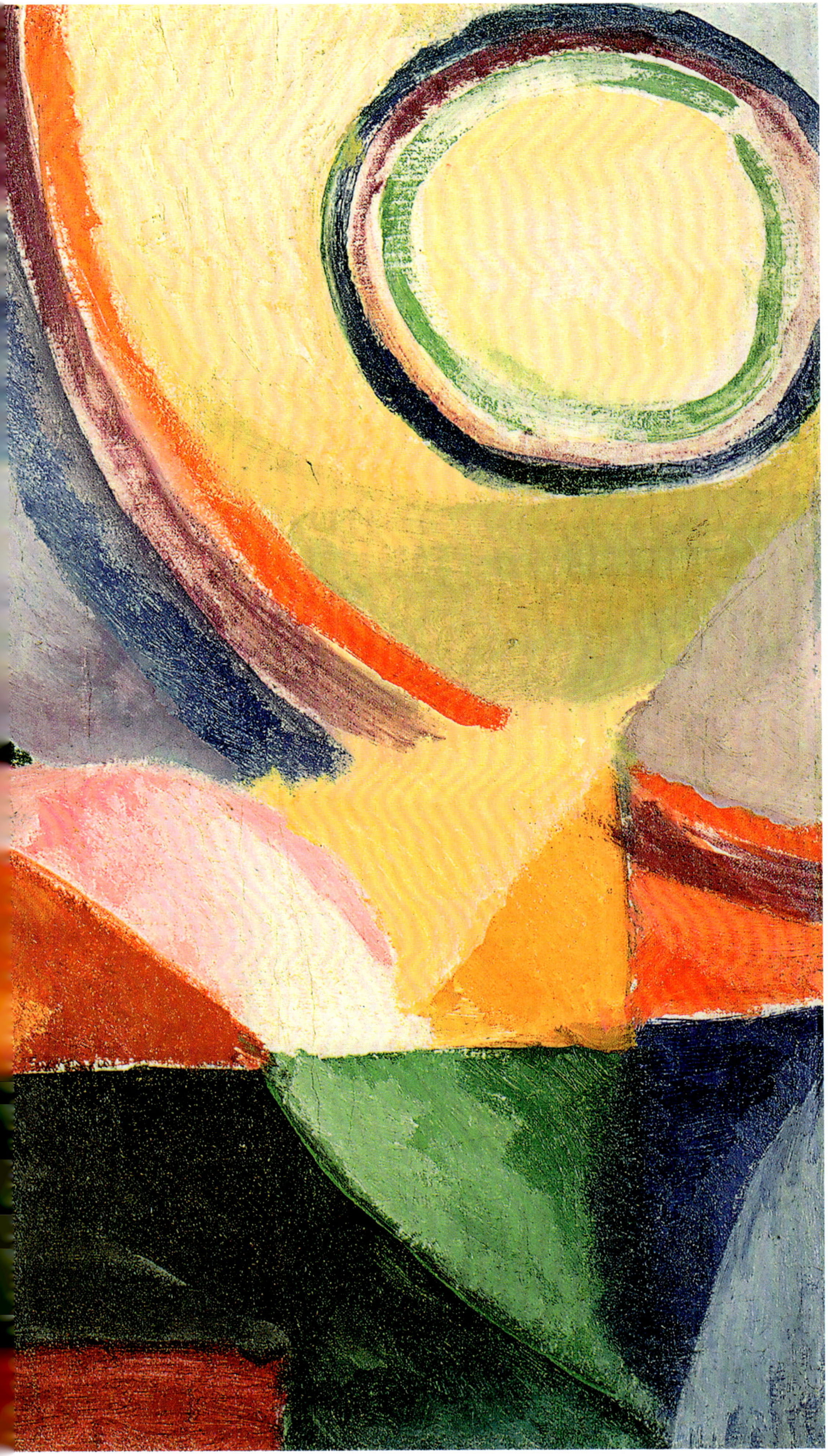

sequence, showing all the reciprocal movements triggered by her walking. In doing this, Duchamp introduced time as the fourth dimension in the painting. Though this nude triggered a scandal at the famous 1913 Armory Show in New York, some recognised the innovative character of this new work, calling it "the light at the end of the tunnel". Duchamp, brother of the painter Jacques Villon, the sculptor Raymond Duchamp-Villon and the painter Suzanne Duchamp, was anything but a consistent worker. His unruly soul quickly led him to experiment with different media and eclectic ideas that shocked the art world. In New York, he became friends with Francis Picabia, with whom he became responsible for Dada.

Simultaneity is the lyric expression of the modern view of life; it signifies the rapidity and the concurrence of all existence and action. Simultaneity for the Futurists was the "lyrical exultation [and] the artistic visualisation" of velocity. It is the result "of those great causes of universal dynamism." Simultaneity was also the focus of Robert and Sonia Delaunay. However, they both interpreted the term in a completely different manner. When Guillaume Apollinaire credited both the Delaunays with the term, the Futurist Boccioni accused them of plagiarism, because he was not prepared to cede this key term to others, much less to two whose interpretation veered so greatly from his own.

The Delaunays did not, like other artists, use this term to mean dynamism. They did not refer to the "*élan vital*" ("vital force") as Bergson did, but rather to Chevreul's theory of the law of simultaneous contrast. This theory, which dated from 1839 and had already played a role with the Impressionists, related colours and the relationship of objects to one another. Chevreul's work was republished in 1890 and thus more present in the collective knowledge of artists. Sonia Delaunay, in her work *Contrastes Simultanés* (*Simultaneous Contrasts*) (pp. 42-43) dared to jump directly into the abstract. Her painting was already a formal reference system of colour rhythms at a time when her husband Robert and artists Klee, Kandinsky, Mondrian and Picasso were still slowly making their way towards detaching themselves from objects.

Robert Delaunay founded Orphism, also known as Orphic Cubism. On account of the orchestration of colour, Guillaume Apollinaire named Delaunay's painting style after Orpheus, the singer of Greek mythology. The origins of his painting style derived from Impressionism, Analytical Cubism and from Cézanne. The new landmark of Paris, the Eiffel Tower, built in 1898, fascinated him. Its elegant design became the subject of the *Windows* series (p. 190). He painted it again and again, in new variations and refractions, using light and bright colour harmonies based on the colour values of light separated by a prism. Emphasising the delicate construction, he ceaselessly offered new perspectives of the monument, showing it in new lights and refractions, and always from a different viewpoint.

Sonia Delaunay,
Electric Prisms, 1914.
Oil on canvas, 250 x 250 cm.
Musée National d'Art Moderne,
Centre Georges-Pompidou, Paris.

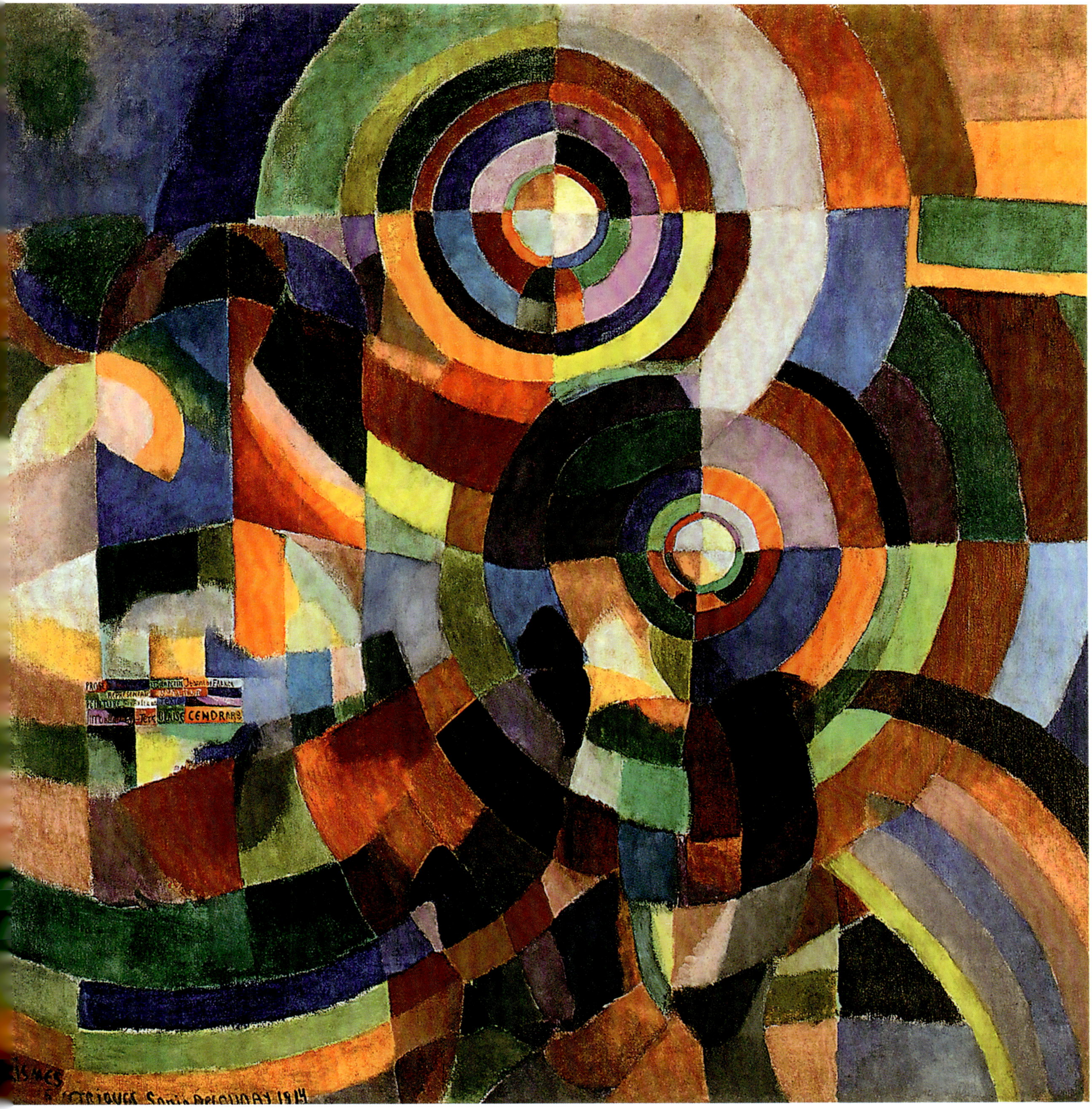
CENDRARS

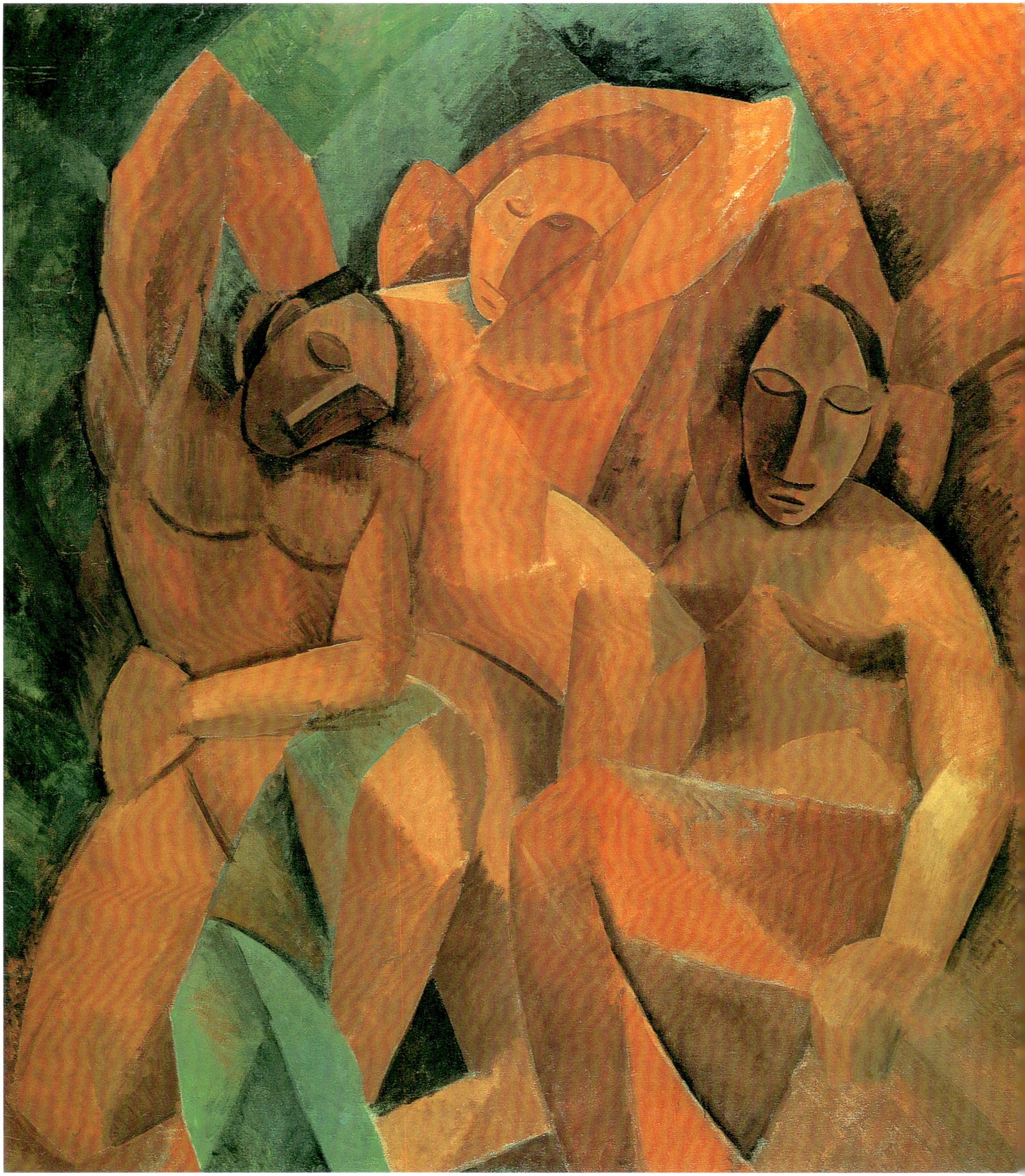

III. Picasso and Cubism

Les Demoiselles d'Avignon: Breaking with the Past

The young artists of the early twentieth century undoubtedly demonstrated an avant-garde spirit of aesthetic radicalism. Yet even the leader of the Fauves, Matisse, was scandalised when he visited Picasso and saw his masterpiece; to him the painting was an abuse of modern art, as he could find no aesthetically justified explanation for it. Could the work indeed be classified (at least in those days) as modern art? Many of its first viewers, at any rate, saw it as "something Assyrian" (that is how Wilhelm Uhde presented it to Kahnweiler). Douanier Rousseau, we know, noted in 1908 that Picasso worked in the Egyptian genre. It has now been proven that during his work on *Les Demoiselles d'Avignon* (p. 6), Picasso had two Iberian stone sculptures with which he "took counsel" in his experiments. Of course, there was certainly Matisse's *Blue Nude* and Derain's *Bathers*, but essentially, Picasso was always a solitary artist: "He was always free, owing nothing to anyone but himself" (Kahnweiler). From the distance of over four decades, here is how the artist himself explained the reasons and essence of the creative breakthrough of 1907: "I saw that everything had been done. One had to break, to make one's revolution and to start at zero."[1]

That break, however, that revolution, was neither instantaneously nor easily achieved. It was carried out amid the conditions of a new spiritual and creative crisis—one far more profound and all-embracing than ever before, because it touched on the technical, spiritual and pictorial possibilities open to the artist ("I saw that everything had been done"). It affected Picasso's future as an artist and, therefore, his existence as an individual. This was a solitary, internal revolution, and perhaps nobody ever understood it as well as Apollinaire, who went through the same kind of rupture and revolution one year later. In *The Cubist Painters* (1913) Apollinaire summed up both his own and Picasso's experience in a theory of artistic creation based on a somewhat surprising criterion: weariness.

While following the conceptual and compositional stages of the painting *Les Demoiselles d'Avignon* and observing the development of its separate images and the parallel appearance of ideas and pictures, we see how Picasso "formulates what he wishes to express", critically studies the creative process itself, stubbornly forces his hand to learn anew and to discard habitual virtuosity and an almost "automatic mastery". "Never was labour less well paid with joys," wrote Salmon,[2] who observed Picasso in his oppressed, troubled, agitated state of mind. Derain did not exclude the possibility of suicide.[3] Yet Picasso's solitude and seclusion were not demoralising. Recalling that period, he said that work had saved him; indeed, will-power helped to overcome the vagueness of his goal as he laboured over the simplest studies and academic models. Each consecutive stage was a new step into the unknown;

Pablo Picasso,
Three Women, 1908.
Oil on canvas, 200 x 178 cm.
The State Hermitage Museum, St. Petersburg.

every step was a violation of the status quo, a transcendence of given limits, a broadening of possibilities. "But what fatigue, imperfection, crudeness!"

What did Picasso gain at the price of "forgetting", with such difficulty, his former vision based on classic pictorial tradition? A new understanding of the plastic arts, in which their formal language has the same relationship with the forms of the visible world as poetic language has with everyday speech. In 1907, in fact, Picasso discovered what had only been implied in the theme of blindness during his Blue Period: the artist has an internal eye of imagination, it sees and feels emotionally (Penrose), and it is therefore essential for the artist "to realise that the world we see is nothing" (as he said many years later to Kahnweiler).[4]

Locked up in his studio, working through the night as was his habit, Picasso stubbornly concentrated on learning anew, changing his taste, re-training his personal feelings. There is a reason why nearly all the works of 1907 have the simplest classroom character: studies of nudes, half-lengths, heads, still lifes; there is also a reason why all of this "academic" work was produced without models, by imagination only. "In those times I worked completely without any models. What I was looking for was something very different," Picasso wrote to Daix.[5] He was seeking the power of expression, but not necessarily in the subject matter, the theme or the object, but in the lines, colours, forms, strokes and brushwork taken in their own independent meaning, in the energy of the pictorial handwriting.

Here he found support in the pre-classic and non-classic experience of mankind: in archaic, "primitive" and "barbaric" artistic systems akin to his own view of himself as a new Adam. On the one hand, the awkwardness and monstrosity of certain 1907 pictures served to re-educate feeling, while, on the other, they corresponded to Picasso's pictorial philosophy at the time. They both activated his emotional perceptions and imbued the image (thanks to their archaic associations) with a certain timeless atmosphere, a certain eternal background. However, this awkwardness may more accurately be ascribed to the feeling of aggressive destruction so typical of Picasso's revolutionary spirit in 1907. André Malraux recalls Picasso's words concerning the need "to always work against, even against oneself",[6] and that, it seems, was also a discovery of the period.

Picasso encountered his revolution having, as it were, lived the lives of several artists, having gone through several phases of growth, several periods (which is why Apollinaire spoke about "forgetting after study"). In addition, Picasso's was the language of concrete visual forms, not the ephemeral material of the word which, equally susceptible to emotions and meanings, easily leads the imagination into areas of theory, of purely intellectual abstractions. And yet it seems that it was precisely at this moment that Picasso was meditating on the effect of words on the imagination: by observing letters and hearing words—as objective realities—we perceive the images with our inner eye, we experience the feelings that they inspire. In keeping with the principle that, in essence, painting and poetry are the same, we must admit that visual elements, when purged of their common narrative function and taken in all their suggestive force, can also produce metaphors like those created with words, giving birth to a internal, poetic perception of images that inspires new sensations, different from any we've ever seen.

Pablo Picasso,
Dance of the Veils (Nude with Drapery), 1907.
Oil on canvas, 150 x 100 cm.
The State Hermitage Museum,
St. Petersburg.

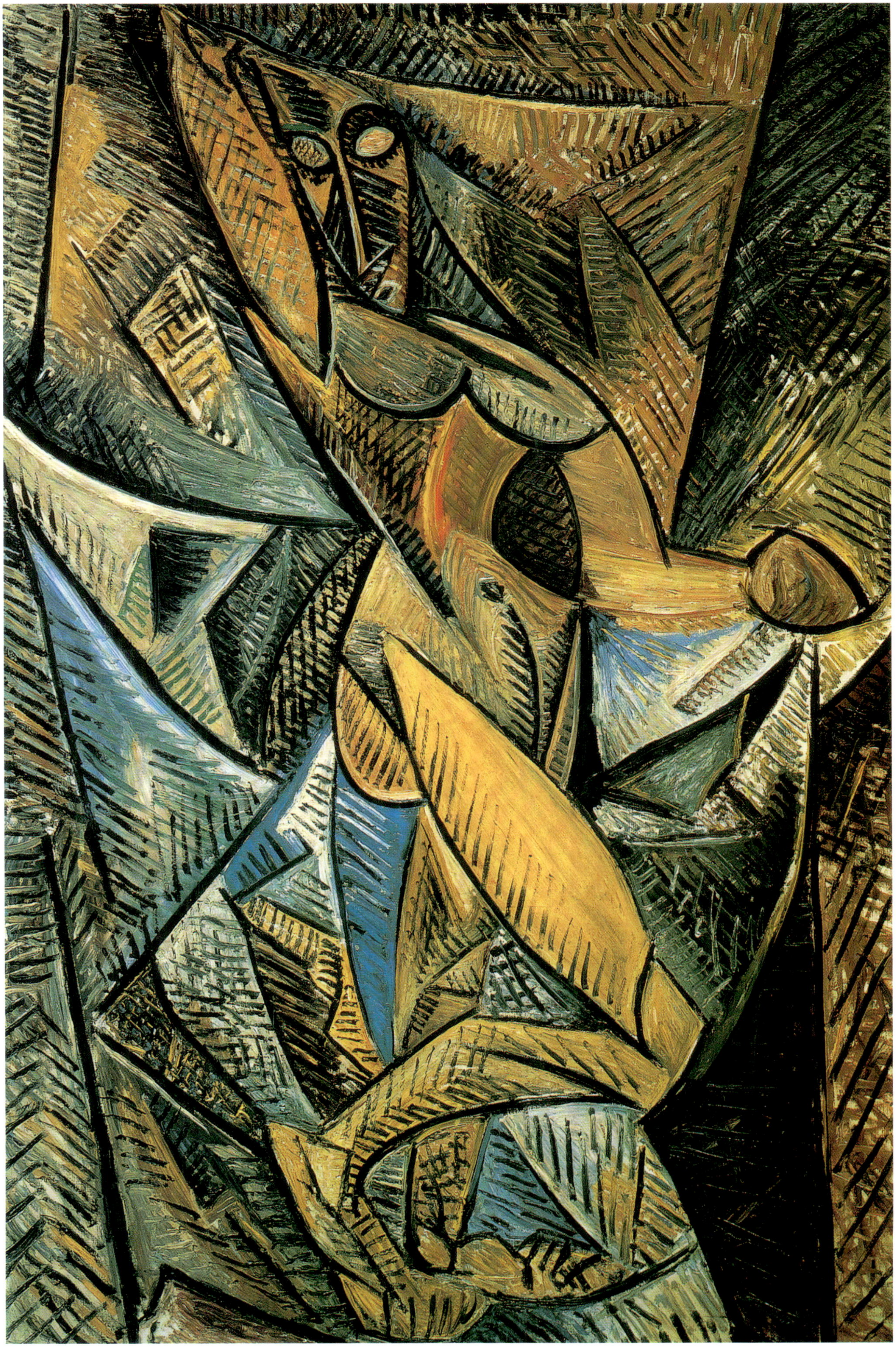

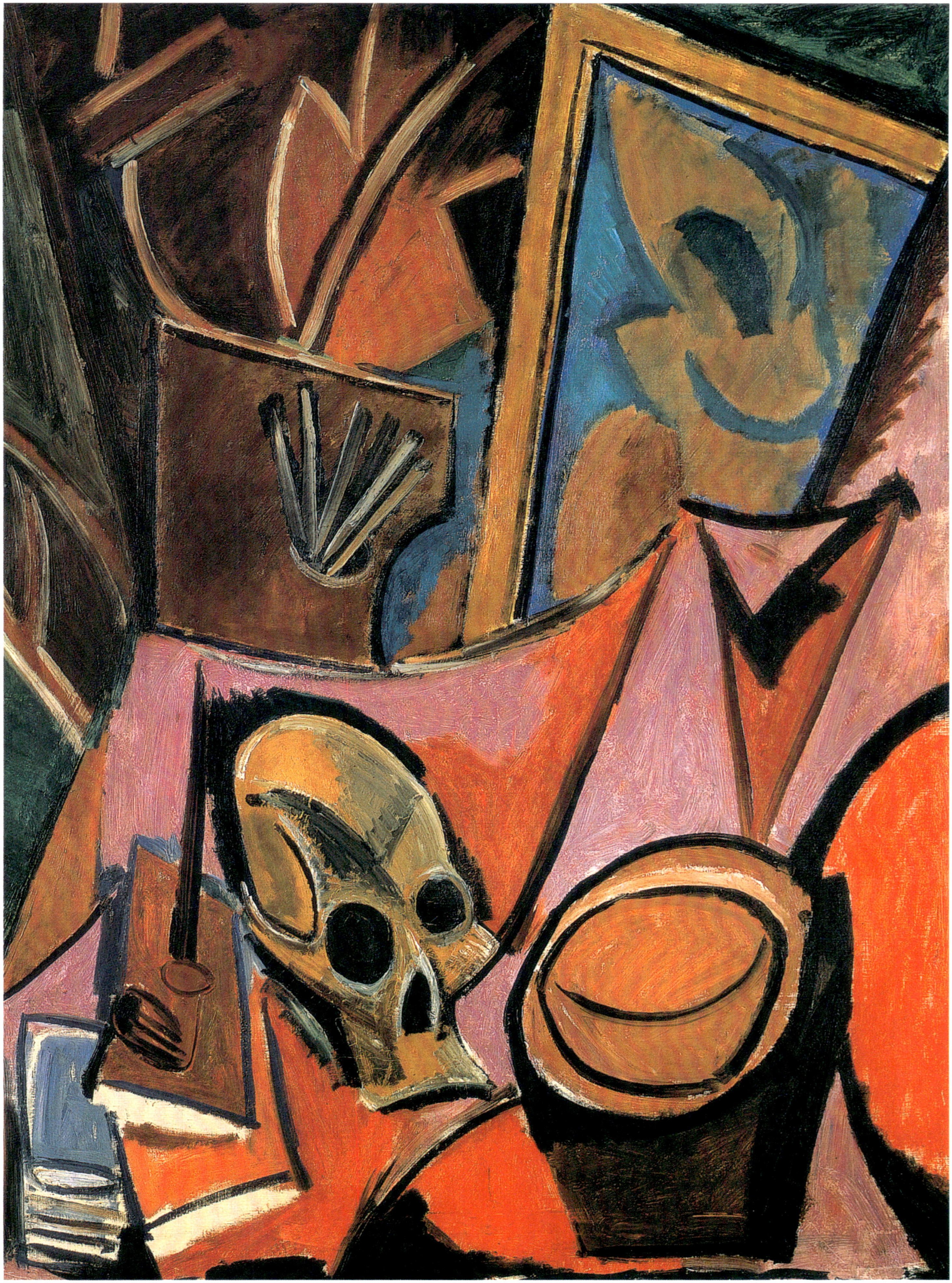

A New Pictorial Language

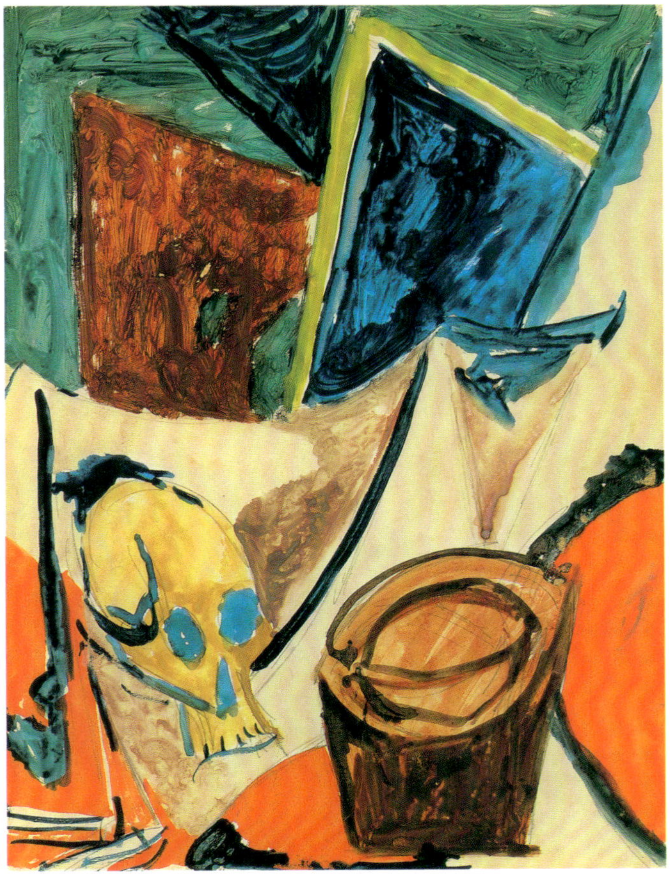

In 1907, while seemingly engaged in a purely formal quest, Picasso continually found in his new language various shades of pictorial meaning, amazing in their vitality and almost psychological essence. Among the great pictorial revelations of 1907 we find two masterpieces in the Hermitage collection: *The Dance of the Veils (Nude with Drapery)* (p. 49) and *Composition with Skull* (opposite). The title *The Dance of the Veils* is mere poetic licence, for in reality the canvas represents a nude against a background of academically abstract drapery academically counterpoised in a typical classroom position. However, in spite of the figure's relaxed and even somewhat languorous pose, the entire image is shot through with such varied and dynamically alive currents of energy that one involuntarily associates it with dance.

Without perhaps noticing it, Picasso in his *Dance of the Veils* returned in essence to the plastic concept of *Acrobat on a Ball*: a triangle standing on its apex and precariously balancing on a round form (there a ball, here an inverted arc); but while in the 1905 painting it was only the subject, the young acrobat, who stands in precarious equilibrium, in the 1907 work the very tectonic structure is caught in tense, dynamic balance, along with the troubled linear rhythm, the texture and tonality—in short, the form itself. Contradicting the academic rules of tectonic structure, Picasso used an effect that shocks the senses—an instability that creates the impression of profound, organic distress. Yet, nevertheless, it is the form that gives the figure and background pictorial and dynamic unity, in spite of its destructive plastic concept and disharmonious polychromic tones, in spite of all its internal conflicts.

The tension of the form immediately grabs the viewer, who perceives it as the real subject of the painting. It is purely visual, and although it can be analysed in formal terms, no description can fully render the impression created by this form-subject, woven, as it were, like a straw basket, yet living the brilliant life of a diamond that amazes us with its "luminous power" (Salmon).

The Dance of the Veils has traditionally—but groundlessly—been regarded in the context of African influences; the entire year of 1907 is referred to as the African Period. However, Picasso's "barbarism" of 1907 is not ethnographic in character, it is negativistic; a "working against, even against oneself", as he was to say later. *The Dance of the Veils* is polemically oriented on the European tradition of painting; it is literally full of various associations with that tradition, more often than not contradicting it. For instance, even without knowing that Picasso, while working on the Hermitage canvas, painted a copy of Ingres's *Grande Odalisque* in the same manner, one can feel the relationship with Ingres's

Pablo Picasso,
Composition with Skull, 1908.
Oil on canvas, 116.3 x 89 cm.
The State Hermitage Museum,
St. Petersburg.

Pablo Picasso,
Composition with Skull (sketch), 1907.
Watercolour, gouache and pencil
on paper, 32.5 x 24.2 cm.
The Pushkin Museum of Fine Arts,
Moscow.

Pablo Picasso,
Seated Woman, 1908.
Oil on canvas, 150 x 99 cm.
The State Hermitage Museum,
St. Petersburg.

Pablo Picasso,
Dryad, 1908.
Oil on canvas, 185 x 108 cm.
The State Hermitage Museum,
St. Petersburg.

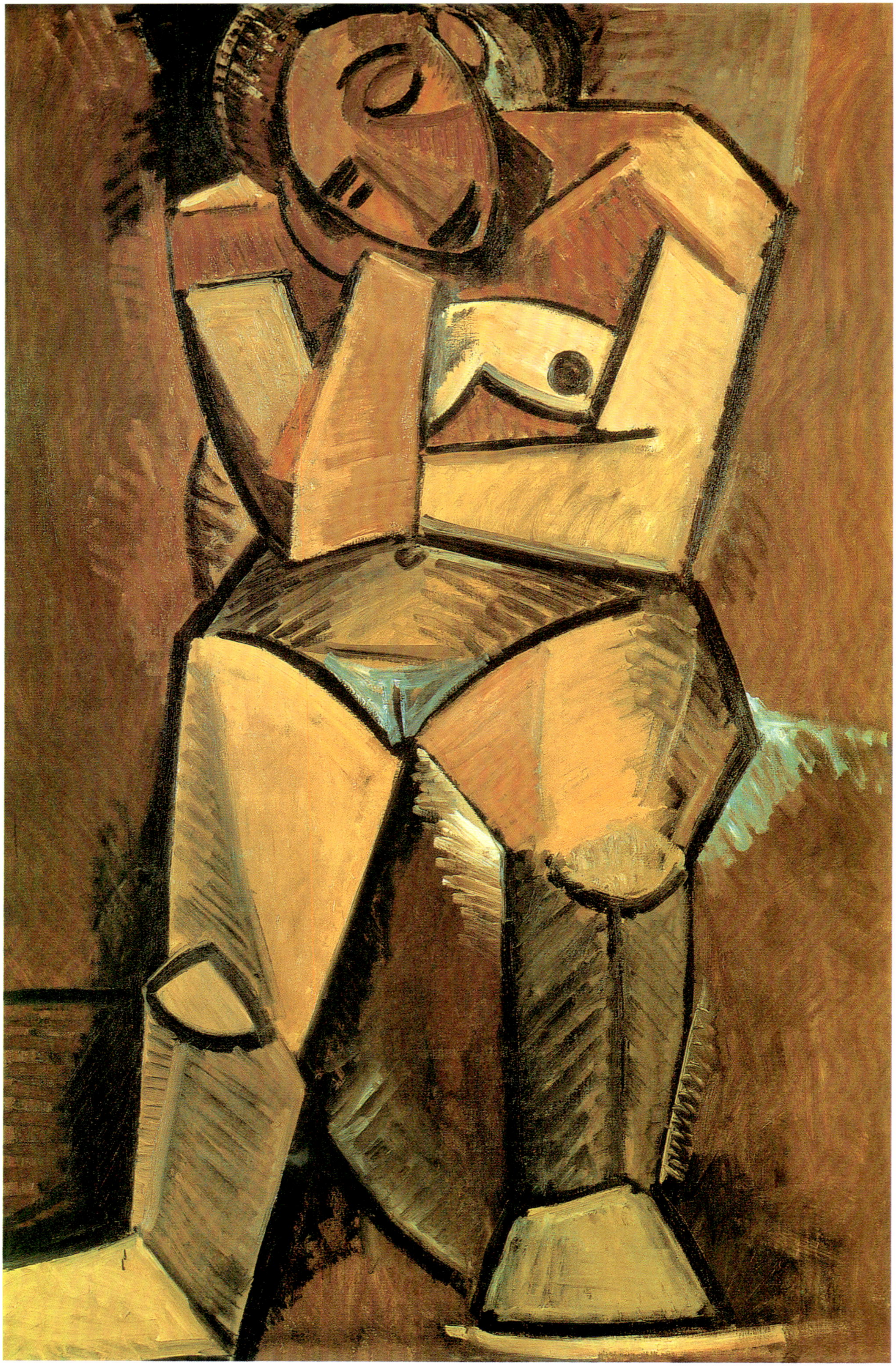

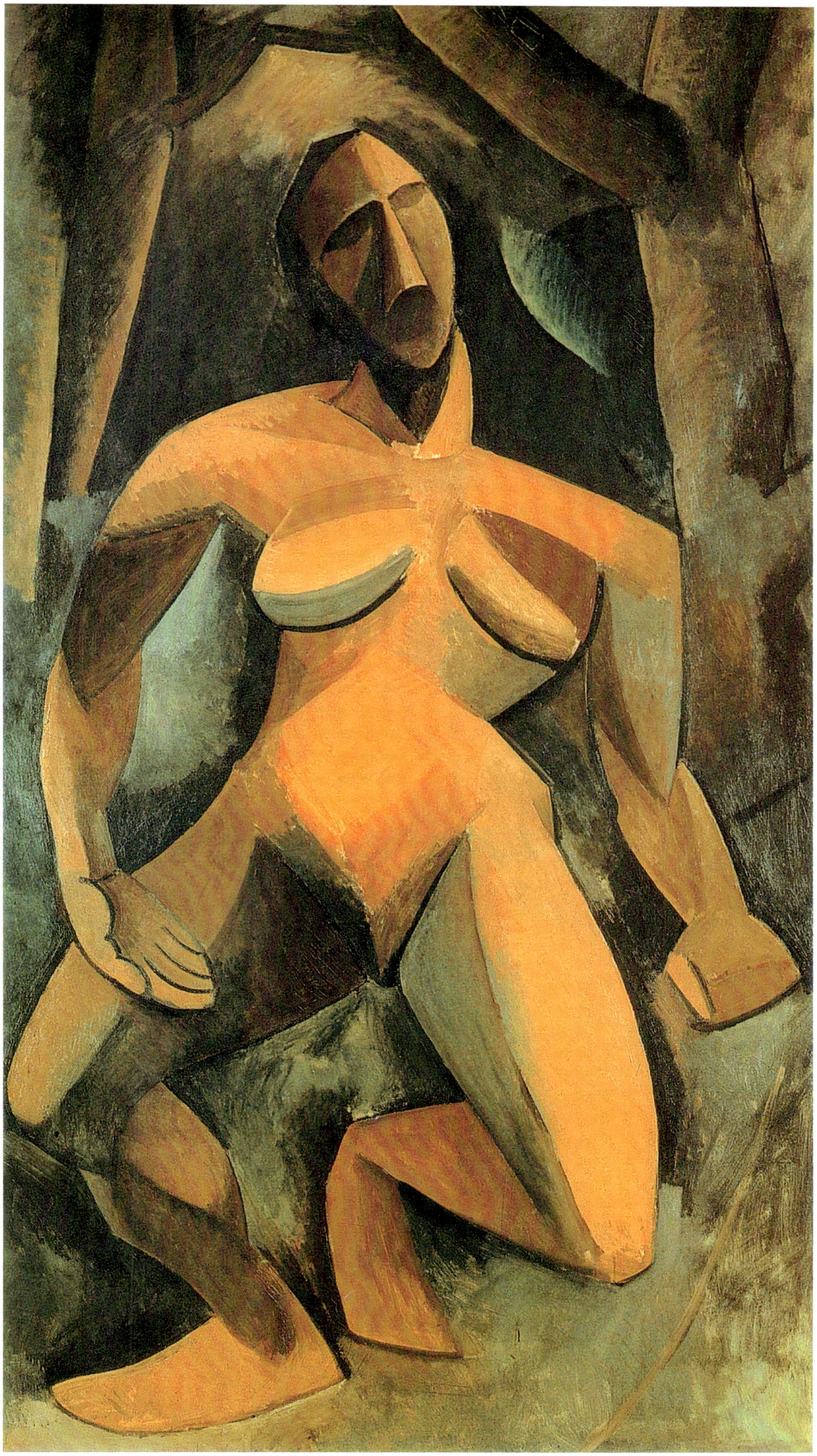

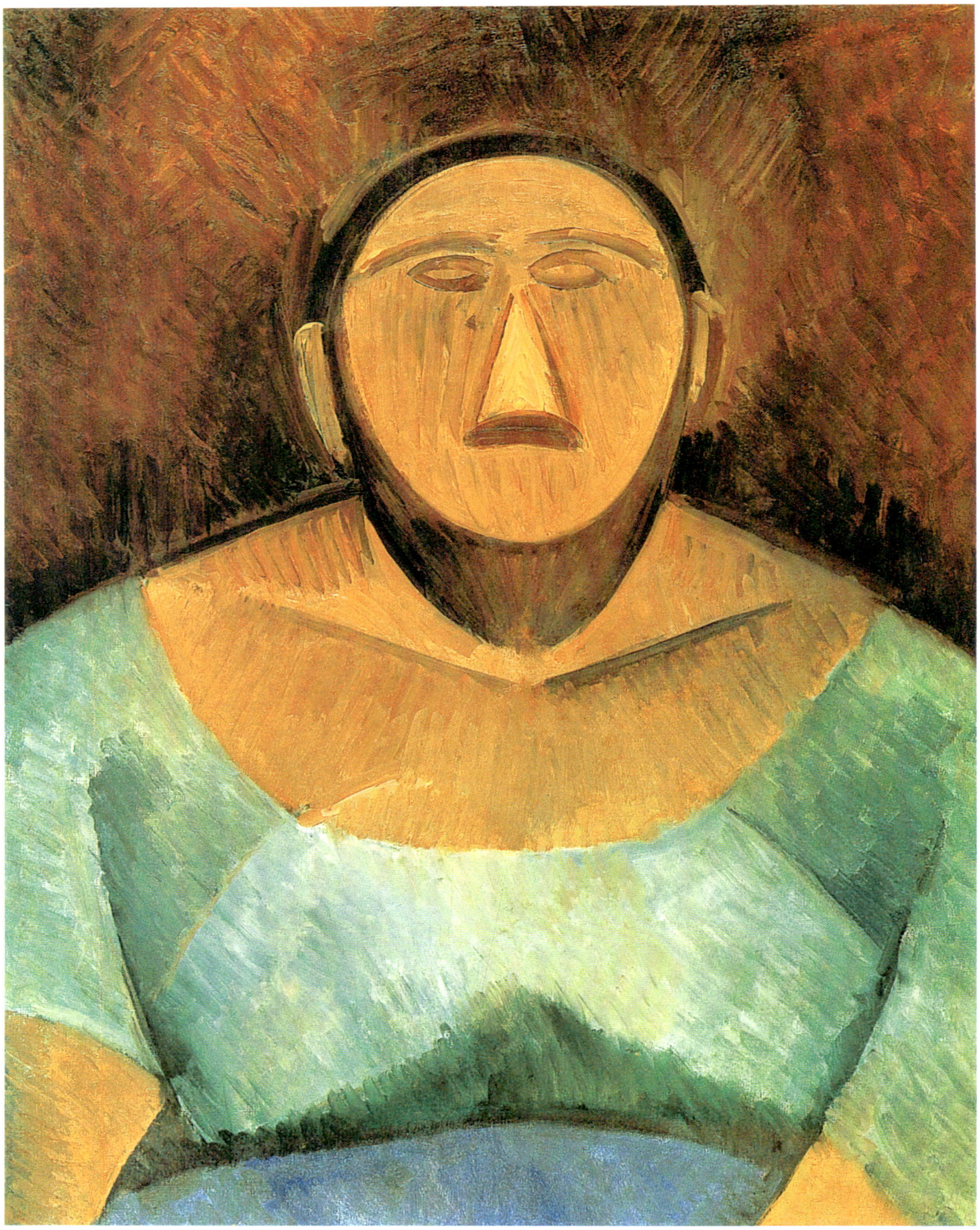

Pablo Picasso,
Farm Woman (Half-Length), 1908.
Oil on canvas, 81 x 56 cm.
The State Hermitage Museum,
St. Petersburg.

Pablo Picasso,
Farm Woman (Full-Length), 1908.
Oil on canvas, 81.5 x 55.5 cm.
The State Hermitage Museum,
St. Petersburg.

La Source, famous for its powerful line. Finally, the texture of the brushwork bristles with such energy that the viewer is bound to think of the expressive, spontaneous technique of Van Gogh.

The same link with the European pictorial tradition, if not as simply discernible, is embedded in the concept of the *Composition with Skull* (pp. 50, 51), which is often, and not without reason, interpreted as Picasso's original variation on the Vanitas theme, so widespread in traditional Western painting. Indeed, the death's head, a traditional symbol of the vanity of life, is combined here with the palette and brushes, painting and books, as well as the pipe, as allegories of intellectual and sensual pleasure, characteristic of that genre.

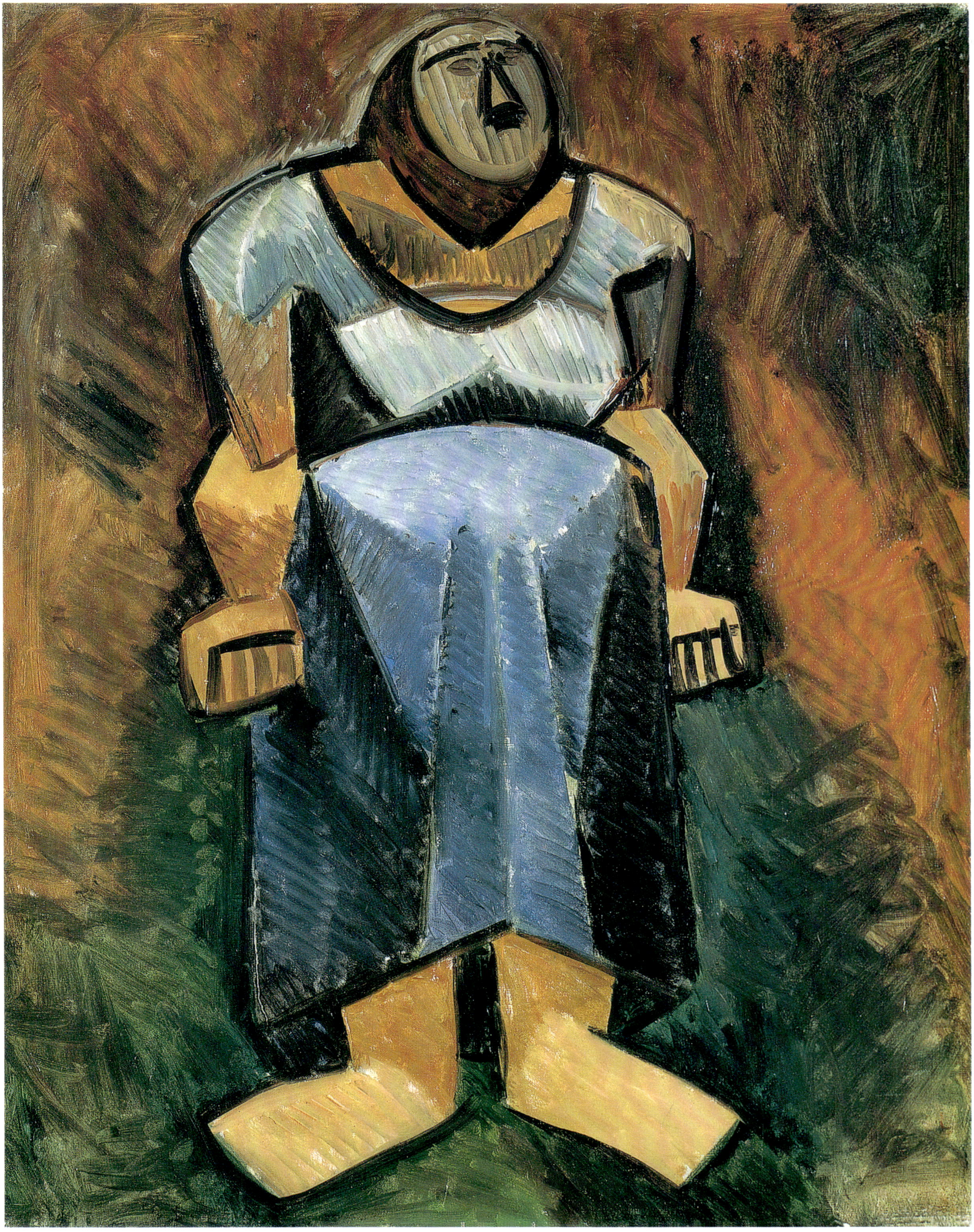

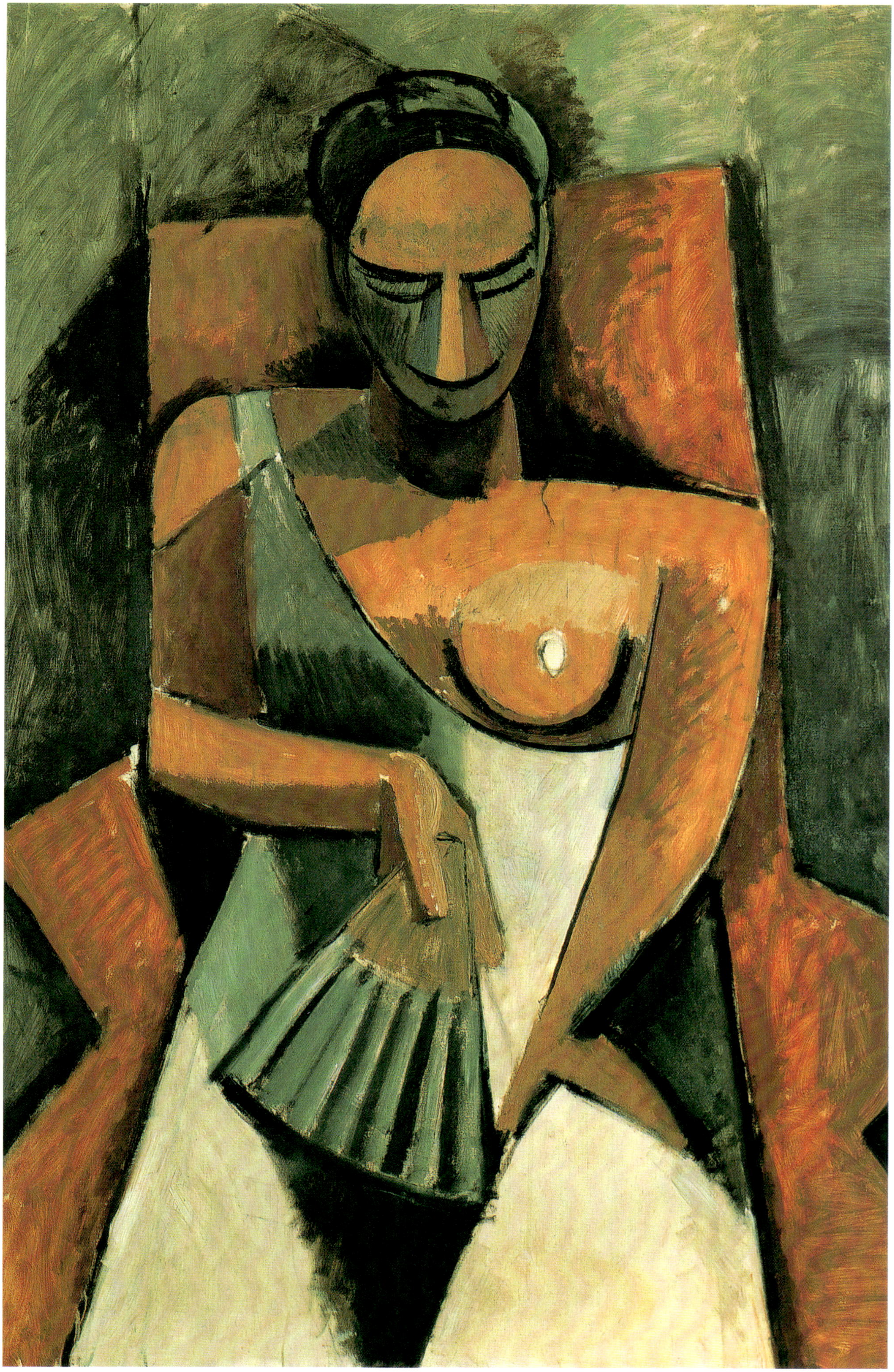

At the same time, the pipe, book of verses, palette, brushes, painting and the skull could be ordinary objects in an artist's studio, and their being thrown together in disorder here is typical of a studio such as Picasso's in the Bateau-Lavoir (to say nothing of all the others he was to occupy). No spirit of wisdom, no ethical preaching of philosophy ("memento mori", "all is vanity") comes from this still life.

On the contrary, the feverish funereal quality of its cold and strident tonalities, the collisions and broken lines of its jagged, sharp surfaces, the headlong fall of its diagonals, all reflect an exalted mourning of a purely personal kind. Much like a huge nugget of raw gold, the human skull serves only to give a final definition to the metaphorical meaning of the form: this is a requiem, though perhaps an unusual one. In the foreground, "face to face" with the death's head, stands an object as mundane as an empty household vessel—a small pail? a pot?—seen even more clearly and impressively in the sketch. In the composition, this object is no less meaningful than the skull—and, perhaps, not only in the composition. Not being a traditional attribute of the iconographic Vanitas theme, such an extravagance in this serious context must have had a very significant meaning, even for Picasso's unorthodox imagination. If the importance of the subject and the clearly agitated mood of the artist reflect a profoundly personal reason for painting this *Composition with Skull*, then this object is the key to its meaning. Its secret may be read through a play on words: an earthenware jar—*jarra* in Spanish—suggests the work is dedicated to the writer Alfred Jarry, whose sudden death on 1 November 1907, could not but have affected Picasso.

In fact, the bold comparison in this memorial composition of a skull and an earthenware jar as two empty vessels is tragically grotesque and full of sorrow. We feel here not only the artist's emotions, but also something of the unconventional, shocking style of Jarry, who was to be remembered as literature's eternal impudent rogue.

Poetic Metaphor

It is not sufficient to understand the revolutionary upheaval of 1907 only as a search for untraditional formal approaches to traditional themes in art, only as a renewal of the language of the visual arts.

The main achievement of Picasso's creative spirit—the result of this revolution and the foundation of his entire subsequent work—was the poetic metaphor, that is to say the creation of an image based on the most unexpected associations, on the interplay and power of imagination. The development of this new poetry would, during the Cubist period, lead to such startling inventions as the inclusion of words as images in a visual context. That was when Picasso, as he was later to say, would paint with words. Perhaps the very first step in that direction was his requiem for Alfred Jarry, *Composition with Skull.*

The appearance of this programmatic painting—this still life on the theme of death—on the eve of 1908 reveals Picasso's need to express his new creative consciousness

Pablo Picasso,
Woman with a Fan, 1907.
Oil on canvas, 152 x 101 cm.
The State Hermitage Museum,
St. Petersburg.

Pablo Picasso,
Friendship (sketch), 1908.
Watercolour and gouache on paper,
61.9 x 47.6 cm.
The Pushkin Museum of Fine Arts,
Moscow.

Pablo Picasso,
Friendship (sketch), 1908.
Watercolour and gouache on paper,
63 x 47.7 cm.
The Pushkin Museum of Fine Arts,
Moscow.

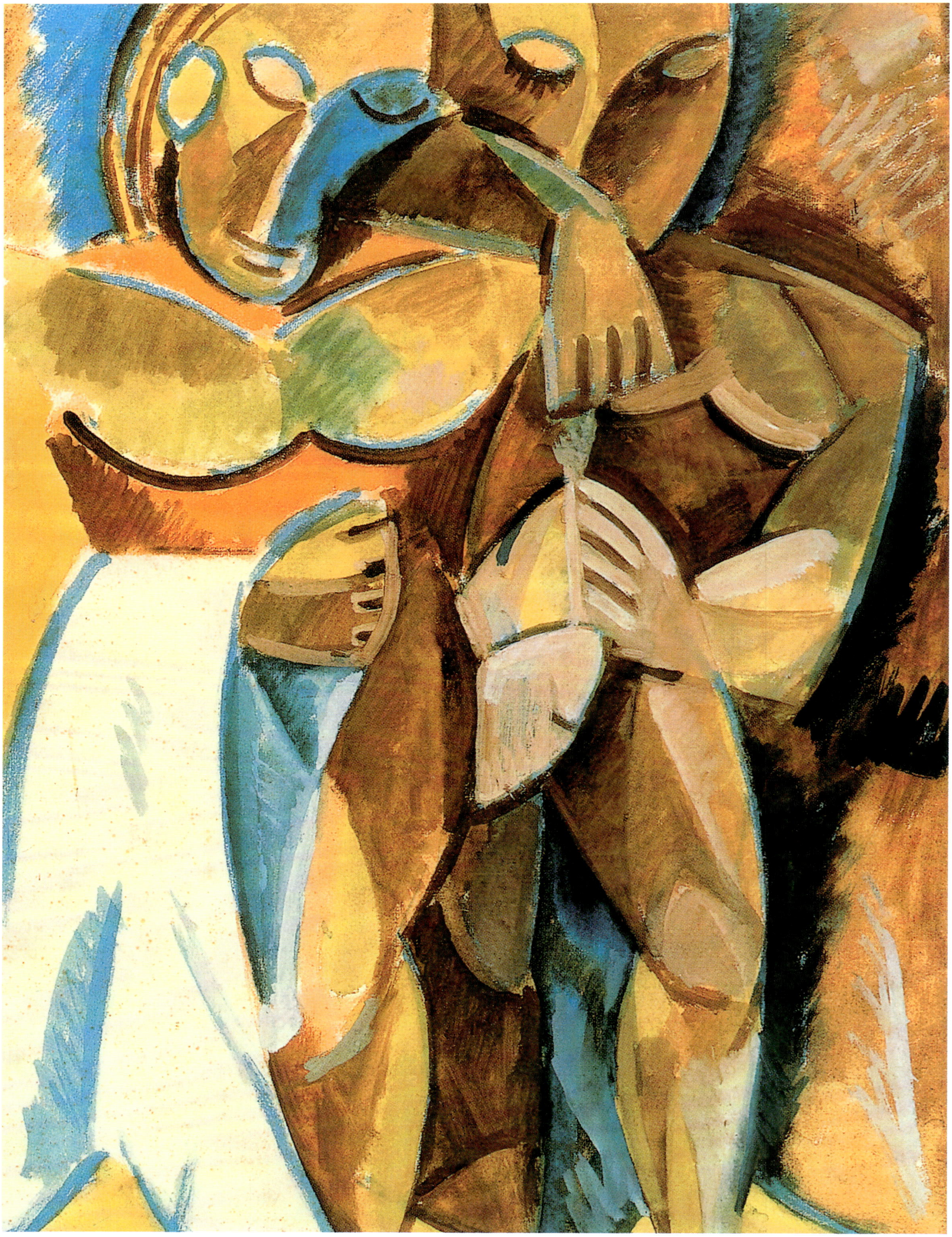

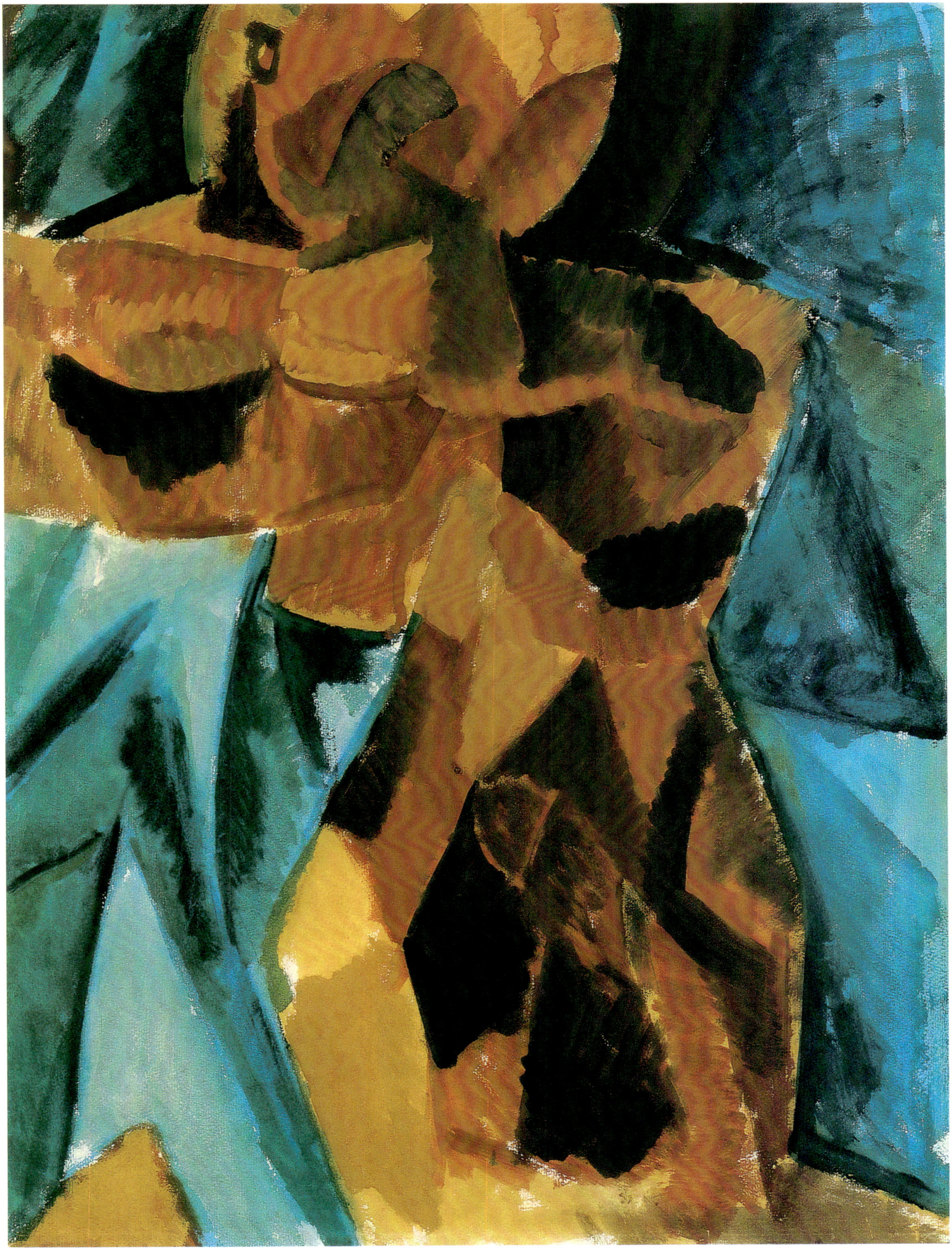

in conceptualised works after a long period of re-evaluation and reassessment. Yet even though from the start of 1908 Picasso had sketched and developed a multitude of subjects, each of which had the potential to lead to a significant composition, hardly any of them went farther than the preparatory stage, and those that did turned out differently from their original concept.

In spite of the attention paid over the past decade to Picasso's so-called early Cubist work and all the efforts made to achieve some order in the understanding of his evolution,[7] the clarity one would like to see in the general comprehension of the period of 1907-1908 is still lacking. The chronology is confused, reflecting a vague understanding of the artist's creative ideas, of their interrelationships and progressions. The issue of Picasso's pictorial philosophy at that time has hardly been examined and, in fact, its importance has yet to be fully appreciated. The formal approach, the preconceived view of works of that period as being proto-Cubist or pre-Cubist (as a proto-stage in the development of Cubism) does not allow scholars to assess the artist in his full significance. Yet it was precisely in 1908, at the height of "proto-Cubism", that visitors to Picasso's studio heard him speak not "of values and volumes", but "of the subjective and of the emotions and instinct".[8]

If one leaves aside the concept of proto-Cubism and looks upon the creative material of 1908 as a single entity, ignoring differences in size and technique between paintings, sculptures and minor sketches, then one sees their organic unity as a monumental ensemble—not of works as such, but of Picasso's creative ideas. One involuntarily thinks of some grandiose concept that was never achieved as a real project: something akin to Michelangelo's tomb of Pope Julius II, where individual sculptures—fragments (often incomplete) of the entire work—have long enjoyed their own separate museum existence, playing a role never conceived by the artist, mysteriously meaningful things in themselves, the independently valuable splinters of a non-existent whole. The same applies to Picasso's works of 1908, which startle one at first glance by their significance and power of expression; but for separate works to acquire their real meaning, one must restore the context of that art. Like Goethe, Picasso could have said (indeed, he did say, although in different words): "All my works are only fragments of one great confession; to understand them, one must know their origins, capture the moment of their conception."[9]

Turning from the paintings to the original ideas—sketches, drafts, studies—one sees everywhere not simply figurative compositions but, as it were, depictions of certain events, ideas for subjects, each with its own internal dramaturgy. It seems as though the new form itself—built on the expressive rhythm of strong, sinuous lines, on sharp, clean, articulated planes, on the internal equilibrium of the entire pictorial structure, this morphologically clear and monumentally impressive form—produced in the artist's imagination impersonal, timeless, powerful images. What could be vaguely felt in the works of 1907 as something existing before time, as some background to eternity, now, thanks to the characteristics of form, becomes objective reality, emerges in the thematic solution itself. Picasso's creative

Pablo Picasso,
Friendship, 1908.
Oil on canvas, 152 x 101 cm.
The Pushkin Museum of Fine Arts, Moscow.

Pablo Picasso,
Bathing, 1908.
Oil on canvas, 39 x 62 cm.
The State Hermitage Museum, St. Petersburg.

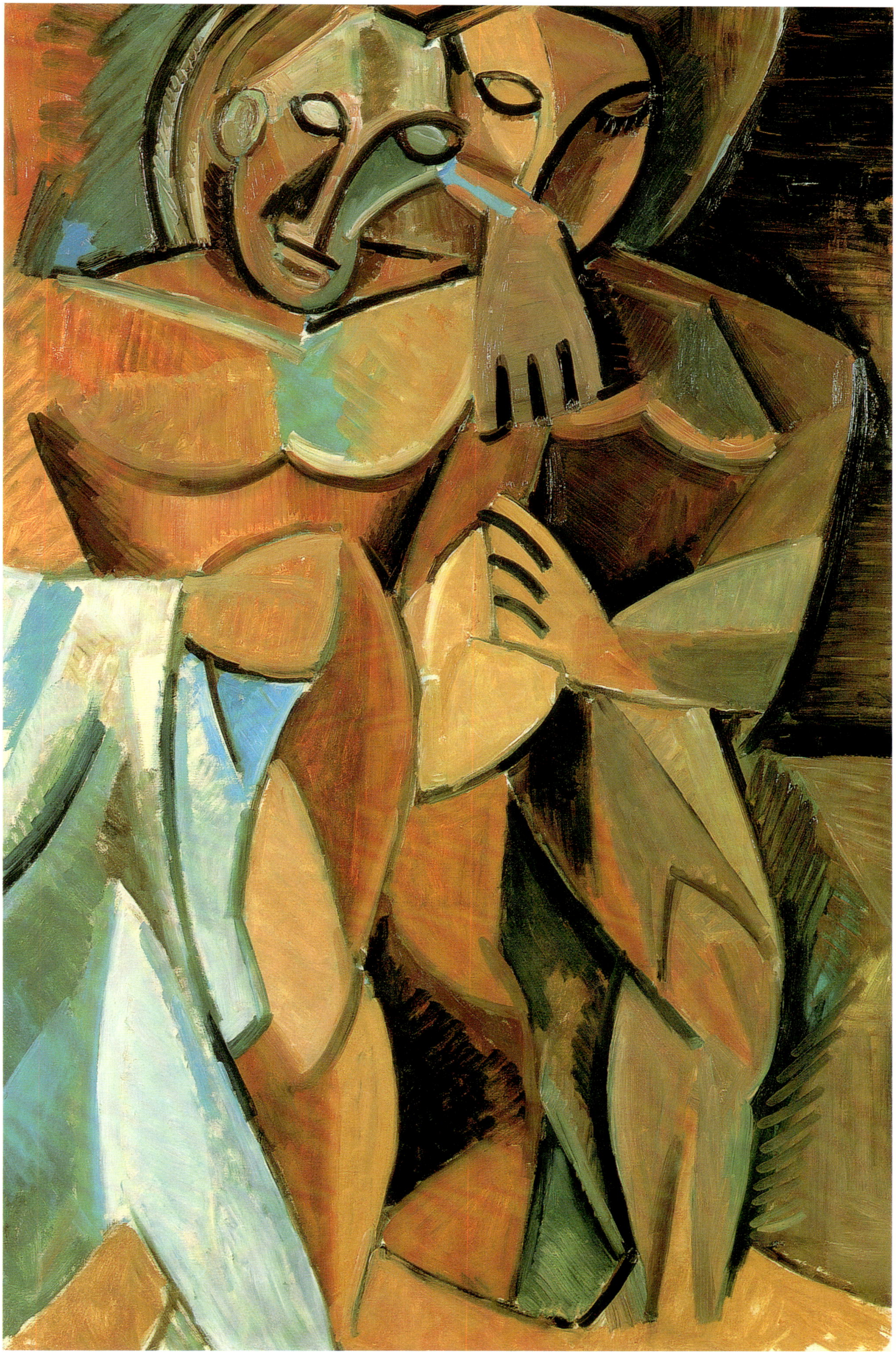

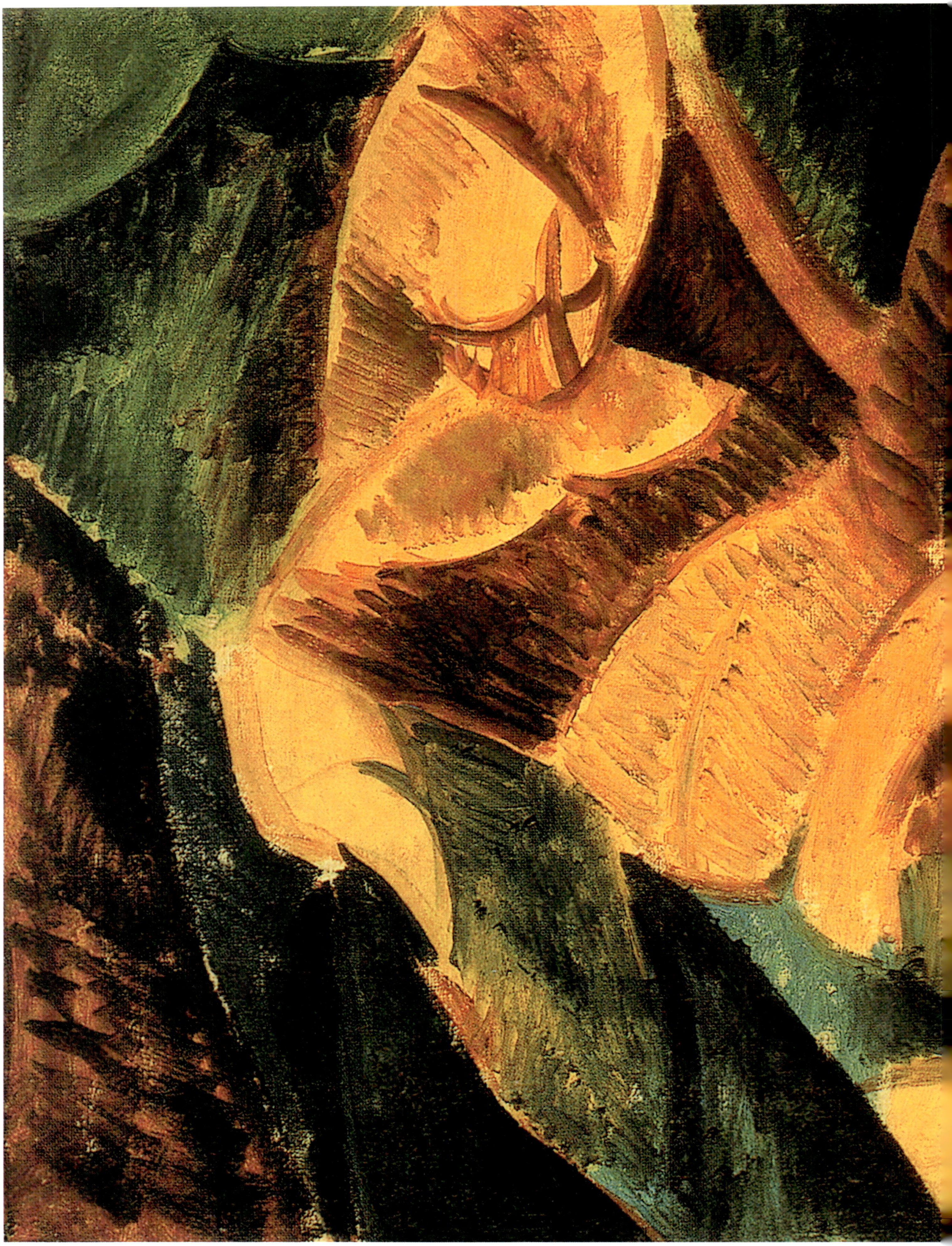

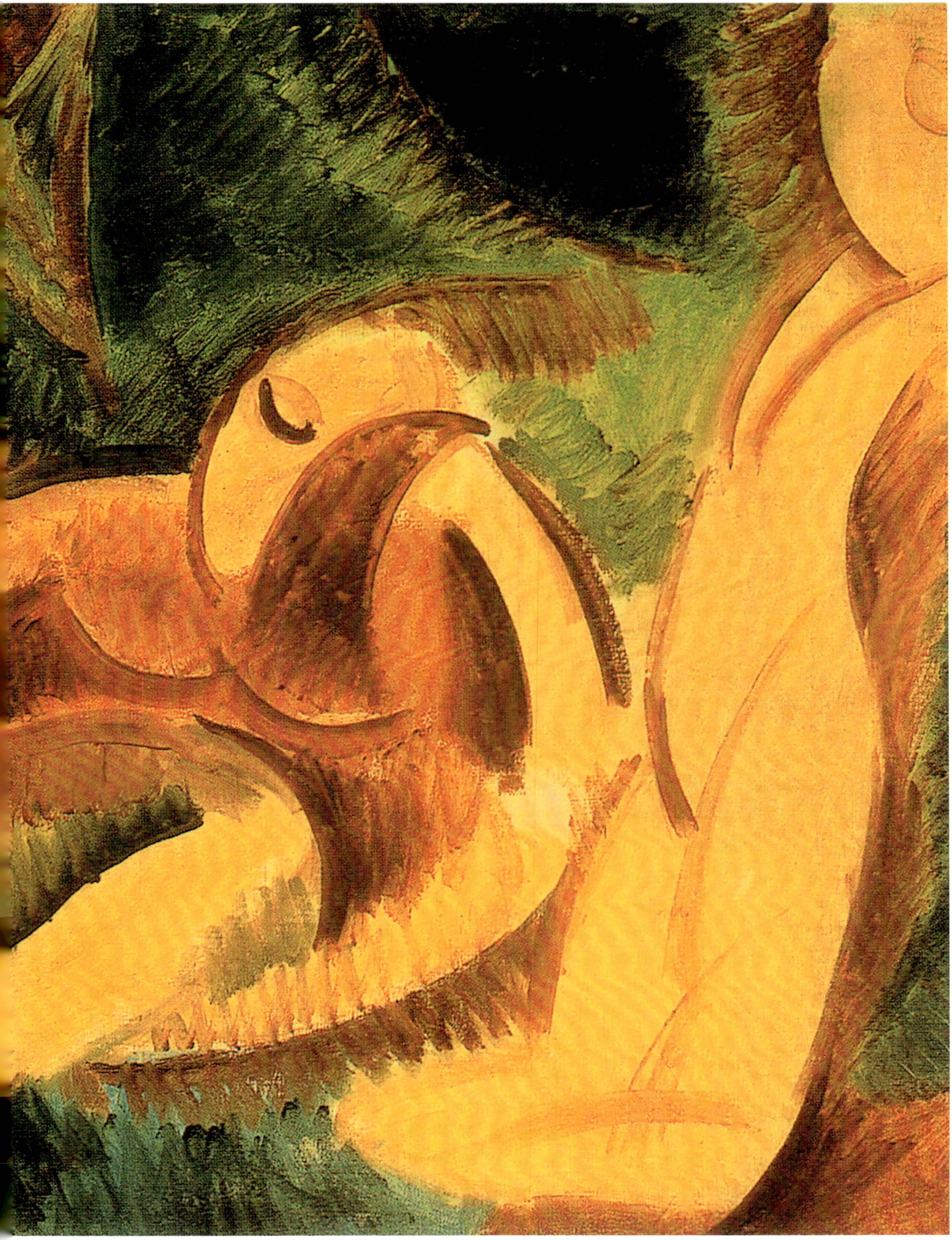

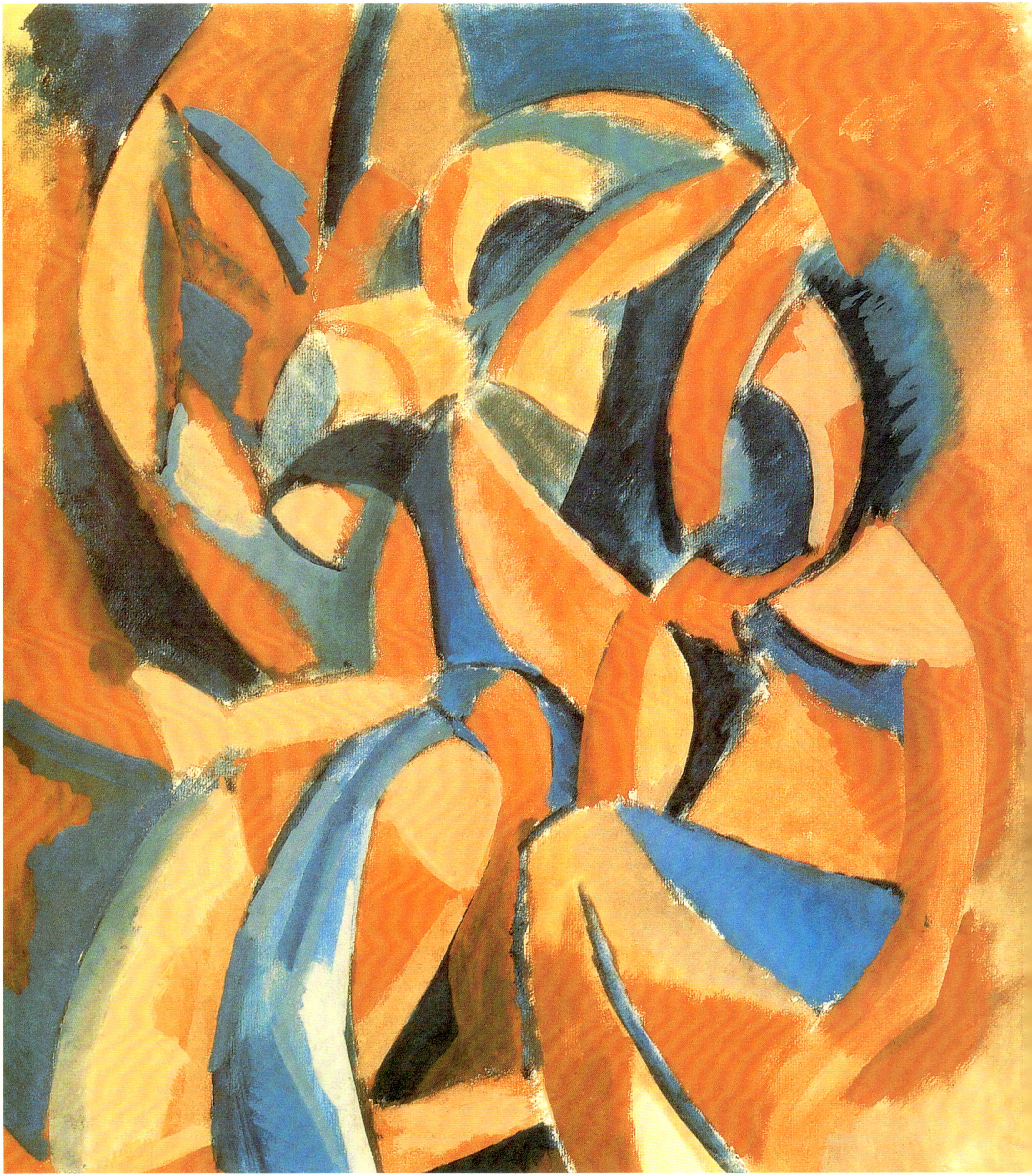

thinking, however, had long before crossed the psychological frontier into the area of ideas that are alien to story-telling-poetic "novels" with narrative and psychological links—but from which prototypes of universal mythological thought emerge. Deeply involved throughout 1907 in the development of a new plastic anatomy for his painting, an anatomy based on the material of the human figure, Picasso imperceptibly, instinctively uncovers and then grasps the corporal-psychological differences of structure between the male and the female archetype: the square form (symmetry and static quality) of the one, and the rhombic form (the capacity for plasticity and the Gothicism) of the other. Basic morphological structure helps him to grasp the metaphorically expressed essential truth of natural phenomena.

By that time Picasso had already discovered African wooden sculpture in the ethnographic museum at the Palais du Trocadero and, like many other artists, had bought several statues and masks. For him these were not only works of incredible outward expressiveness, works in which others sought to find an explanation for his innovations. André Malraux cites Picasso as saying: "Their forms had no more influence on me than they did on Matisse or Derain. For them, though, the masks were sculptures like all others. When Matisse showed me his first African head, he spoke to me of Egyptian art."[10] Picasso, however, immediately saw in them magical objects with their own artistic idioms. And the discovery of African art staggered him by its correspondence to his own deeply personal attitude towards life, his own attitude towards creative work. Just as in the year before, the desire for self-realisation had led Picasso to prehistoric Iberian sculpture, now the irrational, superstitious side of his complex nature led him to grasp the universal goals of art through the magical figures of spirits. During the autumn of 1907 the artist spent long hours carving strange, fetish-like figurines and primitive dolls and making sketches for future sculptures (see drawings and engravings). He was not alone in this passion, for Derain as well was occupied with carving at that time. Unlike Derain's wooden sculptures, however, those of Picasso bore not a hint of decorativeness. These were indeed fetish figurines, and they exude something grave, threatening, dramatic. The same figurines became the characters of his paintings near the beginning of 1908.

Picasso approached the subject as a sculptor, saying, "When it comes to paintings [. . .], it would be enough to dissect them—colours, after all, being no more than the indications of different perspectives—then reassemble them according to the indications given by colour, in order to find yourself in the presence of a 'sculpture'. The dead painting would not be missed"[11]: if painting is always an illusion, something projected onto a screen, sculpture is always an objective reality, the image of the sculpture being present in the character of the object-thing.

The reason for, and meaning of, Picasso's proto-Cubism are normally explained as the artist's desire to radically simplify his pictorial vision of the objective world, to strip away the layers of illusion and reveal its constructive physical essence. It is usual in this context to cite the famous words Cézanne wrote in a letter addressed to the artist Émile

Pablo Picasso,
Three Women (sketch), 1908.
Watercolour and gouache on paper, 54 x 47.7 cm.
The Pushkin Museum of Fine Arts, Moscow.

Pablo Picasso,
Pitcher and Bowls, 1908.
Oil on canvas, 66 x 50.5 cm.
The State Hermitage Museum, St. Petersburg.

Pablo Picasso,
Green Pan and Black Bottle, 1908.
Oil on canvas, 61 x 50.5 cm.
The State Hermitage Museum, St. Petersburg.

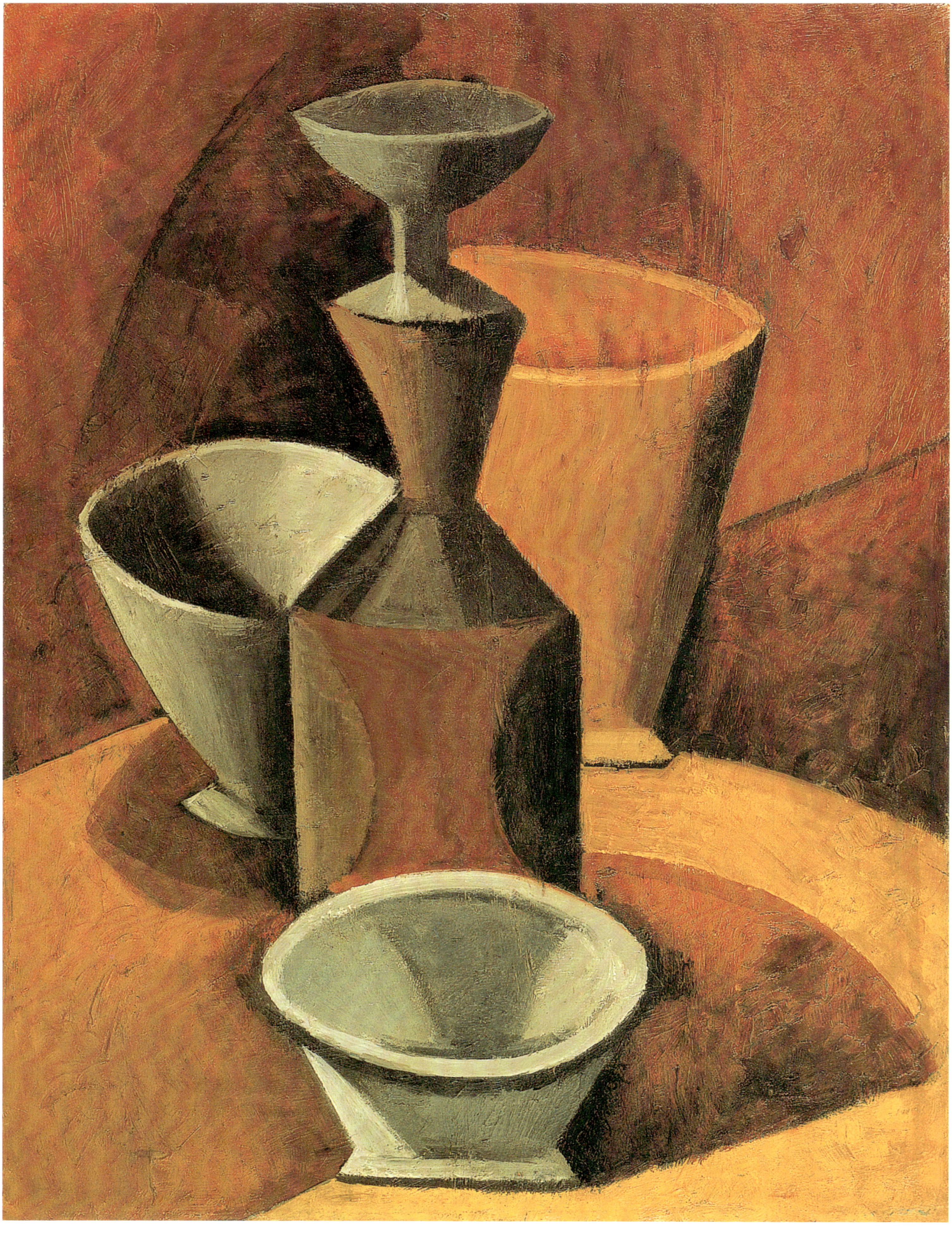

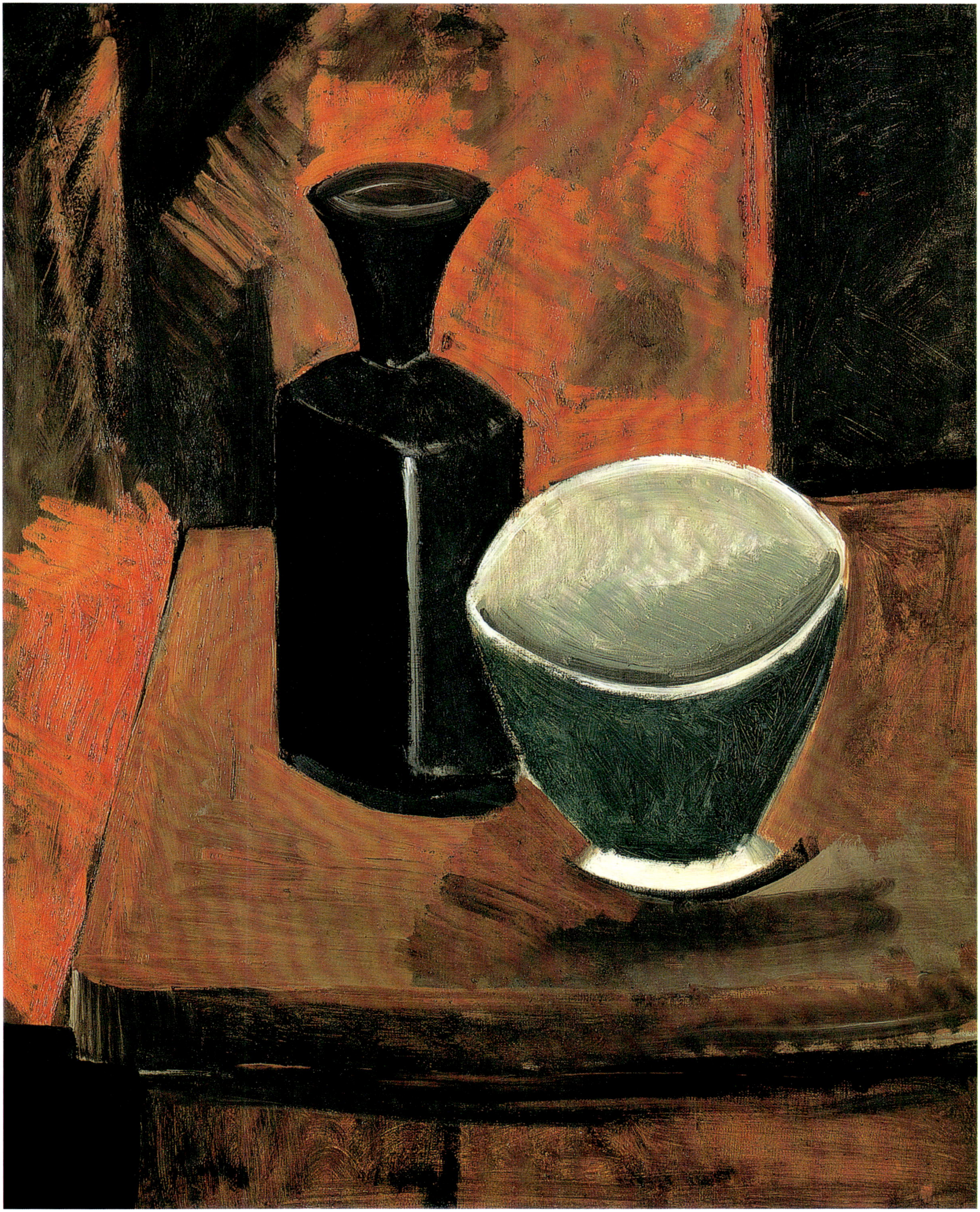

Bernard that was published in the autumn of 1907: "Treat nature by means of cylinder, sphere, cone." Another of the generally assumed points of departure for so-called proto-Cubism is the African influence, which introduced simplification of anatomy and other expressive features. The combination of these two diametrically opposed influences—Cézanne's "perceptualised" art and black Africa's "conceptualised" art—is usually employed to explain the stylistic phenomenon of proto-Cubism as an art entirely preoccupied with the problem of space.

Subjectivity

Yet when we dig deeper into the sources of Picasso's creative ideas—the sketchbooks of early 1908—we find not objective reality geometrised for geometrisation's sake, but rather a desire to lend adequate expression to the artist's subjective truth concerning the primary and most profound essentials of the human world.

Picasso's proto-Cubism of 1908 began with this expression of the eternal differences between man and woman. During that time, drafts of two paintings appeared in his sketchbooks: a seated man and a seated woman, conceived as a pair.

The man is monolithically cubic, like an Aztec statue, with an accented frontal plane and a symmetrical structure: both hands are clasped on the torso, the head is inclined, the eyes are closed, and there is something morose in the entire figure, with its primitive power. The woman's plastic character is more complex: a hieroglyph stressing asymmetry, broken lines expressing suffering (see a ceramic tile of a later date). The male sketches were executed in oil only at the end of 1908 (see *Man with his Arms Crossed*, p. 79). *Seated Woman* (p. 52) was immediately created as a large canvas.

In this painting Picasso was hardly trying to solve the "spatial problem through a brutal geometrisation that here gives the woman the semblance of a mechanical statue."[12] On the contrary, everything in *Seated Woman* is subordinated to expression: not only the figure's sorrowful pose, but also the primitive form and the brutal, graphic style, the depressing brownish colour and the drama of the tonal contrast, even the scarified brushwork—all are part of the metaphor of suffering. Deformation of body and expression has a pictorial meaning here: in these "distortions" one can see an attempt to express the nature of woman as a *machine à souffrir*, as Picasso himself was to say thirty years later, at the time of *Weeping Woman* and *Guernica*.

The second antithesis to the seated man—another facet of woman, expressive but without suffering—is represented by *Woman with a Fan* (p. 56), also originating from the same sketchbook. The harmonious principle of internal equilibrium holds sway in this work: mutual reflections, response patterns of form and rhythm, tranquil shadings of ochre, white and grey tones. First conceived as a portrait of Fernande Olivier, the painting preserved in its formal structure the tranquillity, classic clarity and majestic bearing of the model's character and physical type. And if the compact, reserved image reminds one of seated Egyptian statues, in a less literal way, deep inside, its monumental proportions prefigure the gigantic order of Picasso's so-called classic style of the 1920s.

Pablo Picasso,
House in a Garden, 1908.
Oil on canvas, 73.6 x 60.5 cm.
The State Hermitage Museum,
St. Petersburg.

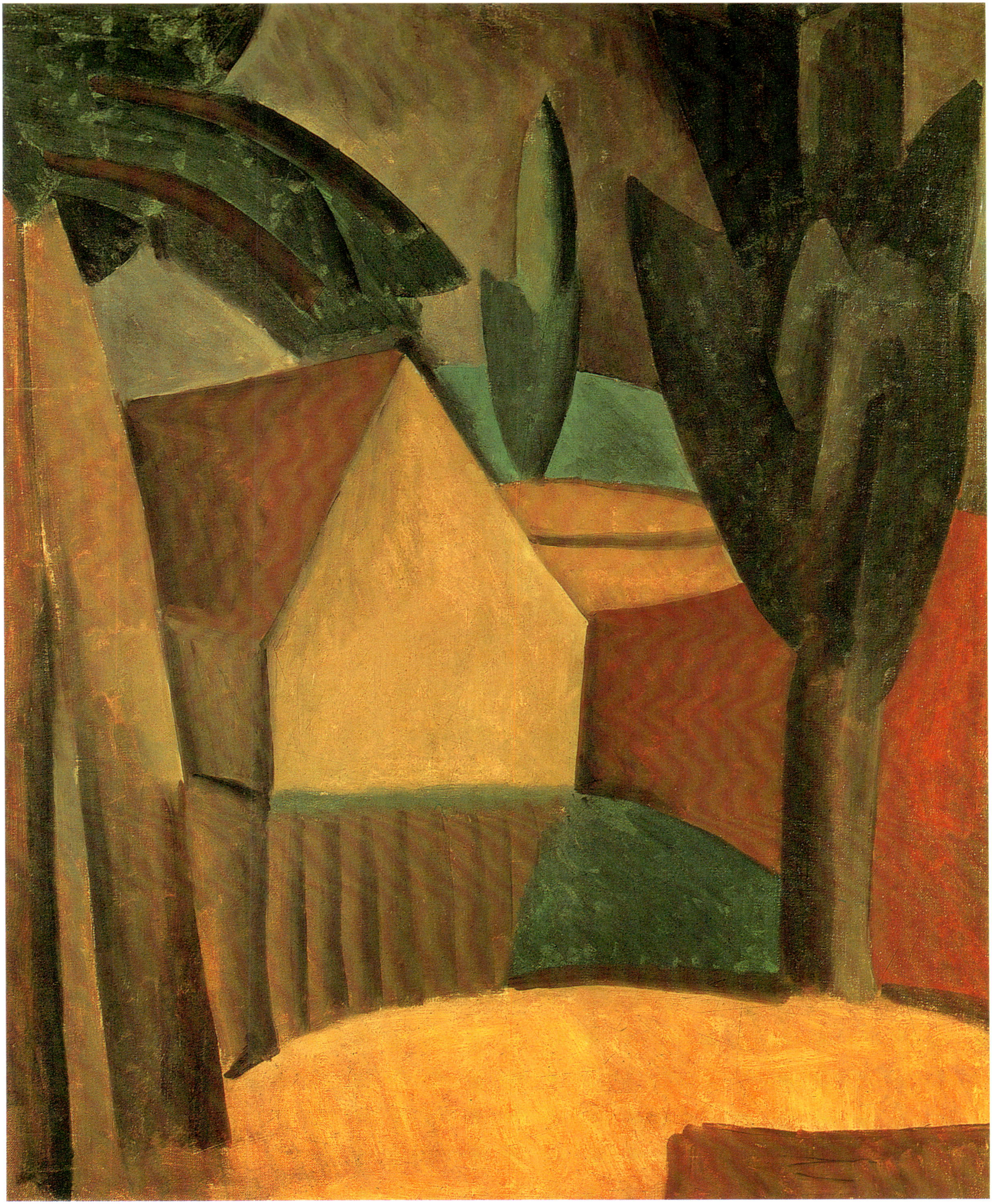

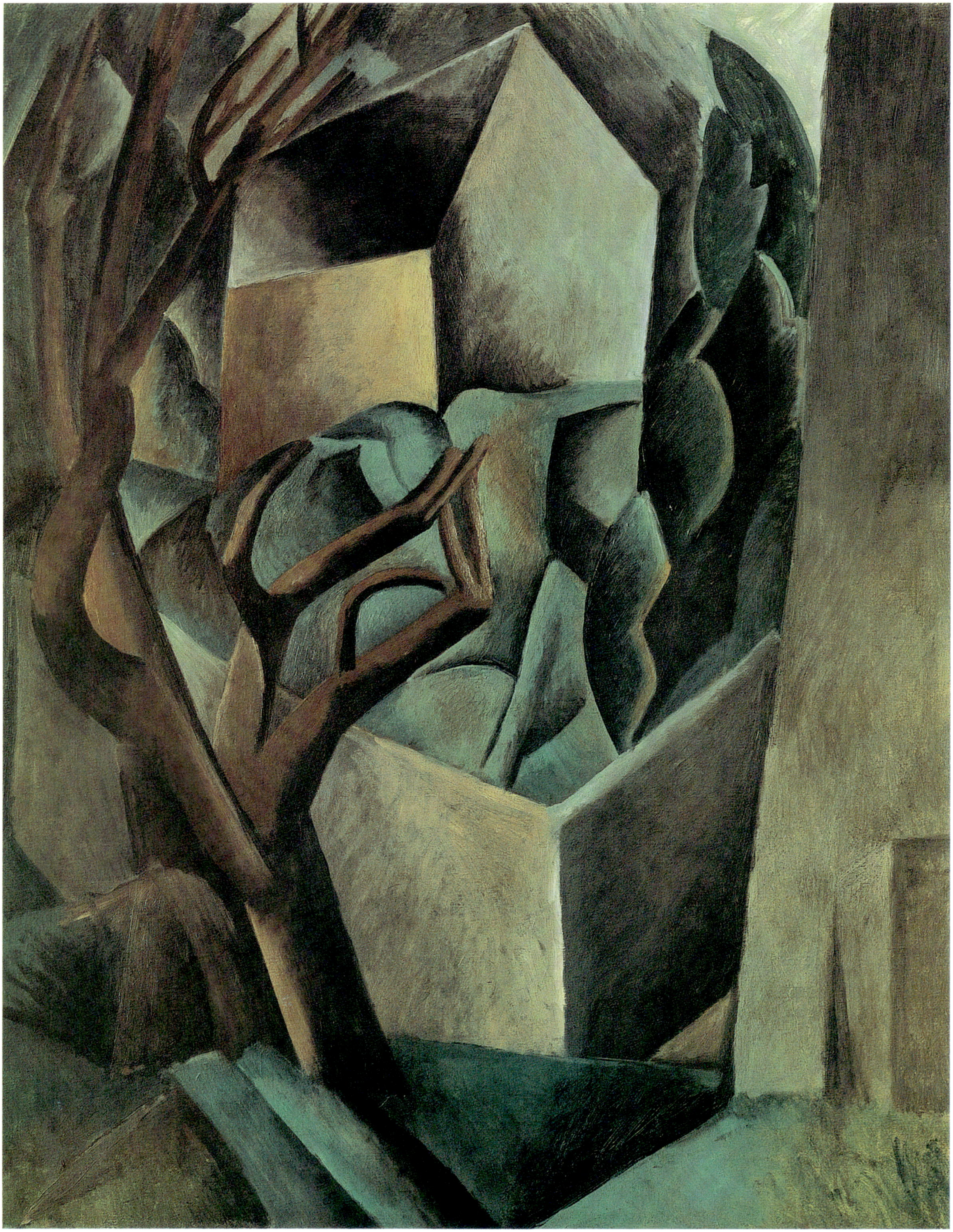

The third variation on the theme of seated women coming from that same sketchbook of the spring of 1908 led several months later to the painting *Dryad* (p. 53), here emphasising the dark, primitive nature of sex. The pose of the nude woman who, in the sketch, seems to be slipping powerlessly from her chair, became transformed in the painting into a threatening gesture of sexual aggression. Advancing on the viewer from the depths of a forest, as if from some niche, the figure is perceived as the incarnation of slumbering, powerful, blind nature, carrying in its loins not only the power of life but the irrational energy of destruction as well. Called *Dryad*, this menacing nude is older than the minor forest deities of Ancient Greece—she is a relative of the great goddesses from mankind's most ancient mythologies.

Here Picasso, in fact, depicted not a woman but some kind of prehistoric female statue, with all its attendant sculptural crudeness and expressively savage distortions. At the same time, it appears that in the pictorial solution he aimed at the same dramatic effect of harshly etched nudity that is so striking in the sombre, melancholy darkness of seventeenth-century religious painting.

Obviously, there was a reason why these paintings struck their first Russian viewers as examples of cult art (whether "diabolical" or "barbarian" is of little importance now), just as there was a reason why Daix, sensitively exploring Picasso's Cubism, even from a formal position, kept returning to the ideas and works of Claude Lévi-Strauss on the subject of myth.[13] Without doubt, Picasso's proto-Cubism—coming as it did not from the external appearance of events and things, but from great emotional and instinctive feelings, from the most profound layers of the psyche—clairvoyantly (as Rimbaud would have said) arrived at the supra-personal and thereby borders on the archaic mythological consciousness.

In formal terms, *Dryad* may be seen as an interpretation of the traditional nineteenth-century theme of a bather in the open air. But in essence, delving deep into the meaning, Picasso strove to reveal behind its bucolic appearance woman's strong ties with the physical world, especially as they express themselves in her powers of generation.

The key work in which both the formal and the pictorial issues of Picasso's proto-Cubism were concentrated was his major canvas of 1908, *Three Women* (p. 46). This, too, took its origins from the bathers theme which he began to work on about the end of 1907, probably under the influence of Cézanne's epic *Bathers*. Picasso conceived a composition involving bathers in a forest in which two figures of *Friendship* (p. 61) emerge, as if from the wings of a theatre, from behind trees on the left and approach the banks of a lake or stream where a group of three naked bathers sit in a moored rowing-boat. The narrative element apparent in the motif of friendship and in the boat on the forest lake, as well as in the general concept, served once again as a springboard for the imagination, leading not to a story but into an anonymous and timeless mythic dimension.

But after going through several preliminary studies, Picasso discarded the narrative elements and, with them, the frieze-like scale of the composition. In *Three Women* all that remains of the original concept of forest bathers is the general structure of the three-figure group on the right and the colour scheme: the red tonality of the bodies, the vibrant

Pablo Picasso,
Little House in a Garden (La Rue-des-Bois), 1909.
Oil on canvas, 92 x 73 cm.
The Pushkin Museum of Fine Arts, Moscow.

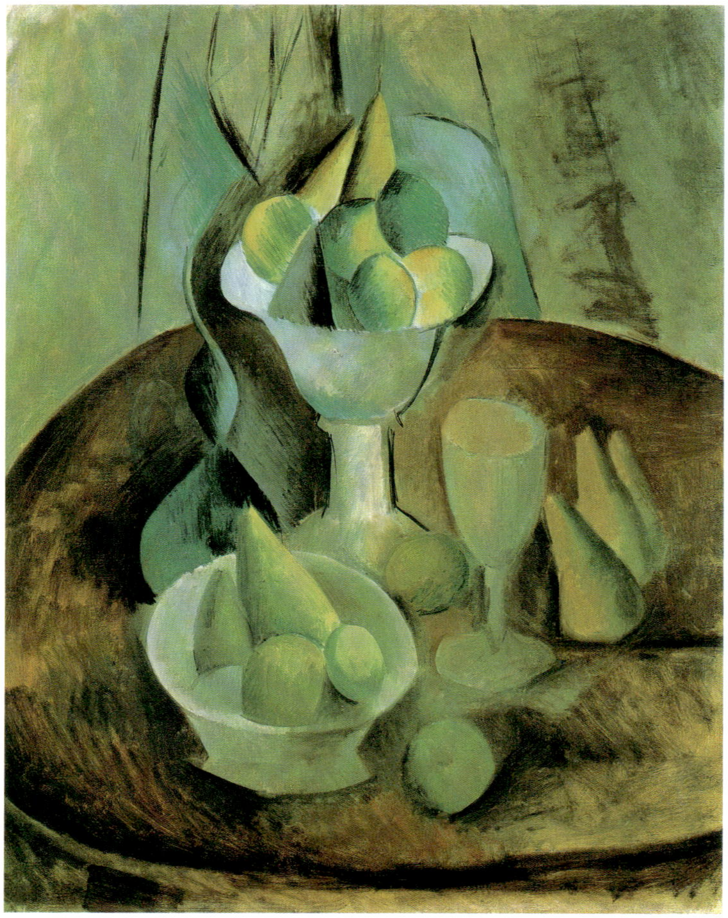

Pablo Picasso,
Fruit in a Vase, 1909.
Oil on canvas, 91 x 72.5 cm.
The State Hermitage Museum,
St. Petersburg.

Pablo Picasso,
Flowers in a Grey Jar, 1908.
Oil on canvas, 81 x 65 cm.
The State Hermitage Museum,
St. Petersburg.

Pablo Picasso,
Woman with a Mandolin, 1909.
Oil on canvas, 92 x 73 cm.
The State Hermitage Museum,
St. Petersburg.

Pablo Picasso,
Queen Isabeau, 1908-1909.
Oil on canvas, 92 x 73 cm.
The Pushkin Museum of Fine Arts,
Moscow.

emerald tones of the vegetation and the silver-grey colour of the water, transposed to the flowing drapery near the figure on the left. As for the three gigantic nudes, who seem to have just emerged from some rock-like source, to be hewn from something more solid than flesh, they are both in spirit and structure more reminiscent of Michelangelo's slaves straining to emerge from the anguish of chaos than of bathers basking in the lap of nature.

Their existence borders on slumber, their somnambulistic poses speak of hidden, unconscious, instinctive driving forces: they have no power over their existence, but in it they are bound together by some design. Studying these figures, one must not ignore the differences which subtly but unequivocally separate one from the other in spite of their apparent homogeneity. These differences are not only the result of each of the figures having been executed at a different time, but also reflect their status as individual images; the compositional and conceptual unity and the internal dramaturgy of this strange scene, steeped in torpor, are built on their correlations. But what are these differences?

The figure on the right is implicitly female in character; it is opposed to the one on the left—implicitly male. Calling attention to this fact, Steinberg notes it would be more correct to call the painting *Two or Three Women.*[14] However, what follows from his interpretation is that the figure in the middle does not depict a woman, but is the personification of a "preconscious hominid, the reserved matrix whence humanity sunders forth, the he and the she of it." This American scholar thus treats the painting's content from a Freudian perspective as a myth of creation, a psychogram of the shaping of human life, in which the separation of the sexes is implicitly dominant. Yet it is precisely this sort of unequivocal and rationalistic interpretation that calls for caution in the case of Picasso's multivalent images, which (borrowing an expression from Goethe) cannot be divided by reason and still result in a whole number as a quotient. Here it is better to remain closer to the material.

Renouncing his original concept of the five-figure *Bathers in the Forest,* Picasso also dropped its thematic conflict no matter how vague it was, that is to say, the drama which was always important to him. He began to develop the three-figure motif of *Three Women,* and here the intermediate stage was the rhythmic version (as Daix called it) of the motif, with its powerful, dynamic image of a spiralling centrifugal vortex bordering on abstraction. Yet even this highly stylised image seemingly implied its own subject, its drama.

This becomes apparent after re-establishing certain links. At the beginning of 1908 Apollinaire revolutionised his creative outlook under Picasso's influence.

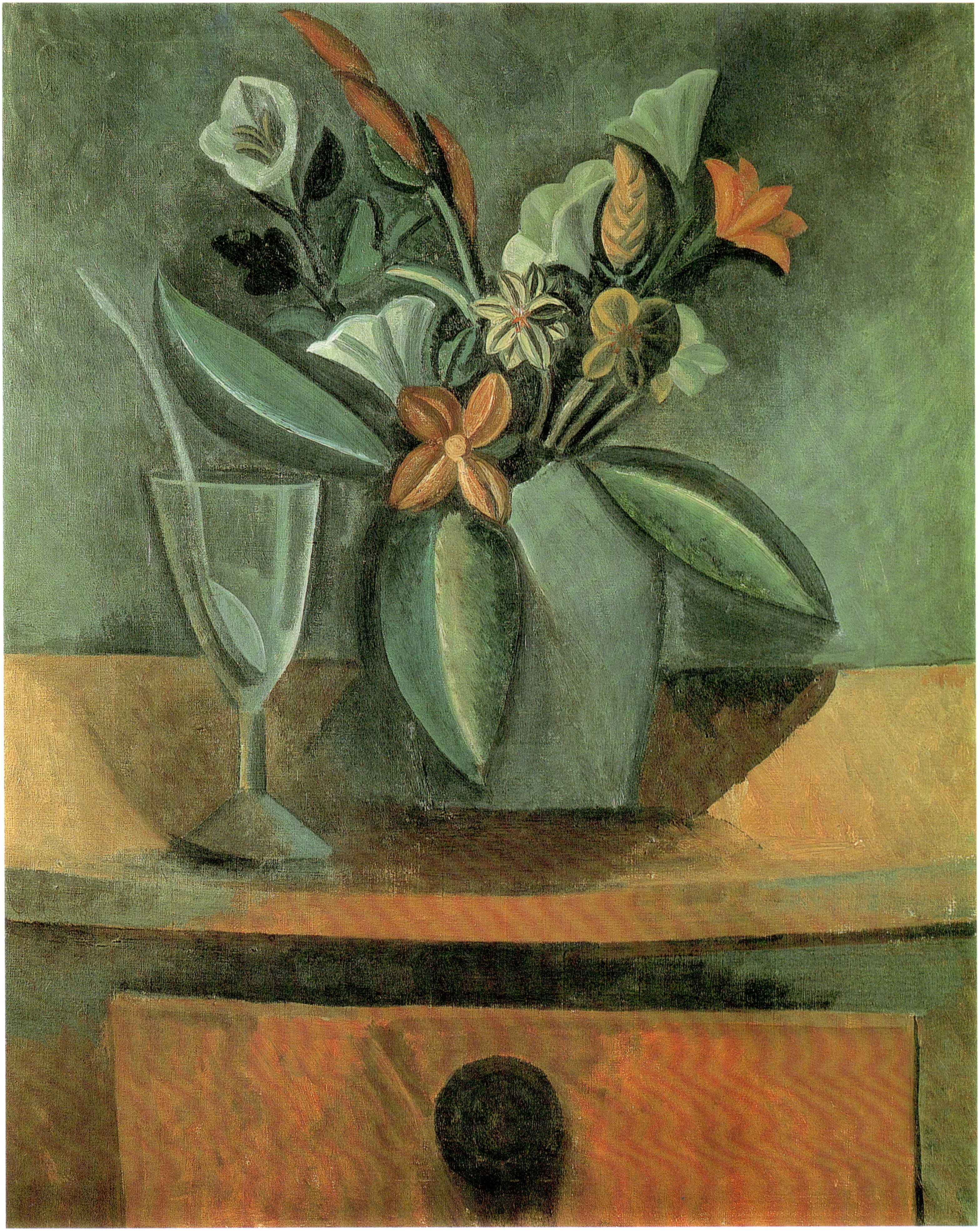

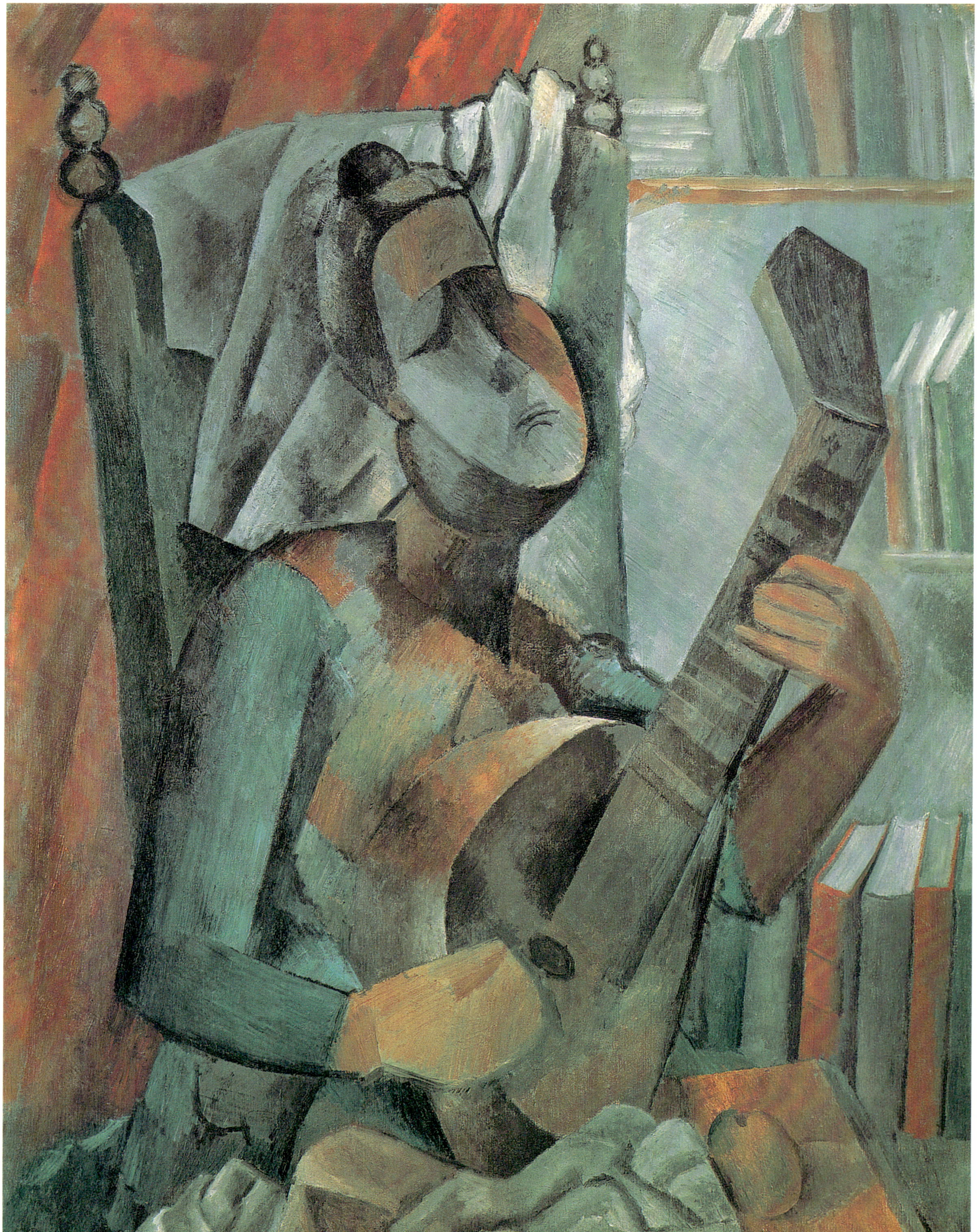

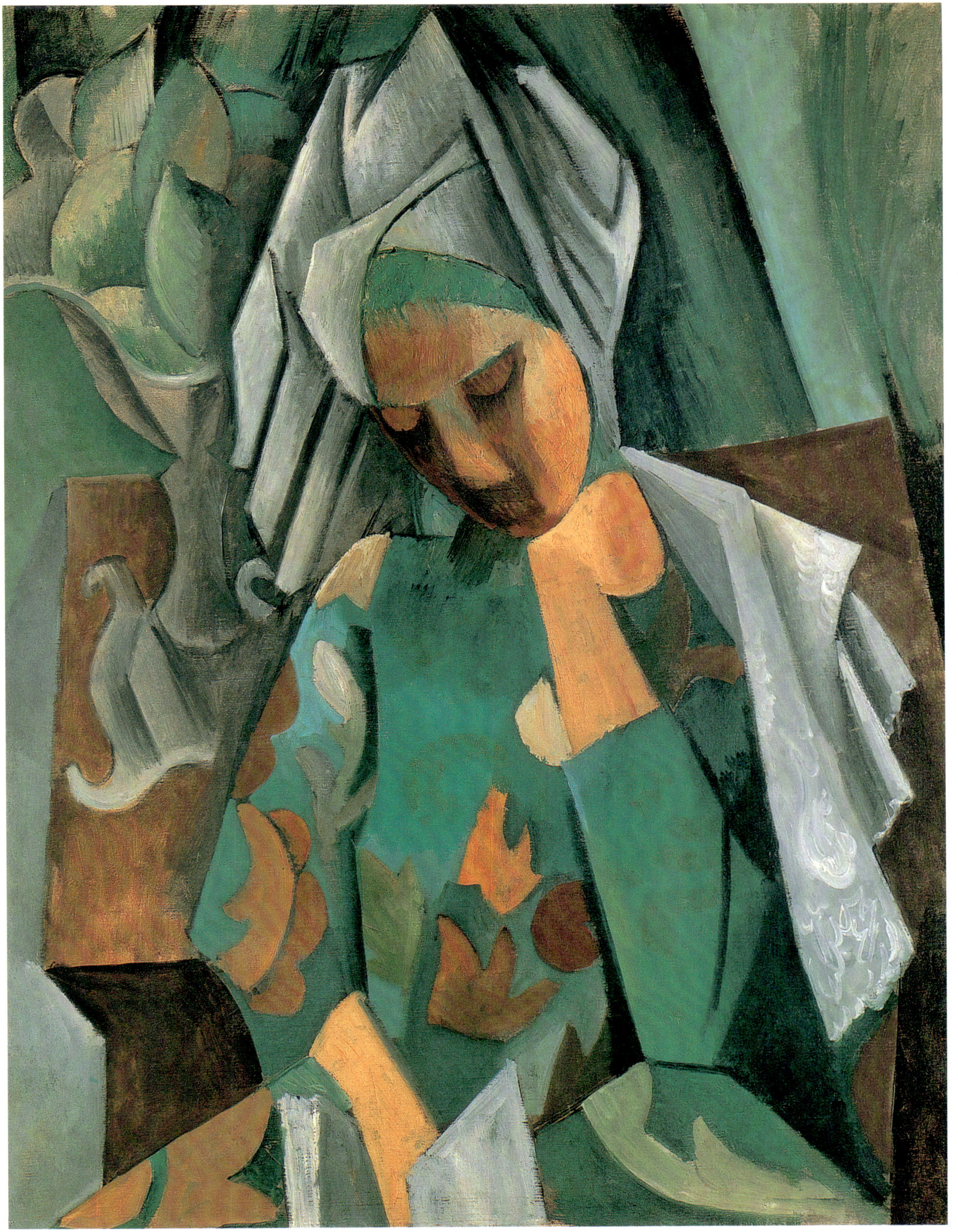

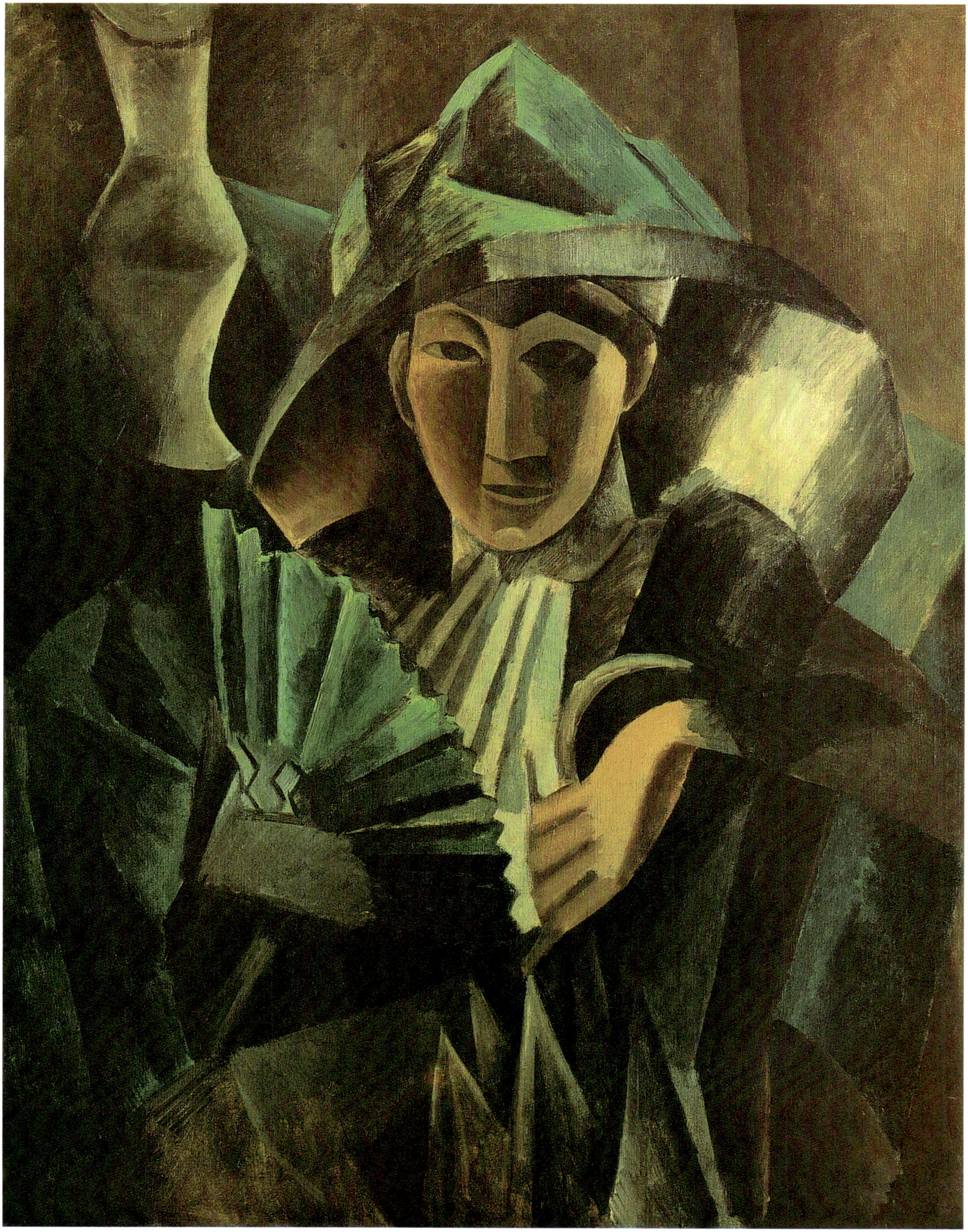

This image was first born in the spring of 1908 in Apollinaire's article on the principles of painting inspired by Picasso's new aspirations and called *Les Trois Vertus Plastiques*. In it the poet postulated the following: "the flame is a symbol of painting and the three plastic virtues burn with radiance." He then examines each of the three: purity, unity, truth.

What is important for us here, though, is the amazing historical and typological parallel between Apollinaire's image of this enormous flame as a metaphor of painting ("A surprising art whose light is without limits") and the rhythmic version of *Three Women*. This version may be seen as a possible metaphor of the flaming vortex cruelly transforming three women's bodies in its image; as such, the work has a magical unity of style and is graced with the supreme persuasiveness of a work of art. In that sense one must note the hot, terracotta red of the figures in all the studies, at times literally achieving a flame-like intensity, the triple unity of the arrow-like forms impetuously driving skyward, and the agonising languor of the poses. As in Apollinaire's article, both a three-forked flame and a heraldic lily, the symbol of purity, are evoked.

Picasso must have known his friend's articles and verses. In the Bateau-Lavoir studio Apollinaire must have seen that immense canvas with its three red, nude colossi, seemingly burdened with the mystery of their existence. Throughout 1908, owing to this new understanding, Picasso and Apollinaire were again reflected in each other's work. Once again, as during the Circus period, their themes and methods had something in common: they both aimed to internalise all depiction and produce the image through layers of subjective association, through the play of metaphors, and both were unabashed by esoteric expression.

Three Women is one of those compositions that do not lend themselves easily to direct verbal interpretation: at the heart of the image is a secret that radiates a tension directed towards the viewer's emotional and intellectual life. In the late series *347 Etchings*, in which Picasso surrendered to the flow of memory and free association, there is sheet No. 38, which seems to echo that distant year of 1908. According to scholars, *Three Women* preoccupied Picasso for many months in 1908,[15] and his efforts during that period evolved, as it were, against the background of this painting, which dominated the studio and bore the results of many other parallel works in both painting and sculpture.

Surreality or Sculpture in Painting

Thus, Picasso's interest in reproducing volumes on a flat surface was inseparable in 1908 from sculpture, and it was not before 1909 that the artist came into contact with Cézanne's purely pictorial experience, moving from the colouring of flat planes, inclined this way and that, to the modulation of volume by means of minute, form-creating daubs. The form of *Three Women* is a sculptor's creation, for one can indeed imagine its being cut out along dotted lines and rebuilt as a sculpture. As for *Farm Woman (Full-Length)* (p. 55) with its powerfully hewn volumes and mass that seems to be

Pablo Picasso,
Woman with a Fan, 1909.
Oil on canvas, 101 x 81 cm.
The Pushkin Museum of Fine Arts, Moscow.

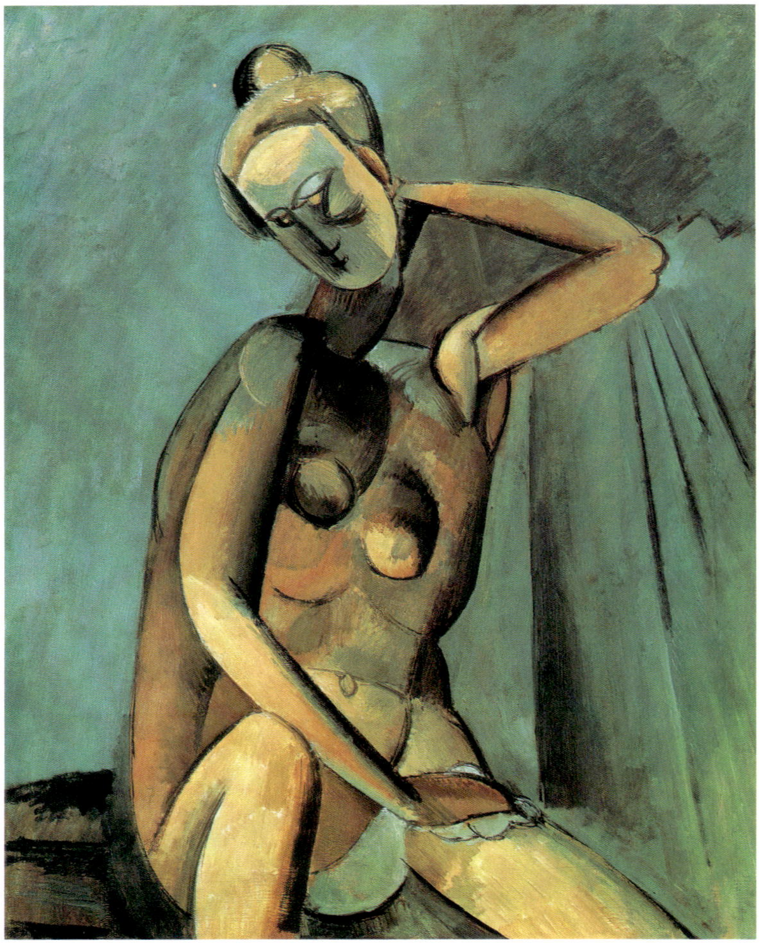

charged with dynamite, it originated directly from work on a carved statue, three-dimensional studies for which appeared in the notebooks. Picasso's true sculptor's temperament, recognised by Julio González, causes him to be very laconic and to reject incidental features in order to lay bare the plastic essence of the image and emphasise its reality. Picasso called such an approach "surreality" and, even in the days of Cubism, considered himself a realist artist. For Picasso, sculpture also served to verify the feeling of reality, in the sense of physical validity, since for him "sculpture is the best comment that a painter can make on painting."[16]

Scholars now cautiously speak not only of a return to the concrete but also of a dramatisation of the surrounding space (Daix) in such works as *Green Pan and Black Bottle* (p. 67) and *Pitcher and Bowls* (p. 66). We are shattered by the dramatic exaltation of *Green Pan and Black Bottle*, an effect one would rather expect from a scene of passion and martyrdom. Forty years before Abstract Expressionism, the pictorial power of the painting's background predicted (and perhaps transcended) that later movement, with its "sorrow of final days", so sharply felt by the critics of Picasso. Such extraordinary dramatic power must have been accompanied by no less extraordinary psychological conditions. From Fernande Olivier's memoirs we know how deeply Picasso was shocked by the suicide of his Bateau-Lavoir neighbour, the German painter Wiegels, on 1 June 1908. While stylistically belonging to the summer works of that period, the *Green Pan and Black Bottle*'s funereal black-and-red tonal chord may reflect Picasso's as yet unalleviated anguish. Yet in the still life *Pitcher and Bowls*, painted soon after, controlled thought dominates over the drama of emotions. This fact is manifested in several ways: in the incontestable logic of the spatial plastic structure, as opposed to illusory perspective; in the monumental grouping of sculptured forms concentrated in an ascending spiral around a common axis; in the overall rhythm of curves and ovals; in the vibrant, yet solid, equilibrium of the entire tectonic structure; in the painting's image; in the contained energy of the brushwork; and, finally, in the desire to achieve perfection in completeness.

In the summer of 1908, Picasso at first turned to the still life genre because of his depressed state of mind and a desire to find support in the world of simple realities. Later, his inquisitive and creative penetration into the specifics of how painting might represent objective realities opened the way to a completely new method of plastic representation called Cubism. It is not accidental that the still life genre, with, as Georges

Pablo Picasso,
Nude, 1909.
Oil on canvas, 100 x 81.2 cm.
The State Hermitage Museum,
St. Petersburg.

Pablo Picasso,
Man with his Arms Crossed, 1909.
Gouache, watercolour, charcoal and paper glued on cardboard,
62.5 x 49.2 cm.
The State Hermitage Museum,
St. Petersburg.

Pablo Picasso,
Brick Factory at Tortosa, 1909.
Oil on canvas, 50.7 x 60.2 cm.
The State Hermitage Museum,
St. Petersburg.

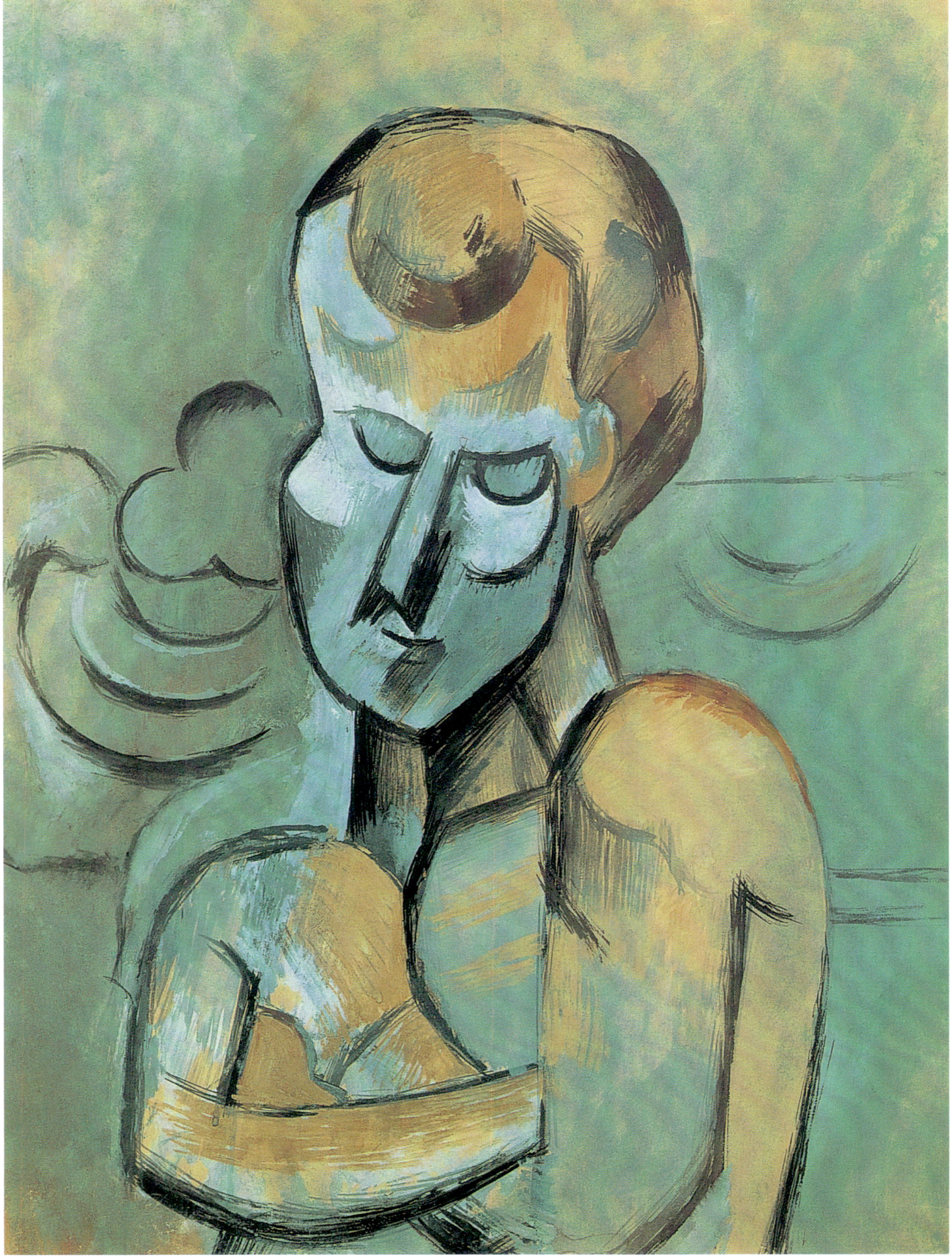

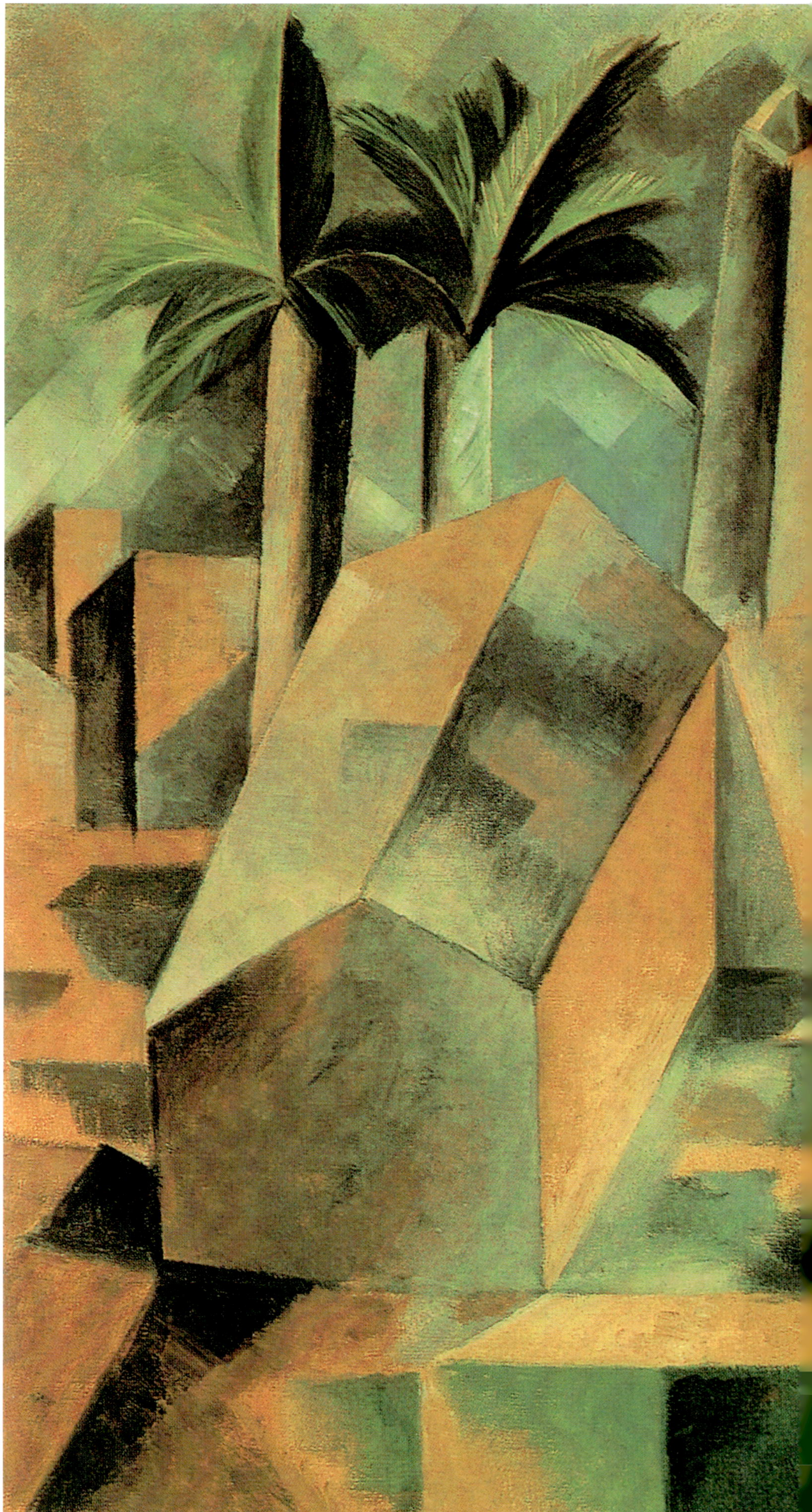

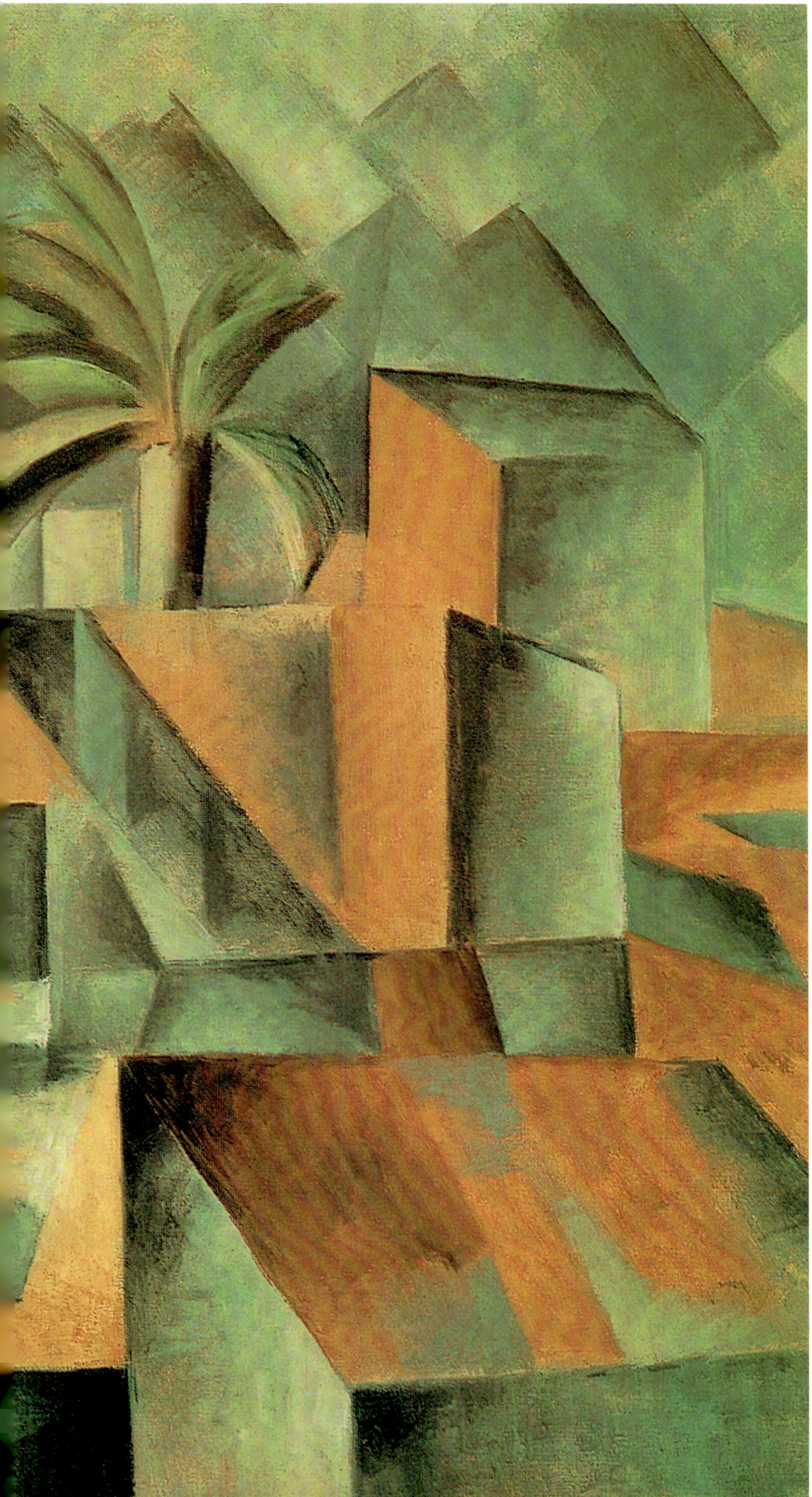

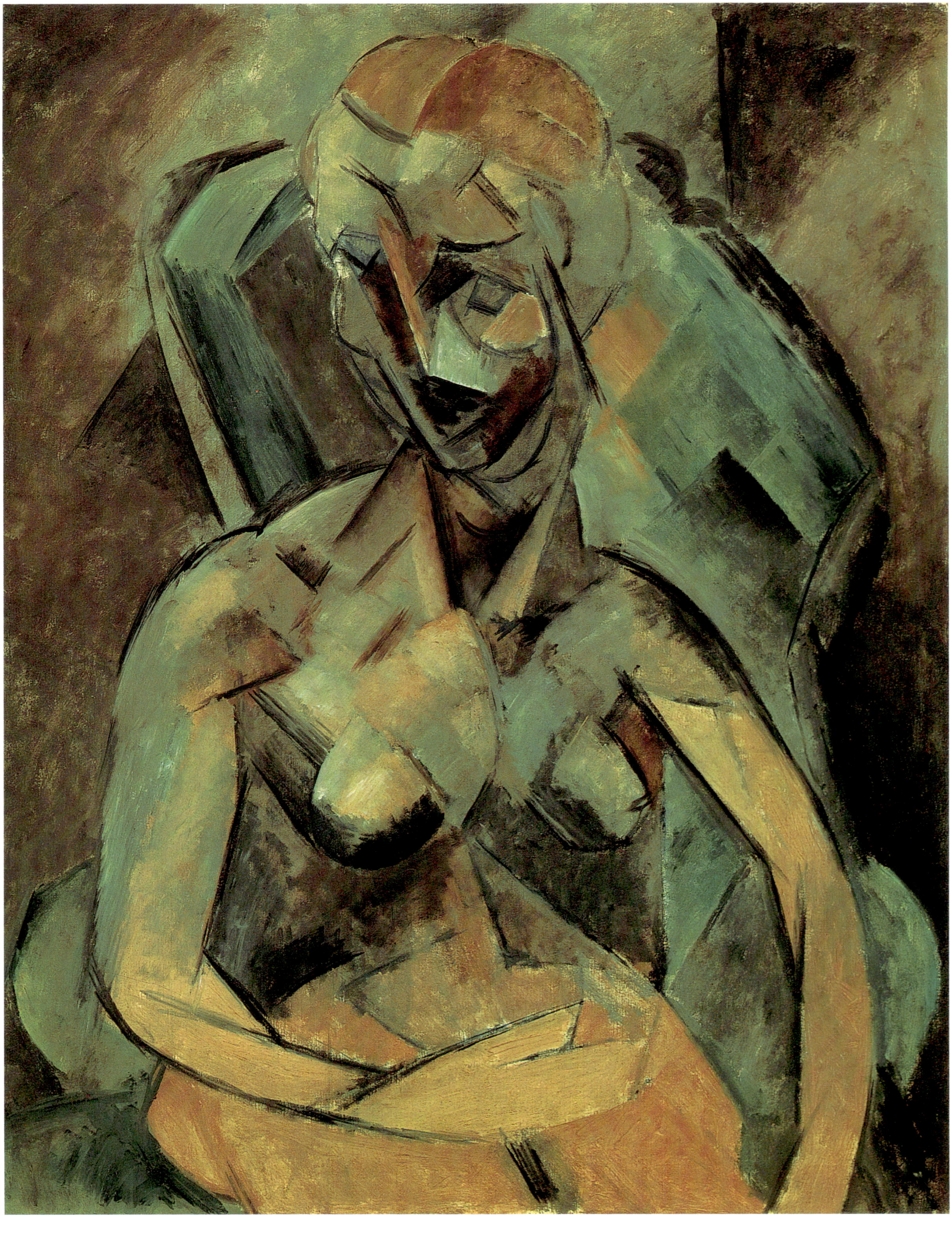

Braque said, its concrete space which one can almost touch,[17] became the favourite subject of Cubist painting.

No other genre was so conducive to a concentrated analytical inquiry into the structural principles of the stable forms in a spatial ensemble, into the controlled rhythmic discipline of a rectangular surface. For Picasso it was normal and logical to move from the form of three-dimensional sculpture to the tangible, objective values of still life compositions. But this movement, in turn, presupposed a shift in his attention from problems relating to sculpture to problems of pictorial expressiveness.

The absence of exact dates, which makes it impossible to determine the absolute chronology of Picasso's proto-Cubism, is perhaps most vexatious for the period between his stay in La Rue-des-Bois in August 1908 and his departure for Horta de Ebro at the end of the spring of 1909.[18] When one considers as a whole all that was done over these eight months—that is, everything created on the very threshold of Cubism—one sees the artist's thoughts flowing in many directions, some of which led to and synthesised new trends, while others temporarily disappeared below the surface. What is needed here is a theory of evolution by which to organise the material and especially an appreciation of the impulse triggering the entire movement. Having a *post factum* knowledge of what might be called the ideal goal of this progression, Cubism, scholars observe the accumulation in Picasso's work between the autumn of 1908 and the spring of 1909 of those formal features which mark the "most important and certainly the most complete and radical artistic revolution since the Renaissance".[19]

Just as African art is usually considered the factor leading to the development of Picasso's classic aesthetics in 1907, the lessons of Cézanne are perceived as the cornerstone of this new progression. This relates, first of all, to a spatial conception of the canvas as a composed entity (Maurice Denis), subjected to a certain constructive system. Georges Braque, with whom Picasso became friends in the autumn of 1908 and together with whom he led Cubism during the six years of its apogee, was amazed by the similarity of Picasso's pictorial experiments to his own; he explained that "Cubism's main direction was the materialisation of space."[20] Not of traditional, optical, illusory space, created by Renaissance methods of perspective, but of a new space which Braque called "tactile, manual", and which he sought by means of still life compositions, tonal spectrums and Cézanne's modulated strokes. "The contact with Cézanne was at the origin of everything. It was more than an influence, it was an initiation. Cézanne was the first to have broken with scientific, mechanised perspective that had been practised by painters over centuries and which had excluded the possibility of any innovation."[21]

If, however, the landscapes and still lifes of the Master of Aix served Braque, first and foremost, as lessons in well-tempered space in which objects are nothing but plastic appurtenances, for Picasso these works constantly conveyed a feeling for the power of Cézanne's attitude towards his subjects: the controlled Romantic drama of feelings and emotions, achieved by a conscious pictorial method, whether it involves pears on a plate, a pine tree on a cliff, the massive Mont Sainte-Victoire, or nude forest bathers. And in

Pablo Picasso,
Young Woman, 1909.
Oil on canvas, 92.3 x 73.3 cm.
The State Hermitage Museum,
St. Petersburg.

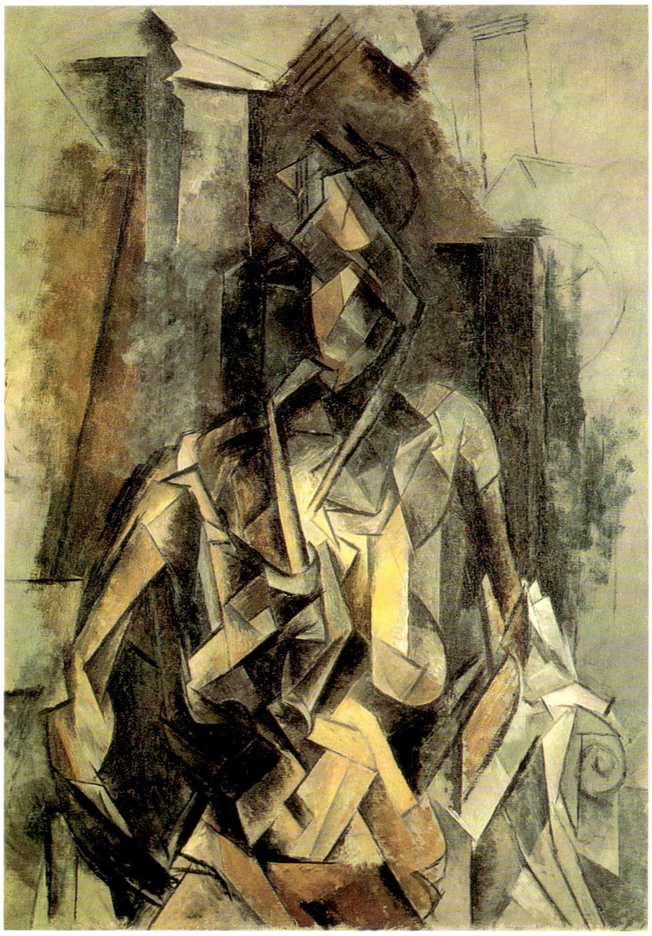

Picasso's so-called Cézanne style (as opposed to Braque's, their technical and stylistic similarities notwithstanding) there always exists a Romantic, and often thematic, feeling for the reality of the depicted image, be it a still life, a landscape, or a figure (the latter held no interest for Braque). It was that element in Cézanne's "wild and yet sophisticated nature" (Pissarro) that Picasso, always sensitive to the instinctive, preconscious origins of art, must have sensed so keenly in Cézanne's paintings.

It was probably around the same time that Picasso painted a small group of still lifes revealing his preoccupation with Rousseau's art.

One was *Flowers in a Grey Jar* (p. 73). Picasso divines in the artificial flowers their other, real nature, then underlines it by comparing it with the unequivocally abstract contour of the goblet, icy in its transparency and yet recalling a flower on a stem. The artist emphasised the value of his motif precisely through the effect of almost solemn representation: the bouquet (which is not free of the coarseness of a cheap, popular decorative print) stands on a massive mahogany chest of drawers, as if on a pedestal, and seems to come to life through the dynamic nervousness of the flowers' "ears" and "eyes", turned this way and that, the "gestures" of their leaves, their muted yet colourful chord struck against the morose and constrained "Spanish" atmosphere of the background.

But Picasso, who knew how to see, had a deep personal conviction about never forgetting the name of what he depicted; he grasped the realities of his objects and found their corresponding pictorial equivalents. Throughout his entire career, the subject—the object-motif—was never irrelevant or arbitrary, for it furnished the poetic impulse of creativity. Even though the Cubist method of total tactile examination provided both of the pioneers of Cubism with a way to completely master the object, the difference was that for Braque it was an object of artistic interest, while for Picasso it was an object of love. Could Picasso, then, ever neglect the pictorial for the sake of a purely aesthetic goal? Could he have been seduced by abstraction? His imagination was full of objects and themes of love, and, even on the very threshold of Cubism (in the winter of 1908-1909), the representational element clearly dominated over the problem of the structural unity of the work.

During this period of multiple and varied pursuits, Picasso does not even seem to have been concerned with the problem of "making a picture" (again differing from Braque); he seems to have had a mania for images, but in the actual process of work this image material, like wax, changes and is transformed, while in his hands, into new ideas. This gave birth to series or, more accurately, families of paintings, drawings, sketches—still lifes, still lifes in interiors, heads, figures, figures in interiors with still lifes, thematic scenes, landscapes, and landscapes with figures forming scenic compositions.

Pablo Picasso,
Woman Seated in a Chair, 1910.
Oil on canvas, 100 x 73 cm.
Musée National d'Art Moderne,
Centre Georges-Pompidou, Paris.

Pablo Picasso,
Portrait of Ambroise Vollard, 1910.
Oil on canvas, 93 x 66 cm.
The Pushkin Museum of Fine Arts,
Moscow.

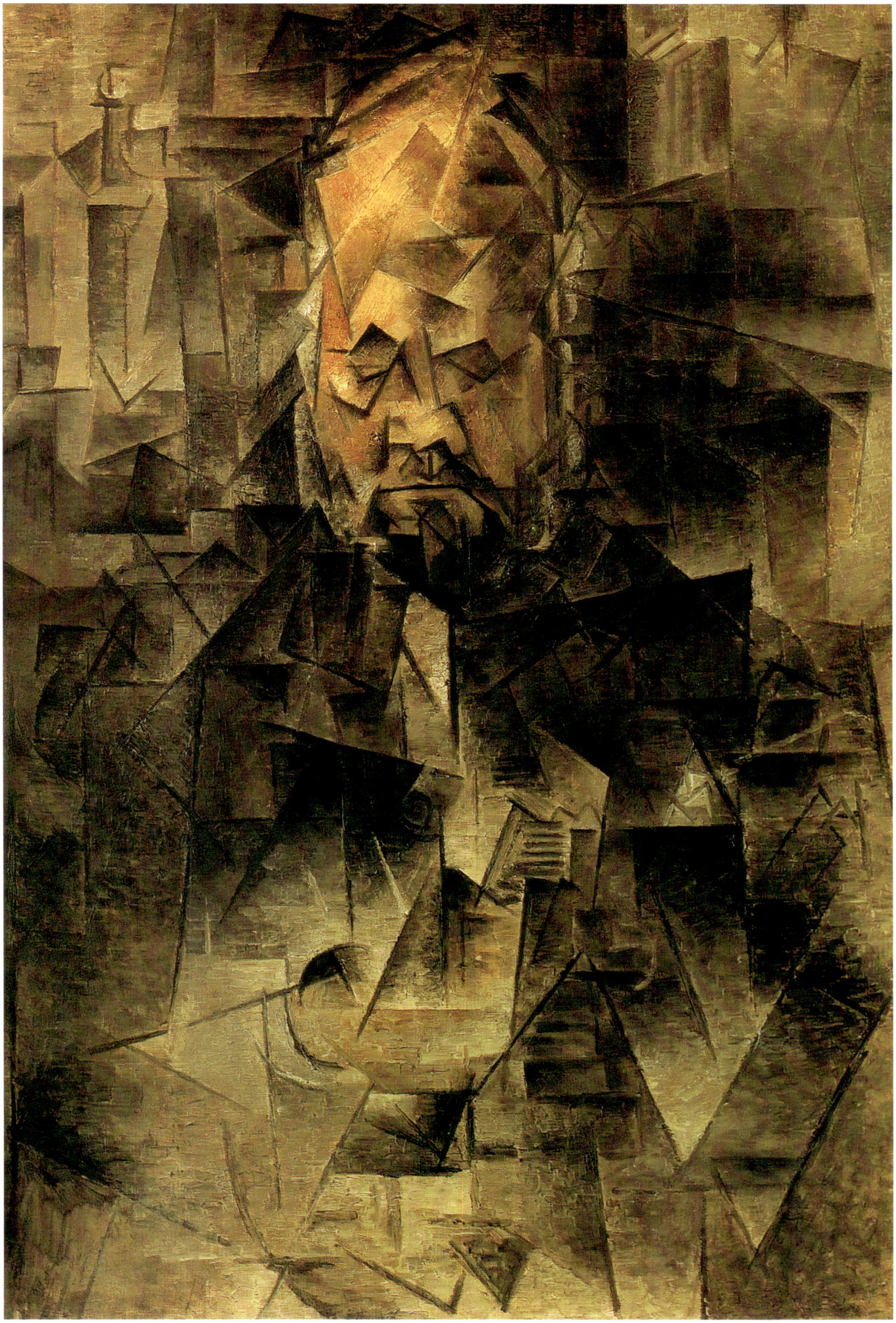

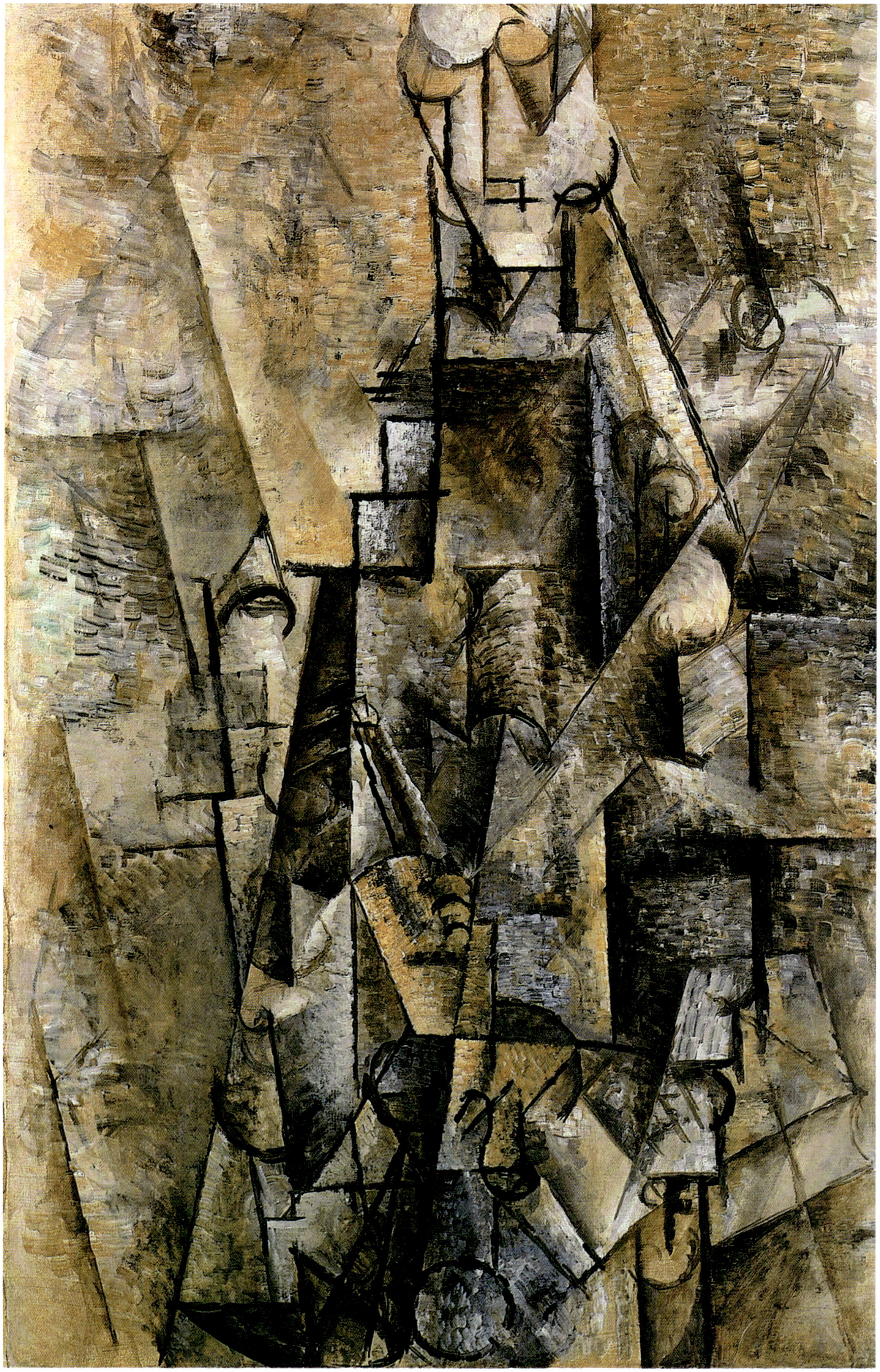

Besides this penchant for the pictorial, several other factors made Picasso more receptive than before to the purely pictorial solution of painters, past and present. Among these were his discovery of Douanier Rousseau as a sort of pre-Renaissance example of the primitive consciousness, unspoiled by academic aesthetics, and also the beginning of his friendship with Braque ("It was as if we were married," Picasso said)[22] which ended his creative solitude and brought an element of the moderation and lucidity typical of the French school. Yet, all of these developments would appear natural in a period of active search and experimentation.

Thus, the Hermitage *Seated Woman* (p. 52), coming from a series crucially important to the Analytical Cubism of the *Bathing* (winter of 1908-1909), seems to be an answer to Matisse (for example, the canvas *Luxe II*, 1908), with his tendency to transform the figure into a flat, coloured arabesque-an organic part of the ripening decorative grand style. Conversely, Picasso is necessarily interested in the figure, the figure as a bodily apparatus which in itself is a powerful tool of expression, as Tugendhold put it so well.

Polarisation of Semantics

The only constructive element is Picasso's artistic will which, heeding the universal law of internal plastic harmony, pulls together the nude's dissociated body parts, her different spatial aspects.

This amazing innovation (which, by the way, dates back to the ancient past-to the pictographic methods of Ancient Egyptian and Assyrian painters) not only established the method of Analytical Cubism, but also opened up a vast area of previously unknown possibilities for the pictorial metaphor. In that sense, the Hermitage *Nude* looks into the future and stands, as Zervos was to note, as the starting point for the poetic element in all of Picasso's subsequent work. Made of formal contradictions—frontal view and profile contours of the torso and left and right halves, lit-up masses balanced by a clear, linear body outline—this nude deliberately has something of Mannerism's unstable style. Its unorthodox anatomy, with its insect-like joints, elongated proportions, and narrowed limbs, seems to be a deliberate recollection of Cranach's angular Venuses, of the sophisticated elegance of the Dianas of the Fontainebleau School, or of the voluptuous curves of Ingres's Odalisques.

Matisse answered reproaches concerning the ugliness of the women in his paintings by saying that he made paintings, not women. Picasso, however, makes women in his paintings. Here he soberly constructs the figure of a female being with youthful forms and an angular gracefulness of motion; and he brings his creation to life by dynamic movements, by the pearly, cool light on the left, which splashes down on the nude's back and which harmonises so well with the warm ochre tones of her body.

Picasso creates a different, male nature in the gouache *Man with his Arms Crossed* (p. 79), using the same pictorial manner of the winter of 1908-1909. This somewhat clumsy, but solidly assembled half-figure speaks less of Picasso's abstract formal pursuits than of his

Pablo Picasso,
Man with a Clarinet, 1911-1912.
Oil on canvas, 106 x 69 cm.
Museo Thyssen-Bornemisza, Madrid.

desire to achieve an expressive character, to reveal the essence in its physical concreteness: the larger-than-life head with its bulging forehead, the powerful neck, the crossed arms that bunch up the shoulders and thus emphasise the athletic and monolithic torso. Yet even now, on the threshold of a new stage in the development of his formal conception, the semantic polarisation of Picasso's pictorial world of 1908, the basic meanings of his personal mythology, is still preserved.

Picasso, of course, did not know then that he was entering the period of Cubism. "To know that we were doing Cubism we should have had to be acquainted with it. Actually, nobody knew what it was."[23] Internally experiencing his art, being the centre and source of that art, Picasso had a more integral, less vague understanding of his goals than did scholars writing about his work at the time. "The goal I proposed myself in making Cubism? To paint and nothing more. And to paint seeking a new expression, divested of useless realism, with a method linked only to my thought—without enslaving myself with objective reality."[24]

If the artist spoke of a quest for new expression, it is because that was his professional concern to find adequate means of expression, an adequate language for the impulses inherent in his thinking. Yet he also said: "In the early days of Cubism we made experiments… to make pictures was less important than to discover things all the time."[25] Today, however, when the formal phenomenon of Cubism has been studied in depth and in sufficient detail, we can look upon Picasso's work of that time not only from the standpoint of the artist's self-development, but with an eye more educated and sensitive to the value of its content.

Indeed, almost every work between the winter of 1908 and the spring of 1909 has its own content, either relating to the development of some theme or, as in the case of the still lifes, situating its object-motif in an atmosphere that seems to vibrate with a strong current. *Bread and Fruit Bowl on a Table* (p. 13), for example, painted during this period, is a still life that is a transformation of the so-called *Carnival at the Bistro* theme, developed in several sketches. In another still life, the artist, as if in Cézanne's honour, depicted a pear, a lemon and Cézanne's hat amid the full folds of a draped cloth which has a luxurious yet controlled leaf-like pattern in the style of the Master of Aix (see *Still Life with Hat*).

The still lifes of that period simultaneously address the sense of reality, the artistic sense, and the viewer's imagination. While composed of real, even commonplace objects (usually fruit, table utensils), they are architectonically organised, and yet at the same time each reveals a certain energetic expression—an epic, dramatic, intimate quality—more to be expected of landscapes.

The Hermitage still life *Fruit in a Vase* (p. 72) is built like a panoramic view (seen from above) of a group of objects situated on the deserted plain of a round table. It was perhaps because he so prized this ambiguous feeling of still life/landscape that Picasso left the painting unfinished, preserving its ghostliness, refusing to make the objects

Pablo Picasso,
Table in a Café (Bottle of Pernod), 1912.
Oil on canvas, 45.5 x 32.5 cm.
The State Hermitage Museum,
St. Petersburg.

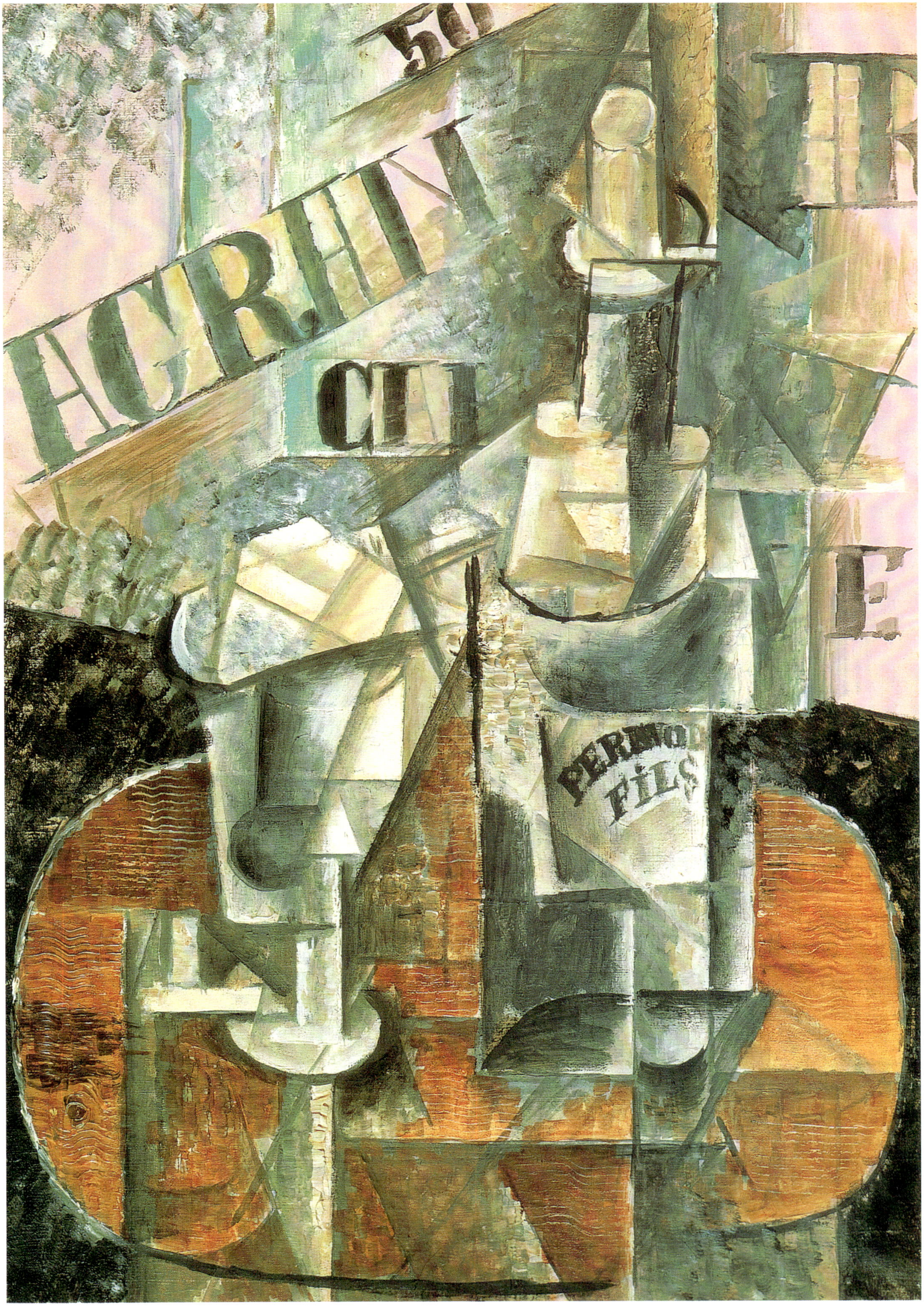

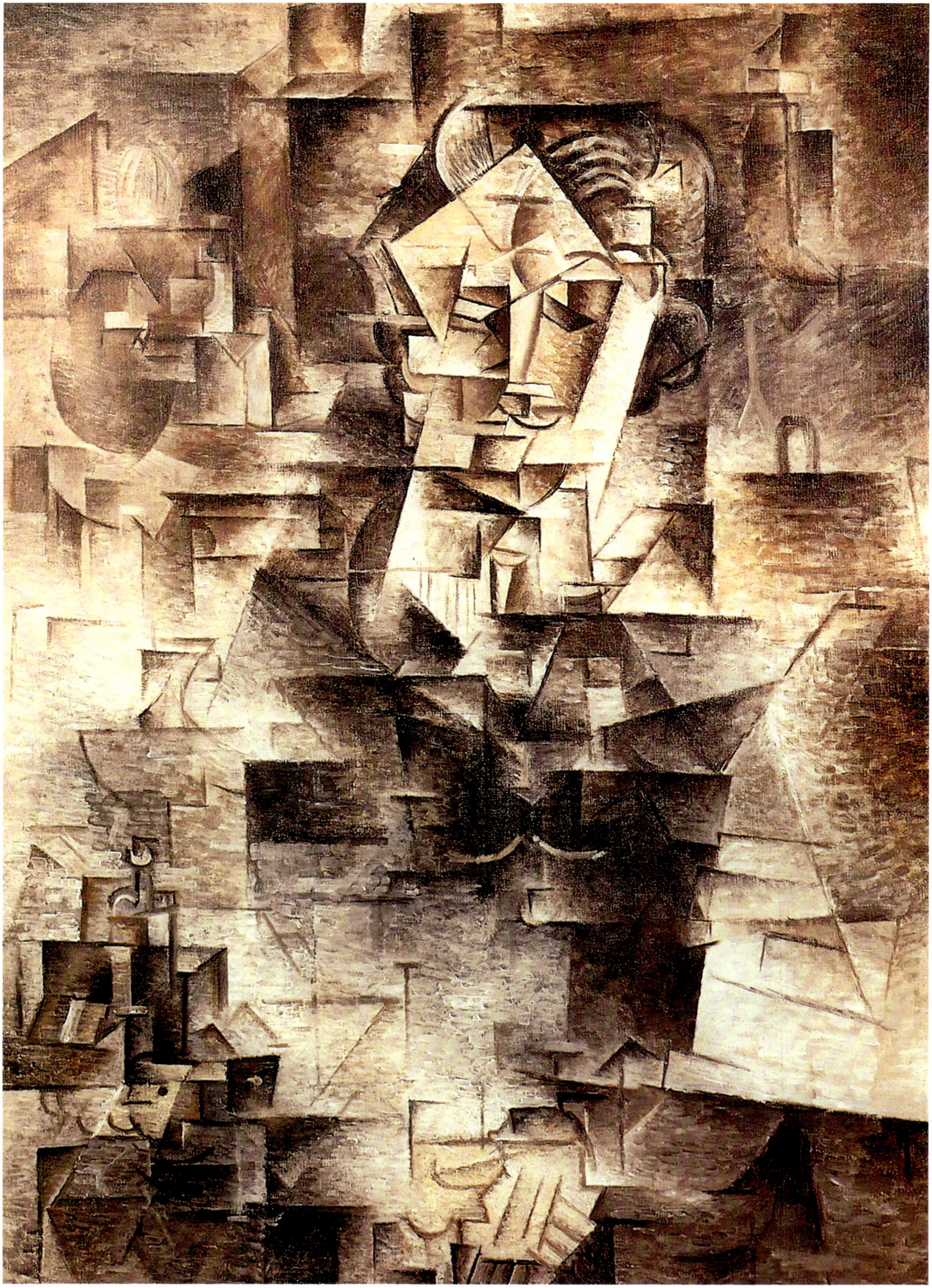

materialise fully. Here, in this concept of still life, with its pauses of empty spaces and its logical interchange of planes, the overall effect reminds one of a landscape's illusory space. In another work, the landscape *Little House in a Garden (La Rue-des-Bois)* (p. 70), Picasso created a three-dimensional impression on the principles of Braque's tactile, manual still life space. And yet in that work, the absence of any sort of analysis, the many smeared forms in the motif, the capriciously rhythmical lines of arabesques, do not speak of a search for real space, but rather tell us that spatial confinement is what the artist needs to heighten the drama of forces locked in battle. One force is Nature with the turbulent, vital energy of its greenery and the pathetic gesticulation of the dead tree; the other is the neatly arranged buildings with their blank walls and sharp, geometric edges.

This drama, heightened by the strictly controlled relationship of the cold mineral colours and the tension of the composition, balancing on a razor's edge, overwhelms the "inertia" of a pure landscape; the painting echoes, as it were, the conflicts of the real world. This final impression corresponds to Picasso's original idea: to make this piece of nature the background for a composition with figures, conceived in the winter and spring of 1909.

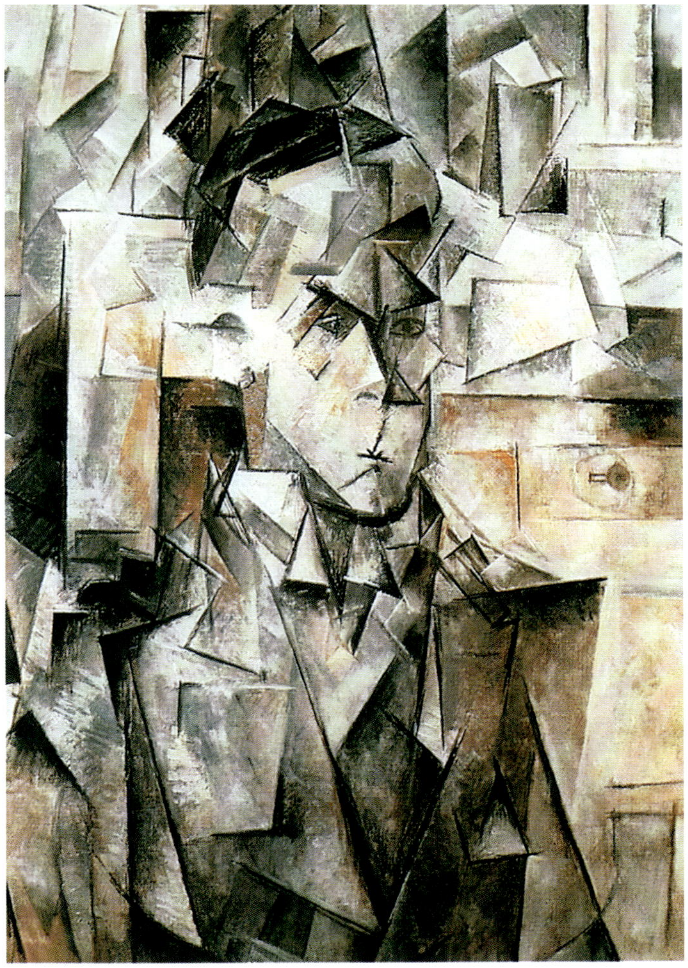

Referring to the transformation of the composition *Carnival at the Bistro* into the still life *Bread and Fruit Bowl on a Table*, Pierre Daix believes Picasso "could not have better expressed the thought that, at that stage, every object or character is, above all, a certain spatial rhythm, a three-dimensional structure which plays its role in the composition through what it brings to the pictorial structure of the whole and not through its own reality. Here he again borders on abstraction. He will treat the *Woman with a Fan* (p. 76) and *Queen Isabeau* (p. 75) exactly like still lifes."[26] Such views, however, are hardly correct, for Picasso at that stage was still very far from abstraction. Actually his desire to achieve a full and unified plastic structure for the pictorial whole (for which he depends on Cézanne's modulated tones which model forms) does not contradict his fundamentally literary quality and does not negate the personal realities of the object and characters. Indeed, the metamorphosis of the figure scene into the *Bread and Fruit Bowl on a Table* clearly reveals the semantic (not just the plastic) value of the still life's object-motifs for Picasso: a bowl of fruit has replaced the female figure in the composition, while the elongated loaves of bread and overturned cup replace the rhythms and forms of the two male characters. An allegorical still life? Whether it is or not, the characteristics of Picasso's objects and figures invariably relate to an internal meaning, as is apparent, for instance, in *Queen Isabeau*, *Woman with a Fan* and *Woman with a Mandolin* (p. 74).

Pablo Picasso,
Daniel-Henry Kahnweiler, 1910.
Oil on canvas, 101.1 x 73.3 cm.
Art Institute of Chicago, Chicago.

Pablo Picasso,
Portrait of Wilhelm Uhde, 1910.
Oil on canvas, 81 x 60 cm.
Joseph Pulitzer Collection, St. Louis.

Pablo Picasso,
Violin, Wineglass, Pipe and Inkwell, 1912.
Oil on canvas, 81 x 54 cm.
Národní Gallery, Prague.

Pablo Picasso,
Violin, 1912.
Oil on canvas, 55 x 46 cm.
The Pushkin Museum of Fine Arts, Moscow.

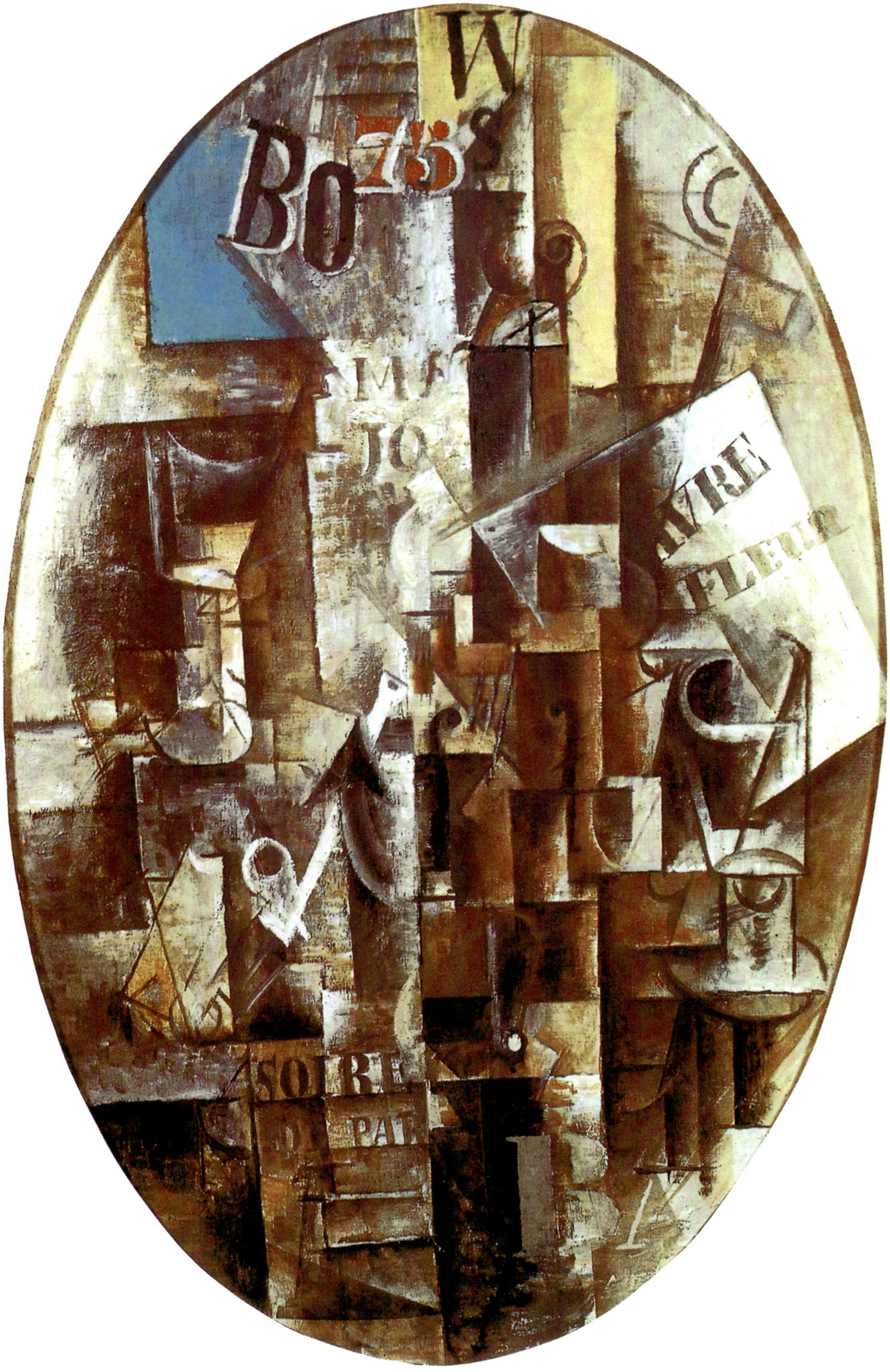
W
BO
75
SOIRE

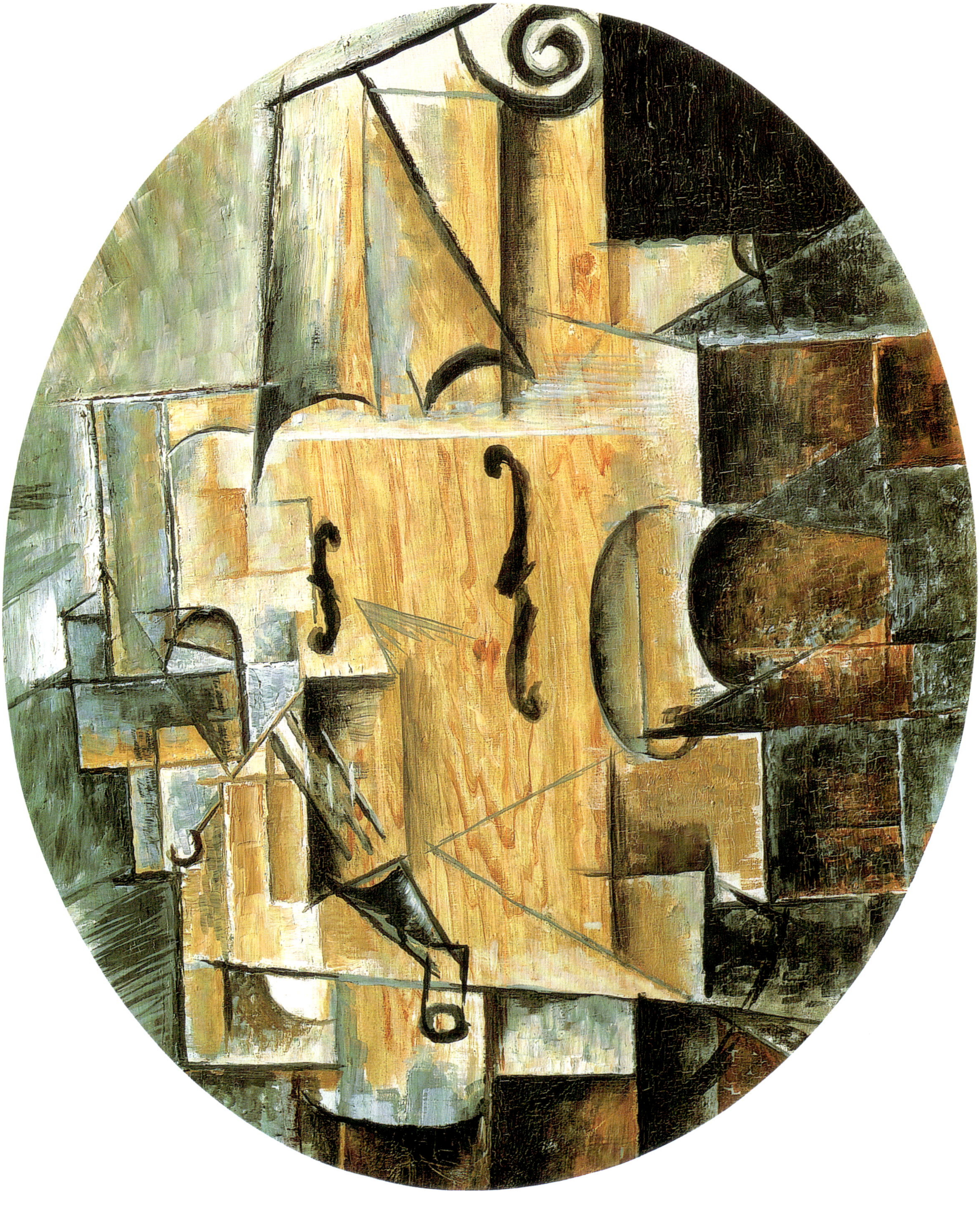

The pseudo-historic Queen Isabeau, a direct descendant of the family of images belonging to the transformed "bistro carnival", is semantically equivalent to Harlequin (one of the carnival group), who reappeared in Picasso's works after a three-year absence. This pensive female Harlequin in her green, leaf-patterned dress and with her pseudo-medieval headdress is accompanied by a bowl in a vegetal form, "gothically" heaped with fruit. The allusion to natural forms serves as a metaphor of the eternal woman, in this case dressed as a medieval "fair lady".

The figure, the stylised arabesques and flat planes, the cool and somewhat mournful decorativeness, give the picture the quality of old tapestries, which Picasso found attractive because of their combination of generalised forms and chromatically graded tones. For Picasso sleep and dream are also elements of the eternal woman, but in this case Harlequin-Isabeau's pensive reverie over a book suggests the character's literary past.

Another fair lady, but of a different era, is depicted in *Woman with a Fan*, in whom some of Picasso's contemporaries recognised an American connoisseur of art. However the resemblance was accidental, even though the painting definitely has something of an actual portrait about it. An elegant woman, wearing a rather audacious hat and a jabot and holding an open fan in one hand and a folded umbrella in the other, sits in an armchair as if posing for the artist. Notwithstanding the obviously new pictorial language of the canvas, all its formal solutions have a wonderful unity that makes one forget the unorthodox manner and react only to the image, its individual expression. The pictorial space—satiated with the interplay of rhythmic planes, graded tonal perspectives and cold malachite and silvery-grey colours—is an attribute of the personality we read in the woman's features. Her fixed, sober gaze from under the brim of her enormous hat hypnotises the viewer; her face, though somewhat generalised, retains its regularity of feature and is treated like a mask, cut and polished by light; the gesture of her hand, holding the umbrella, is both angular and affectedly refined; her entire figure reflects the fashionable style of a woman of the world, a sister of Alexander Blok's mysterious "Unknown Lady" (that was how the Russian Symbolist Georgy Chulkov perceived her).[27]

If, however, Harlequin-Isabeau's inclined head, downcast eyes and pseudo-historical details created the image of a queen from some romantic dreamland, what Chulkov calls a charming monster, then in this other lady we have two strains, differing in expression, two different halves of one mask. This combination of contemporary urban style with awkward, almost sharp rhythms lacking in plasticity creates the image of a mannequin with no more substance than what the eye can see, rather than that of eternal woman. And while Queen Isabeau's femininity was emphasised and expressed by the metaphor of plentiful vegetal allusions (the leafy ornament, the full fruit dish, the emerald green tonality), here the pictorial element characterising the woman with a fan is an empty, jagged vase.

In *Woman with a Mandolin* (p. 74), the interrelationship of the objects and the character is obvious because it is based on a thematic concept: a woman plays a musical instrument,

Pablo Picasso,
Musical Instruments, 1912.
Oil, plaster of Paris and sawdust on oil-cloth, 98 x 80 cm.
The State Hermitage Museum, St. Petersburg.

Pablo Picasso,
Tavern, c. 1914.
Oil and sawdust on cardboard, 29.5 x 38.7 cm.
The State Hermitage Museum, St. Petersburg.

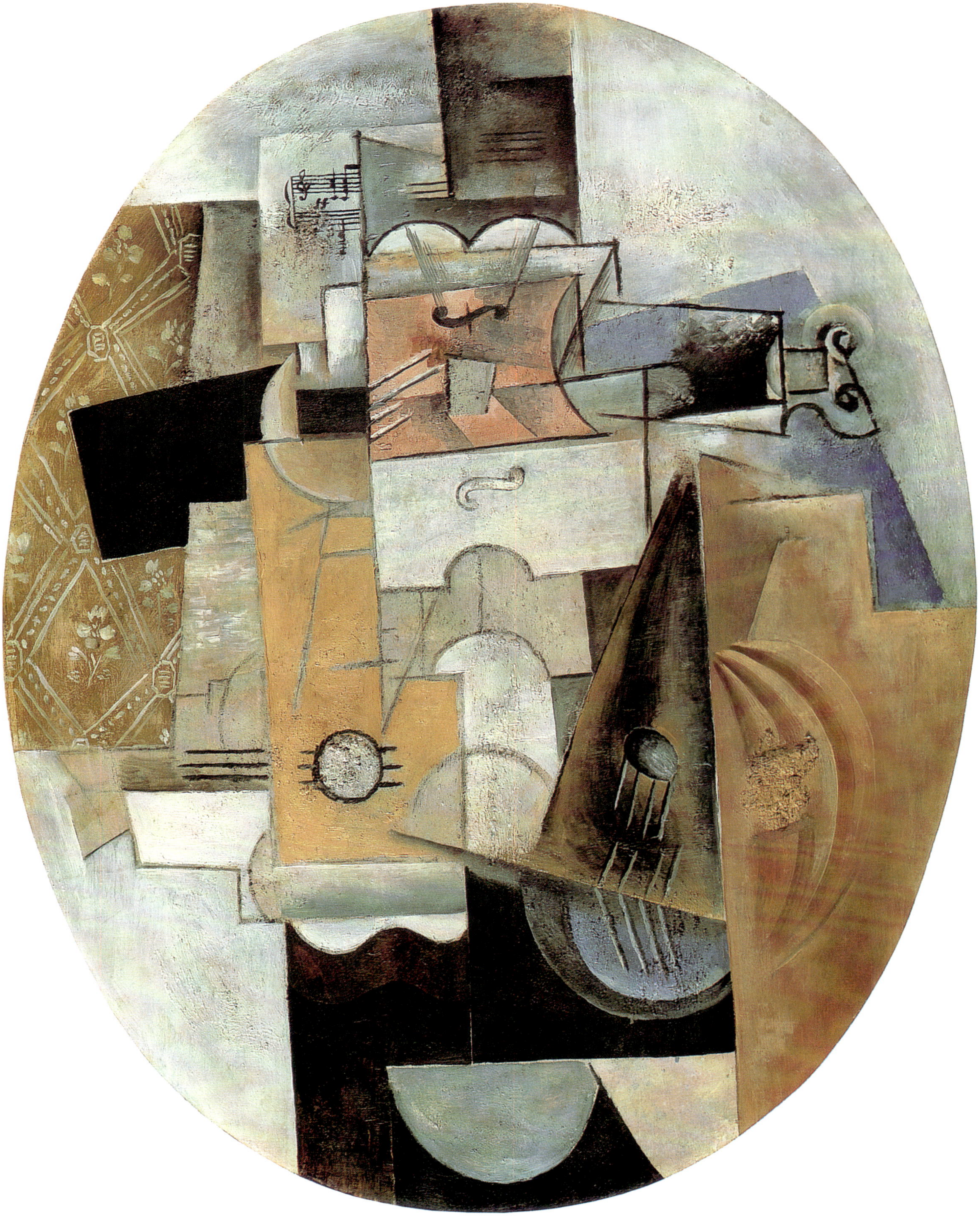

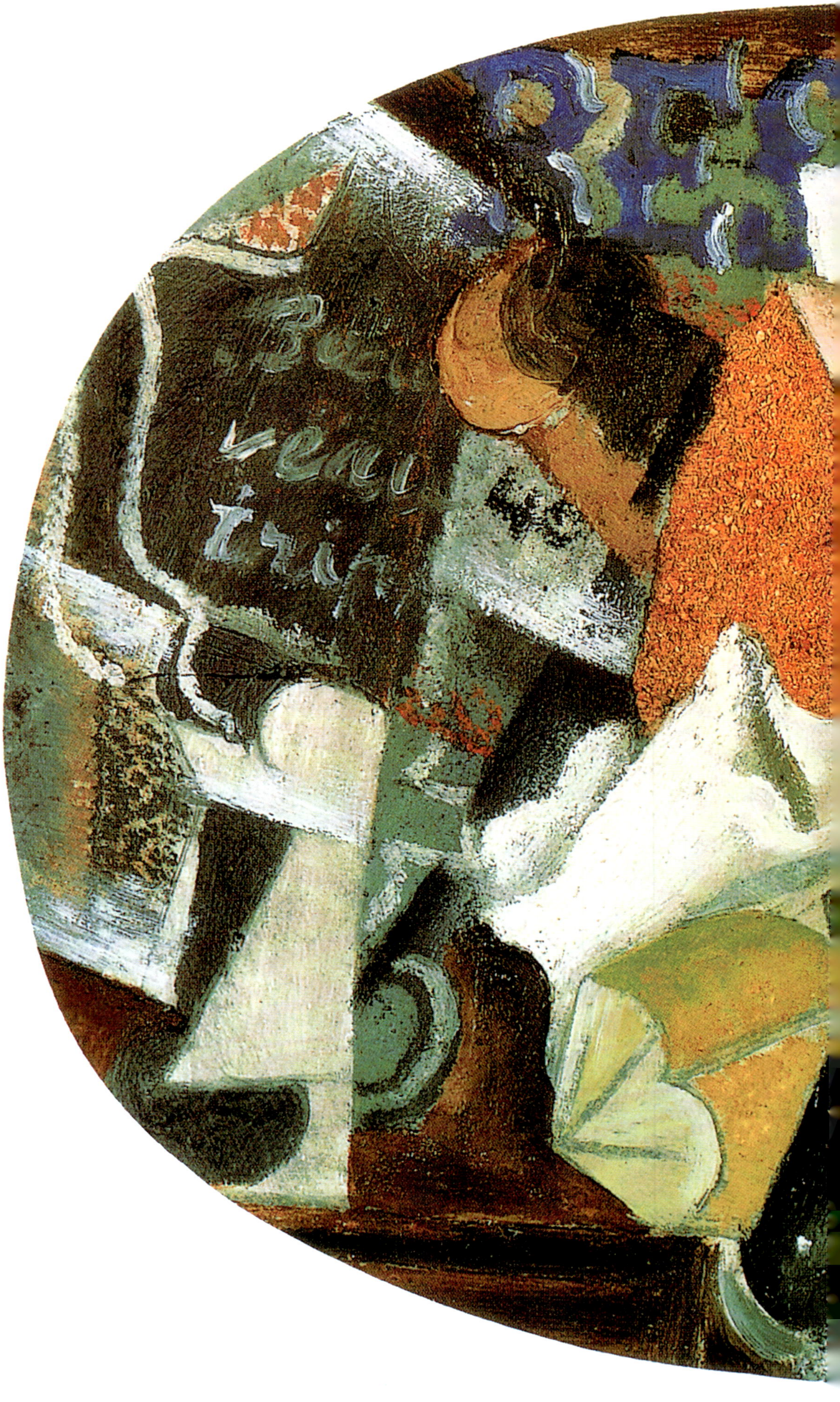

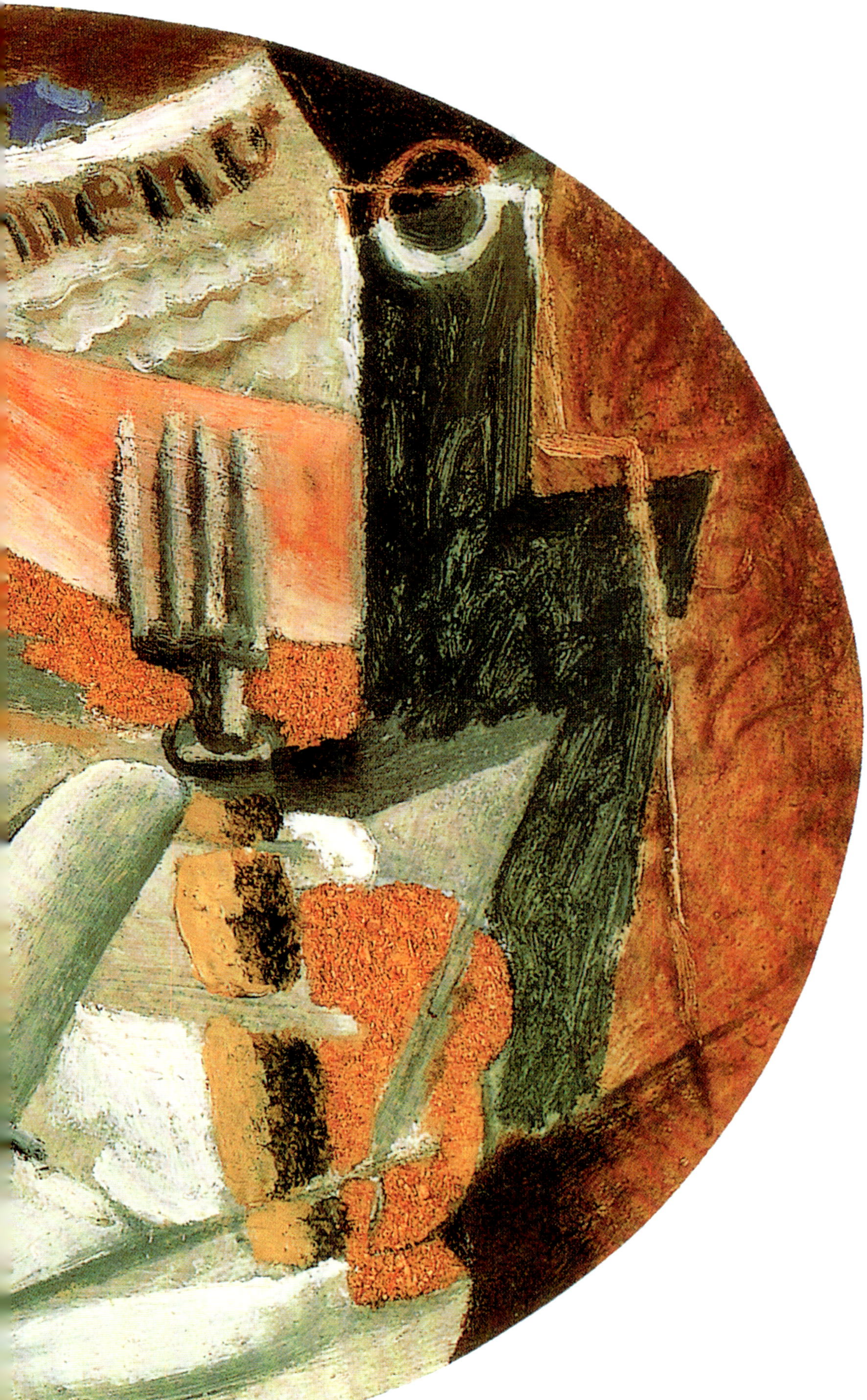

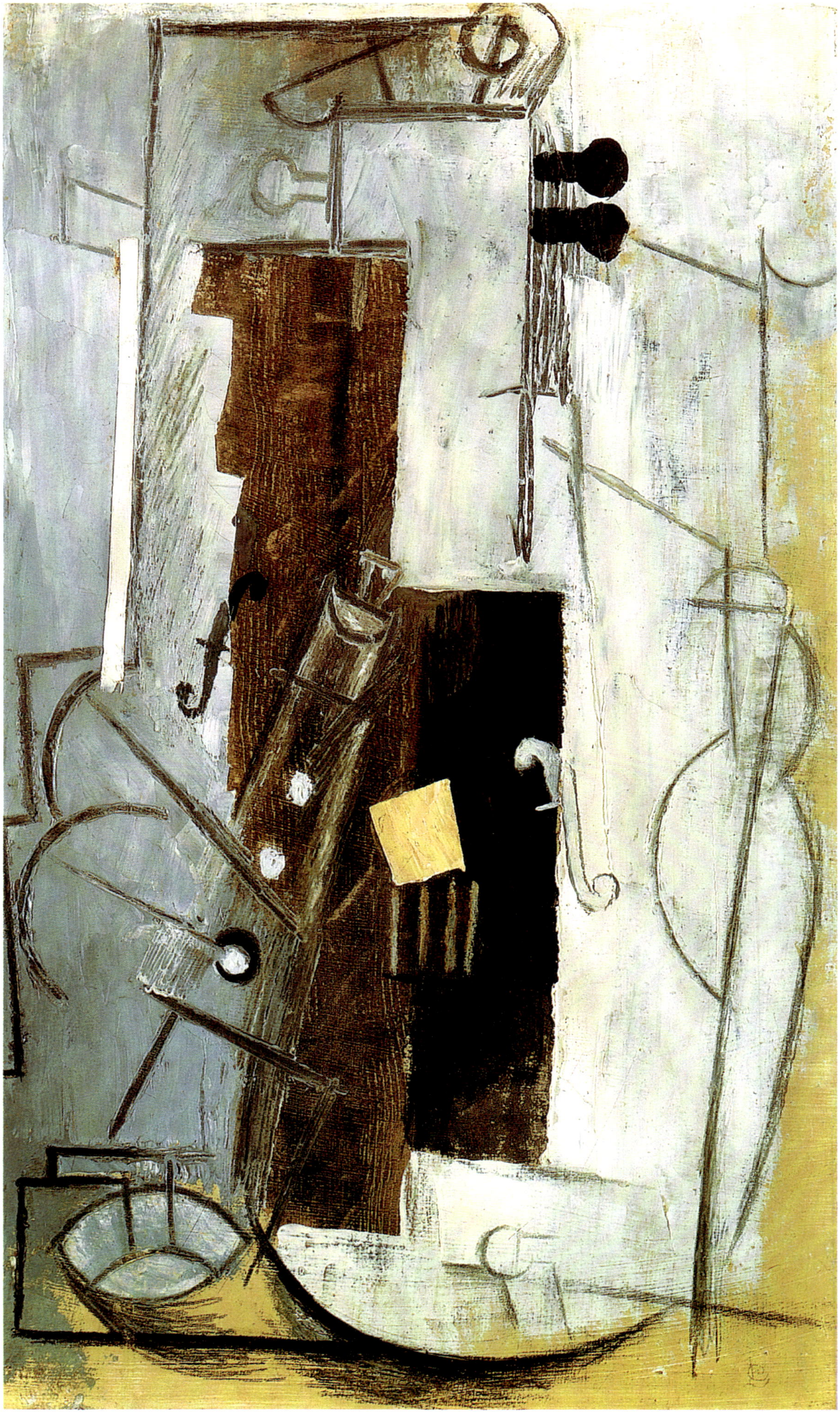

while books serve as attributes of the intellectual atmosphere of music-making. On the other hand, the regulated and ordered lines of the bookshelves contrast sharply with the scarlet waterfall of the drapery and the folds of white cloth streaming along the back of the armchair. These rhythms find their response in the musician's emotional state as she obliviously gives herself to the torrent of music. Picasso rendered this fusion of music and emotion by shaping the contour of the woman's figure like that of a musical instrument (a sort of lute-*cum*-guitar, rather than a small, graceful mandolin) and by giving an analogous structure to the woman's head and the hemispherical body of the mandolin. For the sake of this analogy, Picasso analysed and recreated, with clear lines and simple planes, the sculptural plasticity of the musician's head; he presented it, unlike her hands, not in "flesh", but in "wooden" tones. He likened the woman's head to a mandolin, her body to a musical instrument, and he did so not just in the literary, but in the plastic sense as well.

In *Woman with a Mandolin* Picasso was on the way to a discovery that would in the future radically transform the very principles of his art—the image presented as a visual metaphor. He stood on the threshold of the discovery of plastic poetry. This comment pertains to a visual metaphor that Picasso himself called *trompe-l'esprit* and that was to dominate his work somewhat later, during the period of verbal inclusions and collages. Yet in such pictures as *Woman with a Mandolin*, there is still much of the *trompe-l'œil*, of the desire for plastic concrete form, for a spatially convincing ratio of volumes—which promoted Matisse, for instance, to consider Cubism "a kind of descriptive realism."[28] Basically, from the viewpoint of the development of literary methods, the shift from *trompe-l'œil* to *trompe-l'esprit* is the direction taken by Picasso's evolution of Cubism. The formation of this new creative spirit was accompanied by a renewal of the expressive means themselves and by a realisation of their purity and power. Step by step, Picasso's Cubism freed painting from optical fiction, in order to make it a plastic language suitable for the creation of visual metaphors, to make it the language of poetry. The stylistic differences (even contradictions) between the works of the autumn of 1908 and the spring of 1909, discussed earlier, reflect the absence of any one evolutionary direction at the beginning of Picasso's Cubism (in that sense, Braque has greater integrity and consistency, but is also more formal). Evidently the theme remained the motivating impulse of his art at that time, although it did not always lend itself to verbal expression. "If the subjects I have wanted to express have suggested different ways of expression, I have never hesitated to adopt them."[29]

Psychological Reality

The evolution of Picasso's Cubism was to assume a certain measure of consistency and logic beginning with the canvases completed after the summer of 1909, a season spent at Horta de Ebro, to which he returned a decade after the happiest days of his early youth. In Horta Picasso felt reality with his entire body, with all his senses, with his very conscience; his art once more made contact with his environment. This contact was,

Pablo Picasso,
Clarinet and Violin, 1913.
Oil on canvas, 50.3 x 33 cm.
The State Hermitage Museum,
St. Petersburg.

Pablo Picasso,
Composition with a Sliced Pear, 1914.
Gouache, lead pencil and wallpaper collage on cardboard, 35 x 32 cm.
The State Hermitage Museum,
St. Petersburg.

Pablo Picasso,
Composition with a Bunch of Grapes and a Sliced Pear, 1914.
Collage on paper mounted on cardboard, gouache, size paint, lead pencil and sawdust, 67.6 x 52.2 cm.
The State Hermitage Museum,
St. Petersburg.

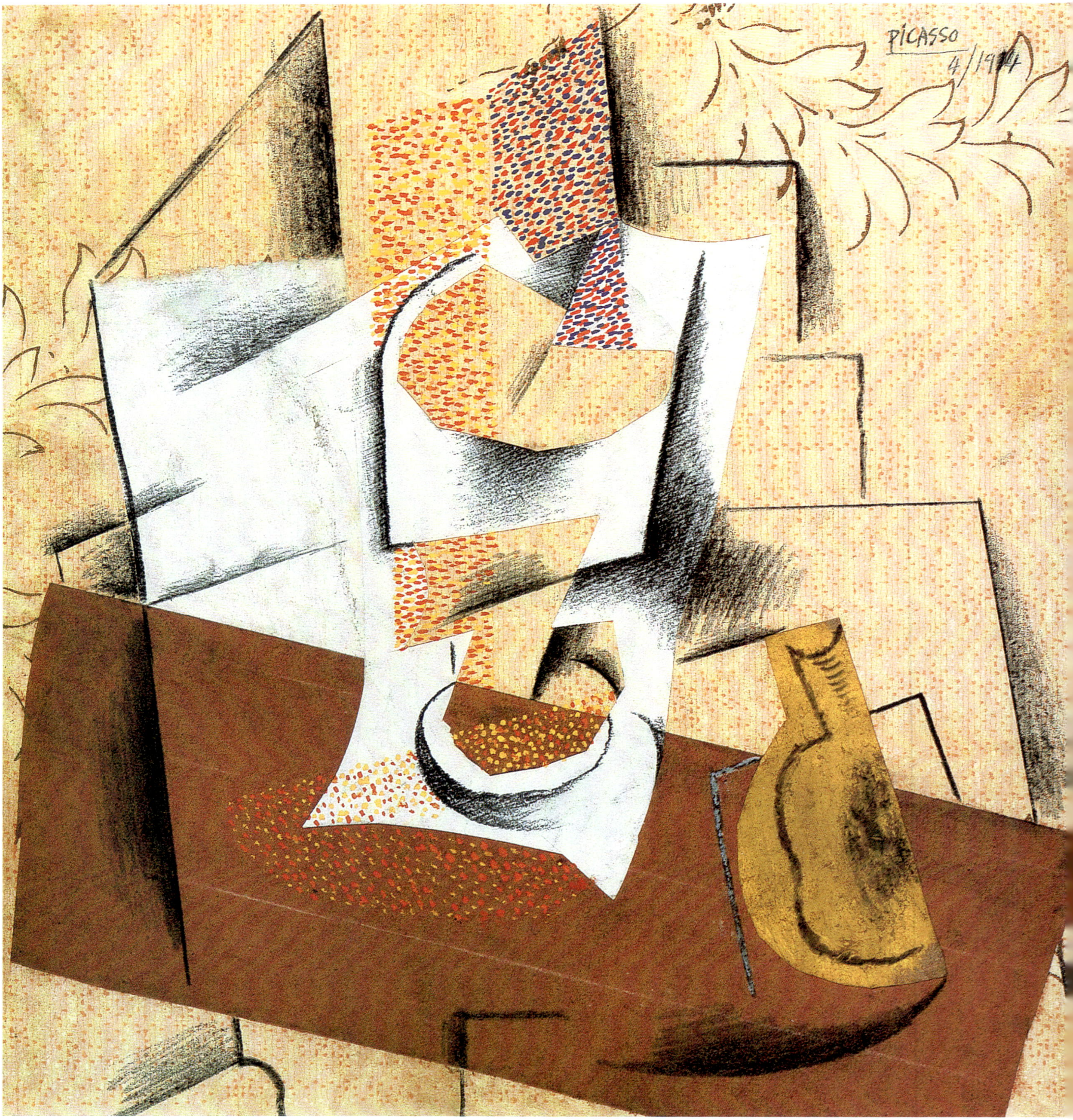
PICASSO
4/1914

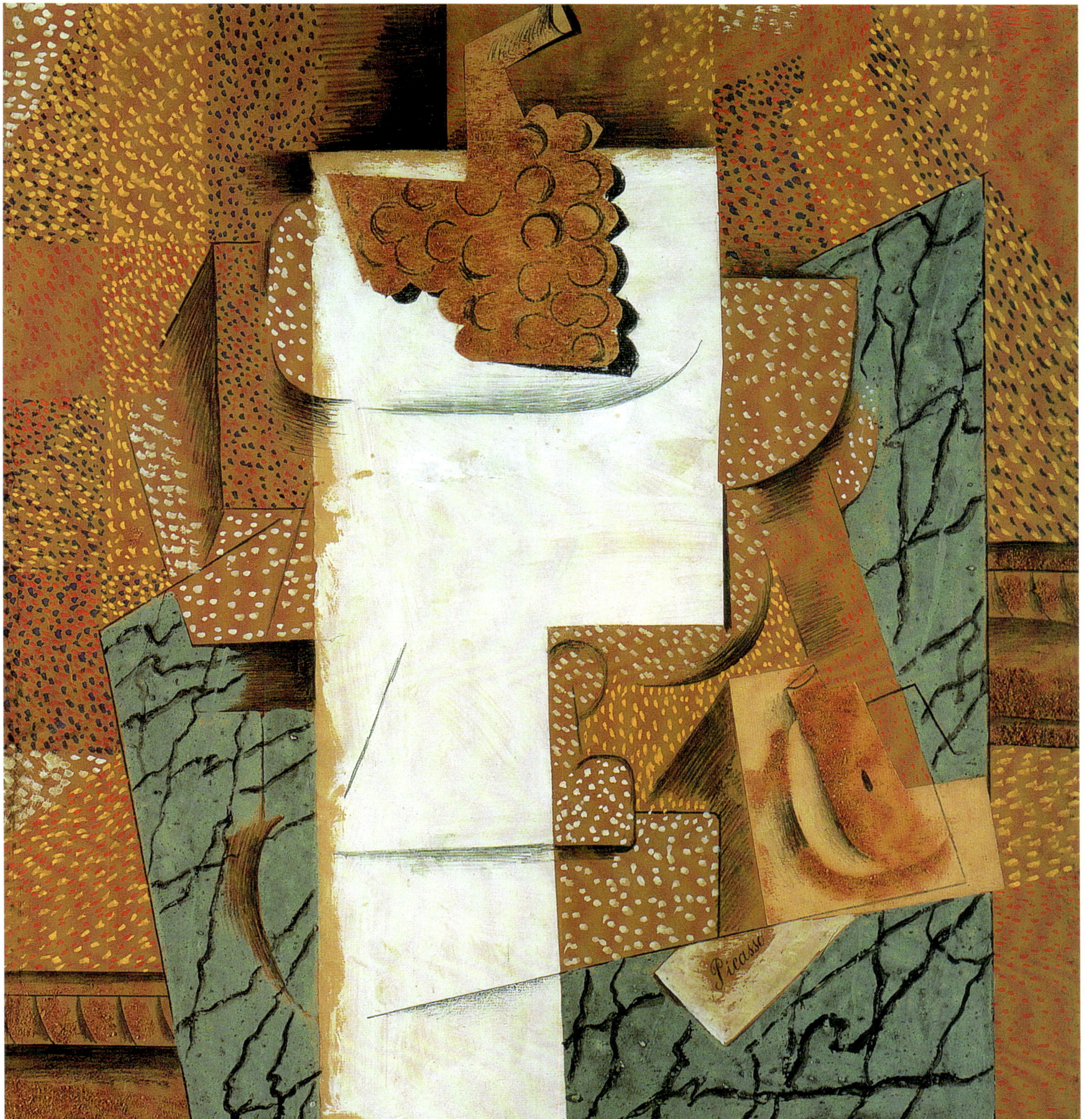
Picasso
Picasso

however, effected with the help of his new "optics", which the artist uses to colour his perception in that stern, mountainous country with its pure, chilly air and cubic structures strewn over the rocky slopes. These "optics" were amazingly purist in their simplicity and clarity. They excluded the accidental, the formless and the secondary; they brought order to nature's chaos and at the same time sharpened to the limit the version of form as the interplay of spatial contrasts, turning a scene into a rich panorama of different aspects arranged according to the character of the subject. They were to serve as the basis of Cubism's formal vocabulary. Let us note, however, that the defining of volume by a detailed faceting of the form did not necessarily result from a preconceived analysis: it came from a feeling for the profound reality of this country, with its landscape baked to a hardened crust under the pitiless light of the Spanish sun. The integrity of that feeling guaranteed the paintings done at Horta de Ebro a certain unity of style, whether landscape, still lifes, or portraits.

The Hermitage possesses one of that summer's landscapes—*Factory at Horta de Ebro.* The title speaks for the reality of the subject, which, however, appears before our eyes in a form cleansed by Picasso's vision and decorated by his imagination. The verdant palm trees that soften the grim view were, as the artist admitted, his own invention (they do not grow in Horta de Ebro or in that region). The group of geometrically simple buildings seem to radiate their angular, fractionalised rhythms outwards like a musical theme that eventually spirals into a sort of spatial fugue. In their magical interplay of silvery-grey and ochre planes the landscape and factory are transformed into a prismatic mirage born from the air of the Catalan mountains, satiated with pure light. This light-carrying air differs from that of the North: it does not embrace and soften forms but brusquely shatters itself upon them. It is depicted here by the striking tonal accents of the sky, an integral part of the overall structure.

The paintings from Horta de Ebro are considered classics of Analytical Cubism. As early as his return to Paris that autumn, Picasso summed up the formal solutions they contain by turning to sculpture, which he called the painter's best commentary on painting. He made *Head of a Woman* in an analytical manner. Without violating the traditional principle of the integrated sculptural mass, Picasso models the surface in a series of spectacular slanted planes; these powerful muscular accents at the constructive joints create an interplay of rhythms, but they also rip open the epidermis of the sculptural surface (Kahnweiler). Recalling *Head of a Woman* decades later, Picasso told Penrose: "I thought that the curves you see on the surface should continue into the interior. I had the idea of doing them in wire." However, Penrose notes, "this solution did not please him, because, as he added, it was 'too intellectual, too much like painting'."[30]

This atmosphere of concentrated intellectual work in the studio is conjured up by *Young Woman*, produced in the winter of 1909-1910. By that time Picasso had moved from the dilapidated Bateau-Lavoir to a comfortable apartment-with-studio on the Boulevard de Clichy at the foot of Montmartre. The large studio window, looking north,

Pablo Picasso,
Glass, Dice and Newspaper, 1914.
Painted wood, iron and wire,
18 x 13.5 cm.
Musée Picasso, Paris.

Pablo Picasso,
Still-Life with Piano, 1911.
Oil on canvas and stencil, 50 x 130 cm.
Private collection.

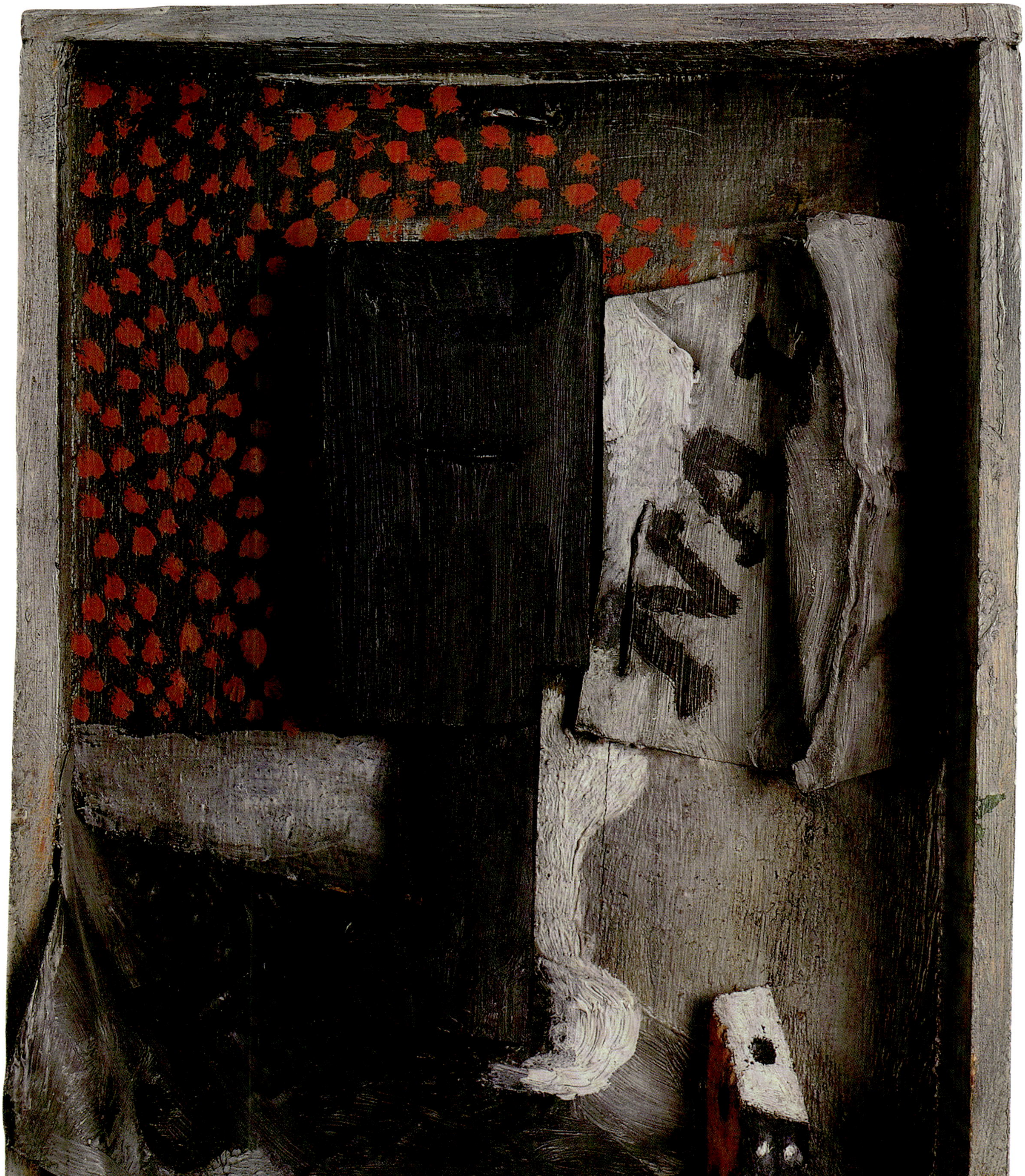

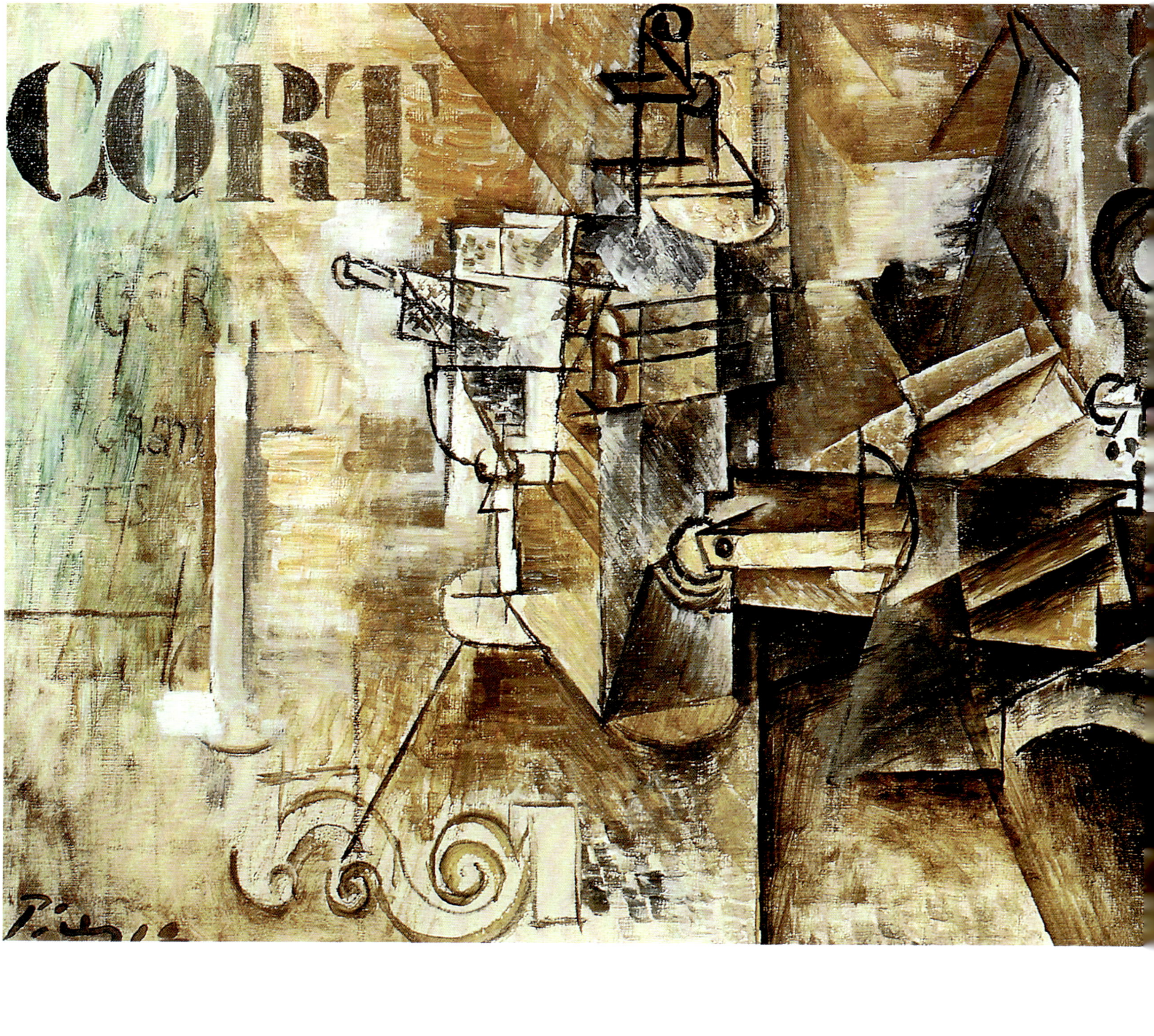
CORT

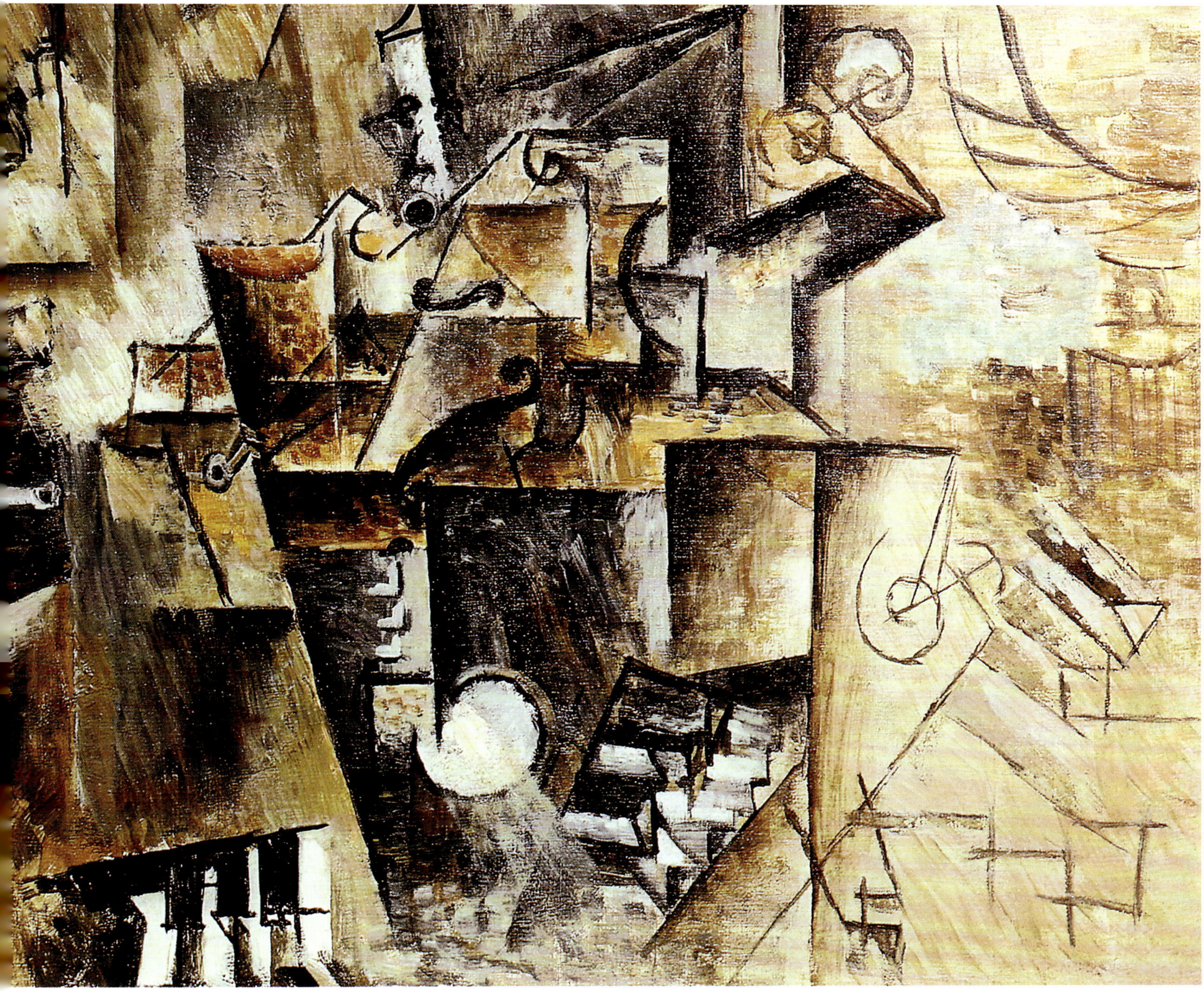

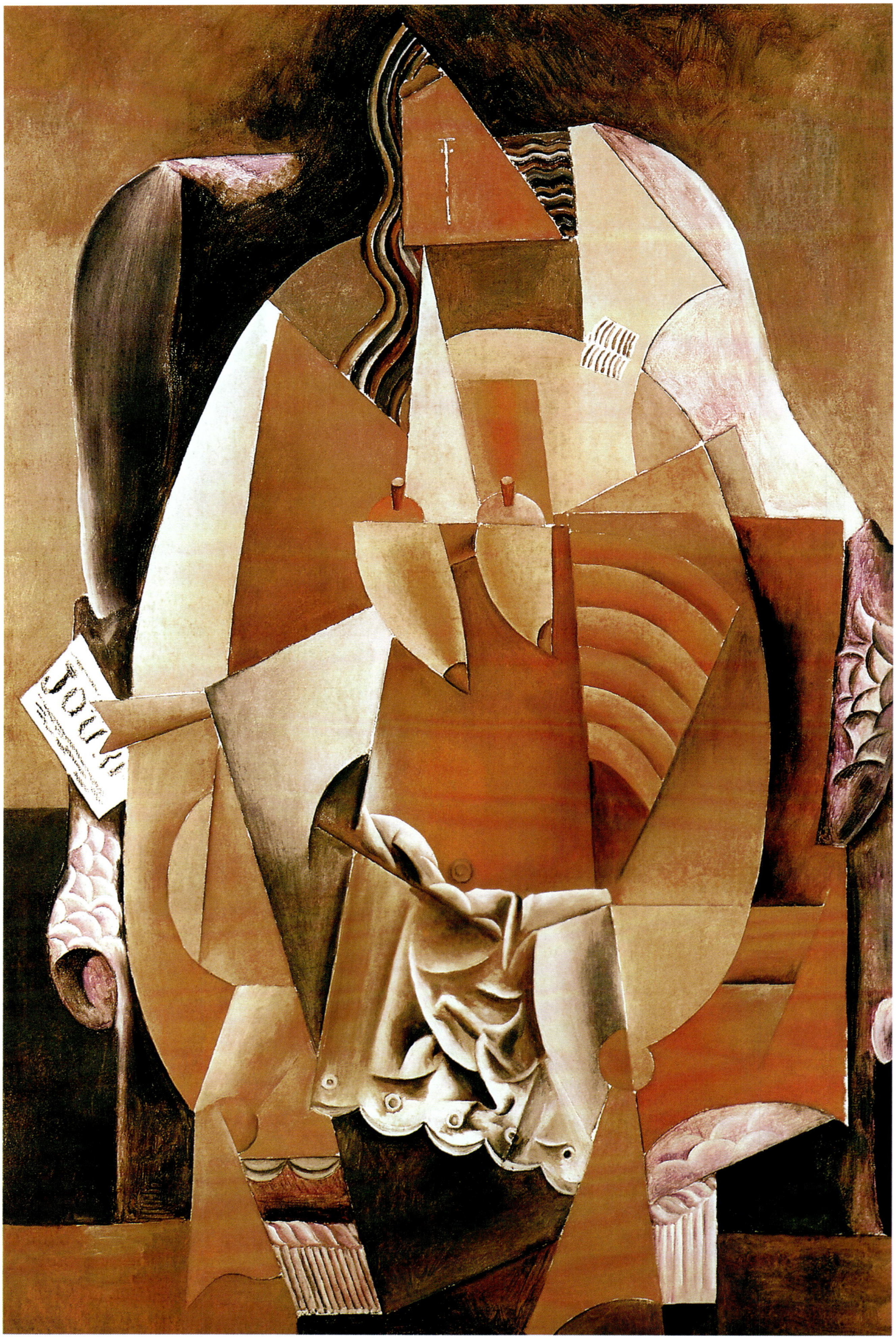

let in the even silvery light so beloved by Corot and Cézanne; that partially explains the unexpected emphasis on colour values evident in the Hermitage painting. The same tones serve to breathe life into the seated nude, treated in a completely untraditional manner: she is a female-like crystal of flesh that at first stuns us with its "deformities". Picasso now painted standing close to the canvas, never stepping back to assess the general effect: it did not interest him. His work is more psychological than decorative. As the Russian critic Innokenty Aksenov was to note perceptively: Picasso stares his objects in the eye, as we look into our lover's face. He must turn his head to see two objects, and so he moves the width of the composition of his canvas into the depth."[31] That is what led Picasso—that painter by calling, innovator by nature, contradiction by temperament (Sabartés)—to such distortions, through which he seems to say: there are no beautiful objects, there is only art (Aksenov). The object of his pictorial studies was not superficial. Braque recalled Picasso and himself in those days: "We were particularly very concentrated."[32] Sometimes Picasso would visit the studios of his friends to draw living models, to become immersed in a given model's character, a woman with individual features, rhythms, proportions. Then, retiring to the seclusion of his studio, he made portraits of his recollections, clarifying their details by his own method. That explains, for example, the impression one receives from *Young Woman* of a concrete character, of an individual modern urban model; the longer one studies her, the more one understands who she is. But from the viewpoint of Cubism, this picture was just one link in a chain of studio works which led to the ever increasing disintegration of volume by means of values and its dissociation into small geometric planes—to the creation of the peculiar esoteric language of Analytical Cubism.

Picasso limited his expressive means to spatial lighting effects: values and planes. Both reflect the relativity of the analytical vision of painters; both are instruments to make order in their visual perception, to create depth on a picture's surface by the use of colour.

This is an enormously difficult problem. Cézanne always complained that perspective eluded him; he organised depth in his painting through receding planes of colour which, like the strips of a wicker basket, he wove into one pictorial whole, vibrating with the vitality of living forms. But colour is a special problem. "In colour," Braque said, "only the aspect of light preoccupied us. Are not colour and space interrelated? So we developed them together… And for that we were called abstract!"[33] Light and space are concrete in the artist's eye, but values and planes are almost as abstract as the letters that make up words expressing thoughts or denoting objects.

Angularly drawn smoky and semi-transparent planes, slanted this way and that, link up like metal pieces around a magnet and incomprehensibly merge in the instantly recognisable *Portrait of Ambroise Vollard* (p. 85). The edges of flat planes become elements of the drawing and mark the characteristic features of the face, the details of clothing (buttons, jacket collar, handkerchief in breast pocket), and aspects of the interior (the bottle on a table). As if trying to square the circle, Picasso builds the dome of his model's head

Pablo Picasso,
Woman Wearing a Shirt and Seated in a Chair, 1913-1914.
Oil on canvas, 150 x 99.5 cm.
Private collection.

Pablo Picasso,
Landscape of Céret, 1913.
Glued papers, pins, charcoal and chalk, 38 x 38 cm.
Musée Picasso, Paris.

Pablo Picasso,
Violin, 1915.
Painted iron sheet and wire, 100 x 63.7 x 18 cm.
Musée Picasso, Paris.

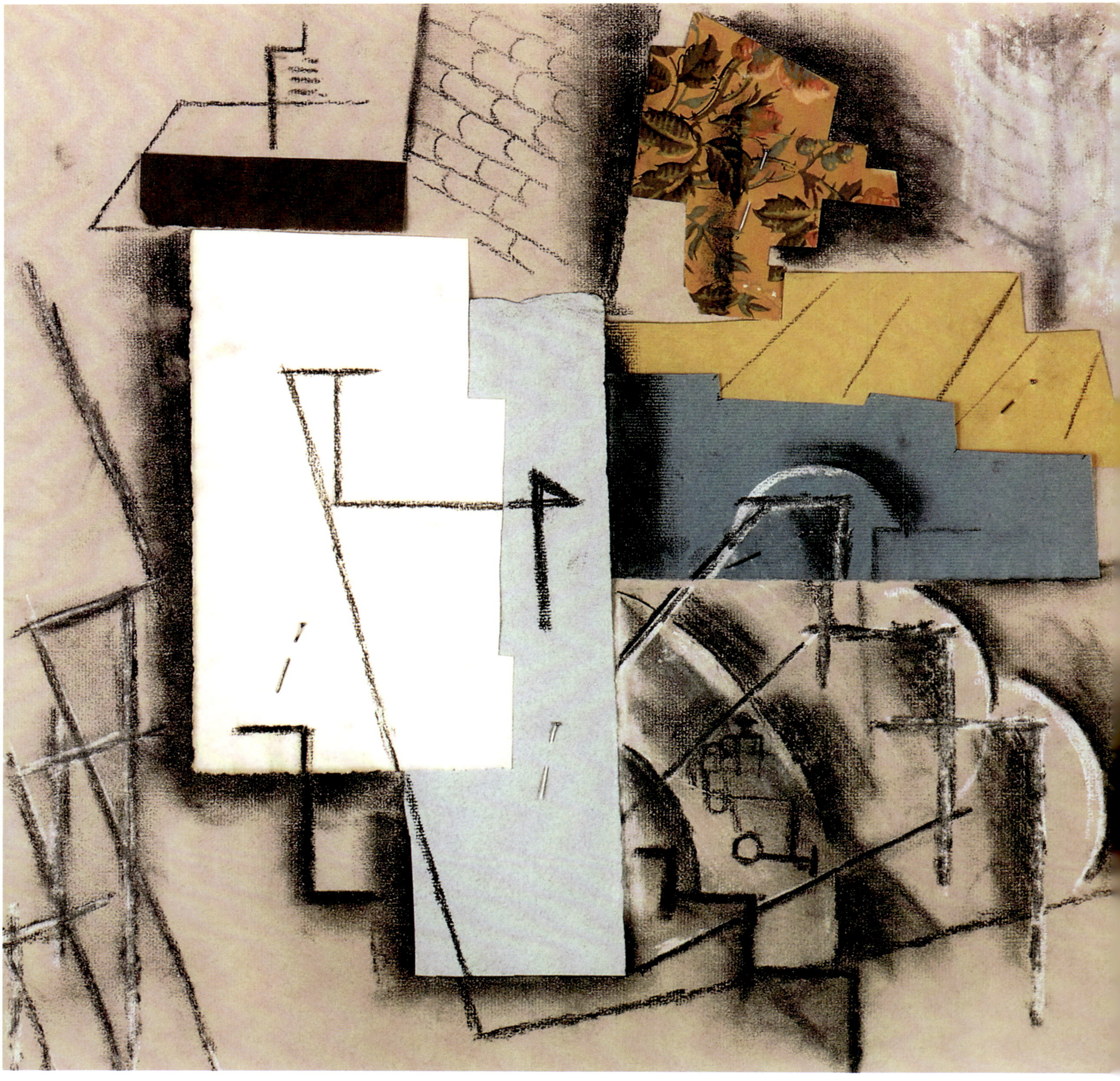

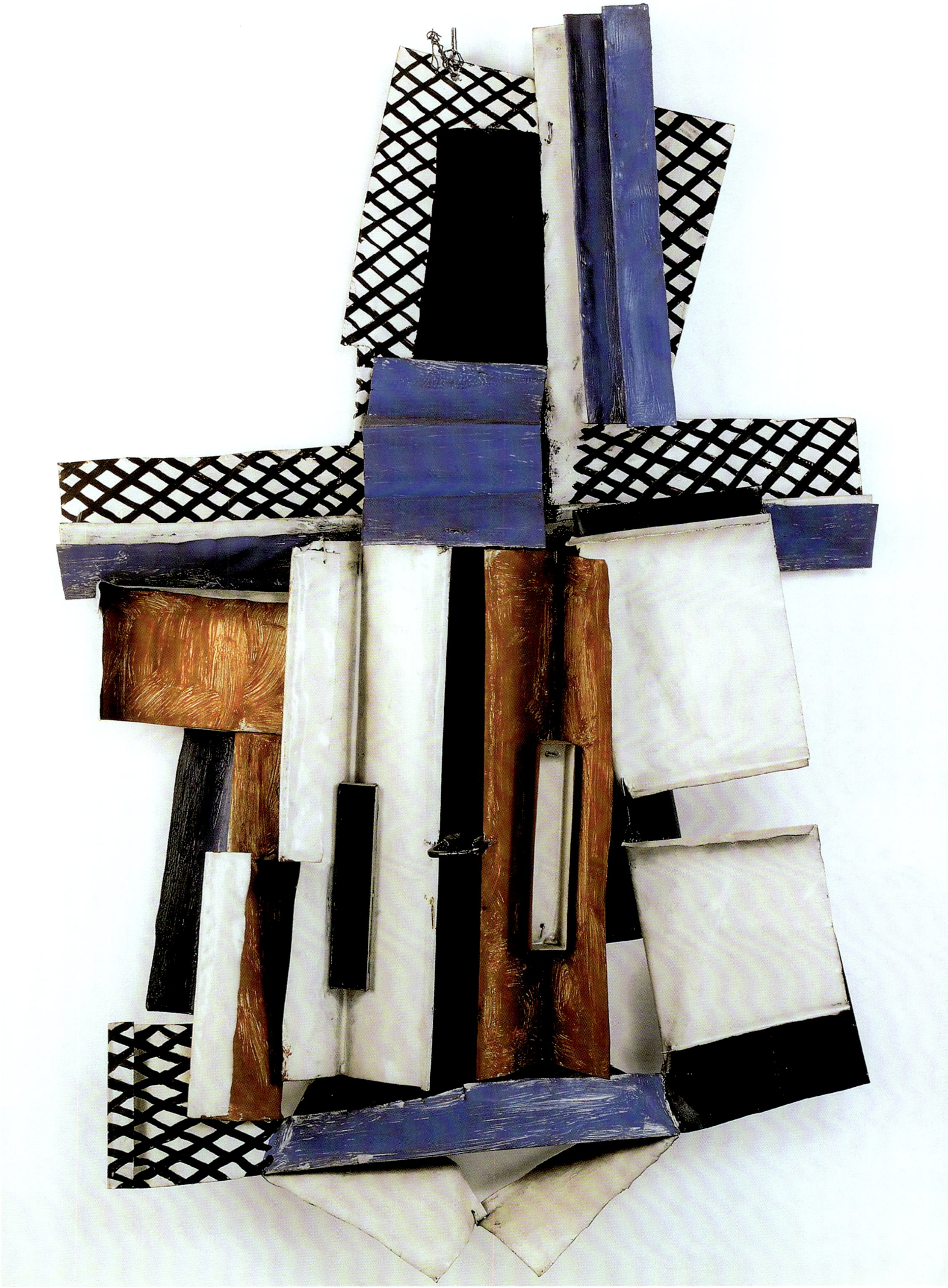

out of superimposed planes. With energetic striation, he marks out the main lines and masses of Vollard's heavy, sleepy face: the small broken nose and the hard line of the mouth. Although there is no imitation in Picasso's plastic language (as early as 1910 he "does not compose from nature, but rather with nature, like nature"),[34] one cannot miss the staggering accuracy of the sophisticated tonal gradations; they give the portrait the power of life despite—or perhaps because of—the obviously relative nature of the forms that compose it. Vollard's face fascinates. Looking into its strong, hard features, one understands why Cézanne, who painted his portrait ten years earlier, called the successful art dealer from Rue Laffitte "a slave merchant". However there is also a tragic element in Vollard's lethargic life mask: it was documented later in photographs, but it also appeared earlier during the periods of black melancholy and somnambulistic torpor characteristic of his nature. It seems he was in that state when he posed for Picasso. Generally considered a masterpiece of Analytical Cubism, the Moscow *Portrait of Ambroise Vollard* is a real masterpiece of psychological realism, illuminating a quality that was perceived in 1910 as one of the Spanish painter's paradoxes, when Metzinger noted: "Picasso openly declares himself a realist."[35]

Already in the *Portrait of Ambroise Vollard* a heightened care for tonal nuances demanded a brushwork technique reminiscent of the mosaic manner of the Divisionists; because of that technique, the material seems to give off a shimmering vibration regulated only by the constructive framework of vertical, horizontal and diagonal lines in the drawing, not all of which can be perceived by the eye. Throughout 1910 and 1911, Picasso and Braque, shoulder to shoulder, developed this hermetic art in which every picture was an autonomous slice of "pure reality" that did not imitate the environment. And even though these works had their own subjects, usually still lifes and the figures of musicians, the reality of this kind of painting was based on more complex, and not always concrete, feelings.

Decades later Picasso was to explain: "All its forms can't be rationalised. At the time, everyone talked about how much reality there was in Cubism. But they didn't really understand, it's not a reality you can take in your hand. It's more like a perfume—in front of you, behind you, to the sides. The scent is everywhere, but you don't quite know where it comes from."[36] In these hermetic paintings Picasso communicated a "scent" of reality that one can grasp through visual allusions: the contours of a glass, a pipe, the elbow-rest of an armchair, the fringe of a tablecloth, a fan, the neck of a violin. This was the concrete reality at the artist's fingertips—in his studio, in the streets, in cafés.

Synthetic Cubism

Soon, in the summer of 1911, another kind of allusion from the real world entered Picasso's painting—street signs, newspaper headlines, words from book jackets, wine bottles, and tobacco labels, musical notes—all of which are thematically linked to the subject of the canvas.

Pablo Picasso,
Portrait of a Young Girl (Woman Seated in Front of the Fireplace), 1914.
Oil on canvas, 130 x 96.5 cm.
Musée National d'Art Moderne,
Centre Georges-Pompidou, Paris.

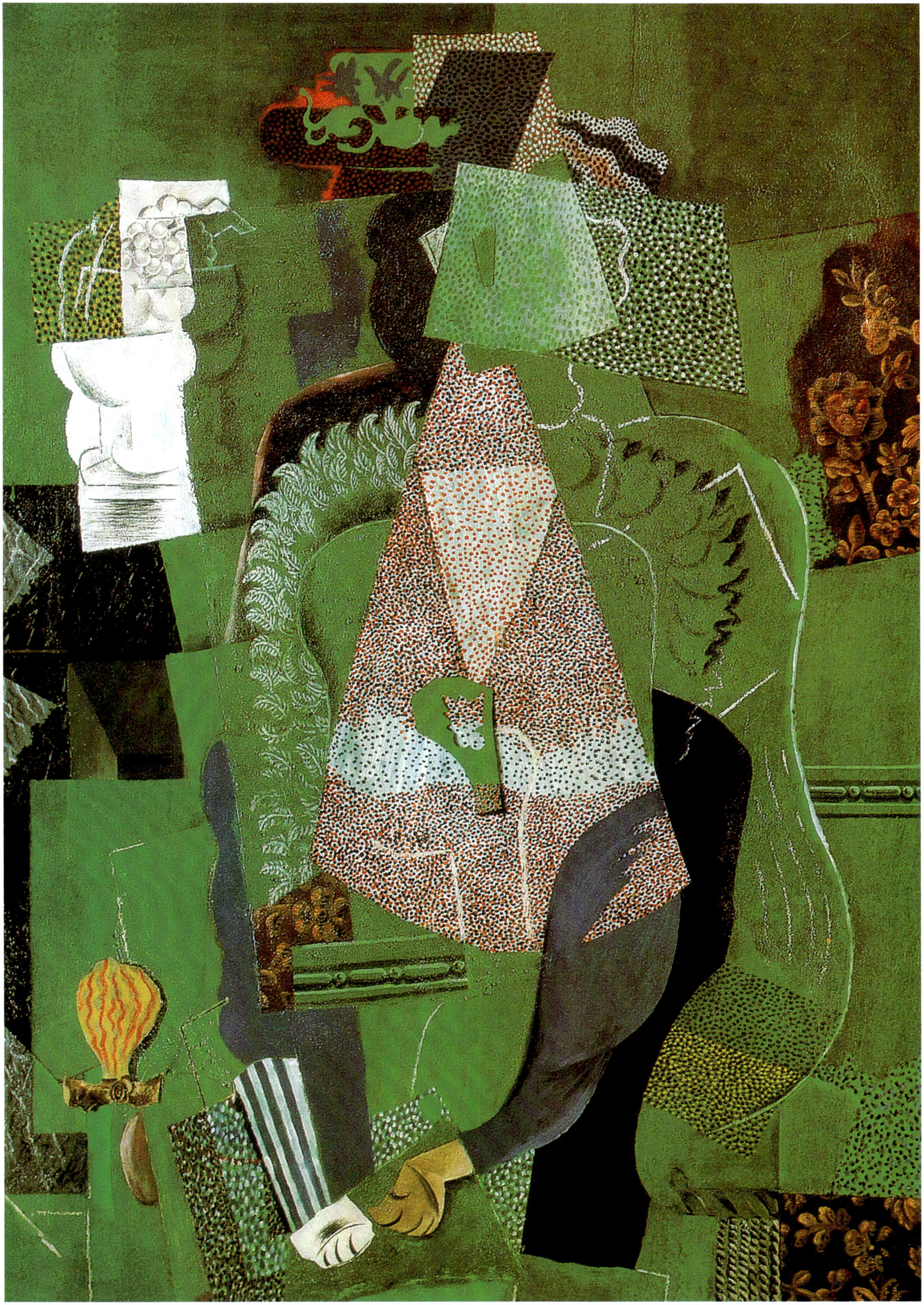

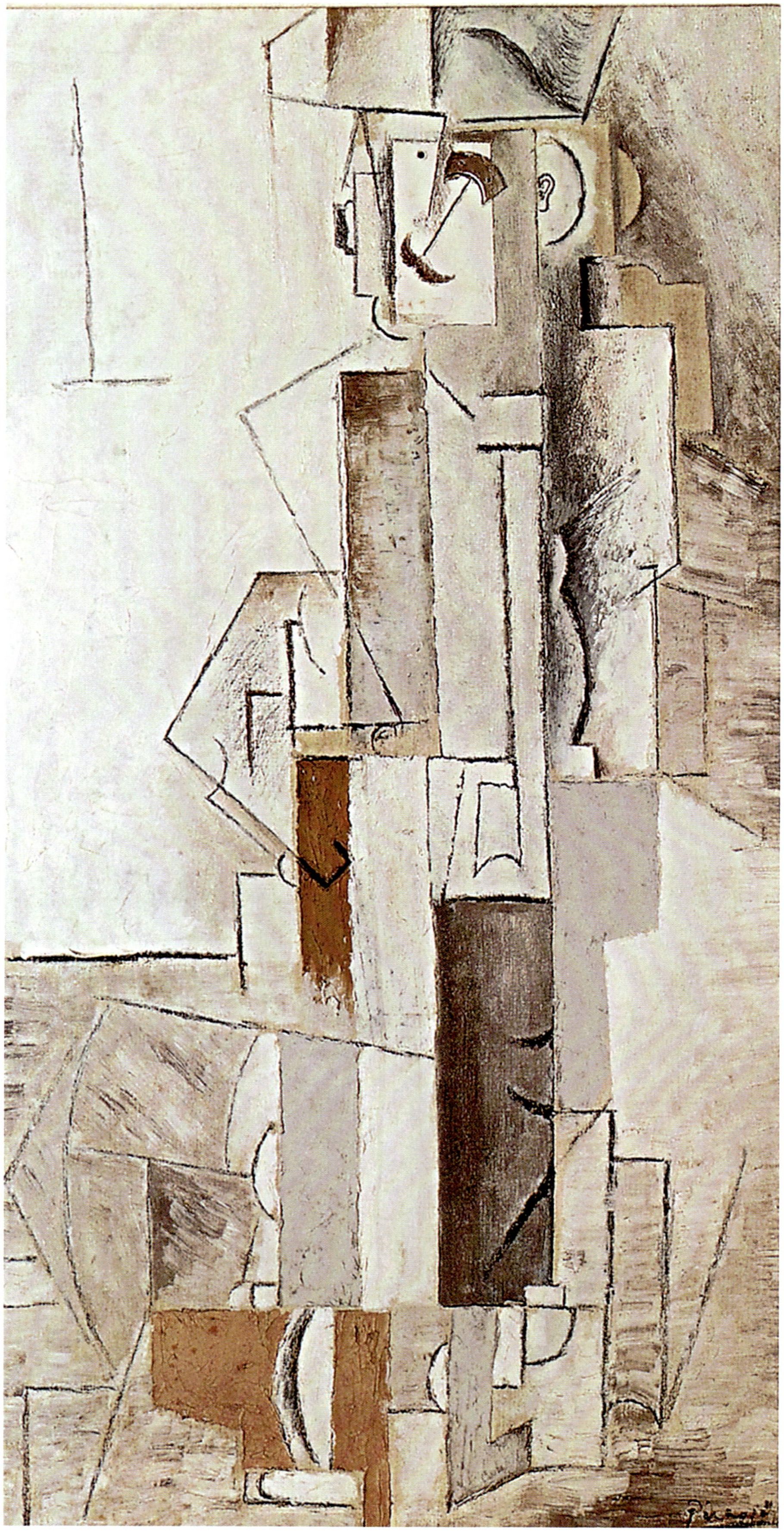

Although such letters and words had appeared before in paintings (for instance, in those of Cézanne and Van Gogh, to mention only Picasso's closest predecessors), in such objects as a newspaper, a book, a sign and so on, the use of verbal elements by Braque and Picasso was of a different character and pursued a different aim. First, for both masters of Analytical Cubism, letters are flat forms that help create the spatial relations of the picture. They are also elements of the surrounding environment that participate in presenting the theme, supporting its subject, which they enter untransformed. Besides that, words and entire sentences, parts of words and syllables, are, to artists who live in close contact with poets (especially to Picasso), also verbal images assuming meaningful relations with the painting's pictorial realities, giving the image a multiplicity of meanings.[37] Having acquired equality in the canvas with plastic forms, verbal print material at the same time heightens the associative meanings of object motifs, stimulates their literal character and, ultimately, their recognisability. Yet this combination of two pictorial levels also leads to the transformation of the picture into a charade with many meanings, a play on words, a total metaphor—an effect that Picasso highly prized.

In the painting *Table in a Café (Bottle of Pernod)* (p. 89), created in the spring of 1912, the letters crossing the background behind the still life are part of advertisements painted on the invisible glass panel of the café window. They endow the picture with the unmistakable look of modern urban life, while the motif—the bottle of Pernod and the glass with its spoon and cube of sugar, placed on the oval table—reveals Picasso's new taste for a material, concrete environment. The artist was clearly enthralled with the contrast between the prismatic refractions of light in the glass objects and the solid, wave-like texture of the warm-toned wood.

At the same time, his imitation of window advertisements imparts an element not merely of reality but of new poetry: by their chaotic nature, as well as by their spatial and semantic relationship to alcohol, these bits and scraps of advertisements echo the perception of modern life as inherently intoxicating and bitter.

According to the generally accepted classifications, during the first half of 1912, Picasso's Cubism underwent a mutation from Analytic to Synthetic. Somewhere at the very start of the year Picasso felt the need to work with tangible forms of reality—to sculpt. At the same time, his introduction into painting of letters and slogans as naked facts of reality opened the way to other facts of reality: in particular, the gluing on of different materials with their own ready-made printed forms, textures, ornaments—and so the collage technique appears. Such are the features of that transition, caused by a host of reasons and events, the most important of which were internal.

The appearance of reality—so direct and unequivocal—signalled the end of the illusory, hermetic and anonymous style of painting called Analytical Cubism, which Picasso developed for a year and a half in such intimate contact with Braque that the other virtually became his double (to the extent that it is difficult to distinguish between their works of 1910-1911). This new orientation was based on a sharpened sensual

Pablo Picasso,
Harlequin, 1913.
Oil on canvas, 88.5 x 46 cm.
Haags Gemeentemuseum, The Hague.

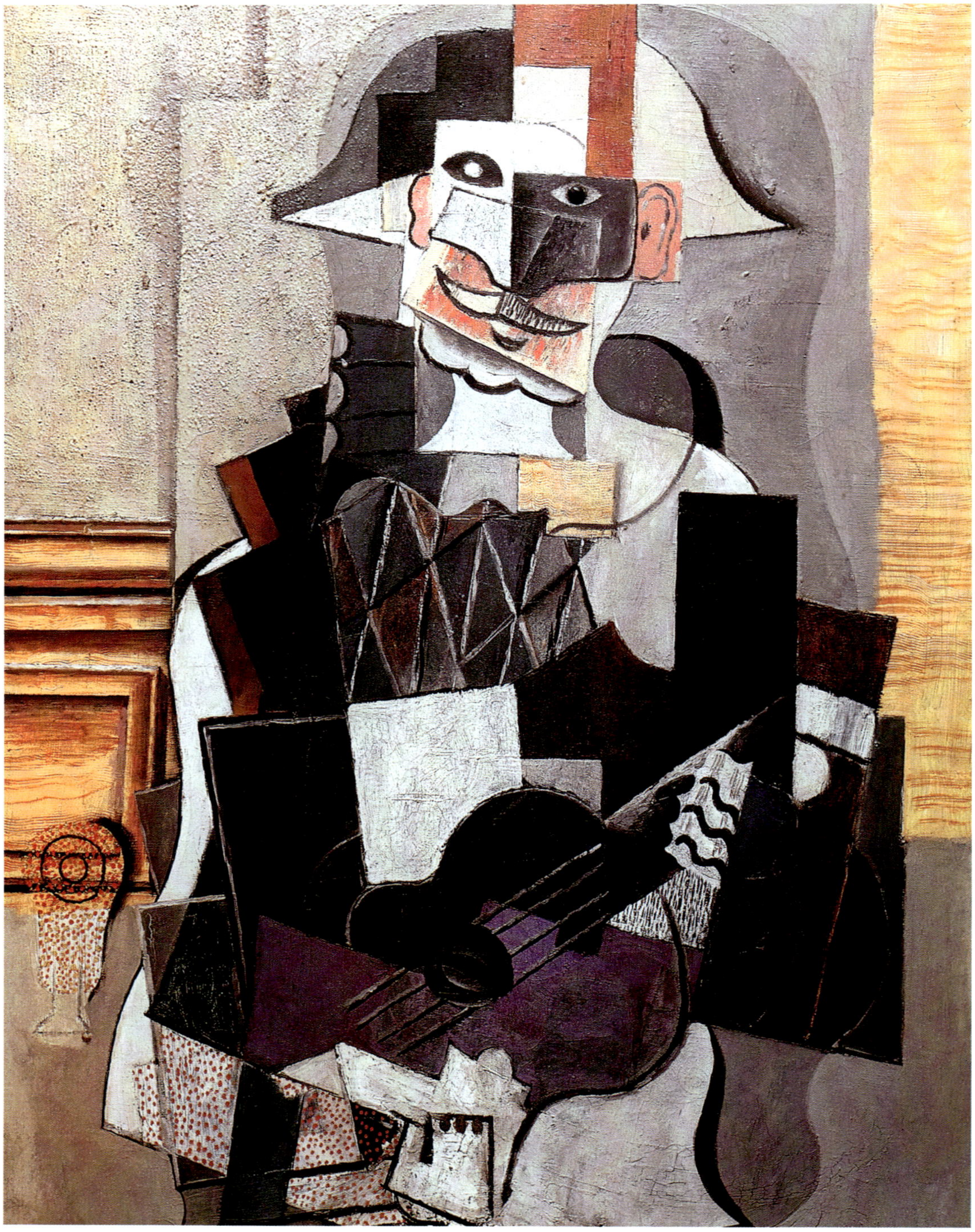

Pablo Picasso,
Harlequin Playing Guitar, 1914-1918.
Oil on canvas, 98 x 77 cm.
Private collection.

Pablo Picasso,
Man with a Pipe, 1915.
Oil on canvas, 130.2 x 89.5 cm.
Art Institute of Chicago, Chicago.

perception of the world, a reassessment of its external stimuli: its variety of colours and wealth of material qualities. This fresh vision was also the echo of an internal event indeed capable of transforming perception and thought, the echo of a new love. This rule had long been clearly established: love brought changes to Picasso's art. Love is what underlies his admiration of textures, for contrasting effects; love is the reason here for the appearance of livelier and more joyful colours. Together with the woman whose very

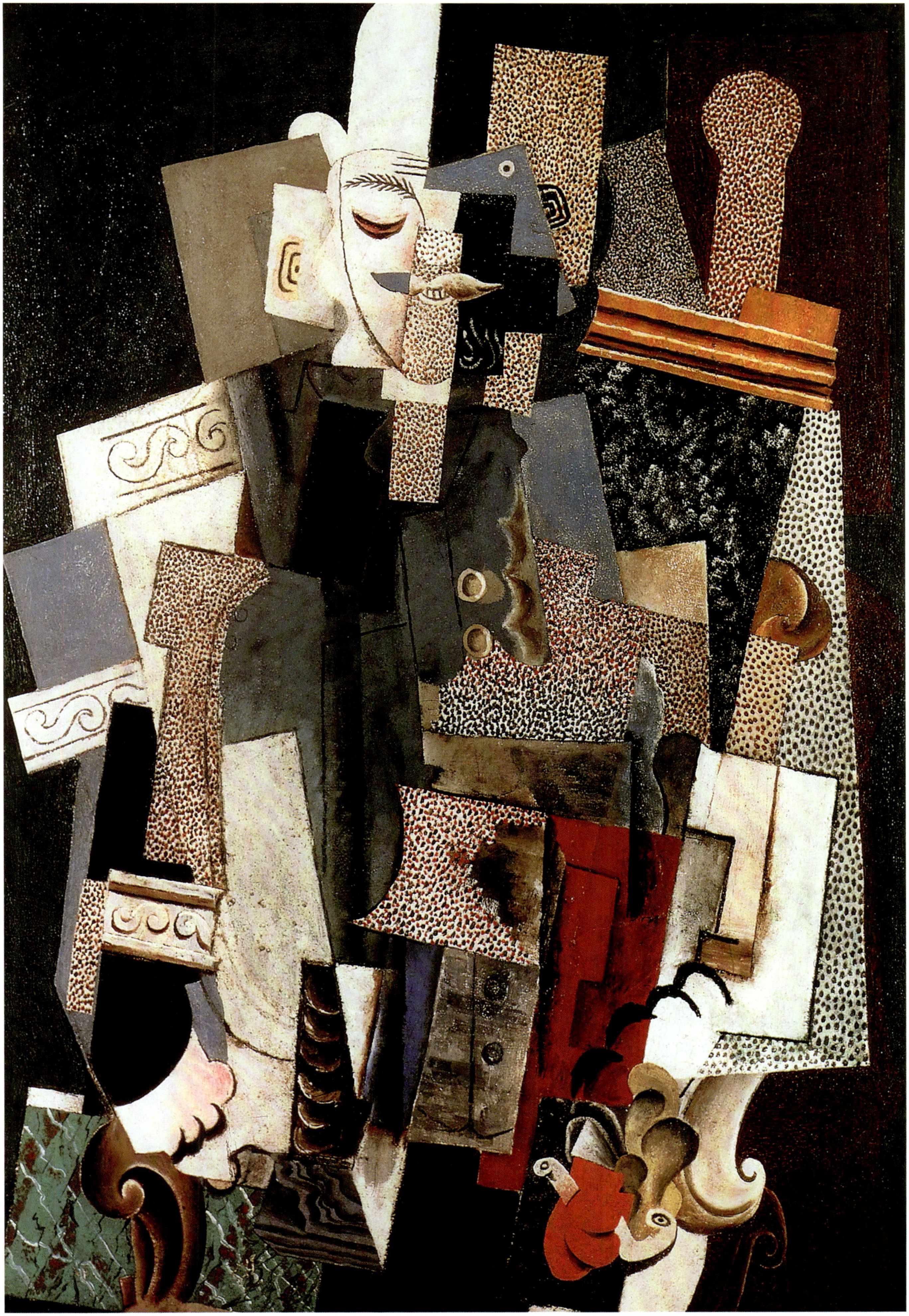

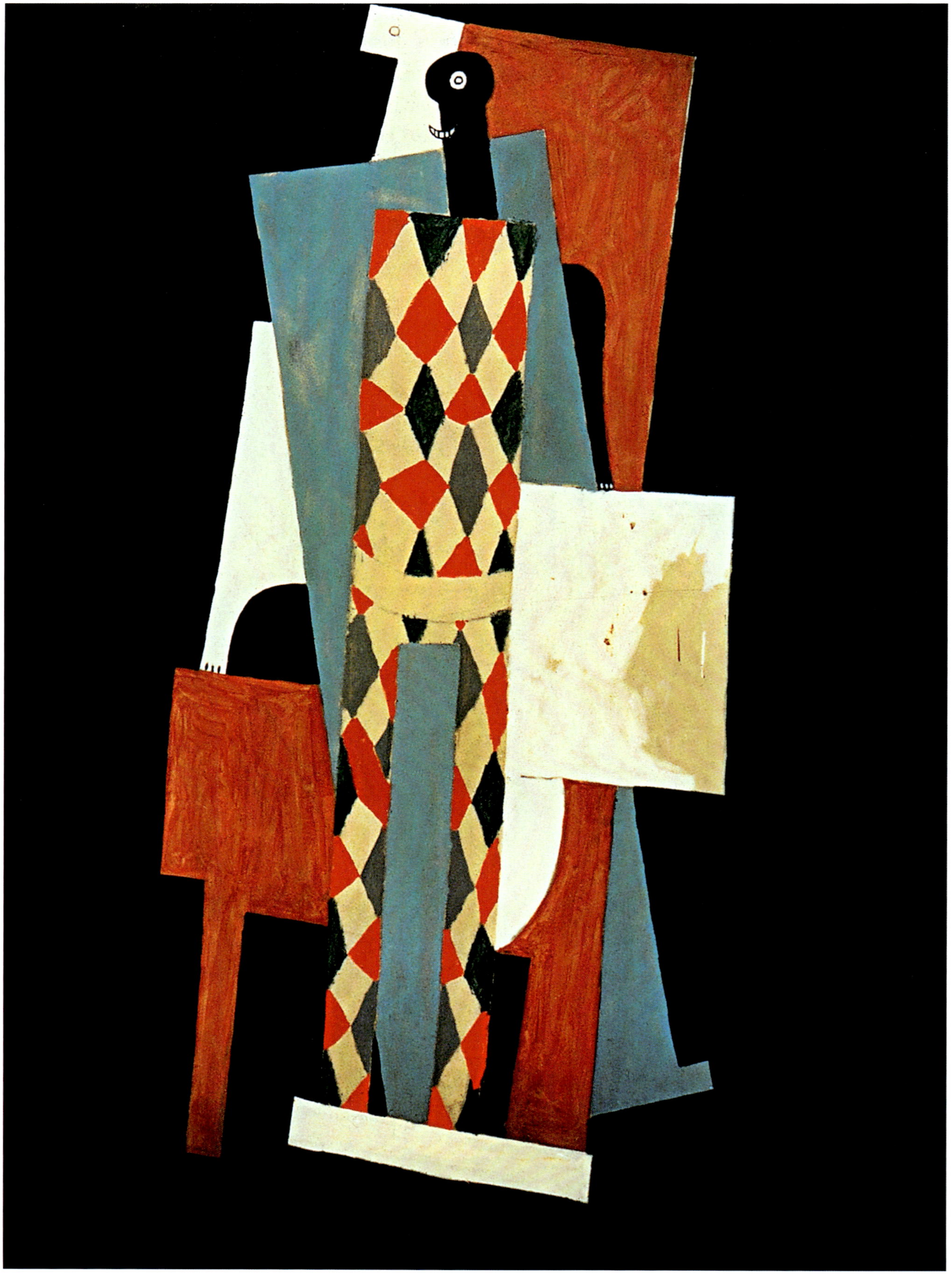

name, Eva, had symbolic meaning for him, Picasso began a new life that introduces new overtones in his art.

In the summer and autumn of 1912, while living with Eva in the town of Sorgues-sur-l'Ouvèze, Picasso was literally possessed by one subject: some fifteen paintings of that season depict violins and guitars. This was lyrical painting, steeped in emotions relating the shapes of these instruments to the female form and aspiring to create a harmonic and tangible image out of different elements of form, rhythm, texture, both of material and painted surface, and colour. This art embraces the world's sensual diversity; not accidentally some of these still lifes bear the inscription: *J'aime Eva.*

Violin (p. 93) is one of Picasso's first and most harmonious works of that period. The painting can hardly be classed as a still life: its formative idea is better expressed by the words *tableau-objet*, which Picasso himself used. Indeed the painted image of the violin is already furnished by the harmonious oval of the canvas; the instrument is recognisably presented in the compositional nucleus by the frank statement of its material qualities (the wavy texture and honey-coloured tones of the wood), as well as of its elegant details (the sound-holes and the curves of the sounding board). This nucleus seems to bulge spherically outwards owing to the passage of fractionalised forms that retreat rhythmically towards the edges of the work. Thus, the entire composition acquires equilibrium, not because of the stability of the object depicted, nor because of the overall pyramidal construction, but because of the daring oval shape (a real tectonic challenge), locked into place by its nucleus like a keystone supporting an arch.

This unstable, vertical ellipse of canvas, which cannot stand but only hang on a wall, tempted the artist to seek new compositional principles for sculptures that would seem to hang or float in the space of an oval form. The painting is presented here by dissociated aspects of its reality—masses, planes and surfaces, contours and elements, symbols of sorts. An entry in his sketchbook tells us that it was indeed in Sorgues that Picasso began to aspire to "find equilibrium between nature and one's imagination."[38]

Musical instruments, considered a lyrical subject by Picasso, continued to occupy his imagination for many months. In the autumn of 1912, in Paris, attempting to realise his new vision, he again turned to three-dimensional sculptural forms to create a family of spatial constructions in the shape of guitars. Made of grey cardboard, these new "sculptures" do not "imitate" real instruments, but recreate their images through spatially linked and partially overlapping flat silhouettes of planes that form open volumes. At the end of 1912, these new lyrical objects as well as the oval *tableau-objets*, destined only to hang on walls, furnished the impulse for endless new interpretations of musical instruments in pasted-paper works (*papiers collés*) and pictures (thus gainsaying the often accepted view that the guitars and violins were cut to pieces randomly, as if by some cruel vivisectionist, and then put together helter-skelter).

Among the works belonging to this period and style we find such pictures as *Violin, Wineglass, Pipe and Inkwell* (p. 92) and *Clarinet and Violin* (p. 98), in which the clearly

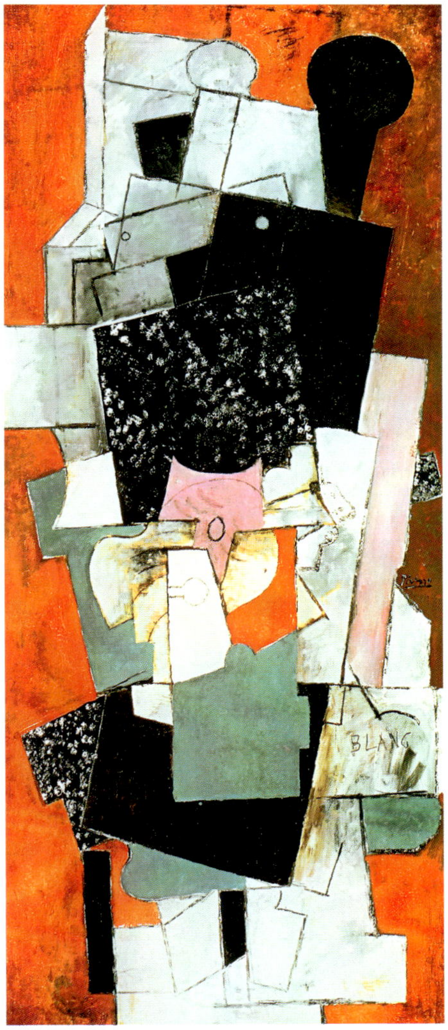

Pablo Picasso,
Harlequin, 1915.
Oil on canvas, 183.5 x 105.1 cm.
The Museum of Modern Art, New York.

Pablo Picasso,
Woman with a Guitar, 1915.
Oil on canvas, 185 x 75 cm.
Norton Simon Fund, Los Angeles.

dominant structural principle of flat, frontal planes points to a link with pasted-paper techniques and sculptured constructions. But if the former seems only a more imposing, assured and decorative version of the small, oval *Violin* from the Moscow museum, the apparently modest canvas *Clarinet and Violin* is both a virtuoso sketch with a new compositional structure and a concise formulation of Picasso's latest pictorial conception (in broader terms, of plastic art), which had ripened over the six years of his Cubism.

An absolutely flat, black plane retreats behind a brown one, to which it is solidly linked by a small, cream-coloured square. This feeling of depth, achieved with such simplicity and skill, clarifies the spatial relations of both instruments, which are sparingly traced by a simple brush drawing. Meanwhile, the colours of the instruments (ebony for the clarinet and a grainy coffee-brown for the violin), although proportional in mass, are dissociated from their shapes and have even shifted from one instrument to the other and changed their spatial relationships.

Presented simultaneously, but not together, the colours of objects and forms, their masses and shapes, are conceived as independent forces that come into play with each other and with our imagination. This astonishing method clearly reveals the anatomy of the plastic metaphor that Picasso called *trompe-l'esprit*, which is actually nothing but a poetic image—that is, according to Garcia Lorca, one "based on the mutual exchange of appearance, destination and functions among Nature's different objects and ideas."[39]

It was with an amazing degree of freedom, resourcefulness and grace that Picasso applied the rule of plastic metaphor to the pasted-paper technique, which revolutionised the possibilities of painting. Here is his own comment: "Aside from rhythm, one of the things that strikes us most strongly in nature is the difference of textures; the texture of space, the texture of an object in that space—a tobacco wrapper, a porcelain vase—and beyond that the relation of form, colour, and volume to the question of texture. The purpose of *papier collé* was to give the idea that different textures can enter into a composition to become the reality in the painting that competes with the reality in nature. We tried to get rid of *trompe-l'œil* to find *tomple-l'esprit*."[40] Not a single one of the *papier collé* components is ever taken in its direct meaning; all are allegories and metaphors.

In *Composition with a Bunch of Grapes and a Sliced Pear* (p. 101) the vertical piece of paper pasted in the centre represents the mass and colour of the porcelain fruit bowl, traced by

Pablo Picasso,
Still-Life in Front of a Window, 1919.
Watercolour and pencil, 32 x 22 cm.
Private collection.

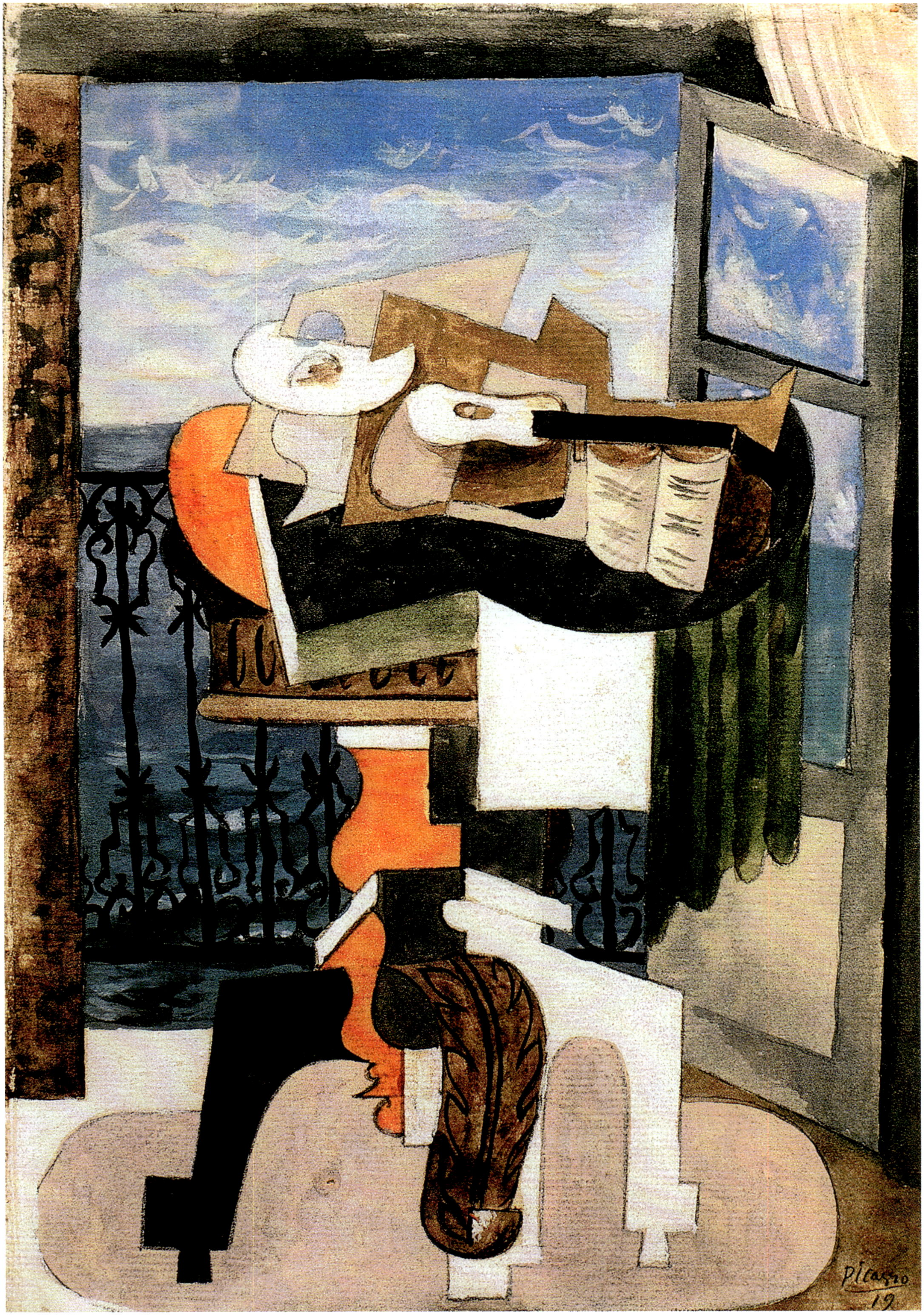
Picasso
19

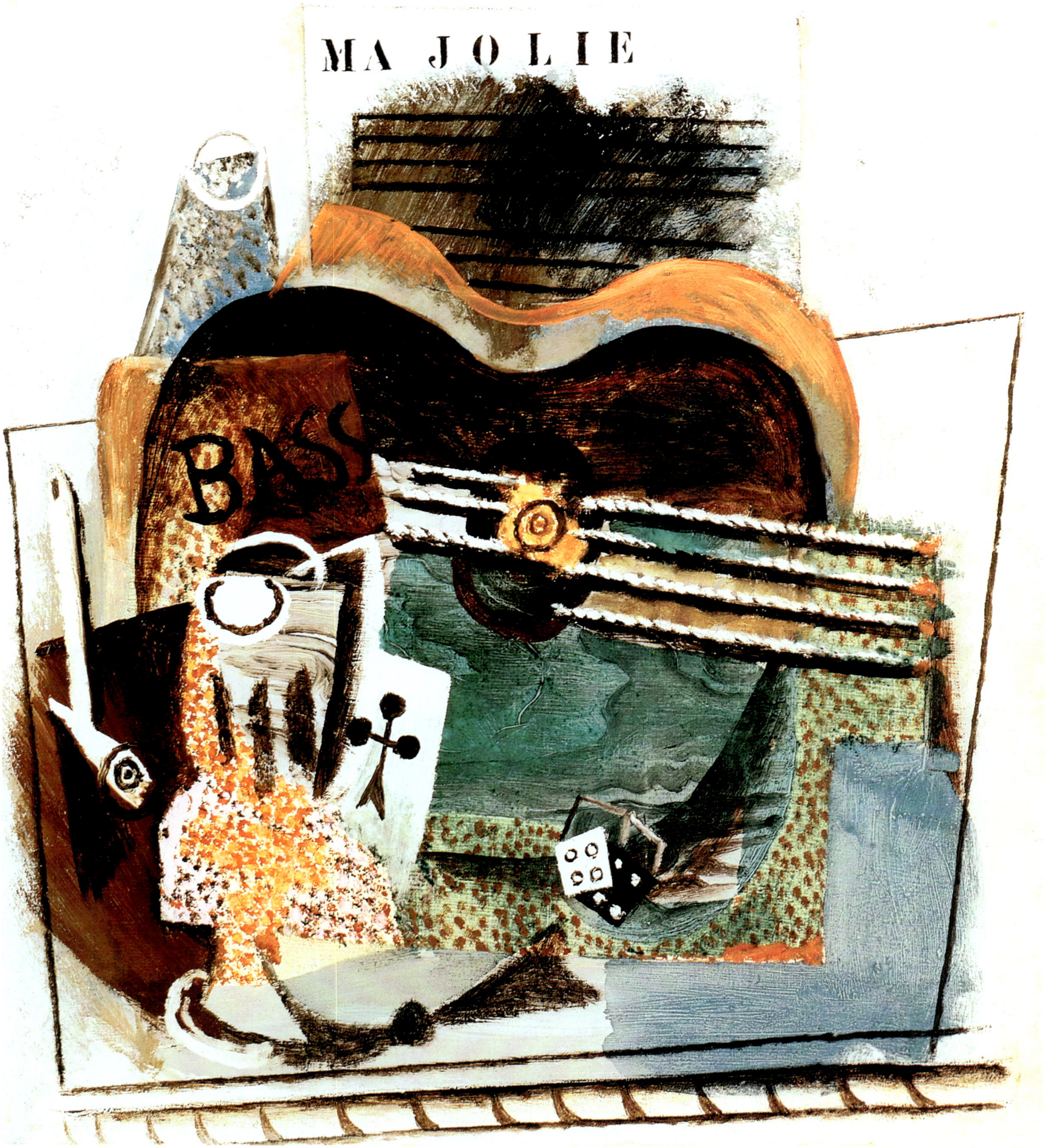
MA JOLIE
BASS

graphic contours, while the cut-out of grey, marbled paper pasted below shows that the fruit bowl, with its grapes, pear and Picasso's personal card, stands on a mantelpiece with a moulded edge. While the glossiness of the fruit and of the stucco mantel are negatively rendered by a velvety, powdered-sawdust texture, the translucence of the space, its airy and sunlit plenitude, are given almost impressionistically through a fairy tale of light and mutually penetrating geometric planes, composed of tiny particles of bright and joyous colours. While not imitating the environment, the artist convincingly transmits the atmosphere of a cosy, sunlit room.

Picasso's Mysticism

The feelings underlying *Tavern* (pp. 96-97) are quite different. This still life was done like a provincial tavern sign. The oval form freed the artist from such considerations as top and bottom, the need to fill corners, and so he arranged the still life with the most amazing ease, like a restaurant table plentifully but chaotically laden with food. A luxurious pink ham occupies the centre, a bottle of beer to the right, and to the left a goblet through which one can read the list of dishes written on a blackboard; in the foreground a lemon and a knife and fork lie on a crumpled napkin; there is a menu and, inscribed in blue letters on the window glass, part of the word "Restaurant". Everything is stated; moreover, it is tangible. The motif is brought as close to the viewer as possible, indeed it seems to fall out from the painting's surface, accentuating the reality of the ham and the lemon, the napkin and the wooden table, the sharp knife and the heavy fork. Unlike the physically tangible real sawdust, the schematically rendered bottle and glass, deprived of any reality of their own, seem to be transparent ghosts—which indeed they are, when empty. While recalling the carnal richness of Flemish masters, Picasso's *Tavern* opposes them, for it invites us to overcome the routine forms of artistic vision that fetter our freedom of perception and to partake instead in a feast of the spirit.

Indeed, mysticism and transcendence are for Tugendhold immutable qualities of Picasso's internal and creative personality—from his debut to his latest works. While, in his opinion, "the blue series promised a major and profound painter in Picasso... He could be a new Puvis de Chavannes, he could be deeper and more religious than Puvis de Chavannes...," the critic discerned nothing less than Faustian, gnomic truths in the formal construction of the early Cubist landscape *Factory*. His analysis of that work is amazing.

Pablo Picasso,
Pipe, Glass, Ace of Clubs, Bass Bottle, Guitar, « Ma Jolie » Dice, 1914.
Oil on canvas, 45 x 41 cm.
Collection Berggruen, Berlin.

"The lines of the factory's walls and roofs do not merge at the horizon... they diverge, running off into infinity. Here no mental point of convergence exists, no horizon, no optics of the human eye, no beginning and no end—only the cold and the insanity of absolute space. And even the sheen of that factory's mirror-like walls, countlessly repeated, reflected from the sky, makes *Factory* an enchanted labyrinth of mirrors, a mad hallucination... For indeed, one could lose one's mind from this thought and temptation that is worthy of Ivan Karamazov: there is no end, no unity, no human being as the measure of all things—there exists only the cosmos, only the infinite fractionalising of volumes in infinite space!"[41]

Yet Picasso told Tugendhold in that period: "A bottle on a table is just as significant as a religious painting."

Neither should one ignore the following piece of reasoning by Yakov Tugendhold, because it is essential for an understanding of Picasso's oeuvre: "He wants to depict objects not the way they appear to the eye but the way they are in out thoughts." Expressed in 1914, that comment by the Russian critic preceded by twenty to twenty-five years the artist's own statement: "I paint not what I see but what I think."[42]

On the metaphorical vision of Picasso-the-Cubist, Aksenov writes: "The mystique of Picasso's objects has the same root as the mystery of ghosts that consist of a chair, a coat and a dangling, starched shirtfront. Practical jokers have roared with laughter at the horror caused by these objects, but this phenomenon is worthy of attention."[43] Therefore, one cannot avoid thinking of the future Surrealist montages, and Picasso's sculptural ensembles of the 1930s-1950s. Here we read about the optical, that is, the real nature of Cubism's so-called distortions: "Picasso stares his objects in the eye, as we look into our lover's face."[44] Did not the artist confirm this himself with his portraits of women in the 1930s?

Aksenov was unaware of the so-called Ingres drawings of 1915-1917, long before the beginning of the so-called Neo-Classicism of the 1920s. Yet he glimpsed what Picasso could be capable of after Cubism: "Now, stealthily, will not this portraitist of countless violins, who leads his careless companions into paper and tin jungles, suddenly turn on them in a frank burst of lofty realism?"[45]

In an epigraph to his book, Aksenov quoted the words of Grigory Nissky: "Some see God as a burning fire, others as a light." For Aksenov himself, however, Picasso was not an infernal, but a creative flame.

Pablo Picasso,
The American Parade Manager, 1917.
Collection du Théâtre Royal de la Monnaie, Brussels.

Pablo Picasso,
Three Musicians, 1921.
Oil on canvas, 200.7 x 222.9 cm.
The Museum of Modern Art, New York.

Georges Braque,
Café-Bar, 1919.
Oil on canvas, 160 x 82 cm.
Kunstmuseum, Basel.

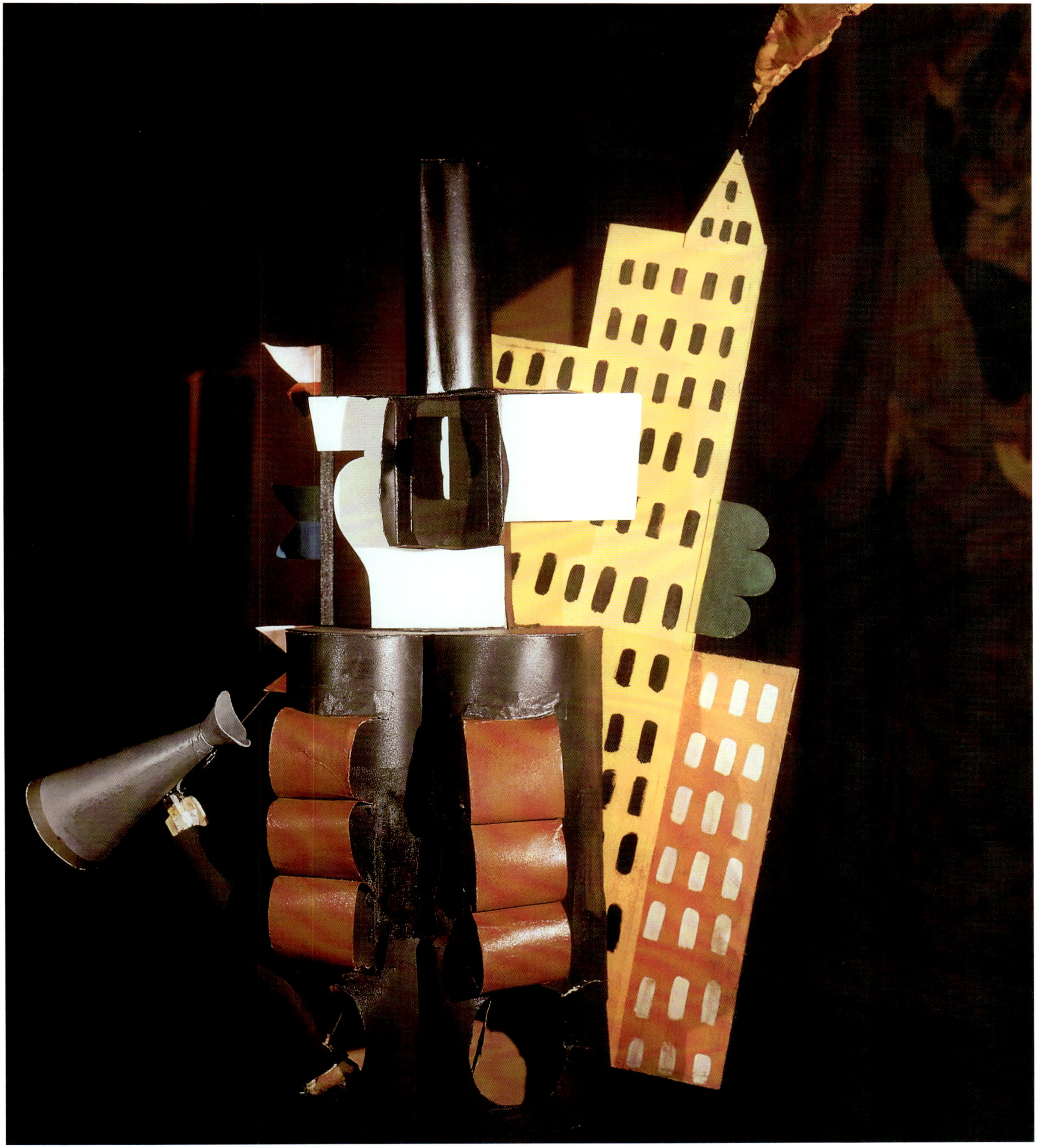

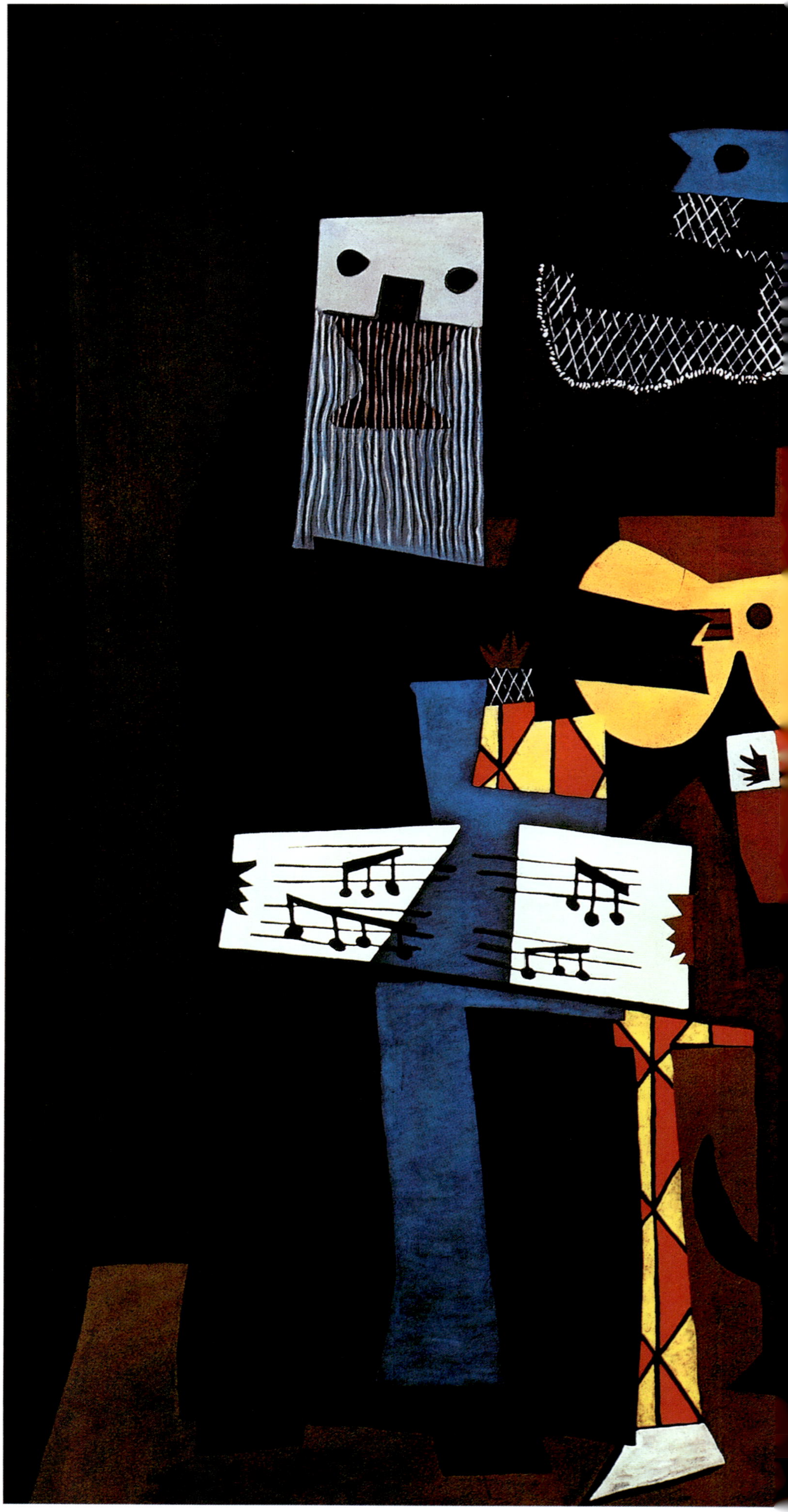

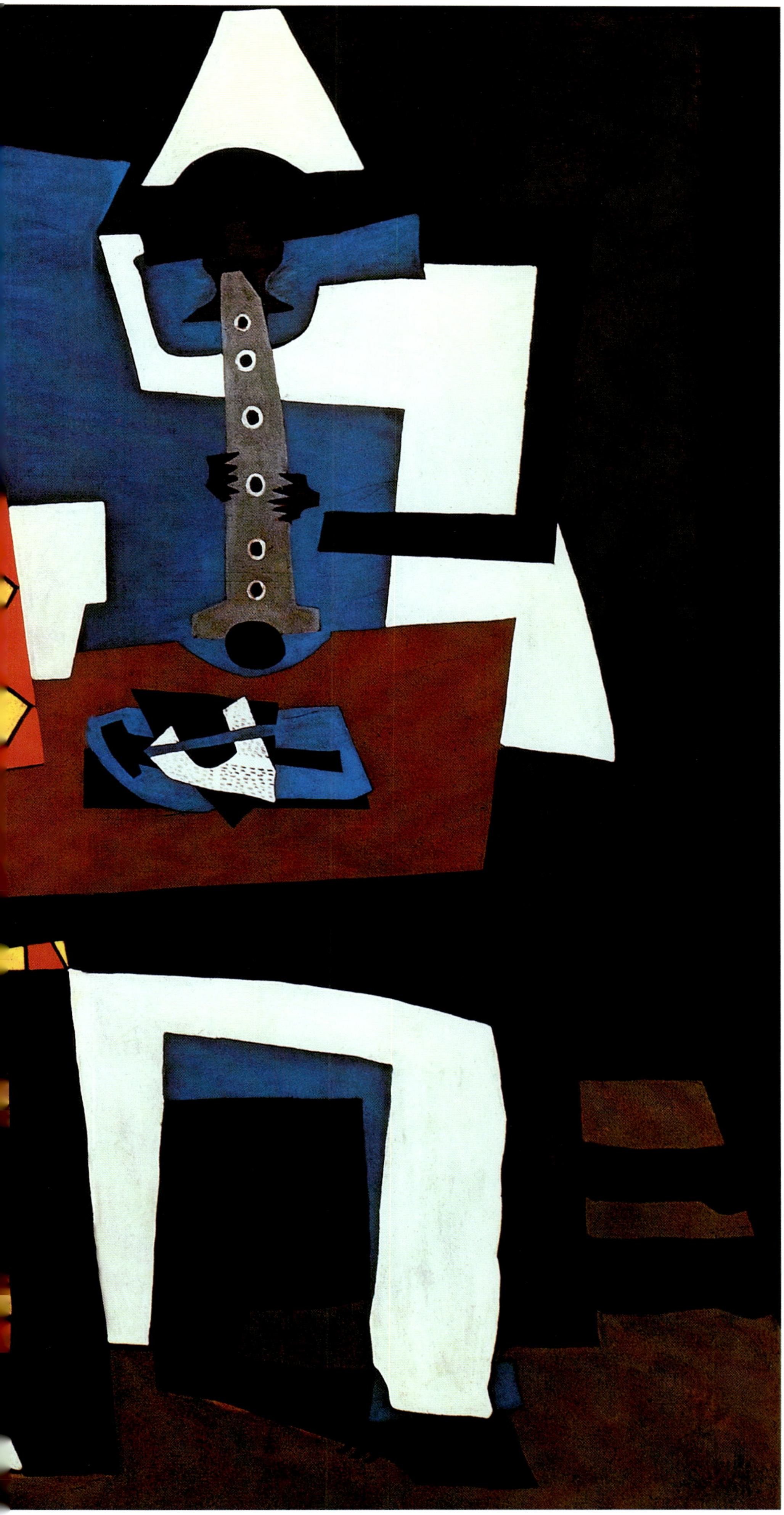

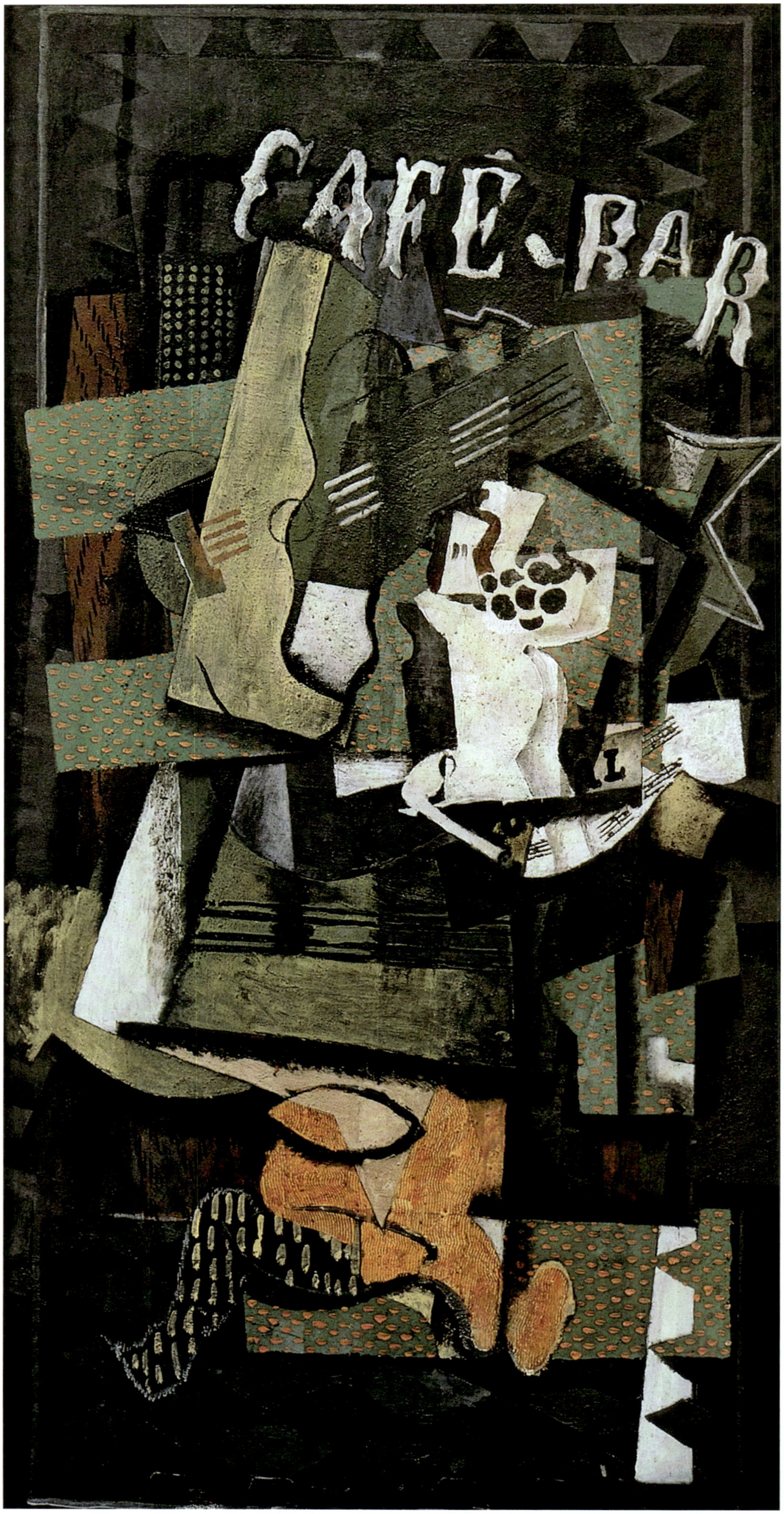
CAFÉ-BAR

Major Artists

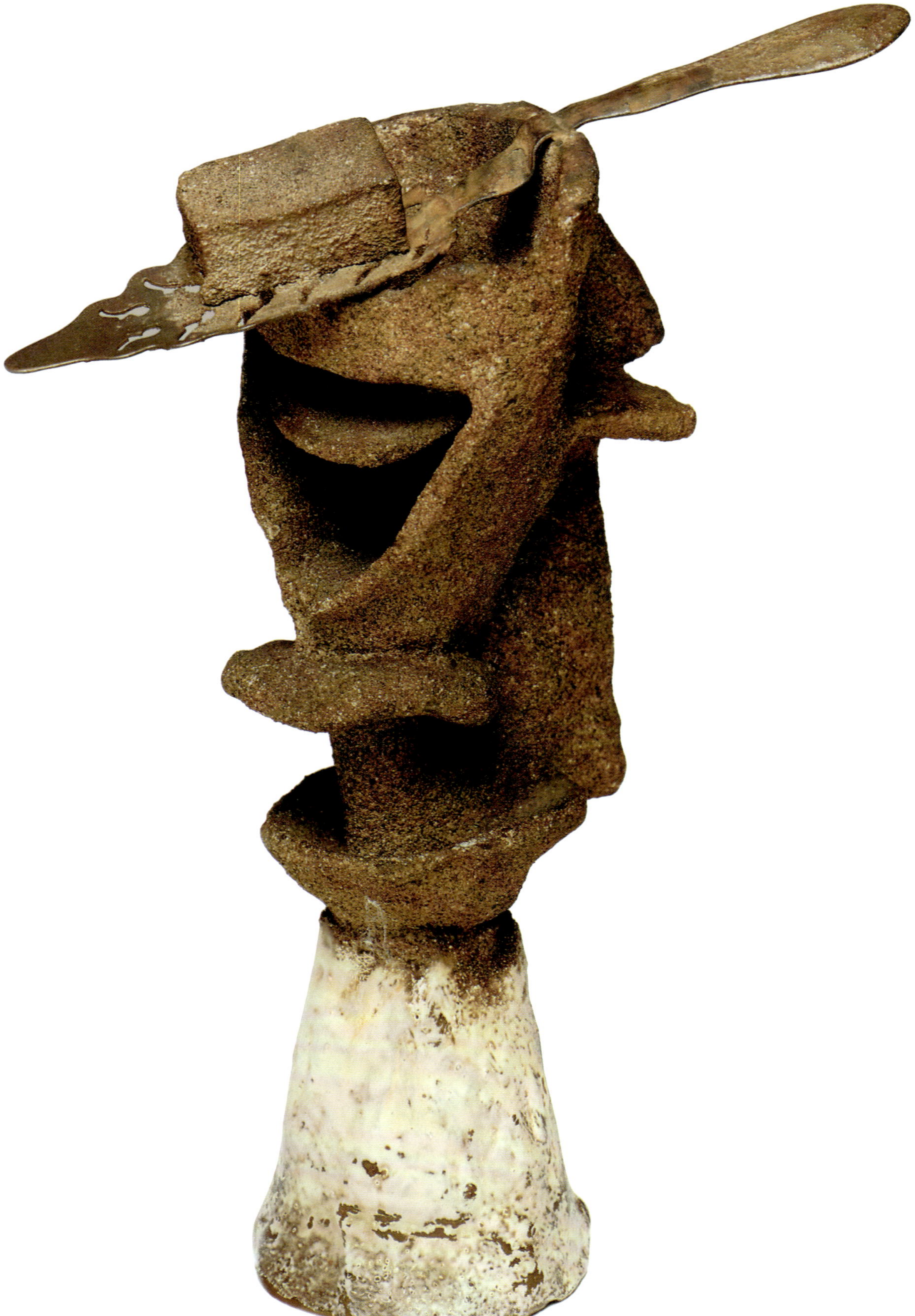

Pablo Picasso

(Málaga, 1881 – Mougins, 1973)

"Picasso always considered himself a poet who was more prone to express himself through drawings, paintings and sculptures." (Pierre Daix).

The great Spanish artist was born to an artistic family. His father, a painter and professor at the School of Fine Art and Crafts, taught him the basics of formal academic technique. He then studied at the Real Academia de Bellas Artes de San Fernando in Madrid, and before his eighteenth birthday he had joined the ranks of the self-styled "modernists", non-conformist artists and writers.

His early works, blue-tinted paintings influenced by a trip through Spain and the death of his friend, Casagemas, were grouped into the so-called "Blue Period" (1901-1904). Towards the end of 1901 the desire to express these feelings of sadness more directly pushed Picasso towards the field of sculpture. The predominance of form in his paintings undeniably testifies to this interest. Picasso began to sculpt because it corresponded to his need to impose strict limits on himself, to achieve the most ascetic means of expression.

Between 1905 and 1907 Picasso entered a new phase characterised by a more cheerful style with orange and pink colours, the "Pink Period".

During the autumn of 1907 the artist spent long hours carving strange, fetish-like figurines and primitive dolls and making sketches for future sculptures. By that time Picasso had already discovered African wooden sculpture in the ethnographic museum at the Palais du Trocadero and, like many other artists, had bought several statues and masks. This "art nègre" influenced his style and especially the idea he had of pictorial representation. At the end of the year, nude females, a subject that had become important for him, were the object of the composition of the large painting, *Les Demoiselles d'Avignon* (p. 6). This painting, undoubtedly the most important painting of the 20th century, was a response to Matisse's *Blue Nude* and Derain's *Bathers.*

Just as African art is usually considered a factor leading to the development of Picasso's characteristic aesthetics in 1907, the lessons of Cézanne are perceived as the cornerstone of this new progression. This was just a first step for Picasso, who still needed to further develop his methods of creation in order to break away from the influent analysis of Cézanne. However, the asymmetry of the frame, the extreme geometrisation of the lines and the violent deformation of the bodies were carrying the premises of a revolution, the Cubist revolution, and above all, the entry in the modern era. The painter Georges Braque explained that: "Cubism's main direction was the materialisation of space." This was followed by a period of intense creativity during

Pablo Picasso,
Glass of Absinthe, 1914.
Painted bronze with absinthe spoon,
21.5 x 16.4 x 8.5 cm,
diameter of base: 6.4 cm.
The Museum of Modern Art, New York.

Pablo Picasso,
Guitar, 1914.
Sheet metal and wire,
77.5 x 35 x 19.3 cm.
The Museum of Modern Art, New York.

Pablo Picasso,
Guitar and Violin, c. 1912.
Oil on canvas, 65.5 x 54.3 cm.
The State Hermitage Museum,
St. Petersburg.

Pablo Picasso,
Head of a Woman (Fernande), 1909.
Bronze, 40.5 x 23 x 26 cm.
Musée Picasso, Paris.

Pablo Picasso,
Head of Fernande, 1909.
Oil on canvas, 61 x 42 cm.
Kunstsammlung Nordrhein-Westfalen,
Düsseldorf.

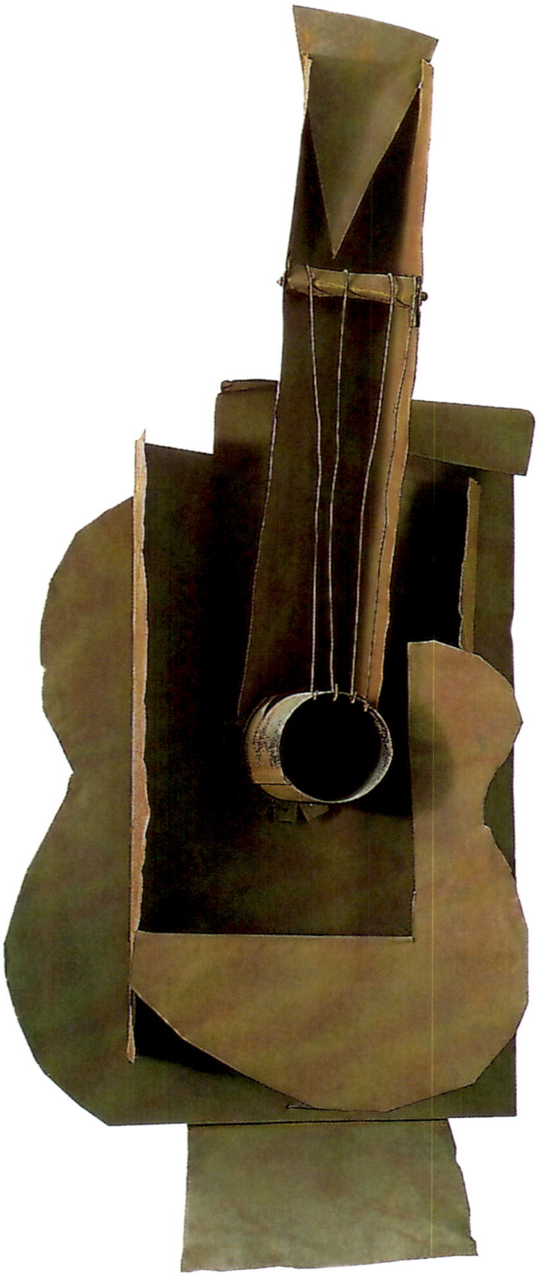

which Picasso, together with Braque, explored all the possibilities this new system had to offer. Painting, collage and even sculpture became outlets for his creativity. Due to his unified vision during this period, his painted and sculpted works were tightly linked and his *Head of Fernande* (1919; p. 153) illustrates the parallel that Picasso could draw between the two media; this work is considered to be the first Cubist sculpture.

In the autumn of 1912, in Paris, Picasso, attempting to realise his new vision, again turned to three-dimensional sculptural forms to create a family of spatial constructions in the shape of guitars. Made of grey cardboard, these new "sculptures" did not even pretend to imitate real instruments, but recreated the images of the instrument through spatially-linked and partially-overlapping, flat, silhouetted planes that form open volumes. After his Cubist period in the 1910s, Picasso returned to a more figurative style and got closer to the Surrealist movement. He represented distorted and monstrous bodies but in a very personal style.

After the bombing of Guernica in 1937, Picasso made one of his most famous works, which starkly symbolises the horrors of war. In this work, we can see that artist has truly surpassed himself, thanks to the unlimited possibilities offered by Cubism in terms of representation of the faces of pain and horror.

In the 1960s, Picasso's artistic style changed again, and he began looking at the art of great masters and based his paintings on those of Velázquez, Poussin, Goya, Manet, Courbet and Delacroix.

Picasso's final works were in a mixture of styles, becoming ever more colourful, expressive and optimistic.

Perceiving painting as sculpture, Picasso approached the subject as a sculptor and saw human anatomy as a plastic construction. His true sculptor's temperament, recognised by Julio González, caused him to be very laconic and to reject incidental features in order to lay bare the plastic essence of the image and emphasise its reality. Picasso called this approach "surreality", and even during his Cubist period, he considered himself a realist artist. For Picasso, sculpture also served to verify the feeling of reality in the sense of physical validity, since for him "sculpture is the best comment that a painter can make on painting."

Picasso died in 1973 in his villa in Mougins. The Russian Symbolist Georgy Chulkov wrote: "Picasso's death is tragic. Yet how blind and naïve are those who believe in imitating Picasso and learning from him. Learning what? For these forms have no corresponding emotions outside of Hell. But to be in Hell means to anticipate death. The Cubists are hardly privy to such unlimited knowledge".

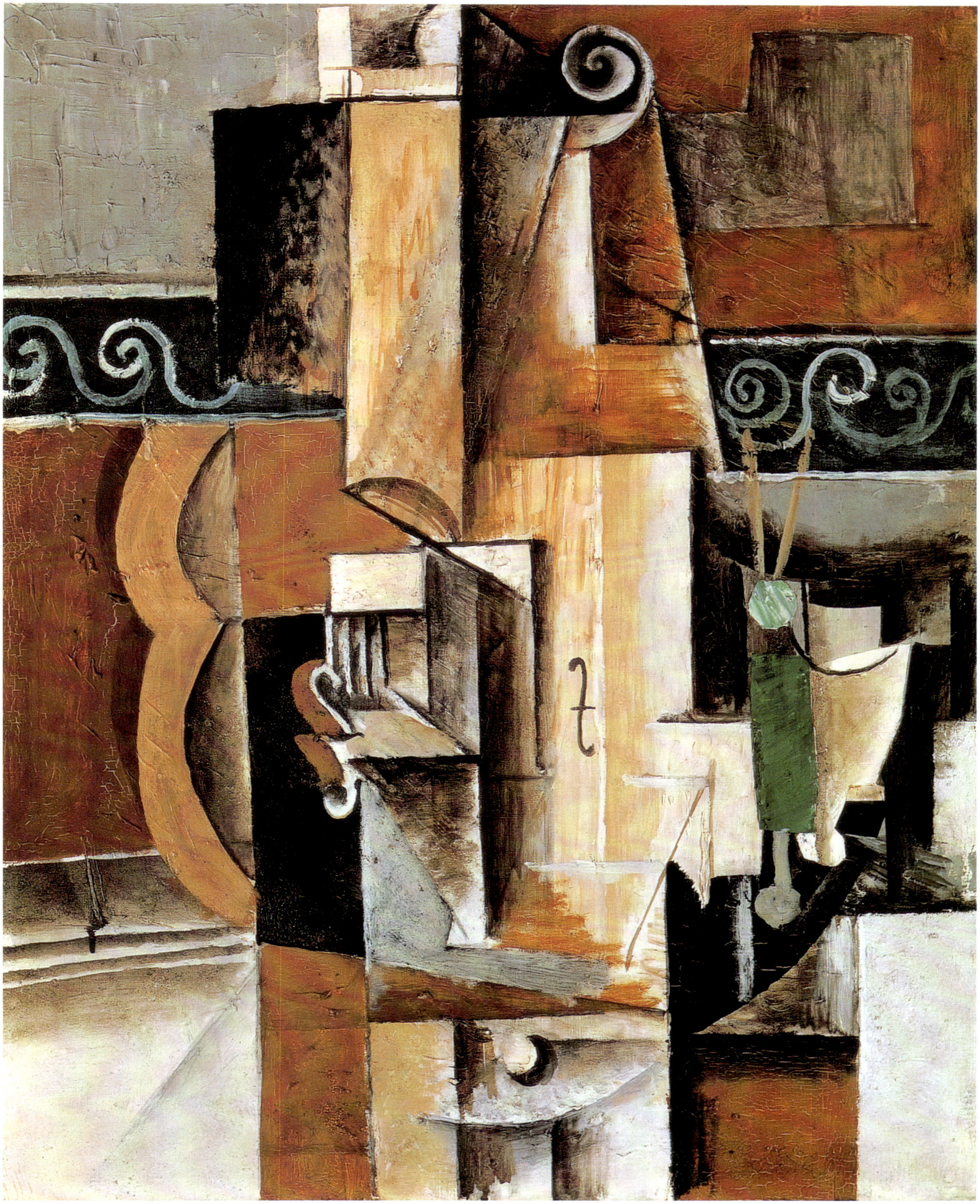

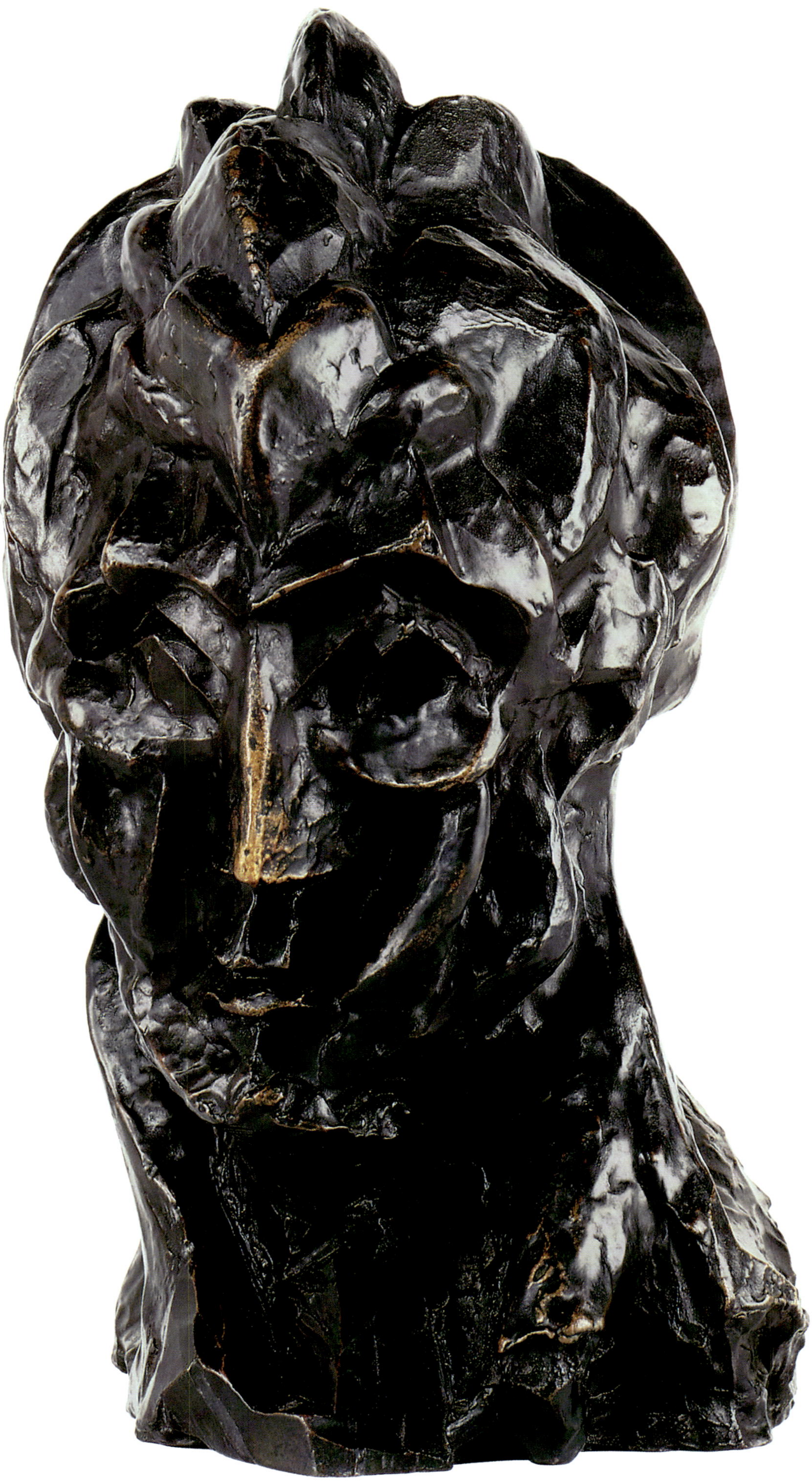

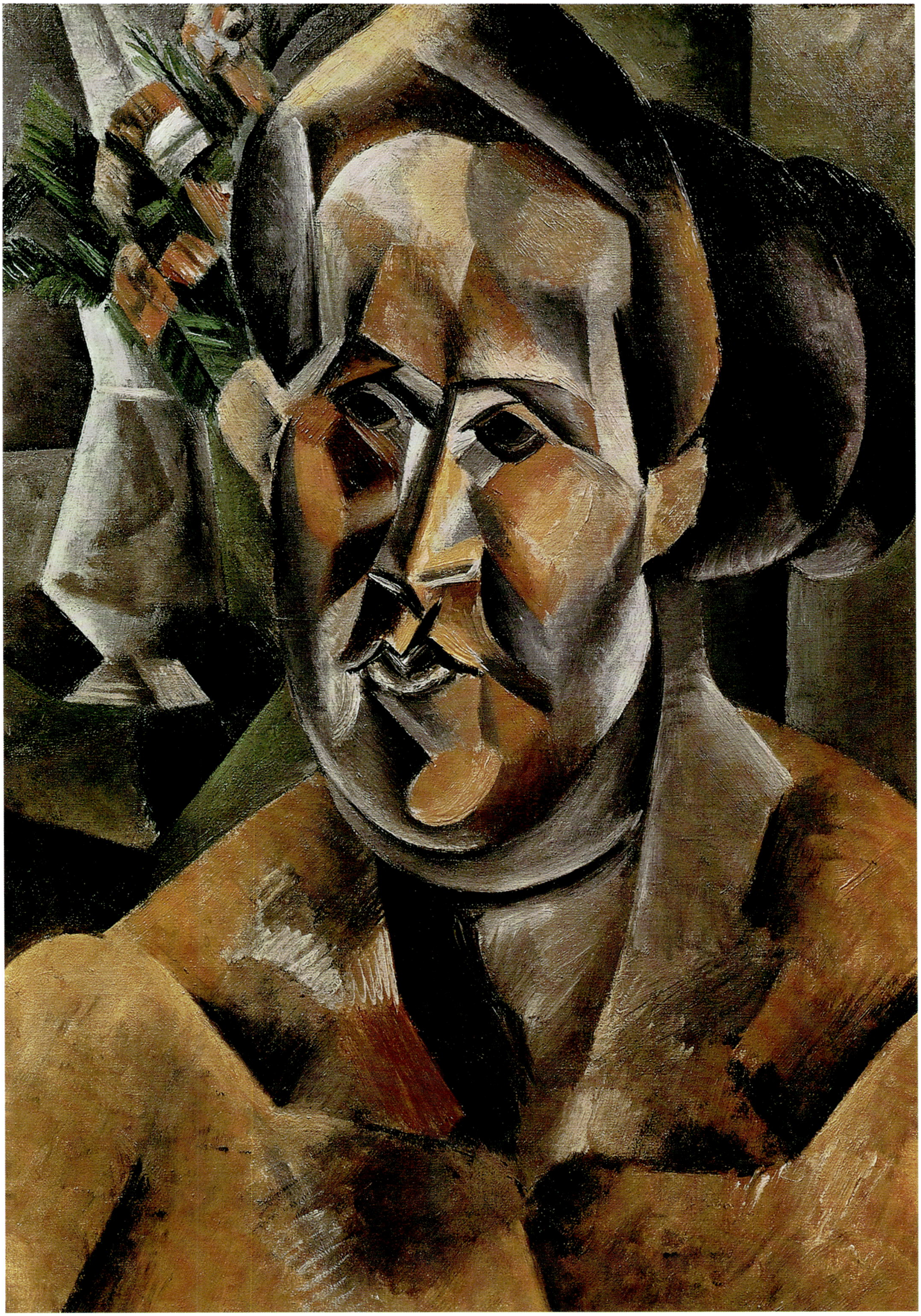

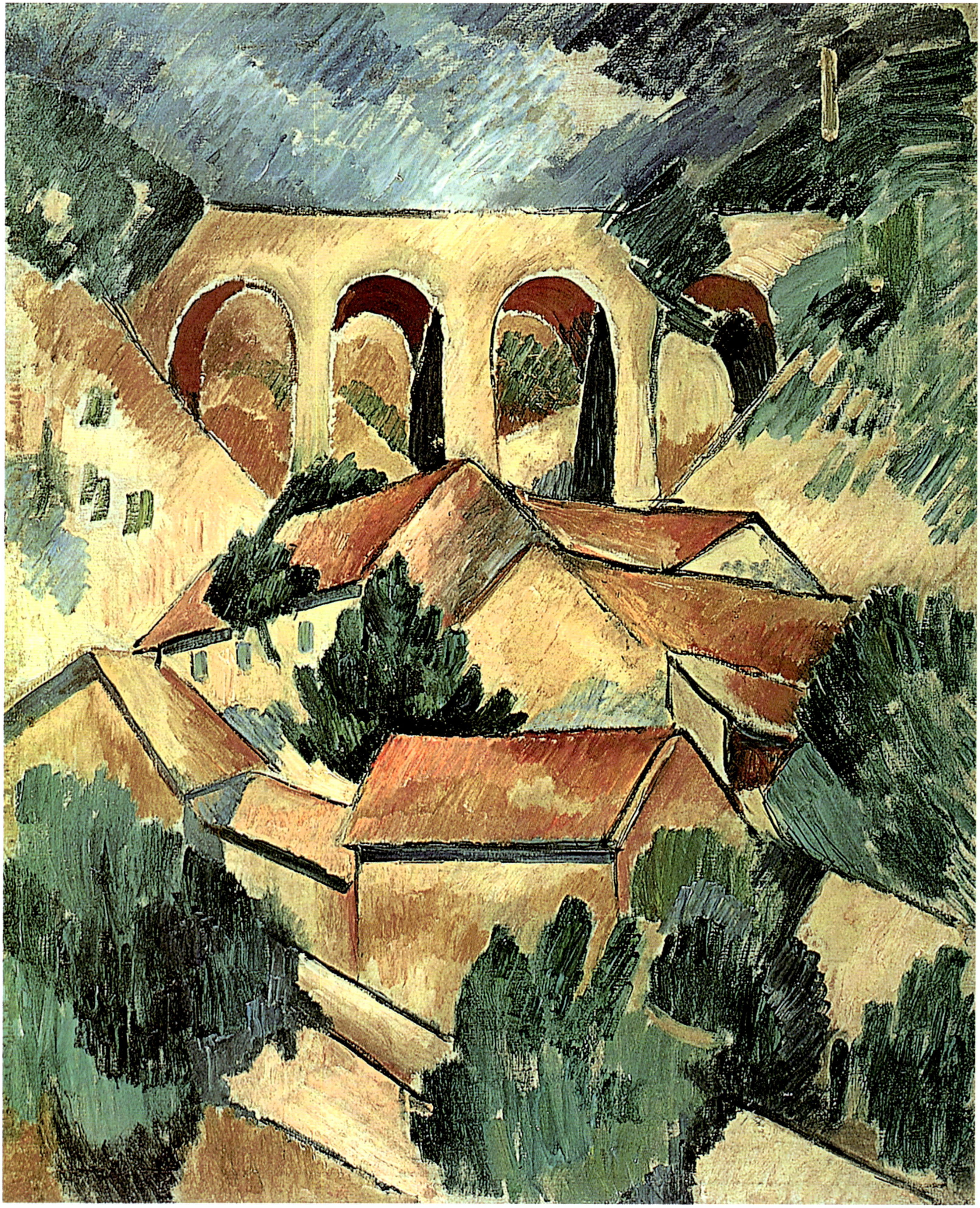

Georges Braque
(Argenteuil-sur-Seine, 1882 – Paris, 1963)

Son of a house painter, Georges Braque grew up in Le Havre. In addition to pursuing his studies at the high school, he attended classed at the École des Beaux-Arts where he became acquainted Dufy and Friesz. In 1900, he left for Paris to work as an apprentice to his father's former employee and took advantage of the trip to study and spend a lot of time in the Musée du Louvre, the Musée du Luxembourg, the Durand-Ruel Gallery and the Vollard Gallery. He attended courses at the Académie Humbert where he met Marie Laurencin and Francis Picabia. In 1905, Braque's aesthetic was overturned by the Salon d'Autumne where he discovered Fauvism, and two years later in 1907, he exhibited for the first time at the Salon des Indépendants with six paintings that were all sold.

Gallery owner Daniel-Henry Kahnweiler signed a contract with him and enabled him to become acquainted with Apollinaire. The poet in his turn introduced Braque to the Bateau-Lavoir neighbourhood, where Picasso was preparing a revolution in the form of his *Demoiselles d'Avignon*. This painting overwhelmed Braque and gave him new creative energy. After a series of journeys to Estaque and La Ciotat in the South of France, Braque returned to Paris with very different paintings (*Houses in Estaque*, p. 138). The colours are markedly more sombre than before and the forms radically geometrical. A true mirror of his retreat from Fauvism, *Houses in Estaque* was nevertheless refused by the Salon d'Automne of 1908 and considered "small cubes" by Matisse, a member of the jury. Following this disappointment, Kahnweiler organised the exhibition of Braque's works from 9 to 28 November 1908, which provoked the appearance of the word Cubism from the pen of Louis Vauxcelles. The next years revolved around the intensification of the relationship between Braque and Picasso. Each of the two artists worked to penetrate the other's creations, drawing from one another a mutual energy and an inspiration. Braque said about his relationship with Picasso: "Those years Picasso and I said things to each other that nobody will say again, that nobody would know how to understand ever again . . . It was a little like being roped together, climbing a mountain".

By means of dialogues and collaborations, both artists created a real plastic language: it was the era of Analytical Cubism. Picasso and Braque officially worked together until 1914, but the perennial quality of their respective works makes them difficult to date. In 1911, Braque stencilled letters in his painting *The Portuguese (The Emigrant)* (p. 137): this formal and concrete element contrasts completely with the abstract concepts governing the structure of the painting. Braque produced *Aria by Bach* (p. 140) before being mobilised for the First World War in 1914. He was hurt on the forehead in 1915 and demobilised in 1917. It was then that he made friends with Juan Gris.

After the war, Braque detached himself little by little from Cubist forms. He exhibited at the Salon d'Automne in 1922, and his reputation grew. In 1924-1925, he designed

Georges Braque,
Viaduct in Estaque, 1908.
Oil on canvas, 72.5 x 59 cm.
Musée National d'Art Moderne,
Centre Georges-Pompidou, Paris.

Georges Braque,
Pedestal Table, 1911.
Oil on canvas, 116.5 x 81.5 cm.
Musée National d'Art Moderne,
Centre Georges-Pompidou, Paris.

Georges Braque,
The Portuguese (The Emigrant),
1911-1912.
Oil on canvas, 117 x 81.5 cm.
Kunstmuseum, Basel.

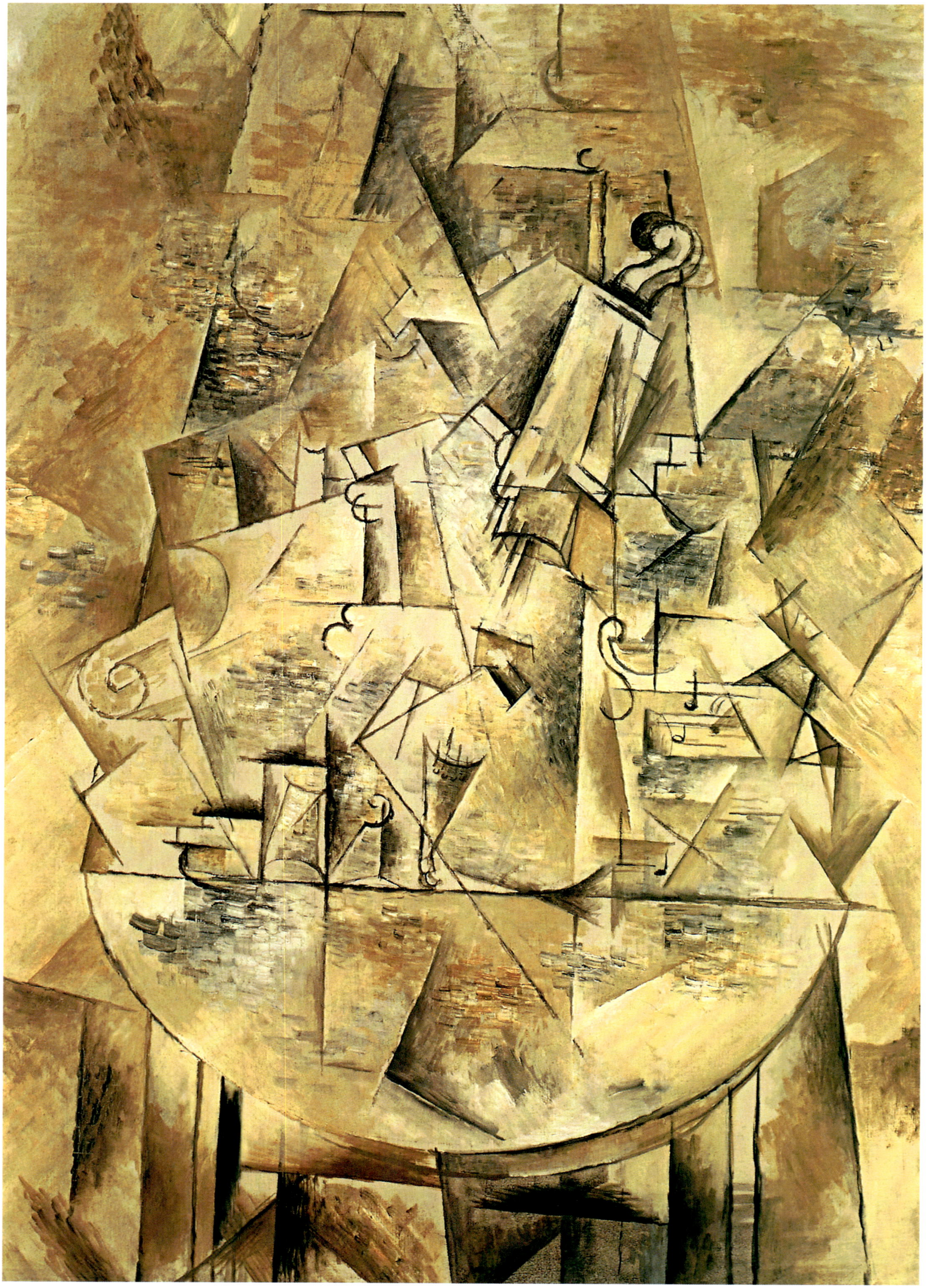

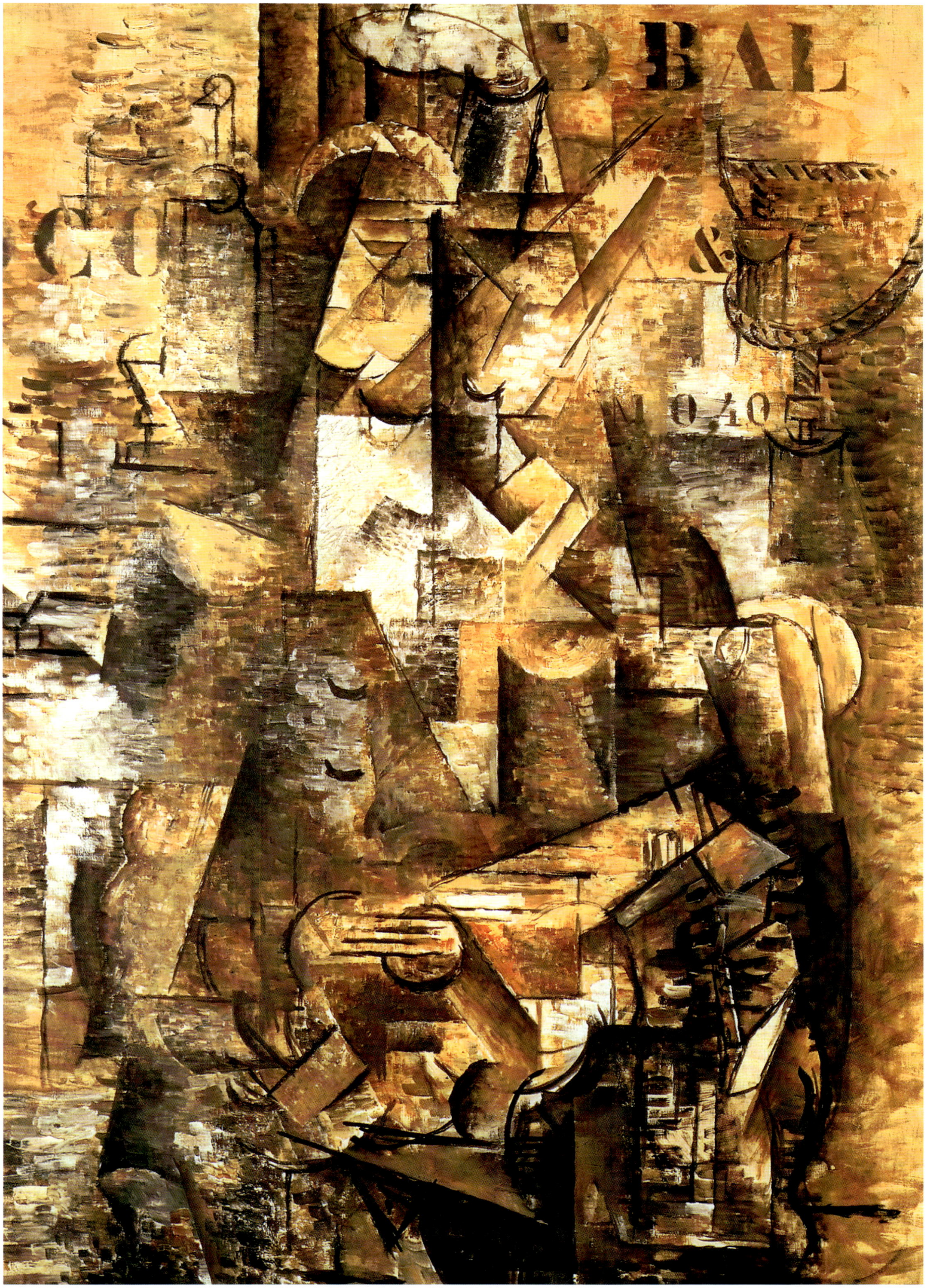
BAL
CO
&
0,40

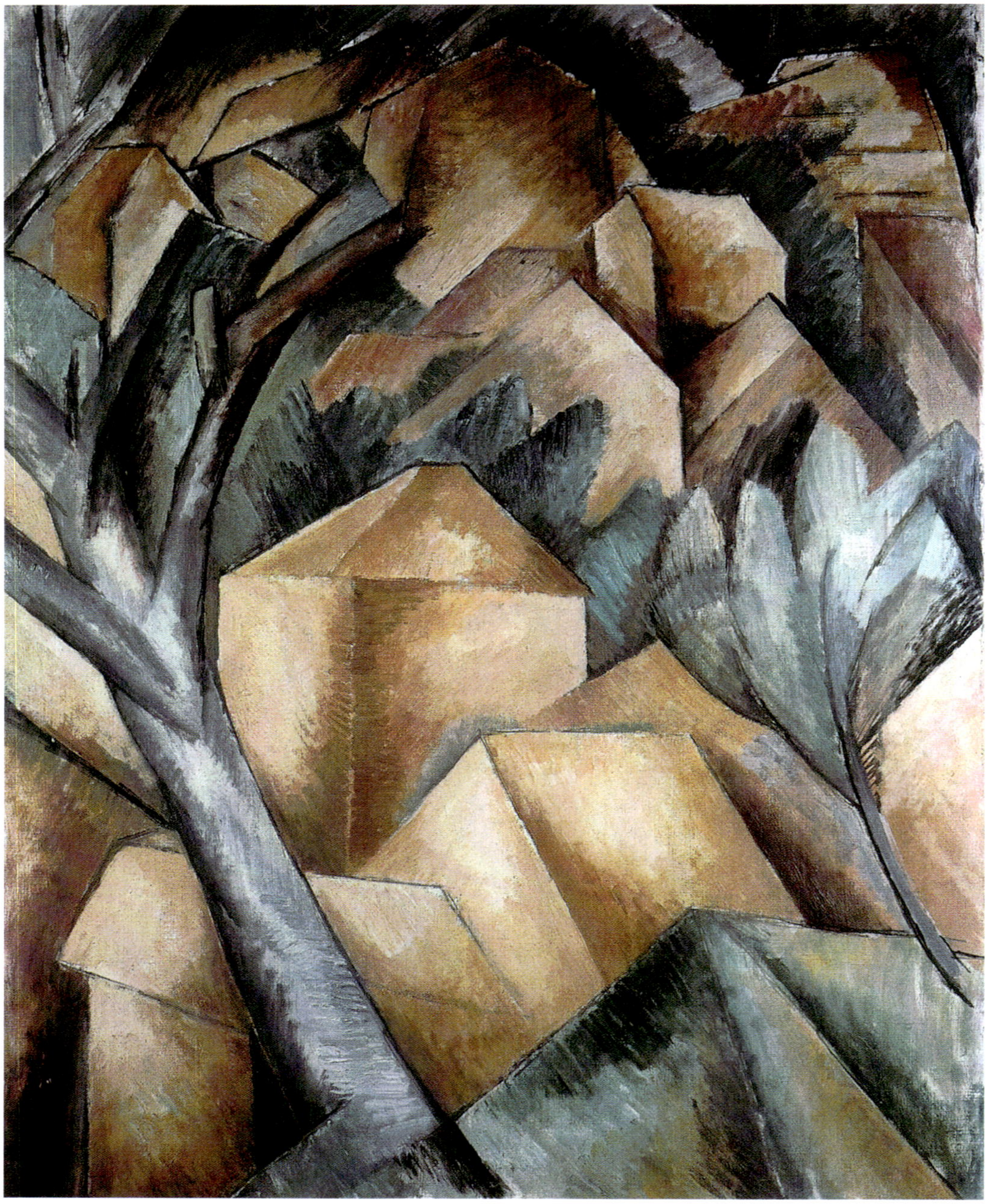

Georges Braque,
Houses in Estaque, 1908.
Oil on canvas, 73 x 60 cm.
Kunstmuseum, Bern.

Georges Braque,
Sacré-Cœur of Montmartre, 1909-1910.
Oil on canvas, 55 x 40.5 cm.
Musée d'Art Moderne Lille Métropole,
Villeneuve-d'Asq.

Georges Braque,
Aria by Bach, 1913.
Collage, 62 x 46 cm.
Private collection.

Georges Braque,
Still-Life with a Violin, 1912.
Glued paper, charcoal, 62 x 48 cm.
Kunstmuseum, Basel.

decorations and costumes for the Ballets Russes. Although he gradually drifted away from Cubism at the end of 1920s, Braque's works nevertheless retained geometrical traces. In 1939, he won the Carnegie Prize in Pittsburgh, and in 1943, an entire room was dedicated to him in the Salon d'Automne. During the Second World War, he stayed in Paris and produced still lifes and interiors ultimately darker than works from his earlier period.

Braque did not confine himself to painting; he also produced sculptures. His art became more and more abstract, personifying the hermetic face of Analytical Cubism. His objects were more coloured. He painted several series of decorative pedestals, tables, mantelpieces, studio furniture, etc. His final design was a bird motif, as if he wished to escape the inert, lifeless world he had created all those years.

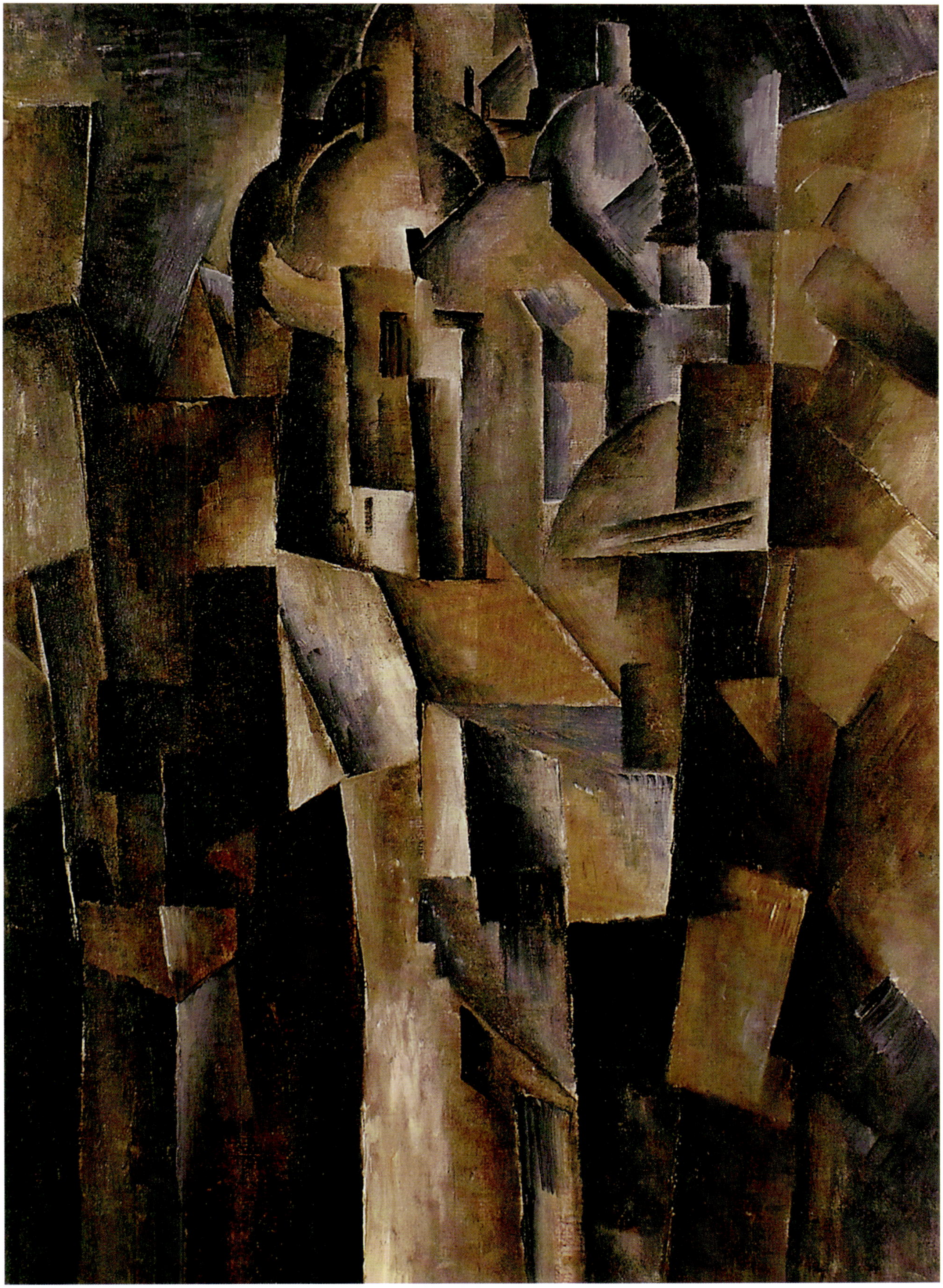

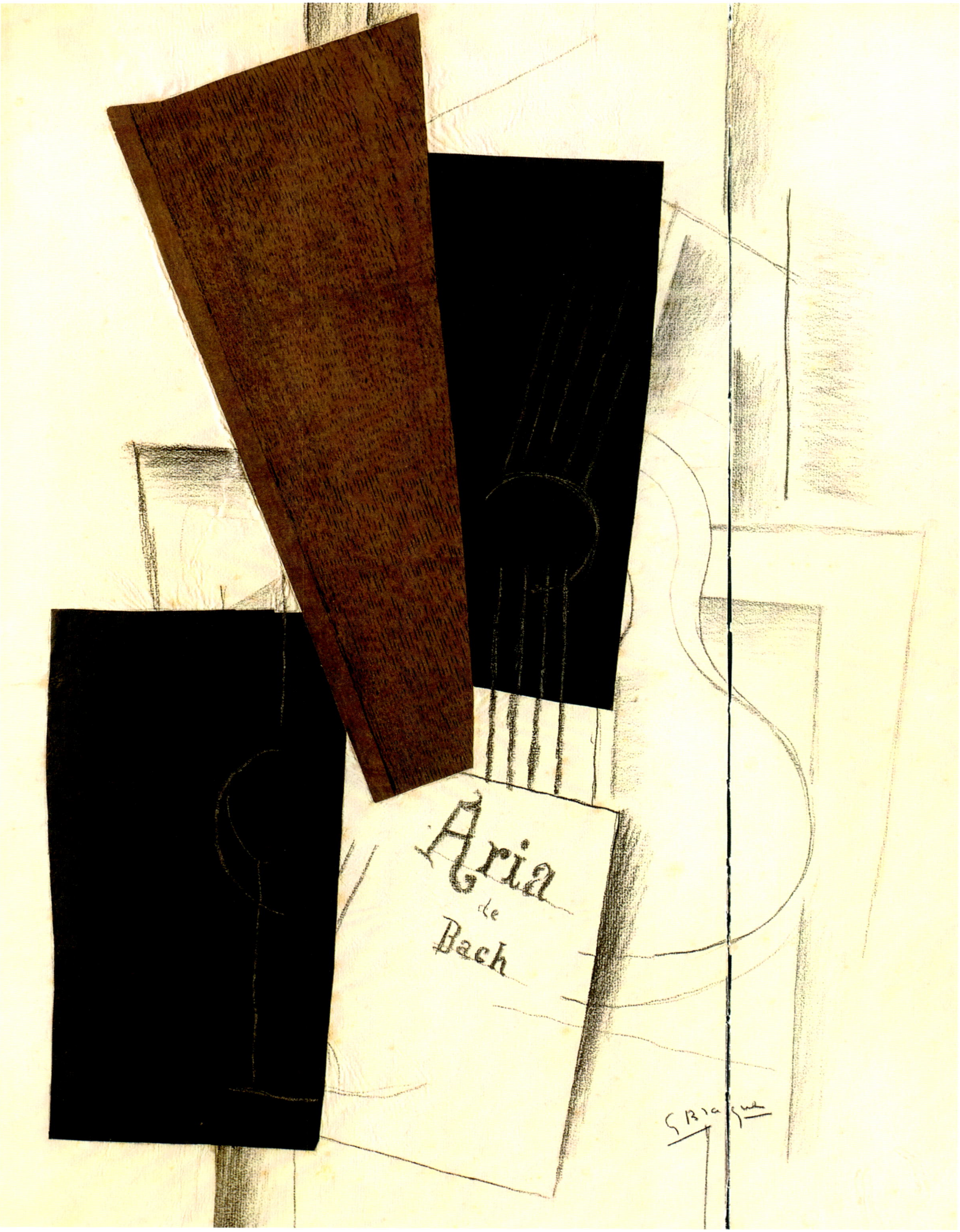
Aria
de
Bach

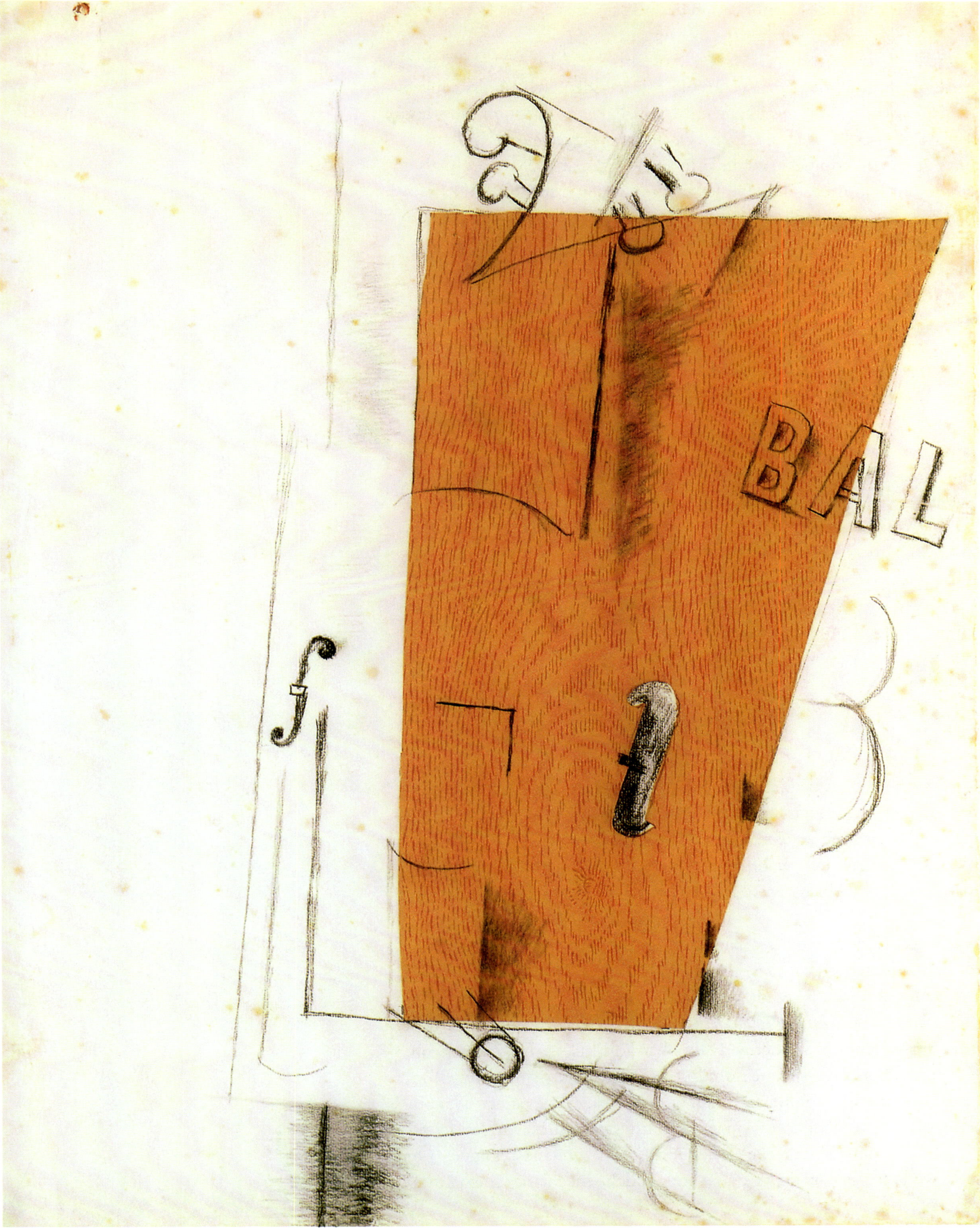
BAL

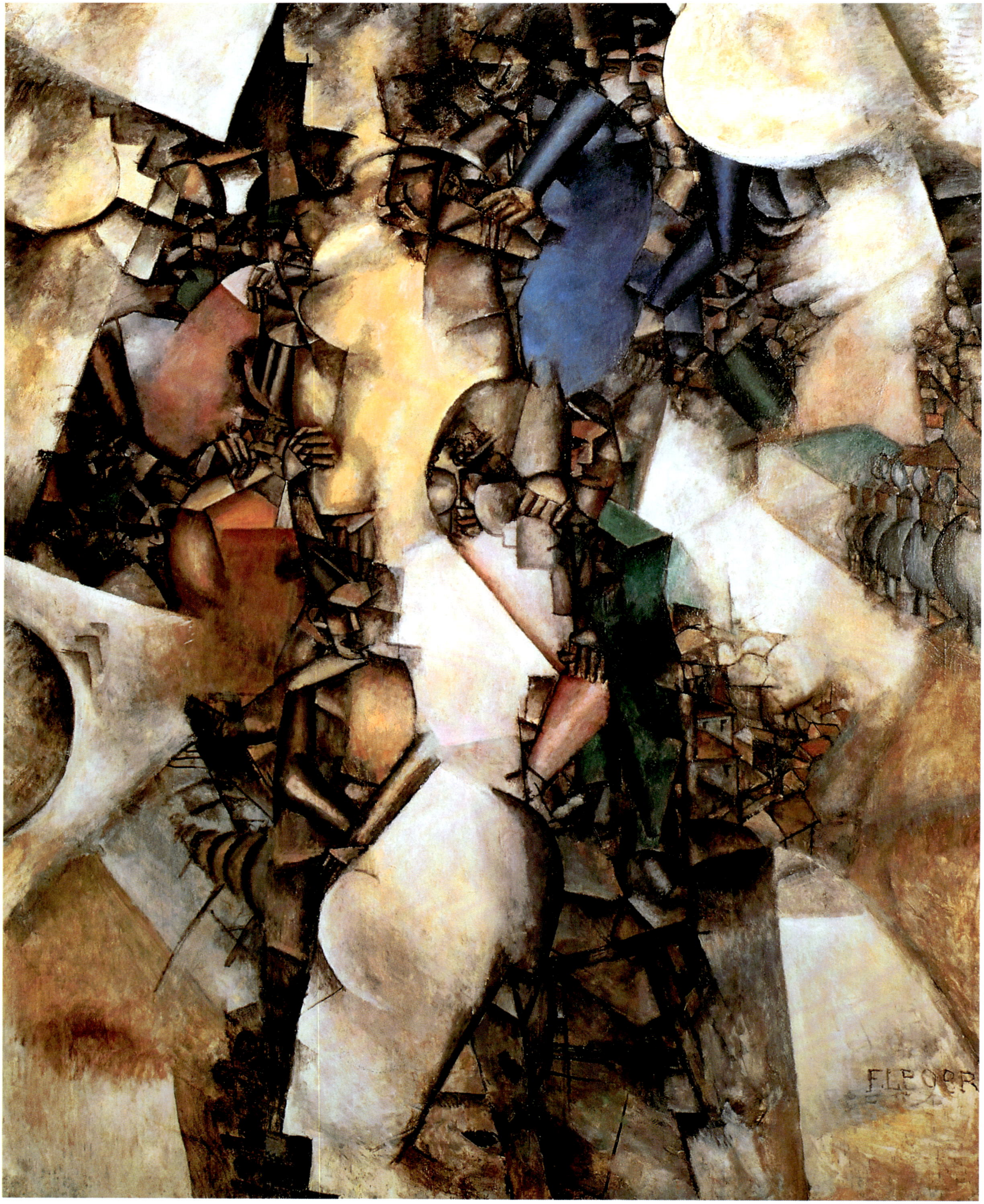

Fernand Léger

(Argentan, 1881 – Gif-sur-Yvette, 1955)

Having lost his father when he was four years old, Léger grew up in the Orne region with his mother and then left his family at the age of nineteen to pursue painting courses at the Académie Julian, having failed to enter the École des Beaux-Arts. He also worked with an architect, which deeply influenced his works, but he never finished his formal education. After a first exhibition at the Salon d'Automne in 1907, the "peasant of the avant-garde" installed himself, in 1909, in La Ruche, where he met Archipenko, Delaunay, Laurens etc.

Léger so embraced the influences of the Cézanne's geometric figures after the retrospective exhibition of Cézanne's work that took place in 1907, that he had to force himself to turn away from abstraction and privilege purely pictorial realism. Only "the lines, the forms and the colors" were pleasing to his eyes. Thus, as one can see in *The Wedding* (p. 142), the commotion and colour that were two founding elements of his art. The big dimensions of the canvas are revealing of his attachment to monumentality that would later confirm itself.

In accordance with the contrast of forms, as suggested vaguely by certain titles of his works, these characters are engaged in "a battle of volumes", overlapping each other in a syncopated rhythm, unified by the cold light, serving as "the exact opposites of Impressionism" and Post-Impressionism, from which he distanced himself. Distorted, its volumes resemble tubes, which drove certain critics, like Louis Vauxcelles, to call him "Tubist" (*Nudes in the Forest*, pp. 144-145; *The 14th of July*, p. 147).

He participated in the workshop of Puteaux and the Section d'Or, accompanied by Delaunay, Metzinger, Gris and others. In 1913, shortly before his departure for the battlefront, he participated in the Armory Show, which opened for him the doors of the Gallérie Kanhweiler. His trench years reversed his apprehension of the world, modernity and the objective world of machines playing important roles in his work. In his futuristic city, clean machines and clear lines of communications cohabitated, all combined but without confusion, in a colourful harmony of popular expressions. The raw, metallic colours that he employed began to transcend the simple chromatic spectrum and became participants (*The Card Players*, p. 146).

From his war years, he also anticipated, in accordance with the image of the anonymous soldier, a way for the individual to plunge himself into the Communist idealised system to which he subscribed. However, in his work, man becomes dehumanised, disembodied and inclines, powerless in the presence of the machine and modernity, as if to combine himself with her. In 1917, he signed a collaborative contract with Léonce Rosenberg that supported him for nearly ten years.

Fernand Léger,
The Wedding, 1911.
Oil on canvas, 257 x 206 cm.
Musée National d'Art Moderne,
Centre Georges-Pompidou, Paris.

Fernand Léger,
Nudes in the Forest, 1909-1911.
Oil on canvas, 120 x 170.2 cm.
Kröller-Müller, Otterlo.

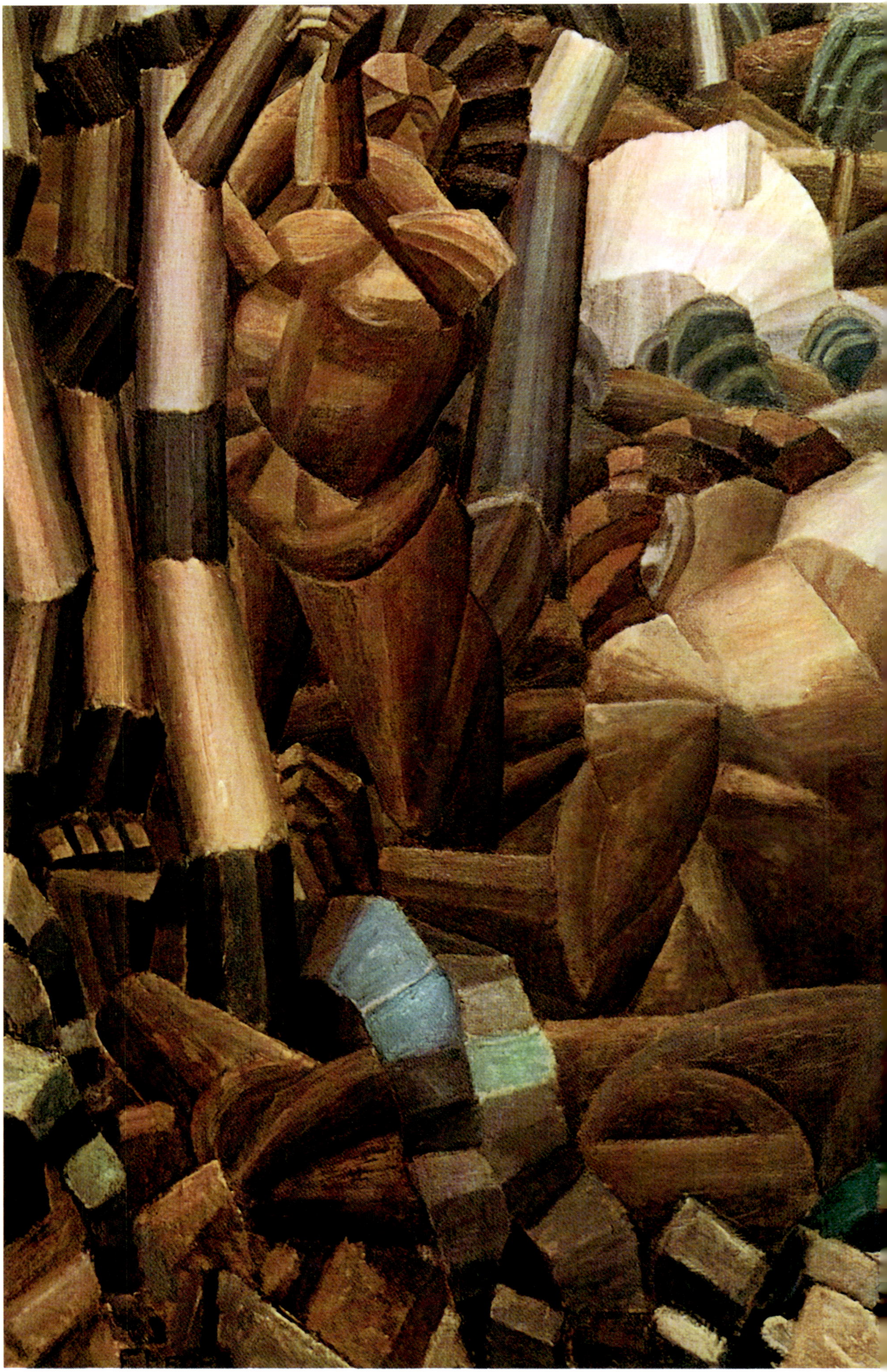

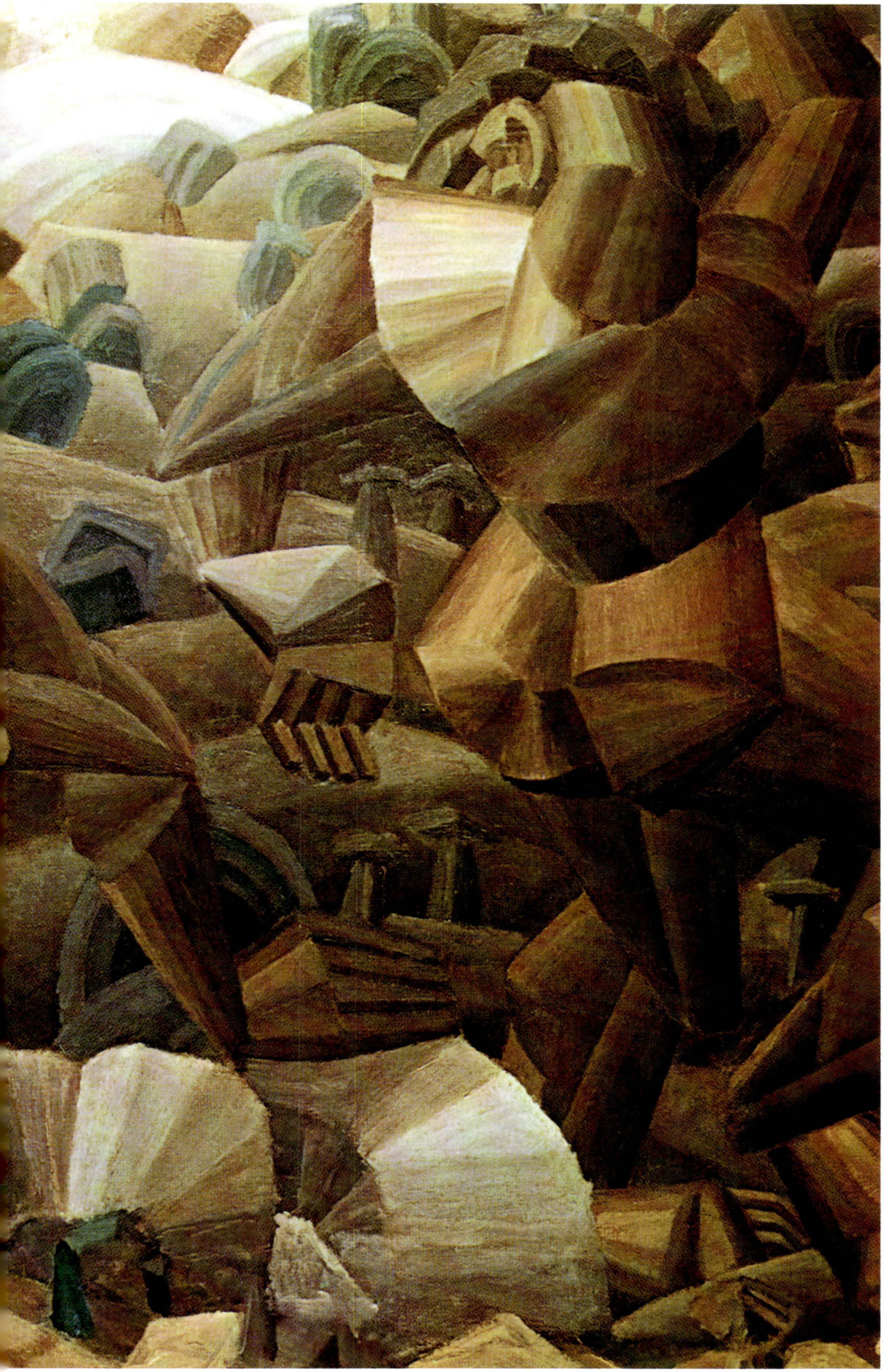

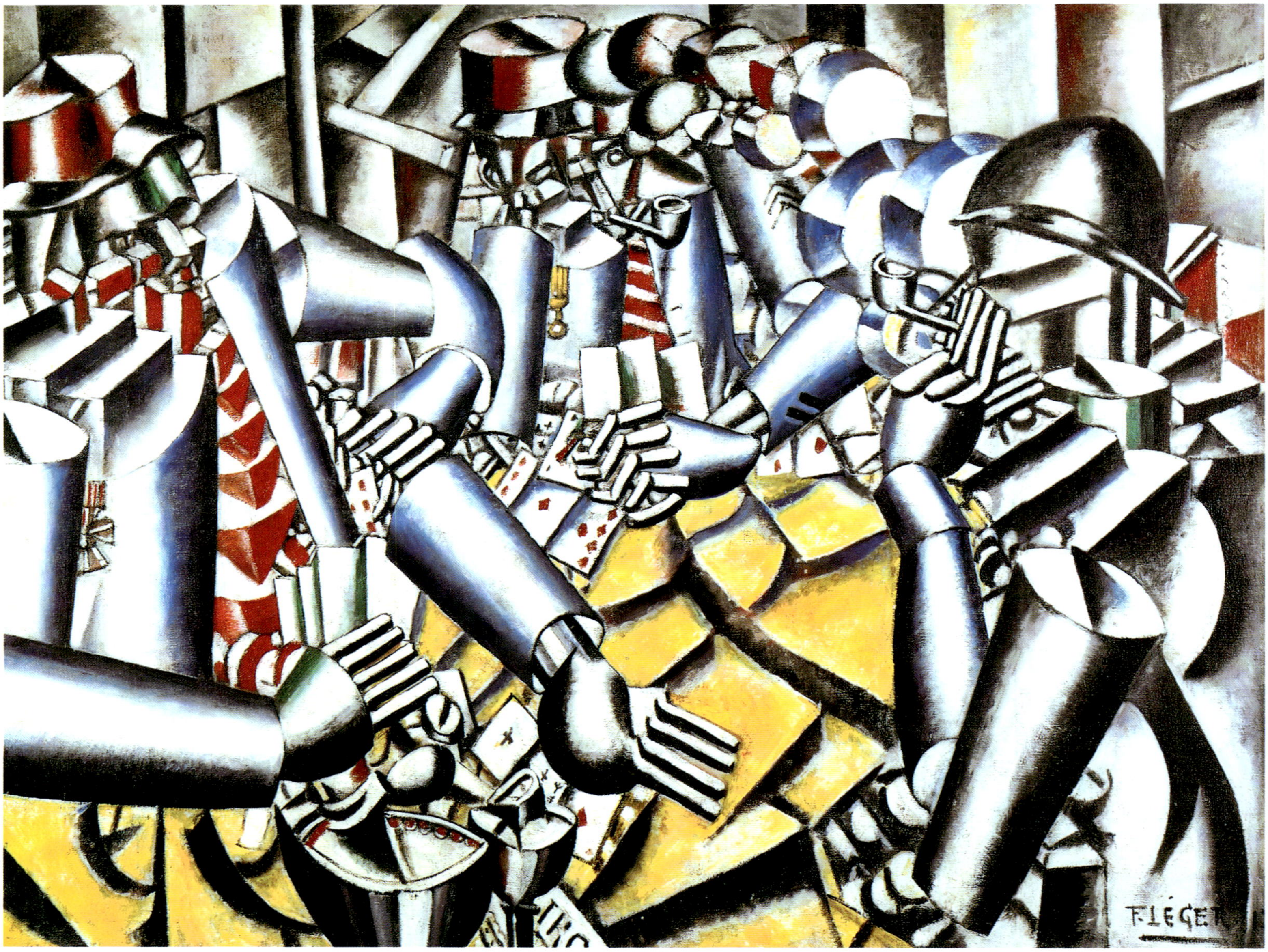

His encounter with Le Corbusier in 1920 confirmed his taste for monumentality; five years later, he painted the first murals for the pavilion of L'Esprit Nouveau for the architect. In addition to this work, Léger created many settings for films and ballets. He travelled several times to the United States, notably during World War II, where he made many important acquaintances, including the Rockefellers and John Dos Passos.

In his last years, he devoted himself to monumental works, one of which is located at the UN (1952). He passed away three years later. While advocating a purification of the plastic language, a return to basic forms and a severe abstemiousness of painting that he associated with ideas and feelings, Léger inspired Apollinaire to classify his Cubism, as he did with the art of Delaunay, as Orphism.

Fernand Léger,
The Card Players, 1917.
Oil on canvas, 129 x 193 cm.
Kröller-Müller, Otterlo.

Fernand Léger,
The 14th of July, 1914.
Oil on canvas, 65.5 x 58.5 cm.
Musée Fernand Léger, Biot.

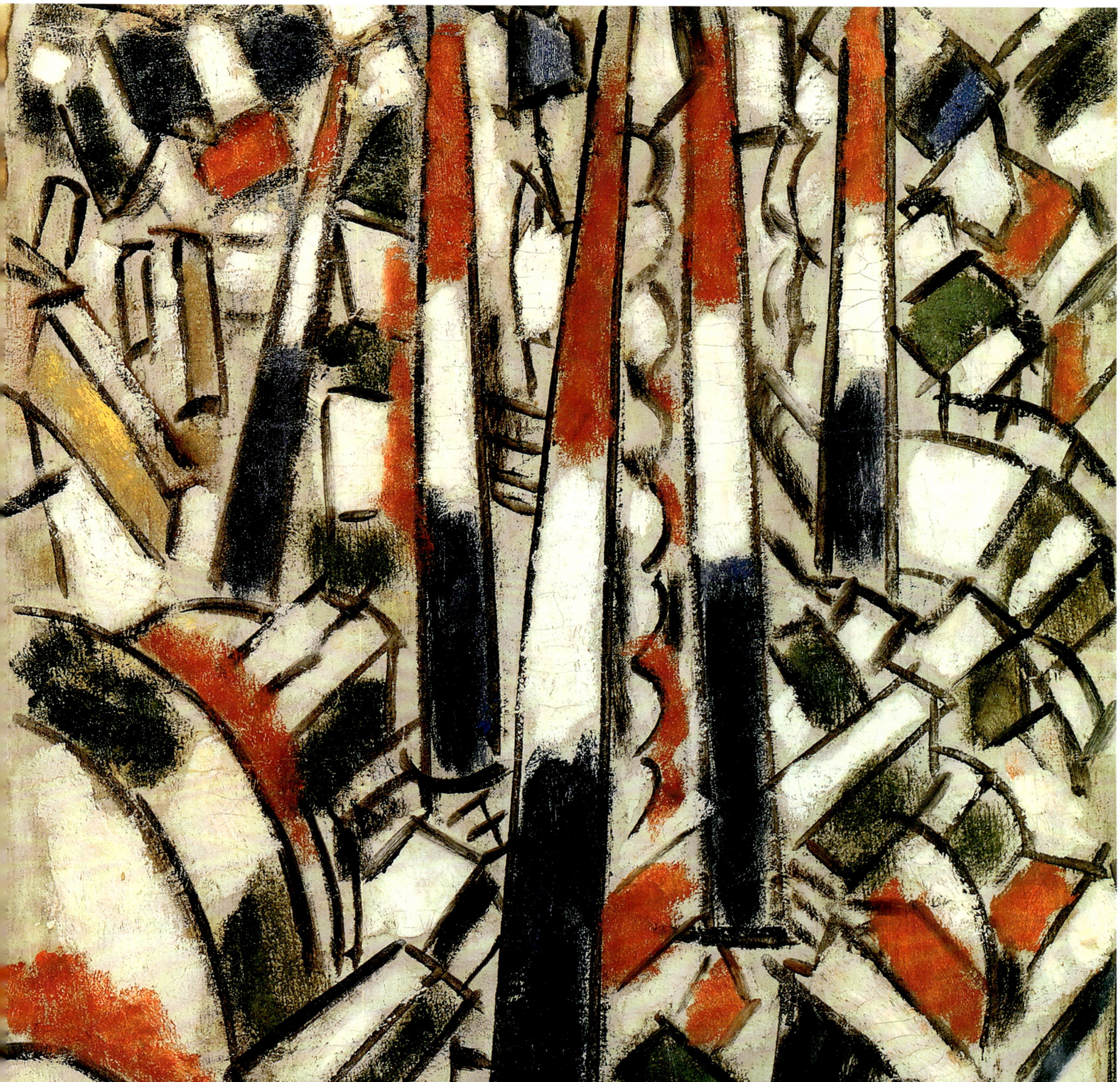
F. LEGER

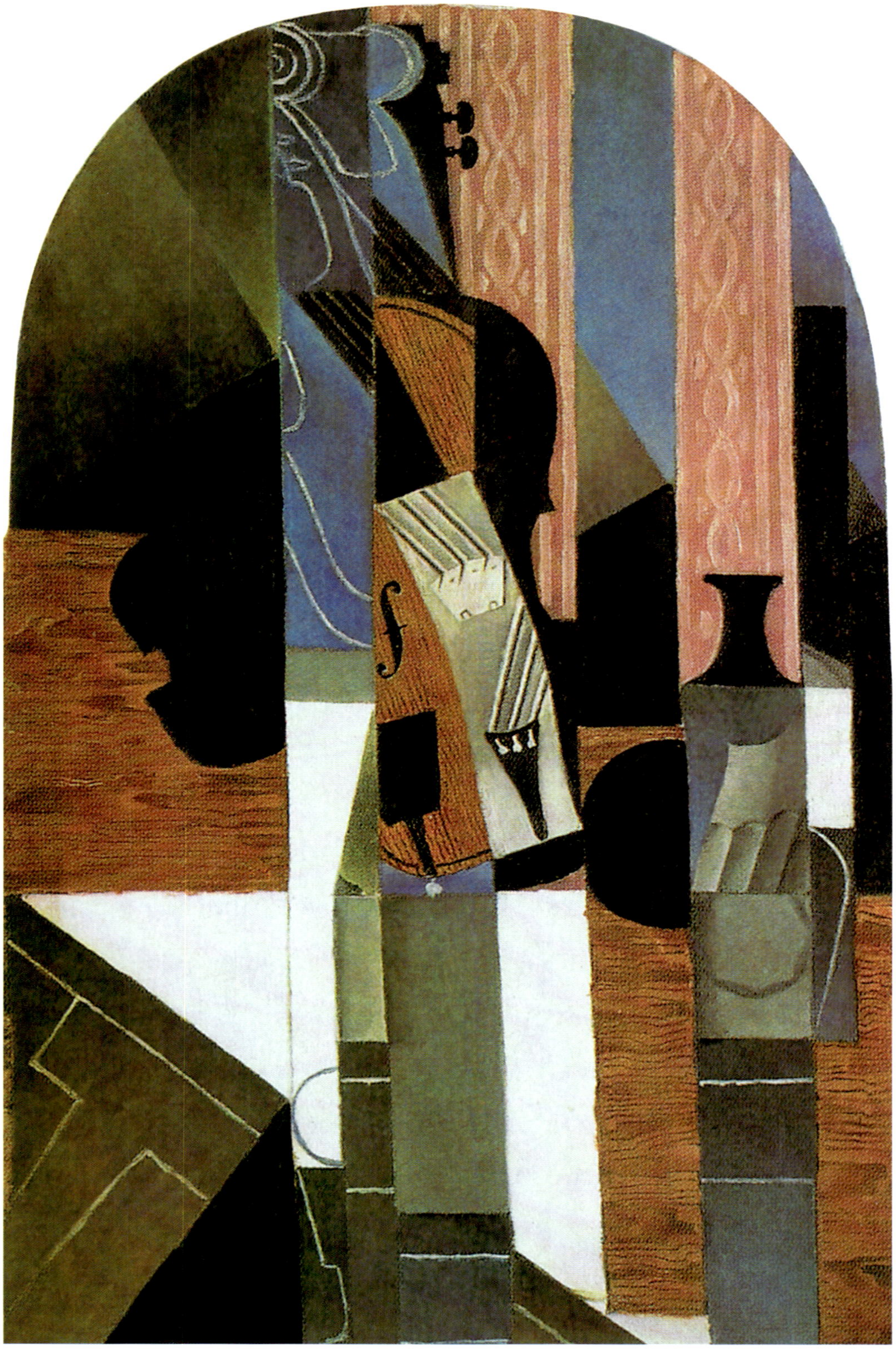

Juan Gris

(Madrid, 1887 – Boulogne-Billancourt, 1927)

Juan Gris was born Juan José Victoriano González Perisies in 1887, and he began his artistic career in the French domain by drawing caricatures for number of newspapers, such as the *Charivari*, *L'Assiette au beurre*, *Le Cris de Paris*, etc. Thanks to the support and immense influence of Picasso, Gris naturally gravitated towards the Bateau-Lavoir. With Picasso and Braque, he participated in the bohemian life enjoyed by artists that lived on Montmartre for around fifteen years, in company with Kees van Dongen, Max Jacob and Pierre Mac Orlan, among others.

In addition to signing a contract with Kahnweiler, Gris saw prosperity when Gertrude Stein, following the example of Léonce Rosenberg, bought a large number of its works. He also knew to surround himself with painters such as Picasso, Modigliani and Matisse, with whom he enjoyed many moments in Collioure, but also entertained poets like Reverdy, Apollinaire and Max Jacob, who he saw often.

Sick since adolescence, the artist was always interested, in spite of his magnificent *Portrait of Pablo Picasso* (p. 150) and his *Portrait of Maurice Raynal* (p. 151), in objects more than men. A homebody, he jostled and reinvented all our daily objects, picking them apart one by one all the better to reassemble them, he the great organiser, as we see in *Still-Life (Violin and Inkwell)* (opposite), *Fantômas* (p. 153) or *Breakfast* (p. 152). Suggesting more than it reveals, his work is a subtle ode to metonymy.

Understanding the whole poetry of his work, Diaghilev commissioned from him a series of sets and costumes for his Ballets Russes in 1922. In 1924, at the age of thirty-seven, he delivered a lecture at the Sorbonne on "The Possibilities of Painting" and passed away three years later, too young, of a uraemia.

Juan Gris,
Still-Life (Violin and Inkwell), 1913.
Oil on canvas, 89.5 x 60.5 cm.
Kunstsammlung Nordrhein-Westfalen, Düsseldorf.

Juan Gris,
Portrait of Pablo Picasso, 1912.
Oil on canvas, 93.3 x 74.4 cm.
Art Institute of Chicago, Chicago.

Juan Gris,
Portrait of Maurice Raynal, 1911.
Oil on canvas, 55 x 46 cm.
Private collection.

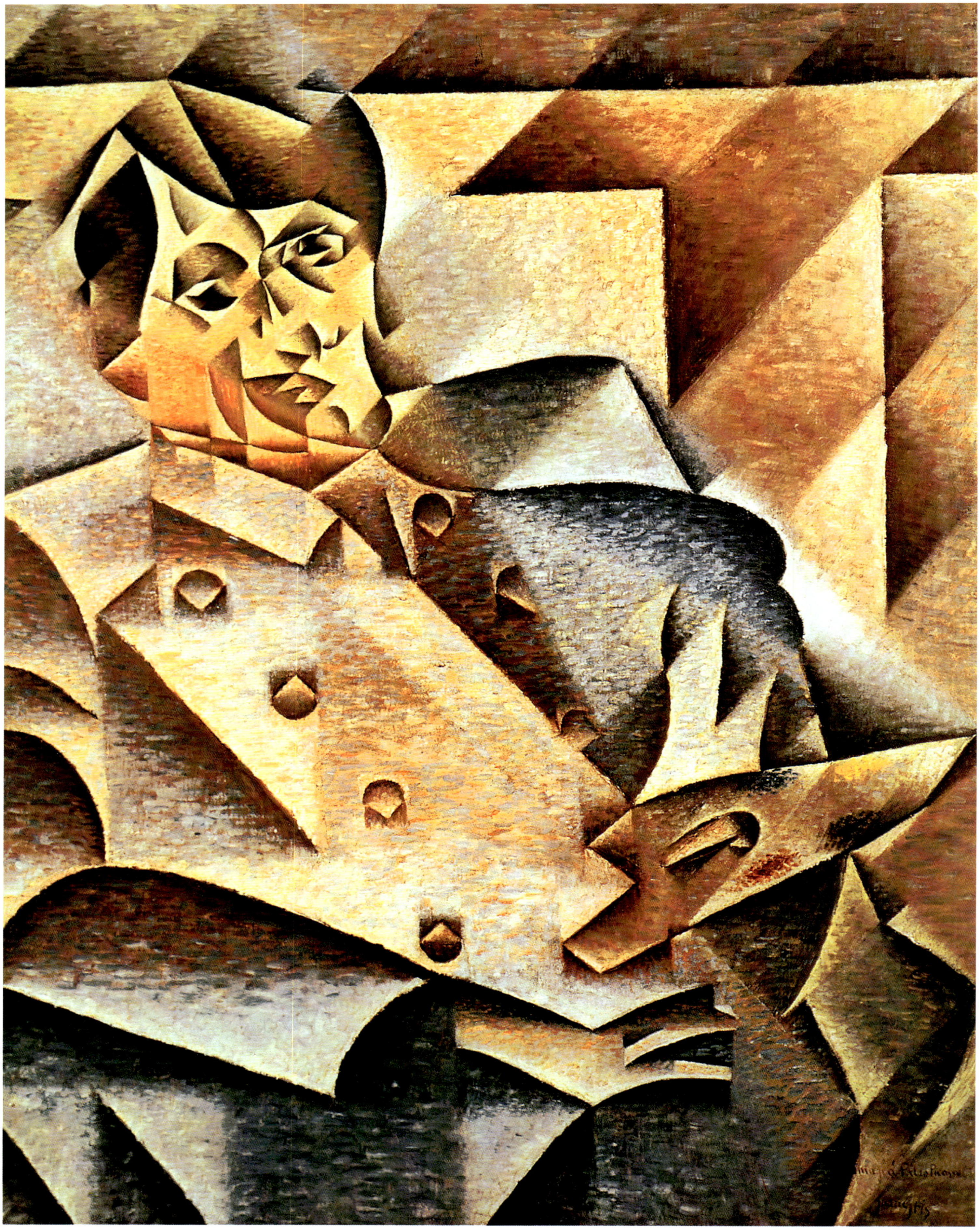

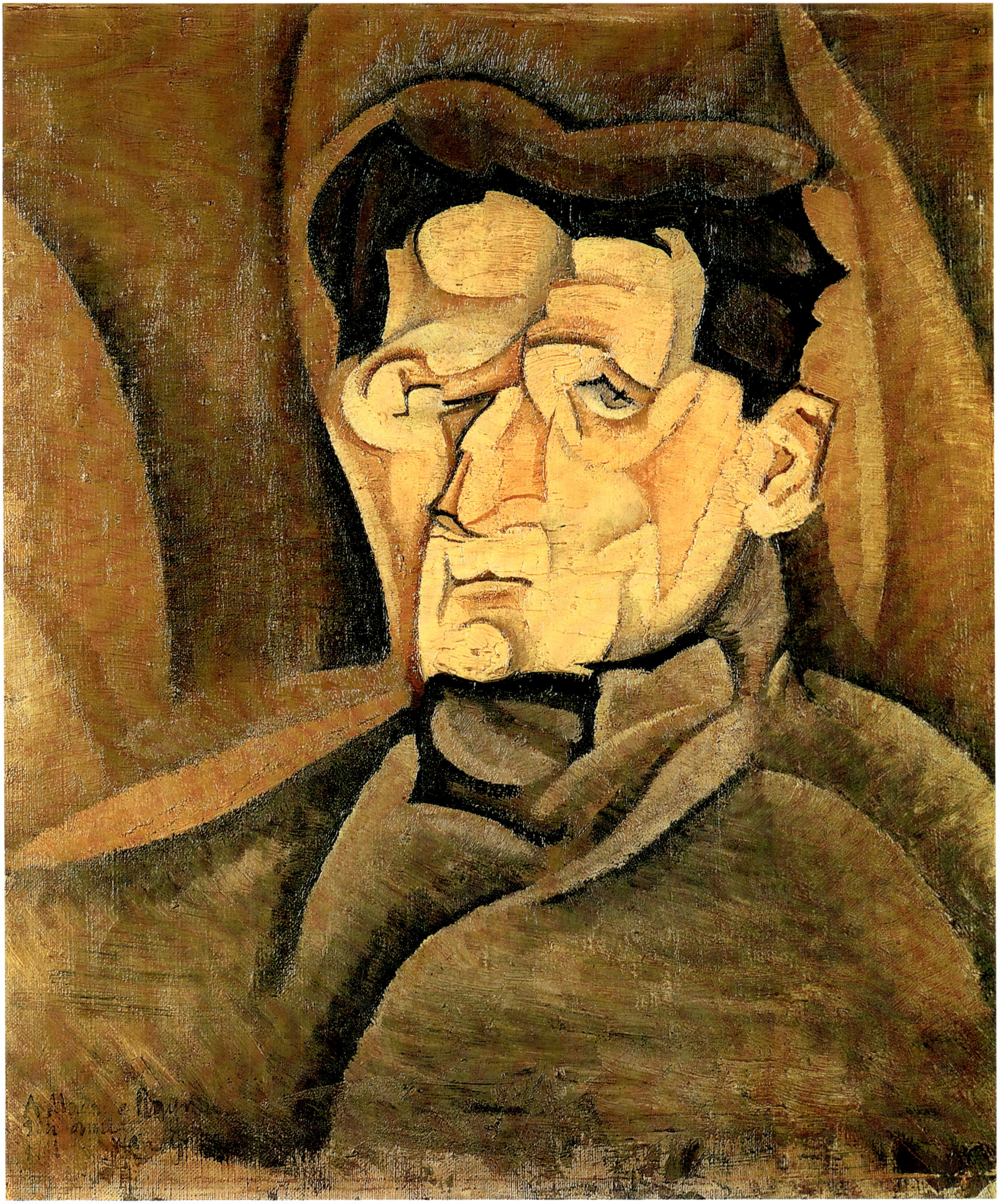

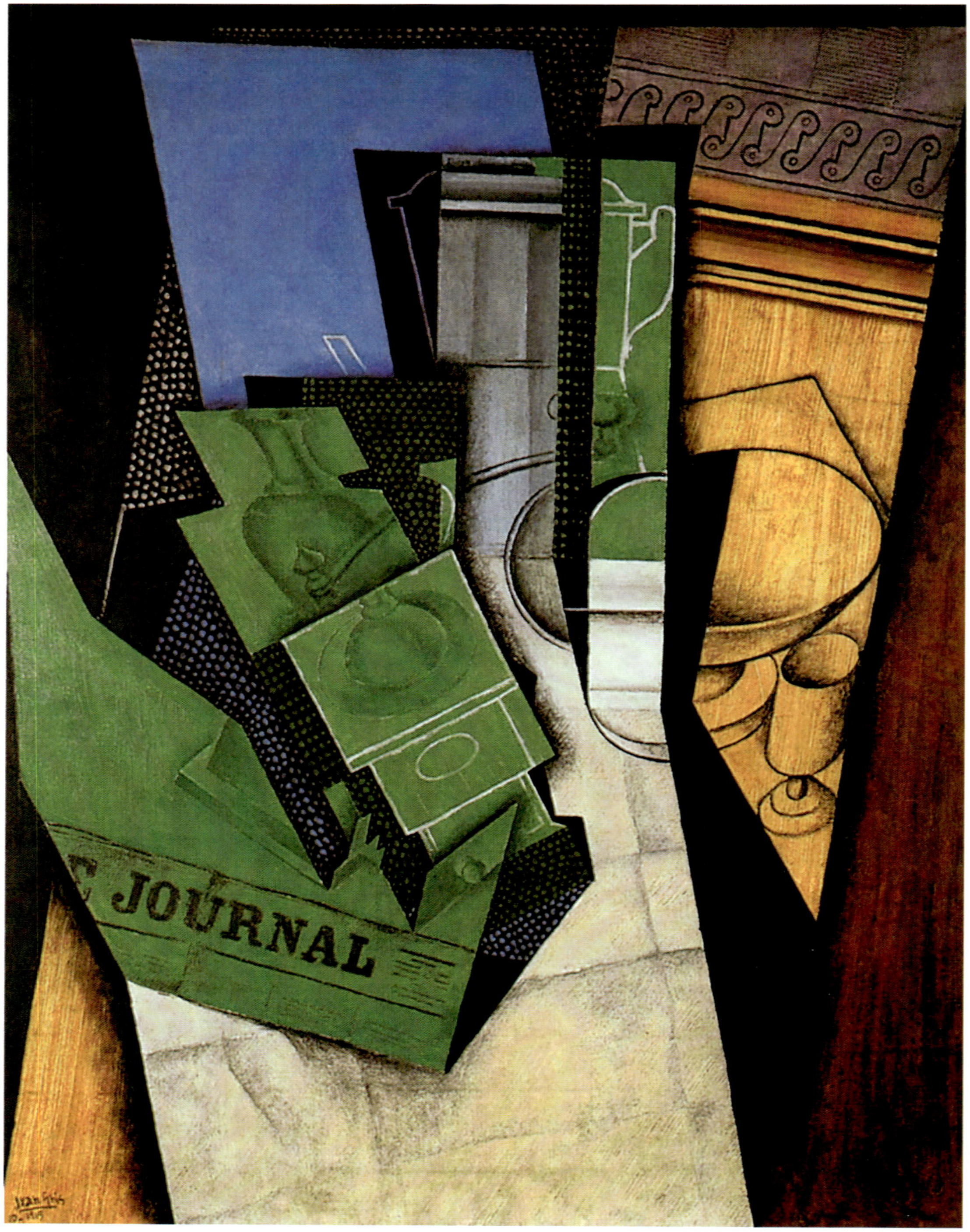

Juan Gris,
Breakfast, 1915.
Oil and charcoal on canvas,
92 x 73 cm.
Musée National d'Art Moderne,
Centre Georges-Pompidou, Paris.

Juan Gris,
Fantômas, 1915.
Oil on canvas, 59.8 x 73.3 cm.
National Gallery of Art, Washington, D.C.

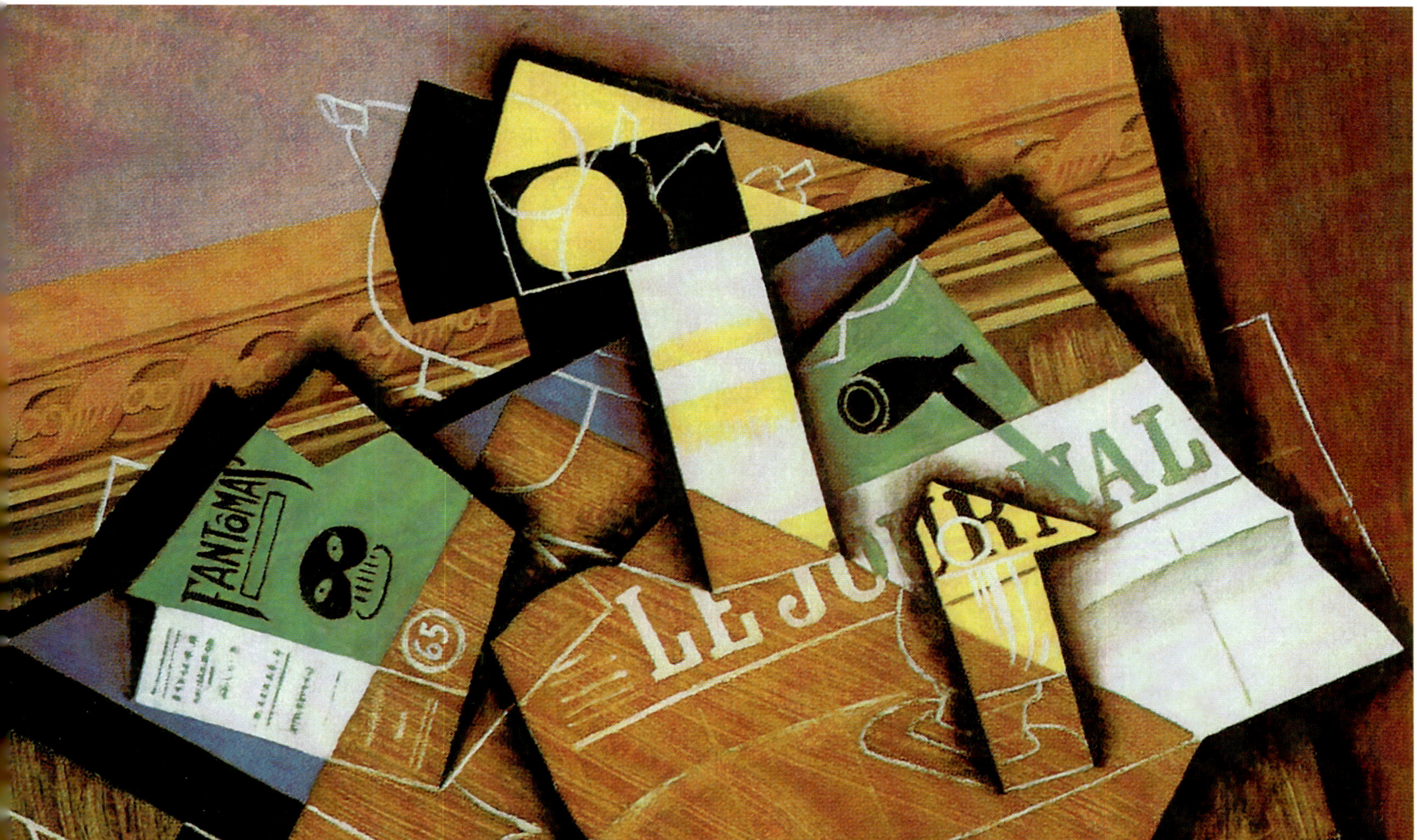
FANTOMAS
65
LE JO

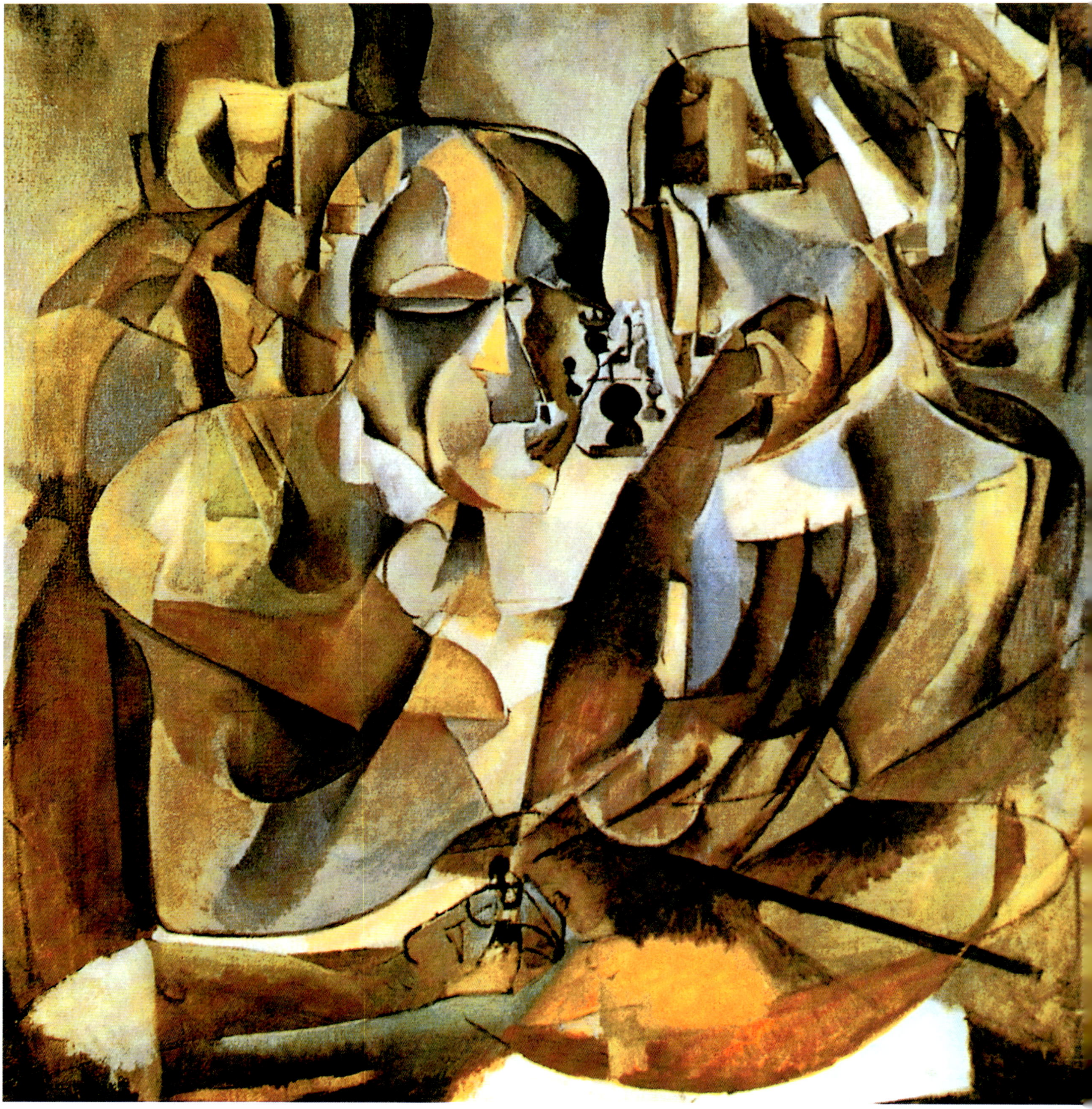

Marcel Duchamp
(Balinville, 1887 – Neuilly-sur-Seine, 1968)

Despite producing a relatively small body of work as a painter and sculptor, Marcel Duchamp exercised a powerful and enduring influence on the art of the 20th century. Coming from an artistic family, he was the brother of sculptor Raymond Duchamp-Villon as well as Jacques and Suzanne Villon. He lived in the Montparnasse area of Paris and studied at the Académie Julian.

Like most artists of his time, his first works were inspired by the art of the Impressionists and the Nabis. But from 1911 onwards, Duchamp attended the meetings his brother Jacques organised with the so-called Puteaux Group that included Fernand Léger, Francis Picabia and Robert Delaunay. While in contact with these artists, Duchamp was influenced by the art of Cézanne, Cubism and futurism, for which a manifesto had been published in 1909 in Paris by the newspaper *Le Figaro.*

Then he started to use an ocre and brown palette like that of the Cubists, and his painting *The Chess Players* (opposite) illustrates this interest for Cubism, with the pieces of chess spread all around the destructured players. One can see the parallel with *The Card Players* painted by Cézanne between 1890 and 1895.

However, Duchamp soon abandoned the analytic Cubism, that had been, as for so many other painters of that time, a way to explore his own style.

For Marcel Duchamp, the goal of personal style was the fragmentation of movement. Following paintings as *Nude (Study), Sad Young Man on a Train* (p. 157), the so-called self-portrait of Duchamp, where he had started his study of fragmentation of movement, he presented, after lots of preparatory sketches, his *Nude Descending a Staircase (No. 2)* (p. 156) at the Section d'Or exhibition in Paris in 1912. The fragmentation of movement then became his preferred subject, growing closer to the Italian futuristic aesthetic. A year later, his *Nude Descending a Staircase (No. 2)* was presented at the Armory Show in New York, where it created a scandal but became a huge success that encouraged the commission of many paintings. However, Duchamp decided to stop painting in 1912, because he thought himself in disagreement with the mercantile system associated with his work.

However, he did not stop working, as we can see in his most ambitious work, *The Bride Stripped Bare by her Bachelors, Even* (1915-1923), which was executed on glass and incorporated a coffee-grinder as a sexual metaphor; this work remains complex and provacative even today. But perhaps Duchamp's most influential contribution to twentieth-century art was the introduction of the notion of "ready-made" or found object pieces. He appeared simply to find an object from daily life, sign it and exhibit it, thus proclaiming it a work of art. He assembled a bicycle upside-down on a kitchen chair for one of his ready-mades.

Bicycle Wheel was exhibited in 1913, followed by *The Bottlerack* in 1914 and the urinal signed "R. Mutt" and exhibited under the title of *Fountain* in 1917. His radical attitude and ironic, sarcastic works aimed at the democratisation of art, making him a great herald of Pop Art and the Nouveaux Réalistes.

Marcel Duchamp,
The Chess Players, 1911.
Oil on canvas, 100.6 x 100.7 cm.
Philadelphia Museum of Art,
Philadelphia.

Marcel Duchamp,
Nude Descending a Staircase (No. 2), 1912.
Oil on canvas, 147 x 89.2 cm.
Philadelphia Museum of Art,
Philadelphia.

Marcel Duchamp,
Nude (Study), Sad Young Man on a Train, 1911-1912.
Oil on cardboard, 100 x 73 cm.
Peggy Guggenheim Collection, Venice.

Marcel Duchamp,
The King and Queen Traversed by Swift Nudes at High Speed, 1912.
Transparent and opaque watercolor, ink and graphite on tan woven paper, 49.1 x 58.7 cm.
Philadelphia Museum of Art,
Philadelphia.

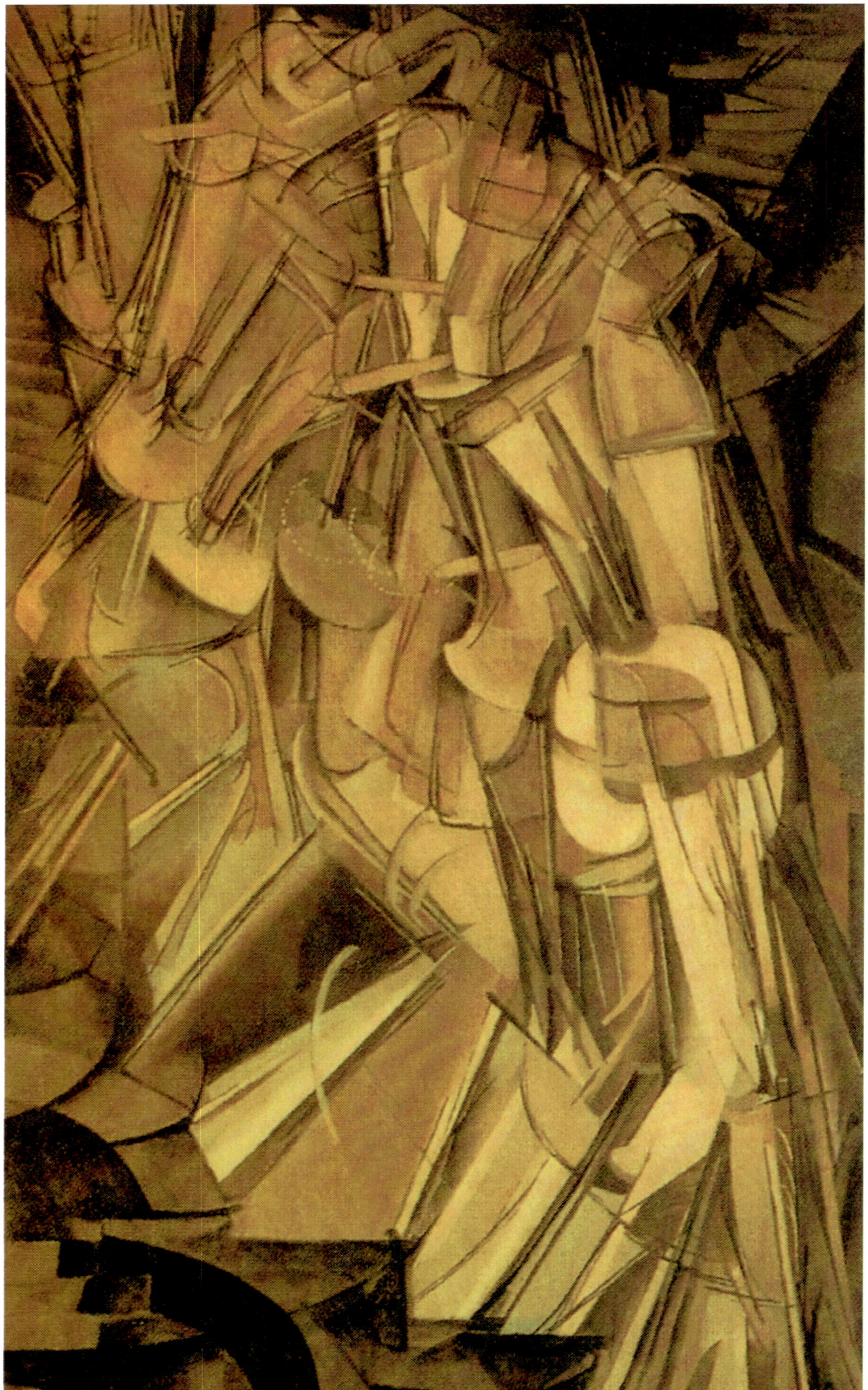

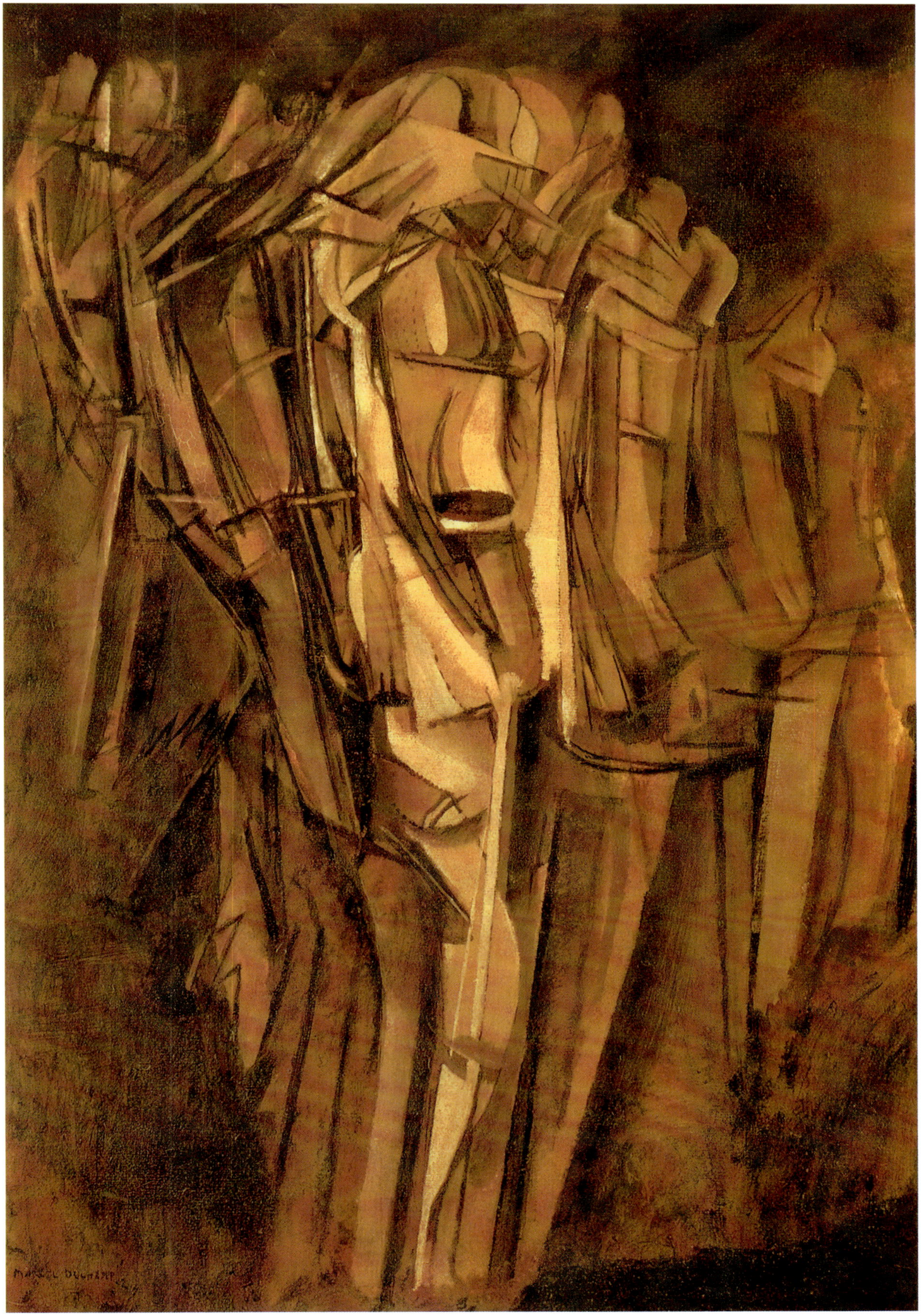

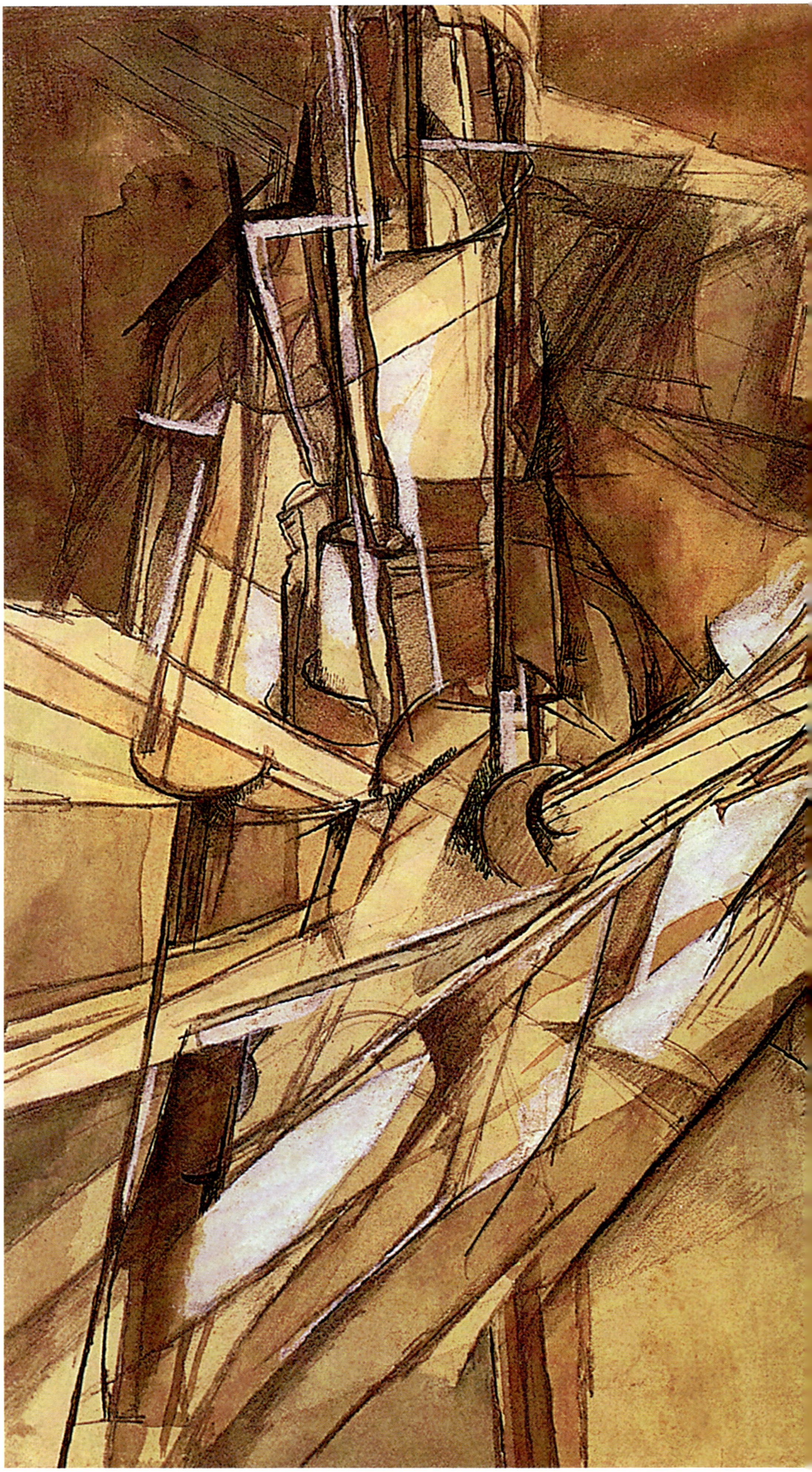

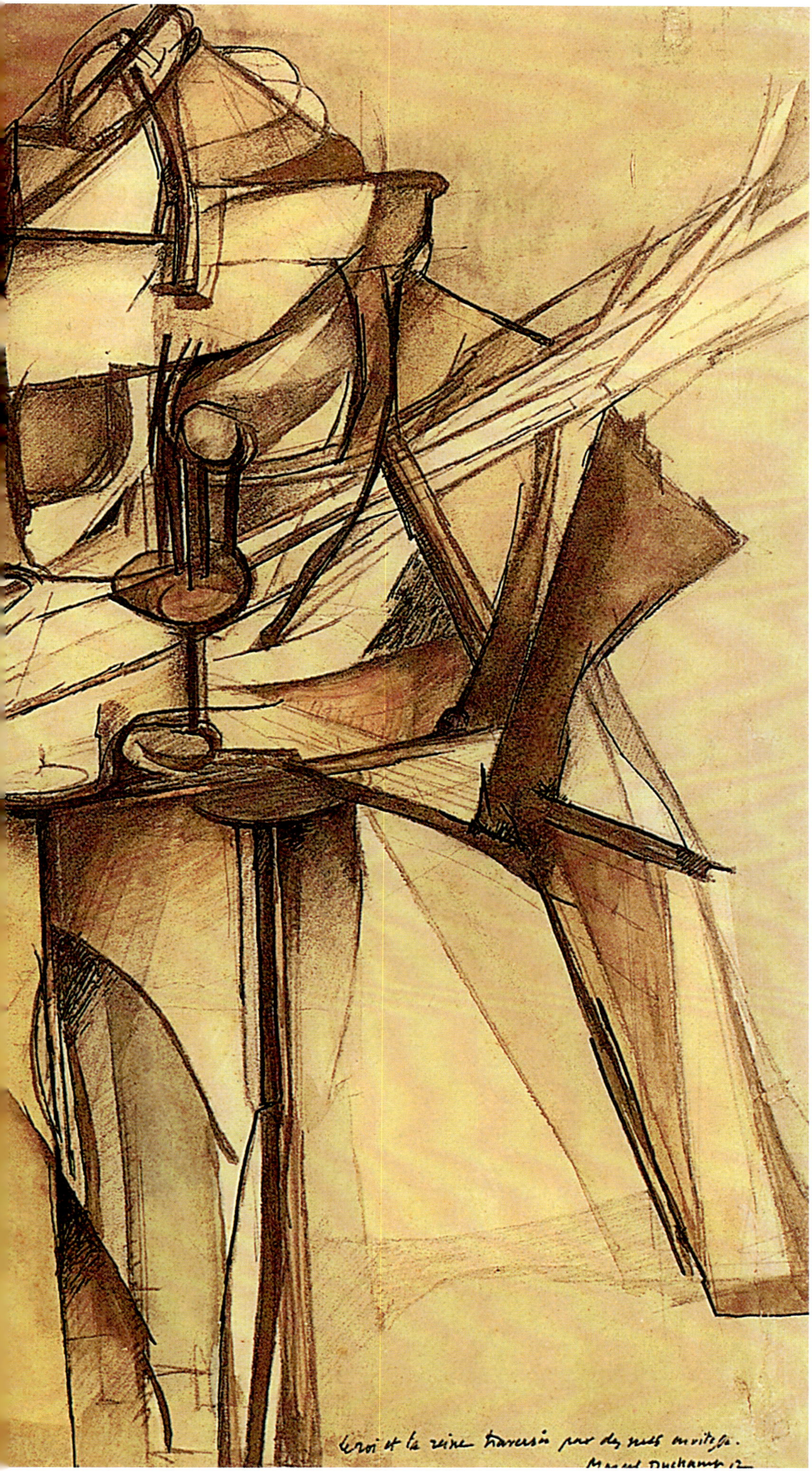
Le roi et la reine traversés par des nus en vitesse.

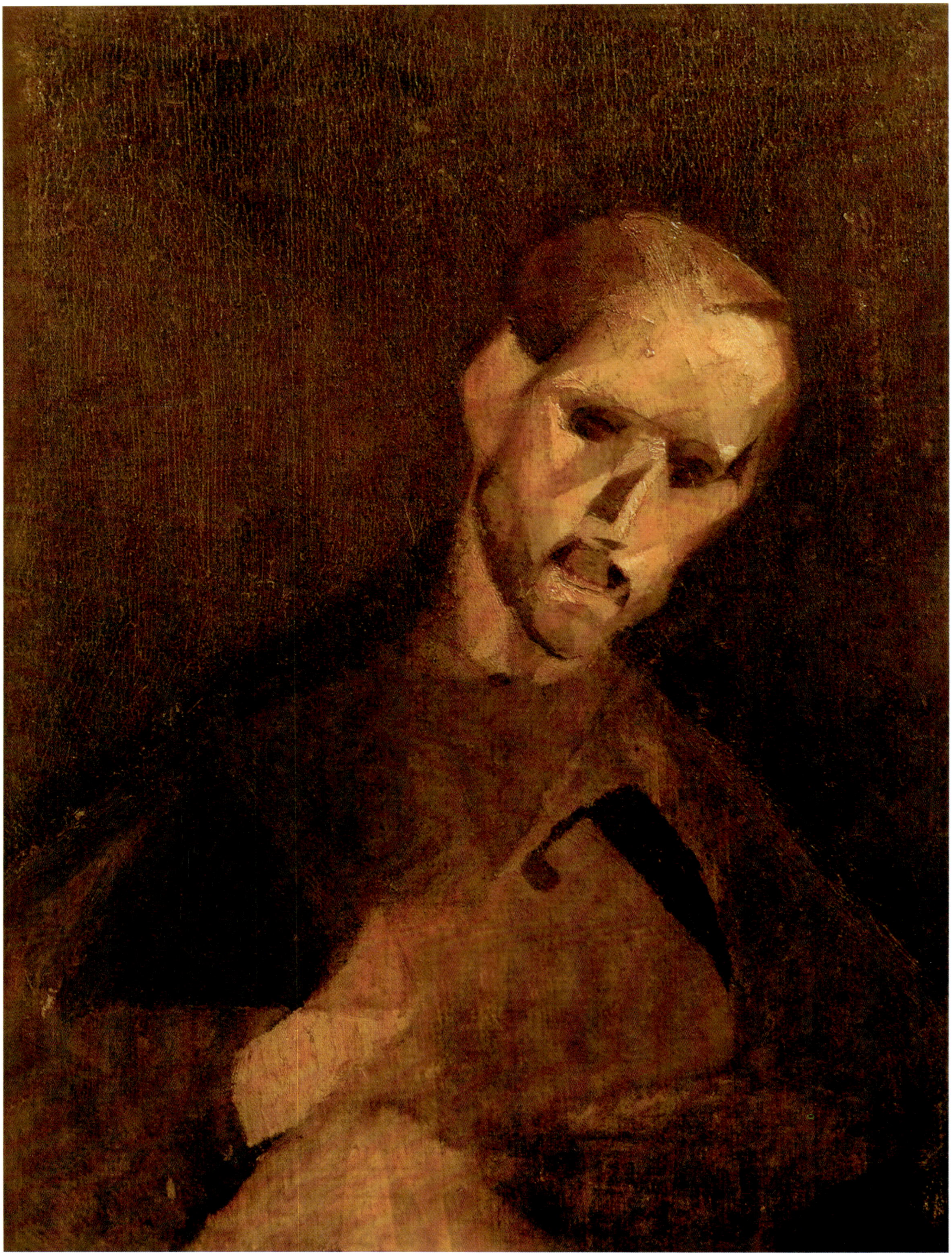

Jacques Villon
(Damville, 1875 – Puteaux, 1963)

Brother of Raymond Duchamp-Villon and Marcel Duchamp, Gaston Duchamp took the pseudonym of Jacques Villon in homage to the medieval poet, François Villon, to distinguish himself from his younger brothers. Arriving in Paris in 1894, having been a notary clerk in Rouen for a short time, he began his studies at the École des Beaux-Arts and was, at the same time, a student in the workshop of Fernand Cormon, as Toulouse-Lautrec had been about ten years before. Evolving in the impetuous environment of the of Montmartre bohemians, Jacques Villon quickly abandoned his law studies to devote himself completely to art. His first graphic works, adopting the style of poster artists of the Belle Époque, like Steinlen or Lautrec, were published in comic magazines like *L'Assiette au beurre* and *Le Rêve*. Already, his sketches communicated the accuracy and confidence that proved characteristic.

Jacques Villon did not move away from Montmartre until several years later, when in 1906 he relocated to Puteaux. Isolated, far from the excitements of the cabarets and other Parisian centres of merriment, the artist concentrated on his painting and consecrated himself completely to the development of his art. At first suggestive of Impressionism and Fauvism, his canvases progressed along the path made by Cézanne that, as it did for most of the artists of his generation, inevitably led Jacques Villon to Cubism.

Beginning in 1911, artists, painters, sculptors and poets began to gather on Sunday evenings in his studio in Puteaux. In the tradition of Mallarmé's "Mardistes", they conversed and theorised together about this Cubism that Braque and Picasso had enabled them to discover. The research of the group at Puteaux sought a harmonious result that they believed could be reached through application of the golden number of the Renaissance. Their interest in this number, long considered the elementary basis for the perfection of all forms of art, was the foundation for the name of the Section d'Or, as the association came to be called. The group held an exhibition in Room 41 of the Salon des Indépendants in 1911. Hung together, the canvases of Villon, Gleizes, Metzinger, Delaunay, Léger and Le Fauconnier provoked a true scandal. Of course, Cubism had already existed for a number of years, but Braque and Picasso rarely participated in formal exhibitions, and the modern movement, until then, was not known to general public. At last, Pandora's Box, which had been opened in 1907, was violently exposed to the eyes of all.

At Villon's studio, the research of the Section d'Or evolved in correlation with futuristic works in terms of velocity and then, little by little, in terms of the power of colour. The weekly meetings came to an end in 1914 when Delaunay turned towards Orphism.

Translating these evolutions, Villon's palette was enriched; pure colours were juxtaposed to give depth to the canvas, then the lines disappeared little by little to leave room for a perfect harmony of hues. Fascinated by the effects of light on colour, Villon valued a rare usage of clear nuances. In the 1930s, he also took part in the group Abstraction-Création, although, paradoxically, he was searching for the means of translating his technique for more conventional subjects at the same time. He was rewarded in 1950 when he received the Carnegie Prize, then the Grand Prize at the Venice Biennale six years later; the work of Villon was the happy symbiosis, in a coloured mixture of tradition and modernity, of abstraction and figuration.

Jacques Villon,
Portrait of Raymond Duchamp-Villon,
1911.
Oil on wood, 35 x 26.5 cm.
Musée National d'Art Moderne,
Centre Georges-Pompidou, Paris.

Jacques Villon,
Marching Soldiers, 1913.
Oil on canvas, 65 x 92 cm.
Musée National d'Art Moderne,
Centre Georges-Pompidou, Paris.

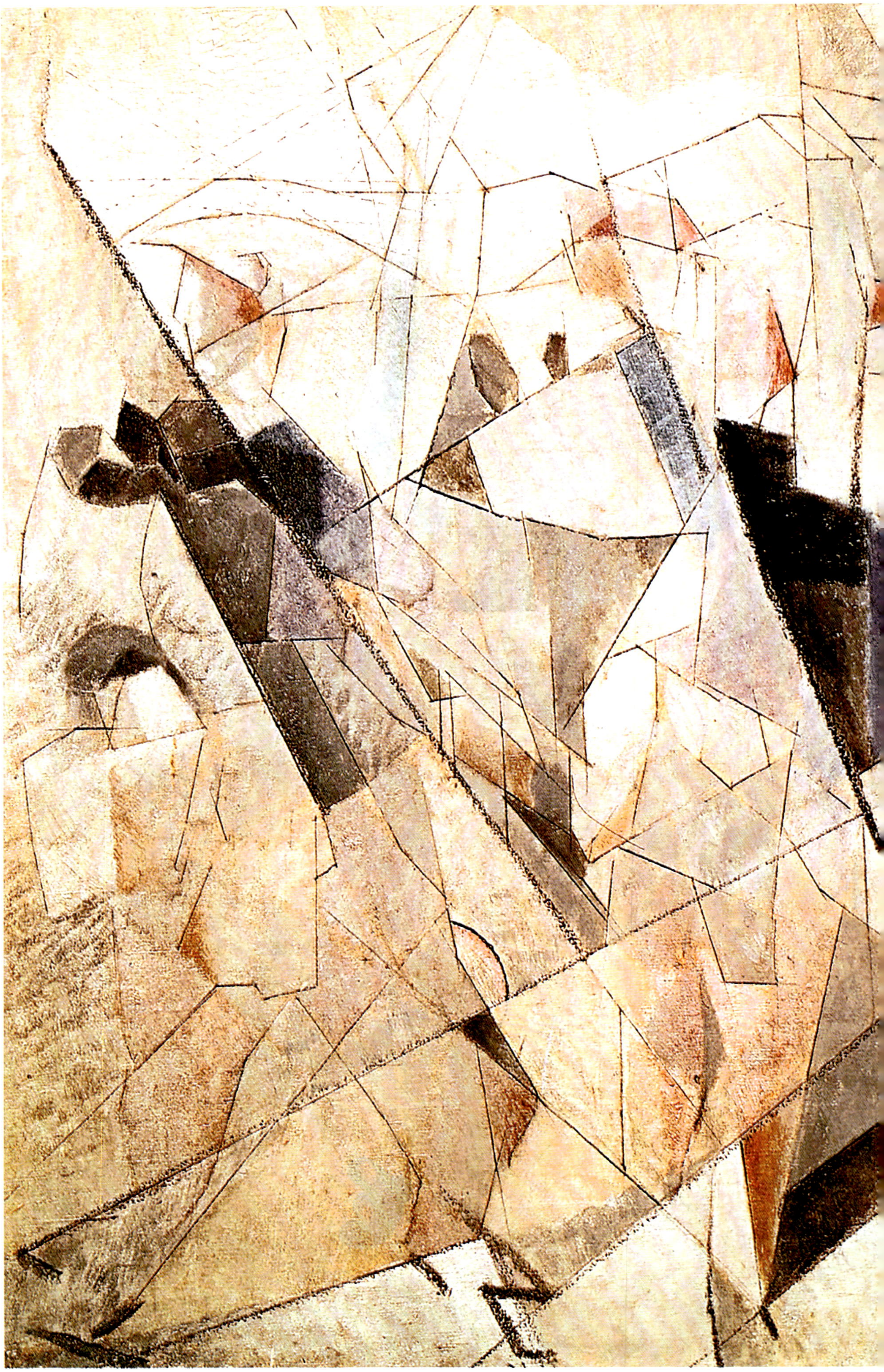

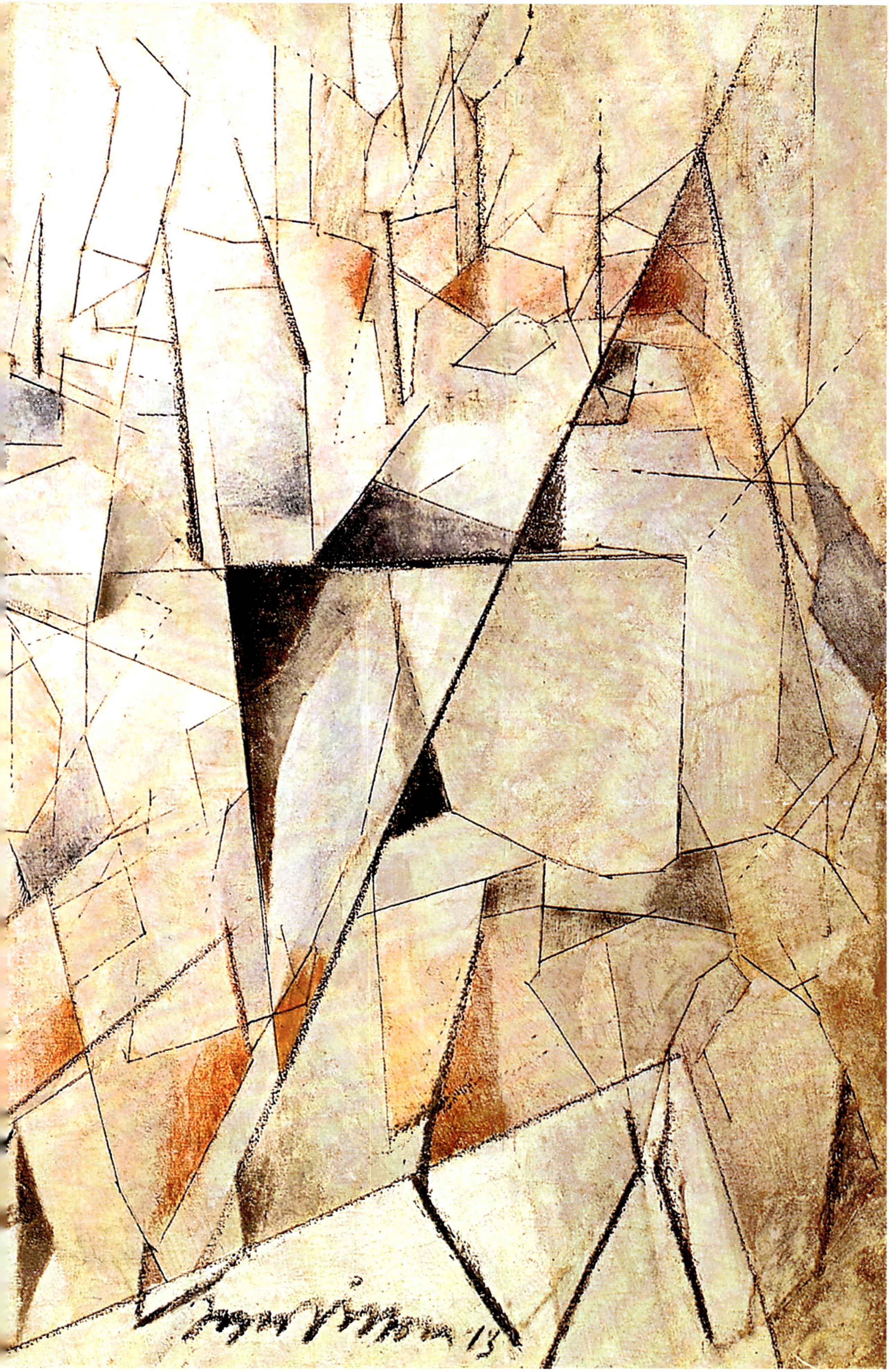

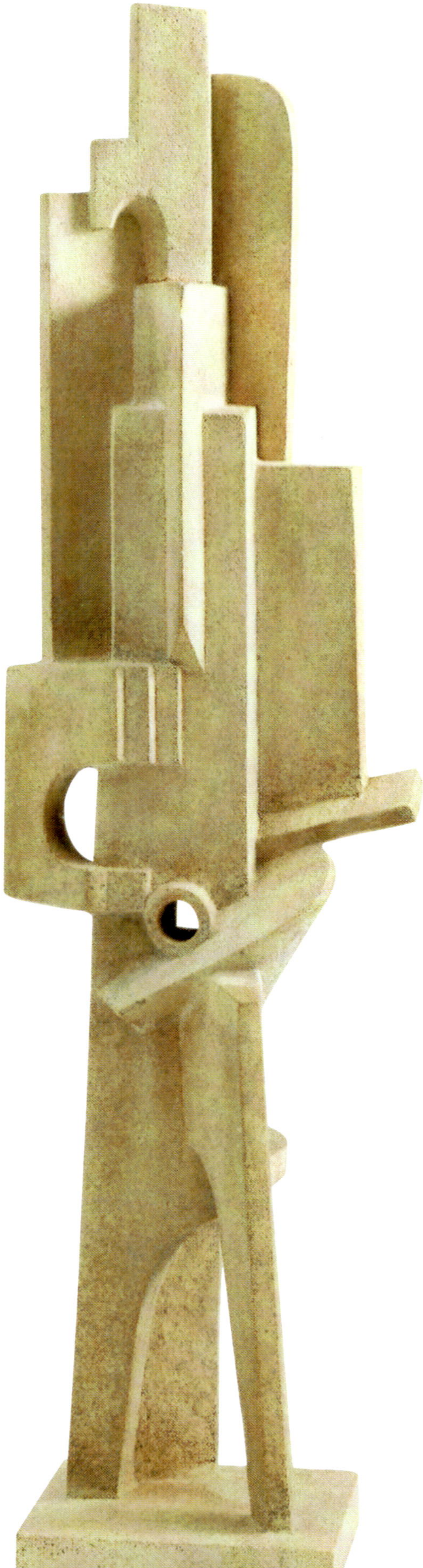

Jacques Lipchitz
(Druskieniki, 1891 – Capri, 1973)

Jacques (Chaim Jacob) Lipchitz was the son of a Jewish building contractor in Lithuania. After initially studying engineering, he was able, with the support of his mother, to move to Paris in 1909 and to devote himself to art, studying at the École des Beaux-Arts and the Académie Julian. Forming friendships with Constantin Brancusi, Amedeo Modigliani, Chaim Soutine, Alexander Archipenko and Diego Rivera, he also met and developed an intense creative relationship with Picasso and Juan Gris. He remained a central figure of the thoroughly international École de Paris until his forced exile to America in 1941. Like many artists of his generation he was attracted to non-European sculptural traditions, and made a study of Scythian sculpture in the Hermitage during a visit to St. Petersburg in 1911.

But it was his encounter with Picasso in 1913 and his discovery of Cubism that was to provide the decisive impetus for the direction his work was to take. From 1916 Lipchitz was represented by the dealer Léonce Rosenberg, who also showed the work of Picasso, Braque, Rivera and Gris. Towards the end of World War I, like Léger and indeed like Picasso himself, he began to feel that experimentation with Cubist form had led him too close to abstraction, and he returned to a more figurative and easily comprehensible, though still Cubist, style.

From the mid-1920s Lipchitz developed a more open and linear style in which voids played an important role. From this time, too, the influence of Surrealism became apparent in his work. After the German invasion of 1940, Lipchitz, like many French-based Modernists, both Jewish and non-Jewish, fled to the South of France and then to America. Lipchitz was well received in America and gained many important commissions there. Though he returned to France in 1946, he continued to be active in America in the post-war years. The events of World War II and the Holocaust quickened his sense of Jewishness, and he was buried in Israel, which he came to regard as his spiritual home.

Jacques Lipchitz,
Man with a Guitar, 1915.
Limestone, 97.2 x 26.7 x 19.5 cm.
The Museum of Modern Art, New York.

Jacques Lipchitz,
Sailor with a Guitar, 1914-1915.
Polished bronze, 77.5 x 29 x 24.5 cm.
Musée National d'Art Moderne,
Centre Georges-Pompidou, Paris.

Jacques Lipchitz,
The Bathers III, 1917.
Stone, height: 71 cm.
Barnes Foundation, Lincoln University,
Merion, Pennsylvania.

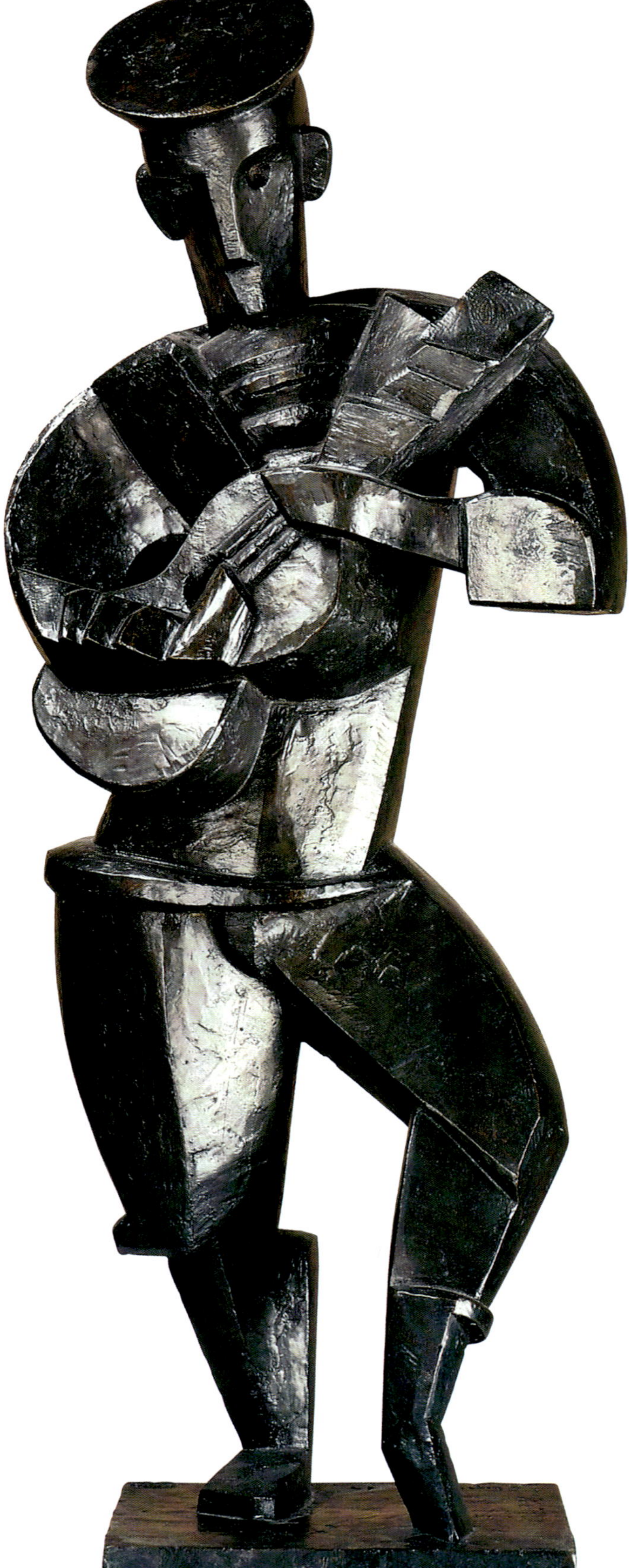

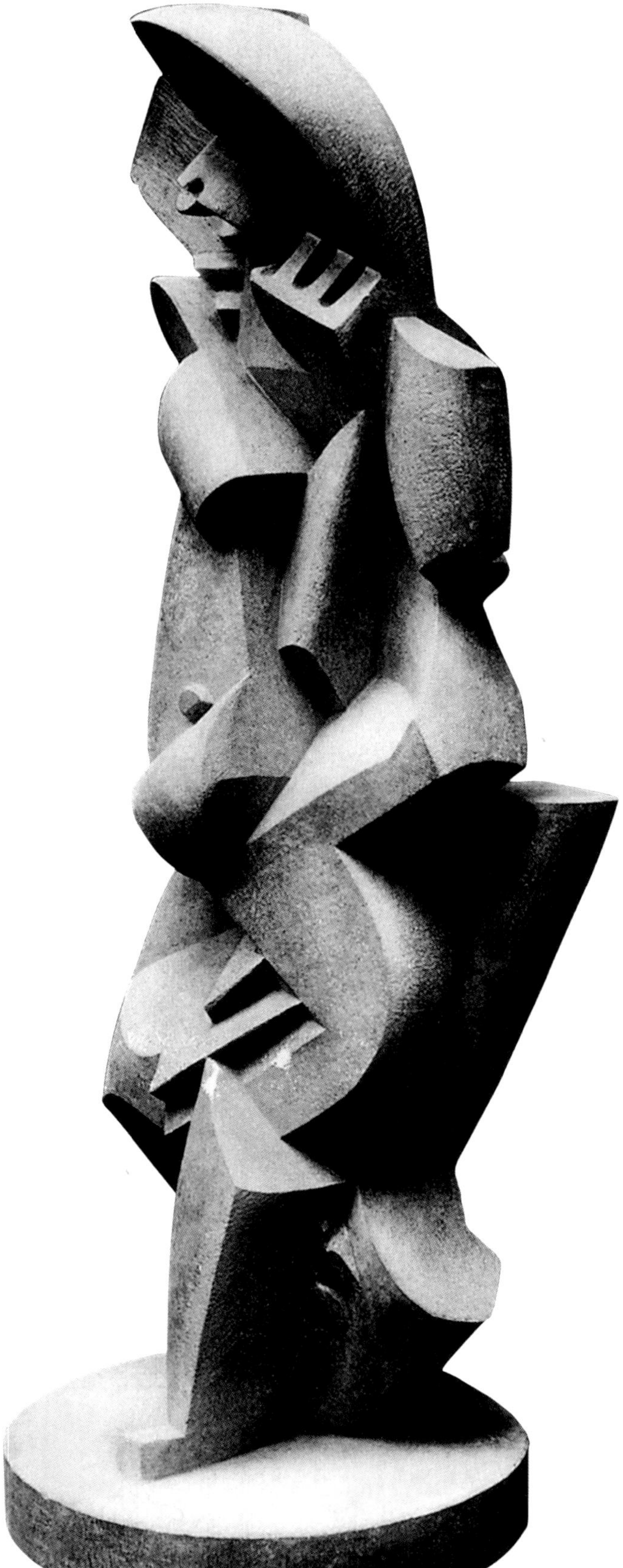

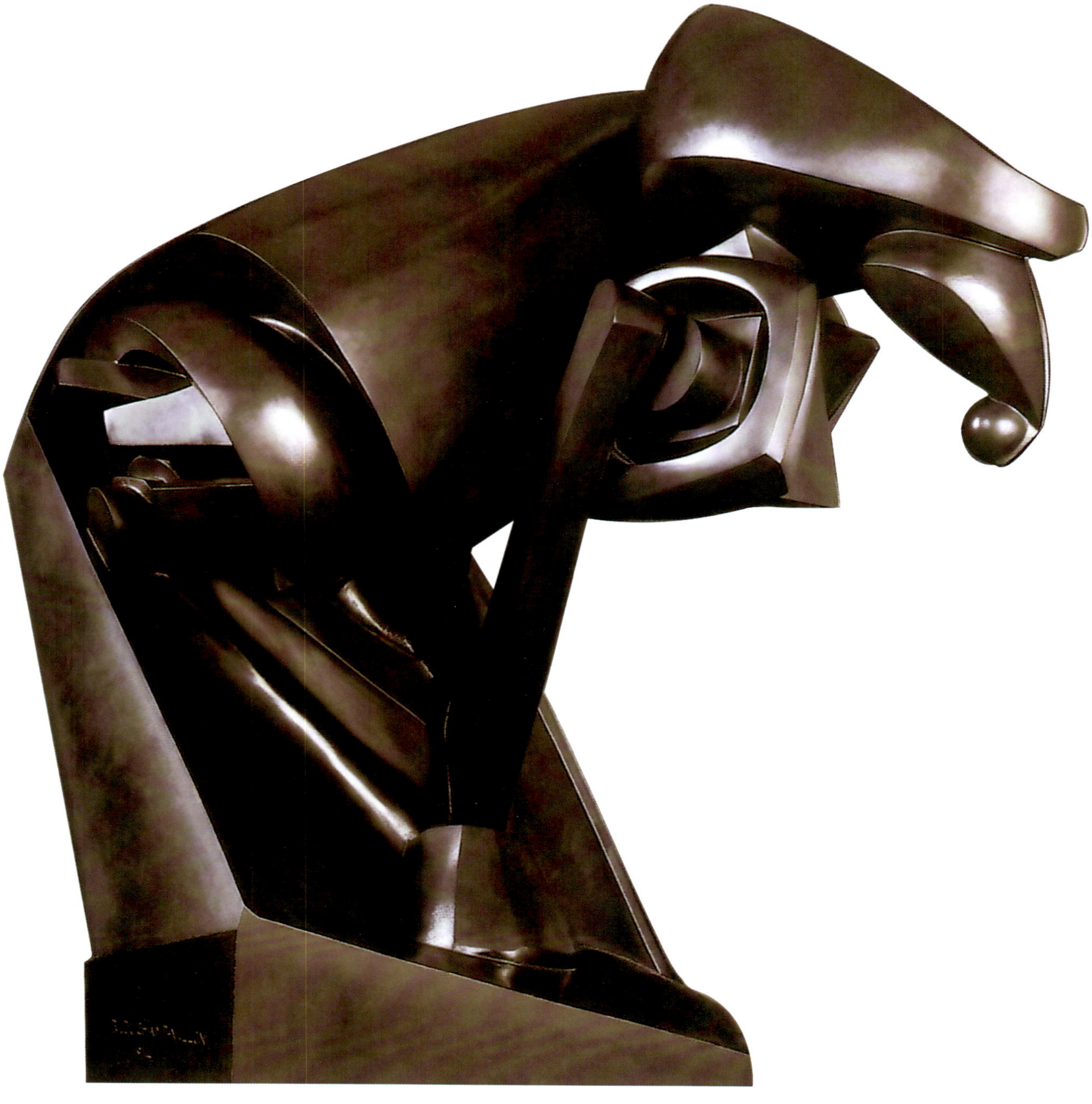

Raymond Duchamp-Villon

(Damville, 1876 – Cannes, 1918)

Raymond Duchamp-Villon was one of the most talented and tragic casualties of World War I in the arts. He died in the final weeks of the war from septicaemia which he contracted while serving as a voluntary auxiliary doctor. Duchamp-Villon was the second of three artist brothers, the eldest being Jacques Villon and the youngest Marcel Duchamp. Duchamp-Villon's studies at the Faculté de Medicine in Paris were interrupted by illness in 1898, and it was while convalescing that he discovered his vocation for sculpture.

Though largely self-taught, he soon attained considerable technical mastery, exhibiting at the fairly traditionalist Salon National and later at the more adventurous Salon d'Automne in a style initially much influenced by Rodin. As with so many artists of his generation, Duchamp-Villon needed to throw off this influence, and Cubism eventually provided the means to do so. In 1906 Duchamp-Villon moved to the district of Puteaux, west of central Paris, where he shared a studio with his brother, Jacques Villon, and with the Czech artist Frank Kupka. After 1910 these studios became a magnet for a group of artists that included Jean Metzinger, Albert Gleizes, Roger de la Frenaye, Henri Le Fauconnier and Fernand Léger. These young artists were all keen to explore the exciting possibilities opened up by the advent of Cubism. They exhibited together at the Salon d'Automne of 1911 and under the group title of Section d'Or at the Galerie La Boétie in 1912.

In the two years that remained to him before the outbreak of war, Duchamp-Villon produced his most innovative and original works. In many ways these works paralleled contemporary work by the Italian Futurists. Like the Futurists, Duchamp-Villon used Cubist devices to represent movement and the dynamism of modern life. His best-known work entitled *The Major Horse* (opposite) was completed while on leave from military service, and was cast in bronze after his death.

Raymond Duchamp-Villon,
The Major Horse, 1914-1976.
Bronze with black polish,
150 x 97 x 153 cm.
Musée National d'Art Moderne,
Centre Georges-Pompidou, Paris.

Raymond Duchamp-Villon,
The Lovers, 1913 (5th cast).
Relief in plaster, 63 x 100 x 11 cm.
Musée National d'Art Moderne,
Centre Georges-Pompidou, Paris.

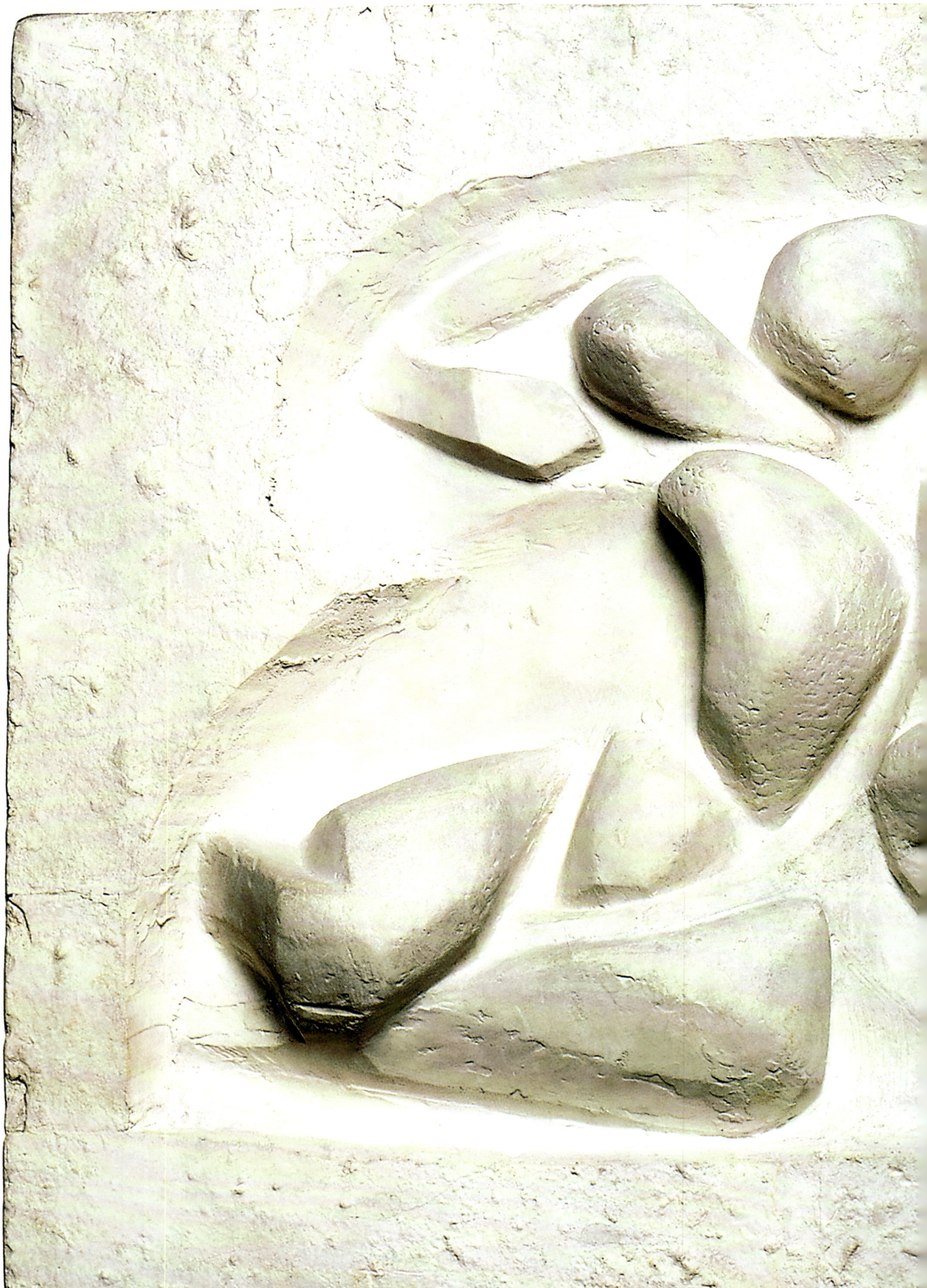

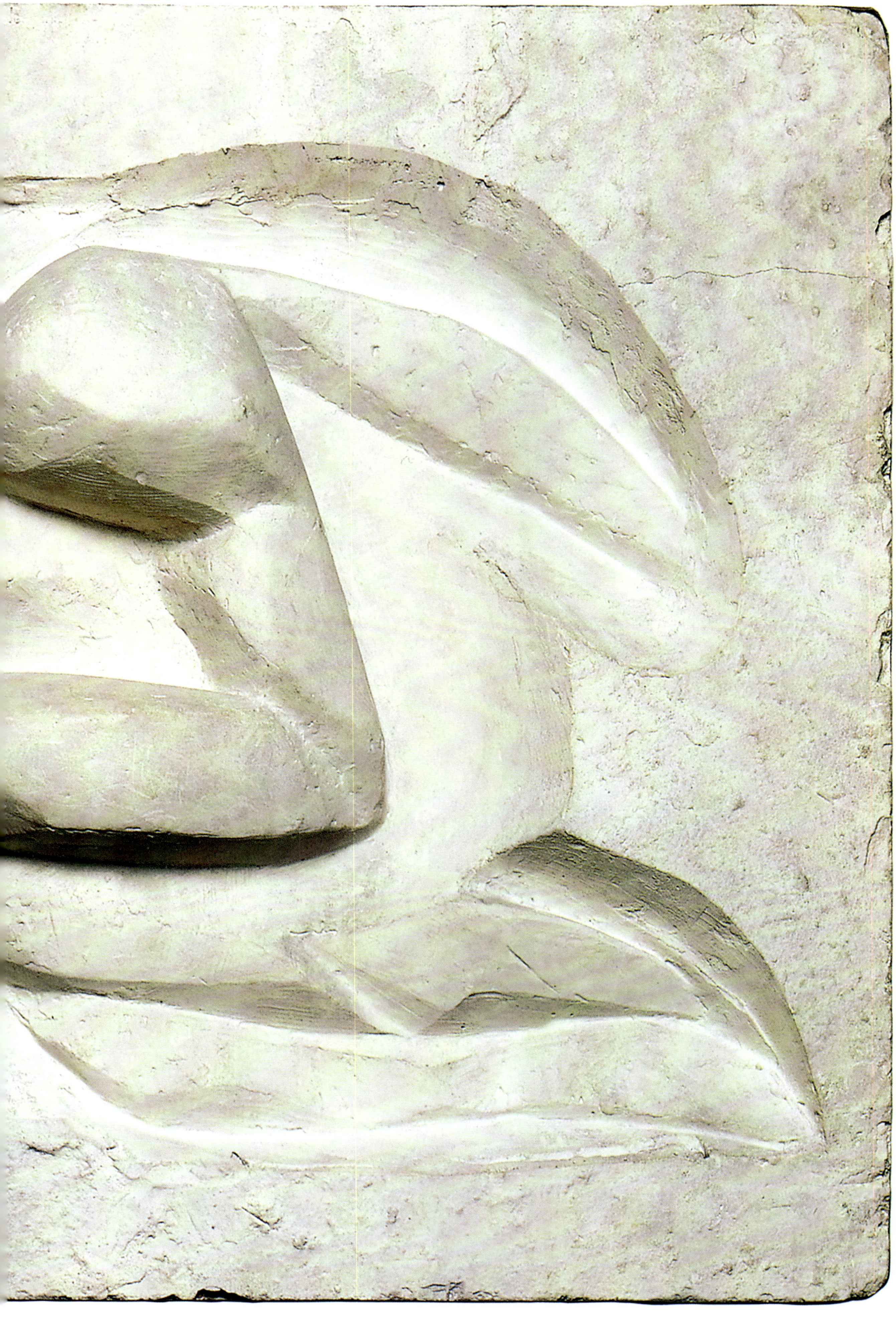

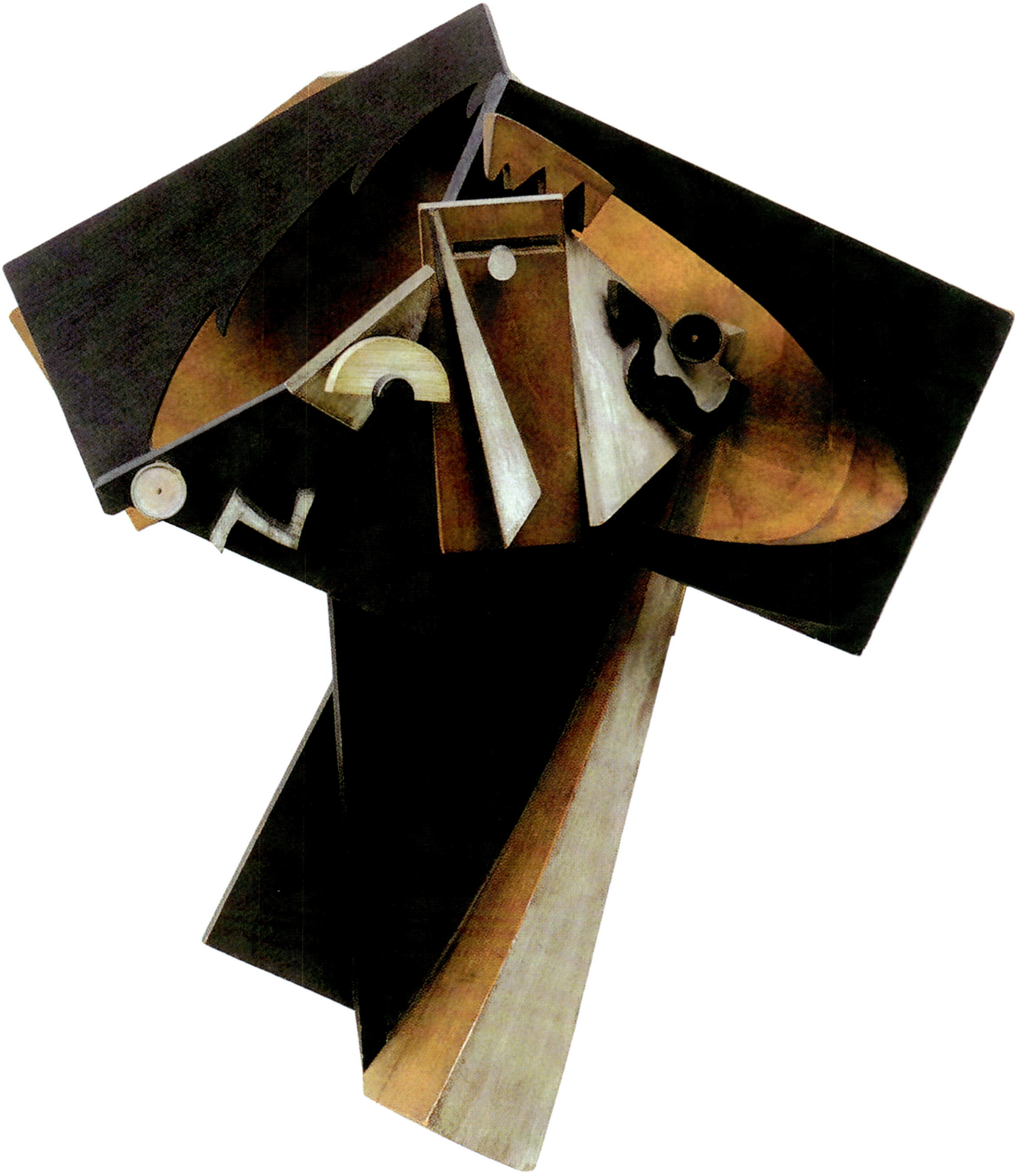

Henri Laurens

(Paris, 1885 – 1954)

Henri Laurens was one of the first sculptors to exploit and develop the innovations of Cubism. His early work, like so much sculpture produced in the early 1900s, was heavily under the influence of Rodin. He turned initially to French Romanesque and Gothic sculpture as a means of escaping the pervasive pathos of Rodin, but a close friendship formed with Georges Braque in 1911, just as Analytical Cubism was giving way to Synthetic Cubism with the introduction of collage, provided a more effective way forward. As one of his legs had been amputated in 1909, Laurens was exempt from the military service that interrupted the career of Braque.

During World War I he expressed his new-found cubist ideas in a series of sculptures entitled "constructions", made in wood and in polychrome plaster, in which he explored the typically Cubist subject matter of fragmented nudes and still lifes of studio clutter (*Bottle and Glass*, 1917 and *Guitar*, 1917-1918). At this time Laurens was represented by the dealer Léonce Rosenberg, along with Picasso, Braque, Gris and Léger. Like most of these he defected from Rosenberg at the end of the war, and moved for a while to the dealer Daniel-Henry Kahnweiler. It was a mark of Laurens' recognition and fashionable status when in 1924 the Russian impresario Serge Diaghilev commissioned him to design the sets for the ballet *Le Train bleu*, set on a beach in the South of France, which combined the music of Darius Milhaud, costumes by Coco Chanel and a curtain by Picasso.

From the mid-1920s Laurens moved away from the angularity of his Cubist style and adopted a softer, more sensuous and organic style, concentrating on the subject of the female nude.

Henri Laurens,
Head of a Woman, 1915.
Assemblage of painted wood,
50.8 x 46.3 cm.
The Museum of Modern Art, New York.

Henri Laurens,
Grape Basket, 1918.
Painted wood and metal,
68 x 62 x 47 cm.

Henri Laurens,
Construction, Little Head, 1915.
Wood and iron polychrome cover,
30 x 13 x 10 cm.
Musée National d'Art Moderne,
Centre Georges-Pompidou, Paris.

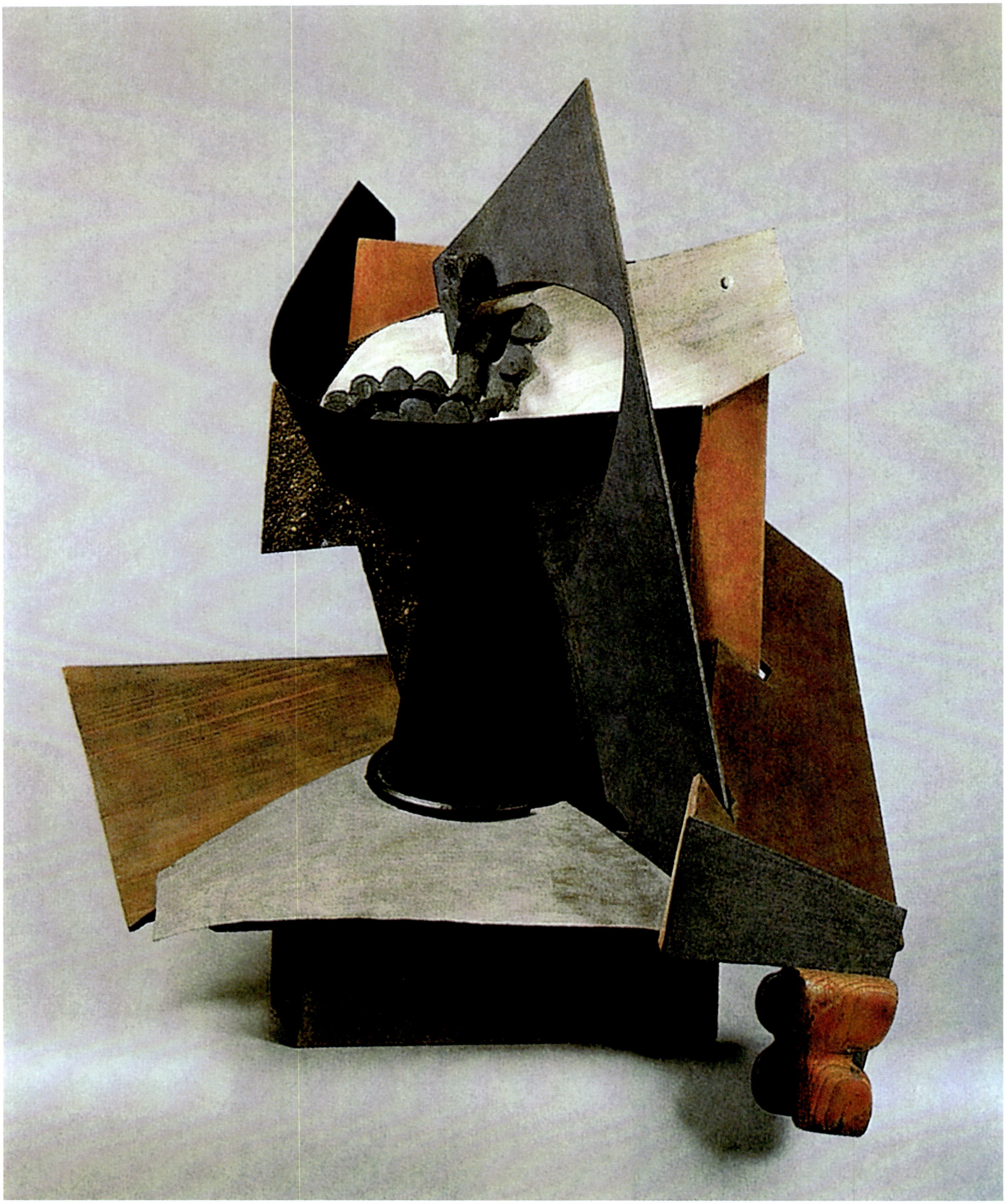

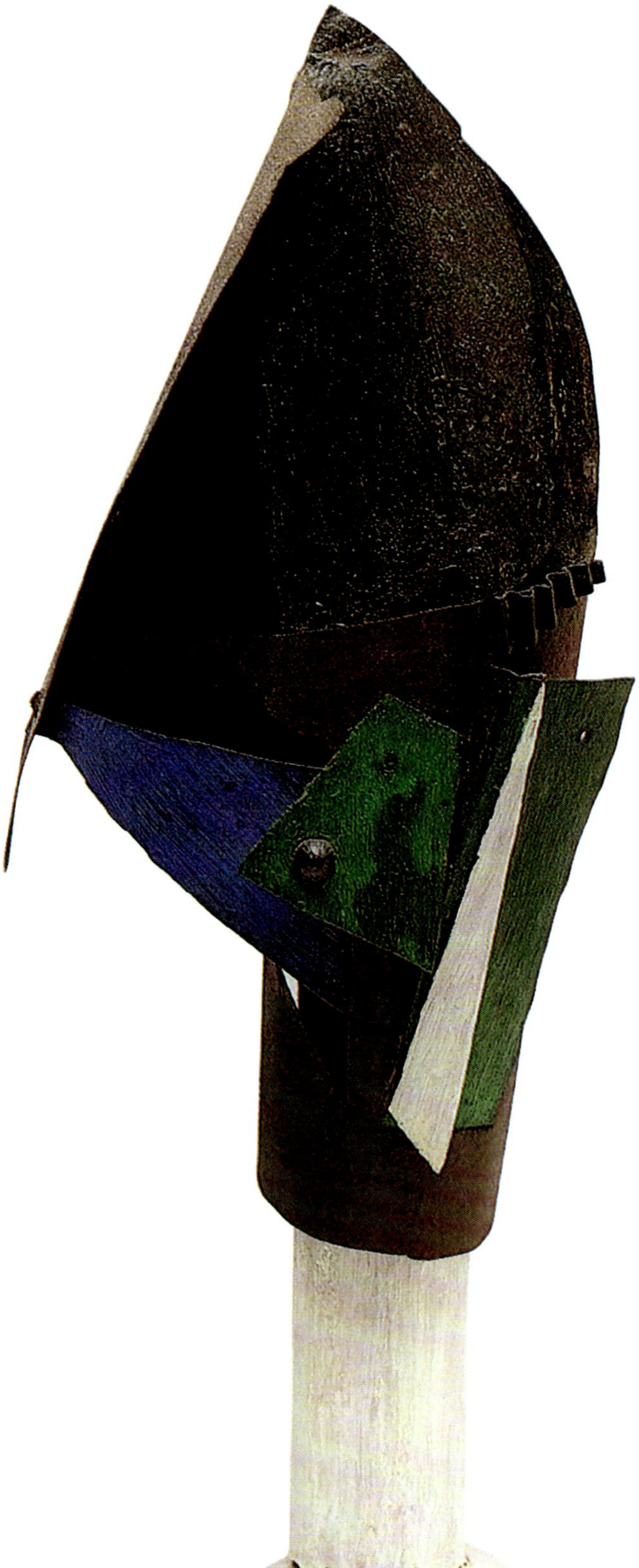

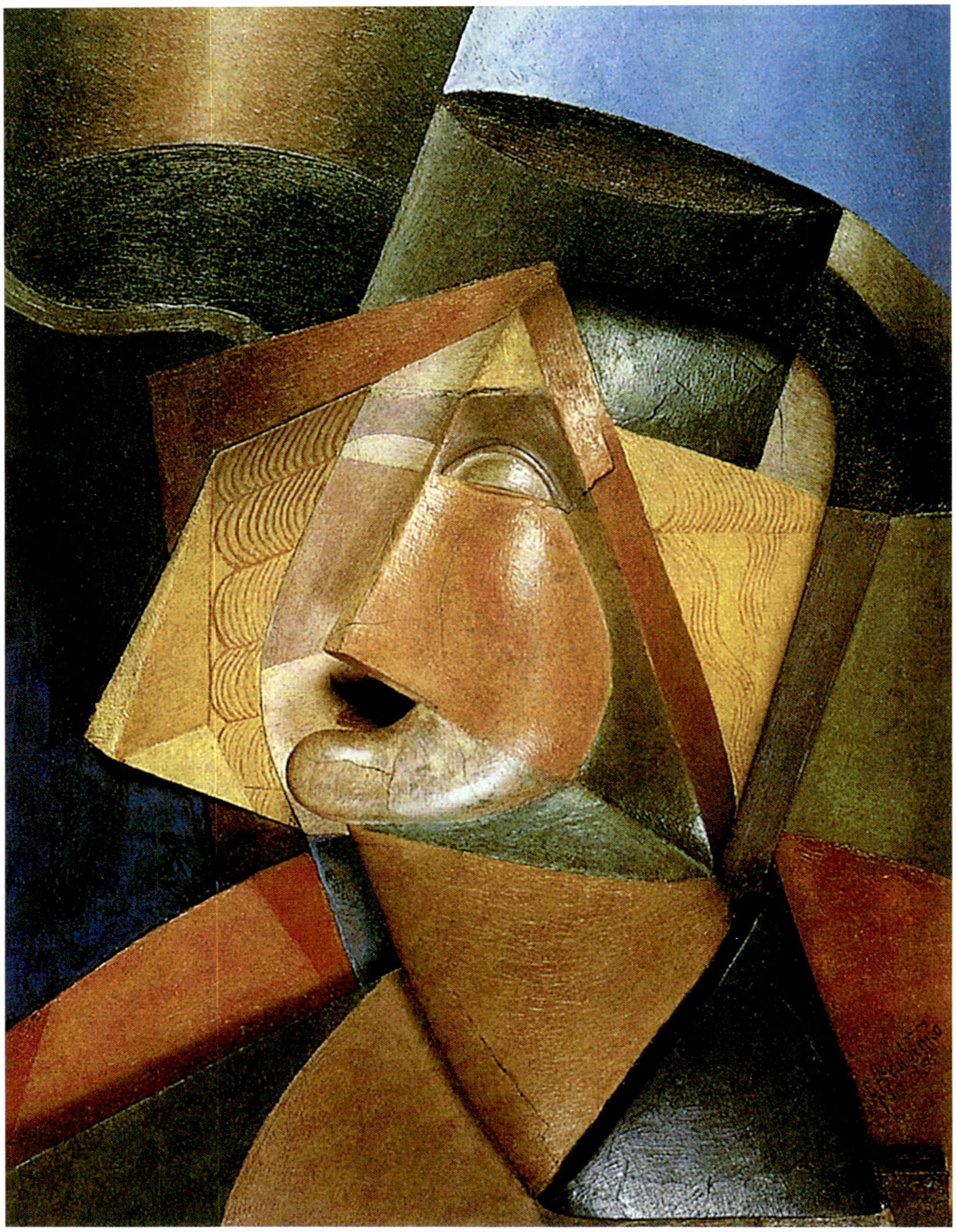

Alexander Archipenko
(Kiev, 1887 – New York, 1964)

Expelled from the Kiev Academy of Fine Arts for criticising the overly academic teaching of its professors, this American of Ukrainian origin settled in Paris in 1908. Quickly disappointed by classical French teaching, he studied the relics in the Louvre on his own. A year later he met Modigliani, Léger, Apollinaire, Cendrars and others at La Ruche. The year 1910 saw his first Cubist exhibition with the Duchamp-Villon brothers, Gleizes, Léger, Le Fauconnier, Metzinger, etc. Then he opened an art school in Paris and participated in the Section d'Or in 1912 along with numbers of other Cubist artists.

The Cubist influence of painters such as Picasso or Braque is visible in his sculptures: like the *papier collé* techniques that he used, his work adheres itself to the goal of illustrating the interpenetration that exists between painting and sculpture, colour emphasising the difference of material, revolutionising the genre from then on (*Medrano II*, p. 178). After all, didn't Archipenko declare, "My painting and sculpture represent a reciprocal connection between the form and colour. The one stresses or diminishes the other. They are unified or contrasted on the visual and spiritual plan. All depends on the aim sought after"?

Shortly before World War I, he participated in the Armory Show in 1913, and his first independent exhibition opened its doors in Berlin. He spent the conflict years in the South of France, along with Cimiez, Matisse, Foujita, Modigliani, etc. In 1923, he settled down with his wife in New York and established another art school. He founded another art school in 1935 in Los Angeles before teaching at the Bauhaus in Chicago upon the urgent request of Maholy-Nagy. Throughout the United States, land of favourable promise in his imagination, he gave many lectures, and his art was the centre of many exhibitions. His wife died in 1957. His last independent exhibition took place in 1964; he died the same year, immediately after having completed his final sculpture: *King Solomon.*

His Cubist period, the most fertile and innovative of his career, lasted from 1909 to 1921. Not without a certain amount of elegance, Archipenko knew how to introduce geometry into his sculpture, giving the human figure, his favourite subject, a revolutionary aspect in sculpture. In addition to his geometric tendencies, Archipenko revived, with his *Medrano II*, polychromic hues in sculpture, forgotten for too long in the mysteries of the Middle Ages. The explosion of the Cubist pictorial surface was redemptive for him, and he devoted himself to giving a rhythm to space. Alternating hollowness and convexity in his work (*Marching Soldier*, p. 179), this sculptor of space actually knew how to master emptiness and make the void his matter of predilection, transforming emptiness into figuration.

Alexander Archipenko,
Woman with a Hat, 1916.
Oil, papier mâché and gauze on wood in a wooden frame, 35.5 x 26.5 cm.
Private collection.

Alexander Archipenko,
Medrano II, 1913-1914.
Iron, wood, glass and oilcloth,
126.6 x 51.5 x 31.7 cm.
Solomon R. Guggenheim Museum,
New York.

Alexander Archipenko,
Marching Soldier, 1917.
Bronze, height: 116.8 cm.
Private collection.

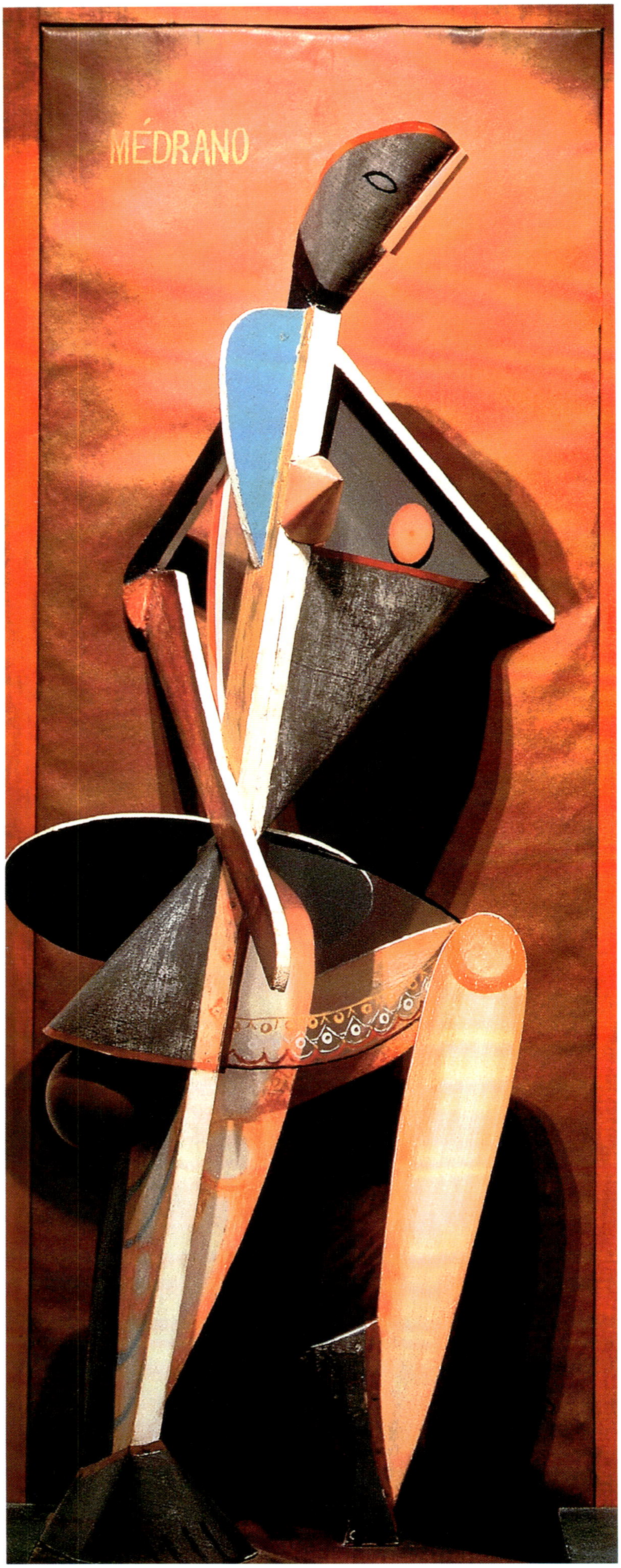
MÉDRANO

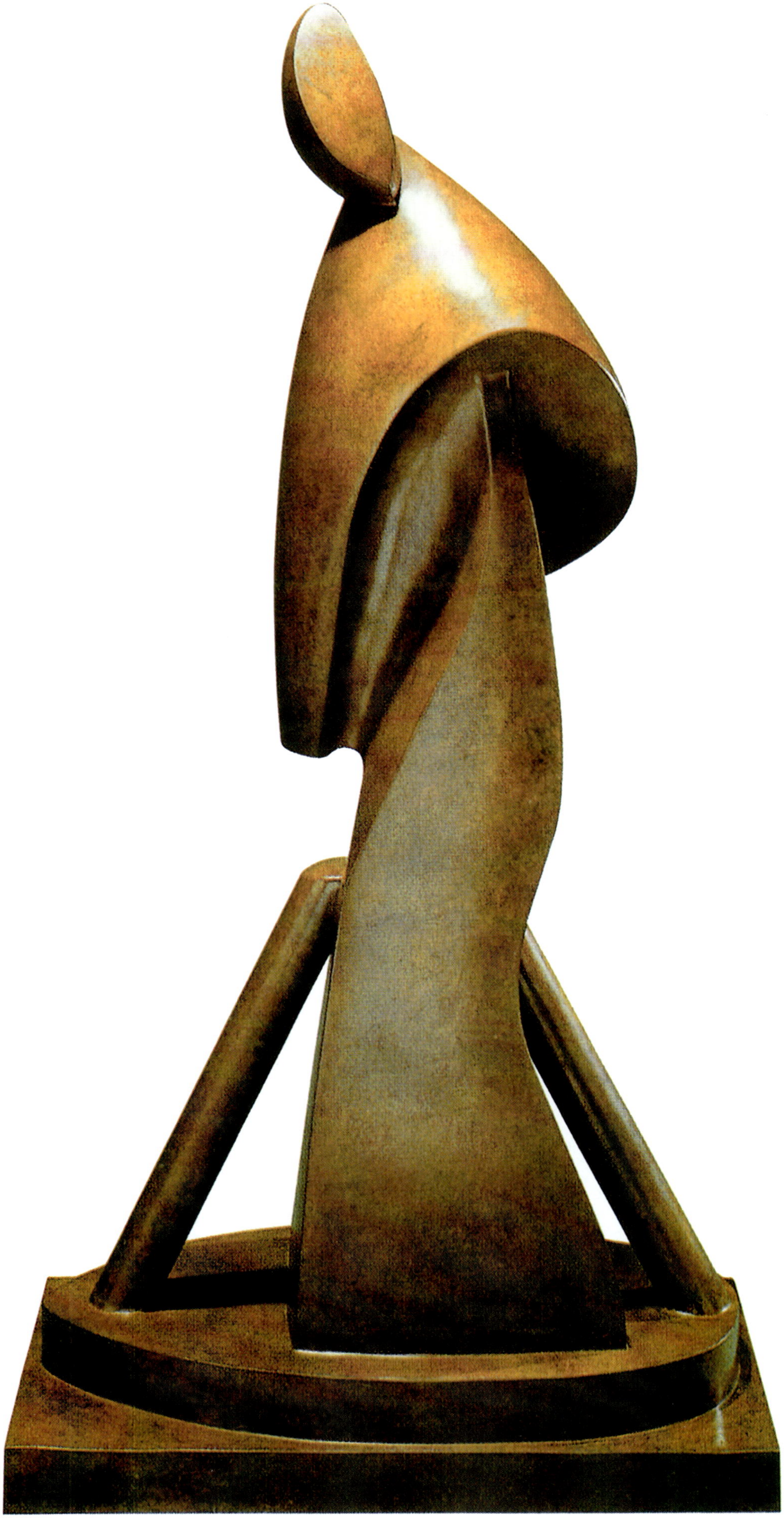

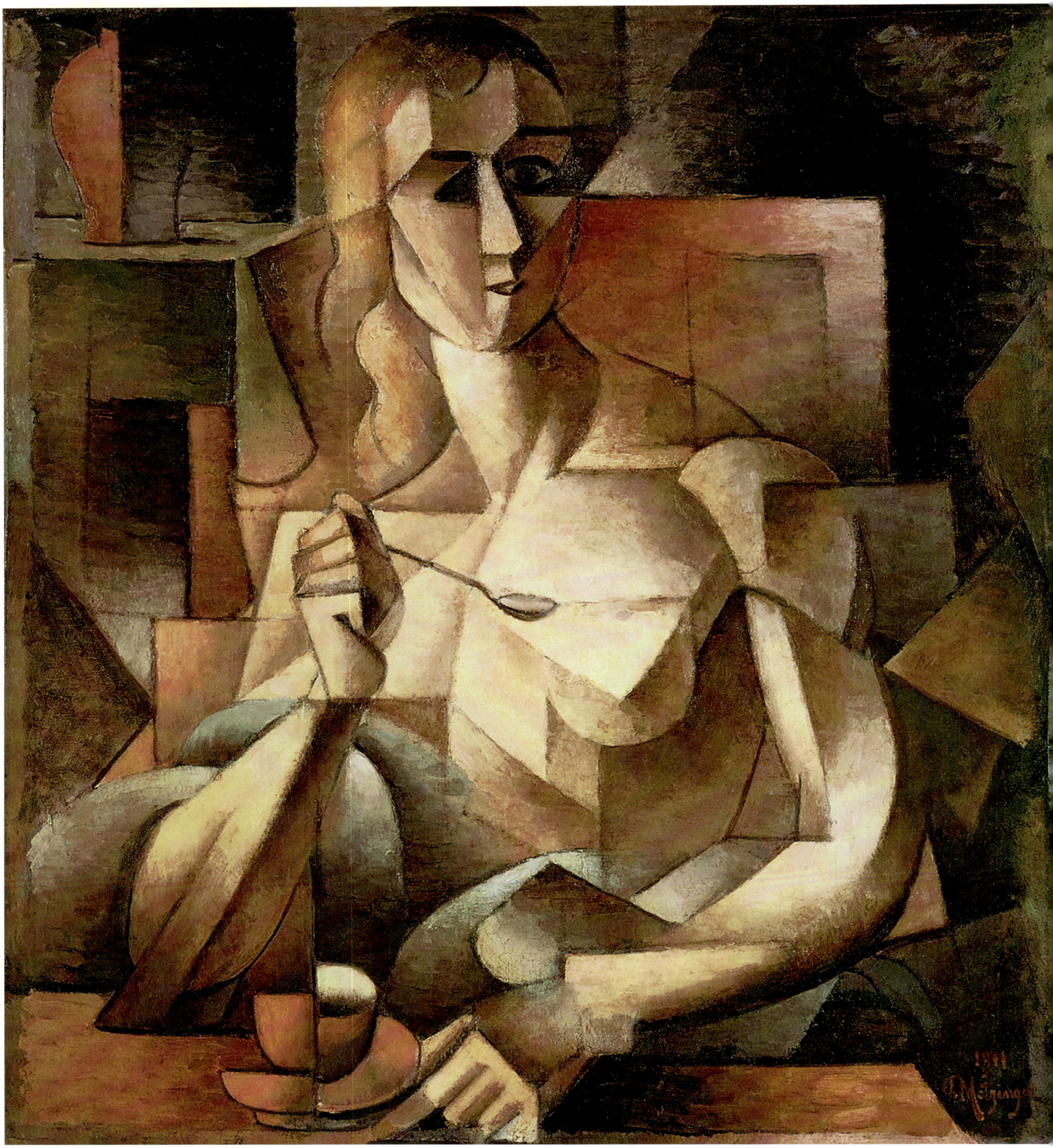
1911

Jean Metzinger

(Nantes, 1883 – Paris, 1956)

Inseparable from the Cubist movement, Jean Metzinger was more of a Cubist theorist than a representative of the style. Co-author with Albert Gleizes of the work *Du Cubisme* (1912), Metzinger enabled wider recognition of this trend by putting words to activities that were going to revolutionise modern art.

Born in Nantes in 1883, Jean Metzinger received an academic education while taking courses of painting with the portrait painter Hippolyte Touront. Although classically trained, he quickly focused his work on the modernity proposed by the Neo-Impressionists, particularly Seurat. This renunciation of gradations and mixed colours also pushed him to experiment with Fauvism for a while.

His first avant-garde works having earned him admission into the Salon des Indépendants, he came to Paris around 1903 to study medicine. He continued to work in order to develop his style and between 1905 and 1908 proposed works that were almost mosaic-like, having from then on the will to depict the world using a multitude of coloured facets.

During the Salon des Indépendants of 1910, he presented his *Portrait of Guillaume Apollinaire*, an important work that earned him a place in the circle of Cubist painters. Indeed, the artistic exchanges he made though contact with the painters Braque, Picasso and Gris had led Metzinger to discover in Cubism a new way of representing reality that perfectly suited his mathematical spirit.

However, his Cubist style always remained less disjointed than that of the movement's pioneers: as a follower of the Section d'Or, Metzinger looked more for a harmony in composition than the total fragmentation of the picture. The following year, *Tea Time (Woman with a Teaspoon)* (opposite) already offered a synthesis of his style: rechristened the "Mona Lisa of Cubism" by the critic André Salmon, this work, still figurative, proposed the reconsideration of a classic theme by placing in the foreground a cup seen from various angles. The quiet atmosphere of this painting seduces by means of the bridge it creates between two periods. Actually, although Metzinger's style had passed through an analytical phase, it now concentrated more on the idea of reconciling modernity with classical subjects, as in *The Bathers*, now preserved in Philadelphia, in which we find his Cubist organisation and monochromes structured by the effects of shadows and light, all revolving around the subject.

Before sharing his reflections on Cubism with Albert Gleizes, Metzinger had published a first work in 1910, *Notes on Painting*, in which he presented his theories. *Du Cubisme* confirmed the theorist's talent and earned him teaching positions in the Académie de la Palette and, later, in the Académie Arénius.

Jean Metzinger,
Tea Time (Woman with a Teaspoon), 1911.
Oil on cardboard, 75.9 x 70.2 cm.
Philadelphia Museum of Art, Philadelphia.

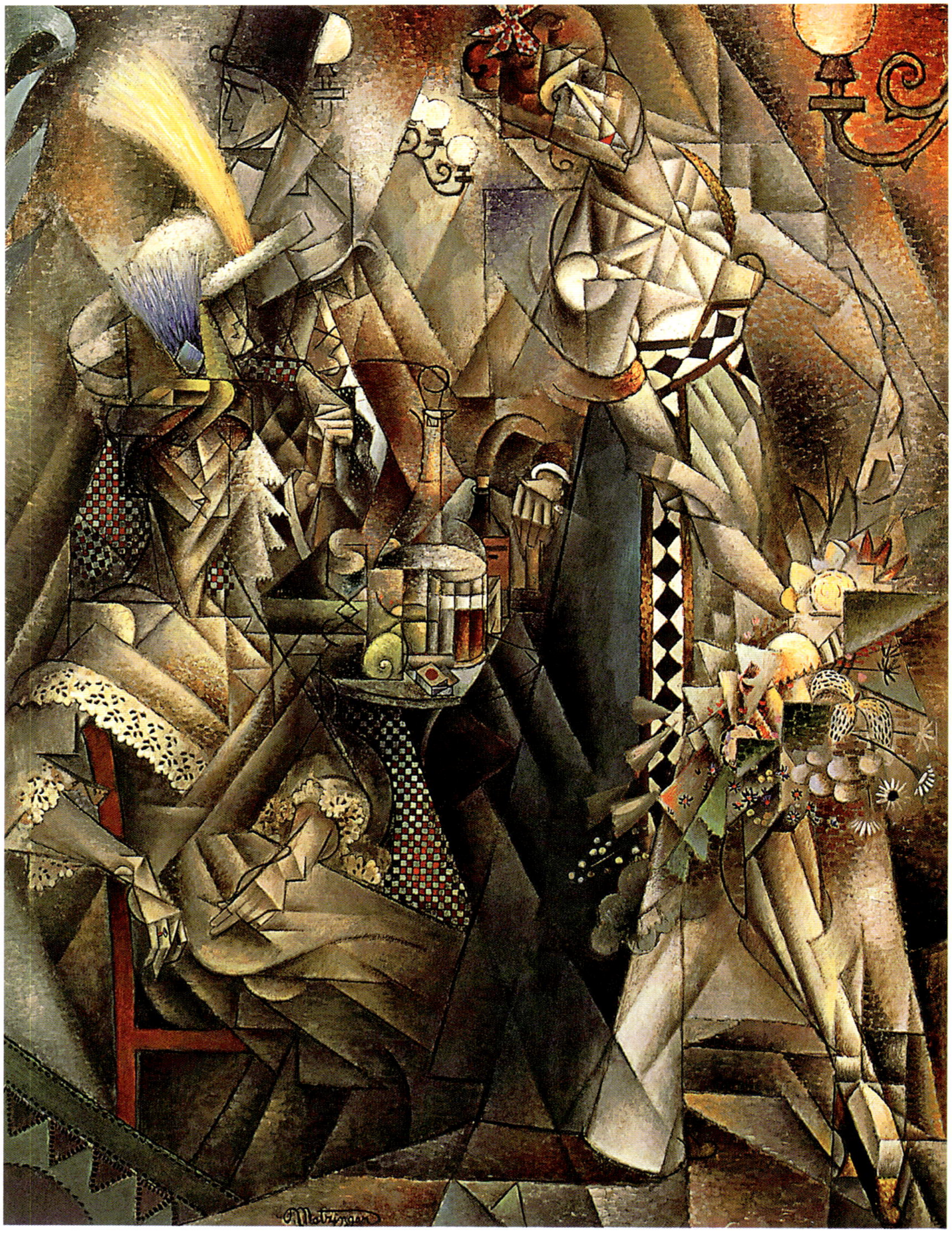

Jean Metzinger,
Dancer in a Café, 1912.
Oil on canvas, 146.1 x 114.3 cm.
Albright-Knox Art Gallery, Buffalo.

Jean Metzinger,
Au Vélodrome (At the Bicycle Race Track), 1912.
Oil and collage on canvas,
130.4 x 97.1 cm.
Peggy Guggenheim Collection, Venice.

Although featured regularly in Parisian salons and aclaimed throughout the world, his best-known works remain those from the period before World War I. The war definitively hindered the development of Metzinger's career, even though he only served in the war until 1915. Detached from Cubism in the 1920s, he lived in the South of France in Bandol, but eventually returned to Paris in 1943. In 1950, he became a teacher at the Académie Frochot, and in 1952 an important retrospective exhibition of his work took place. He died in 1956.

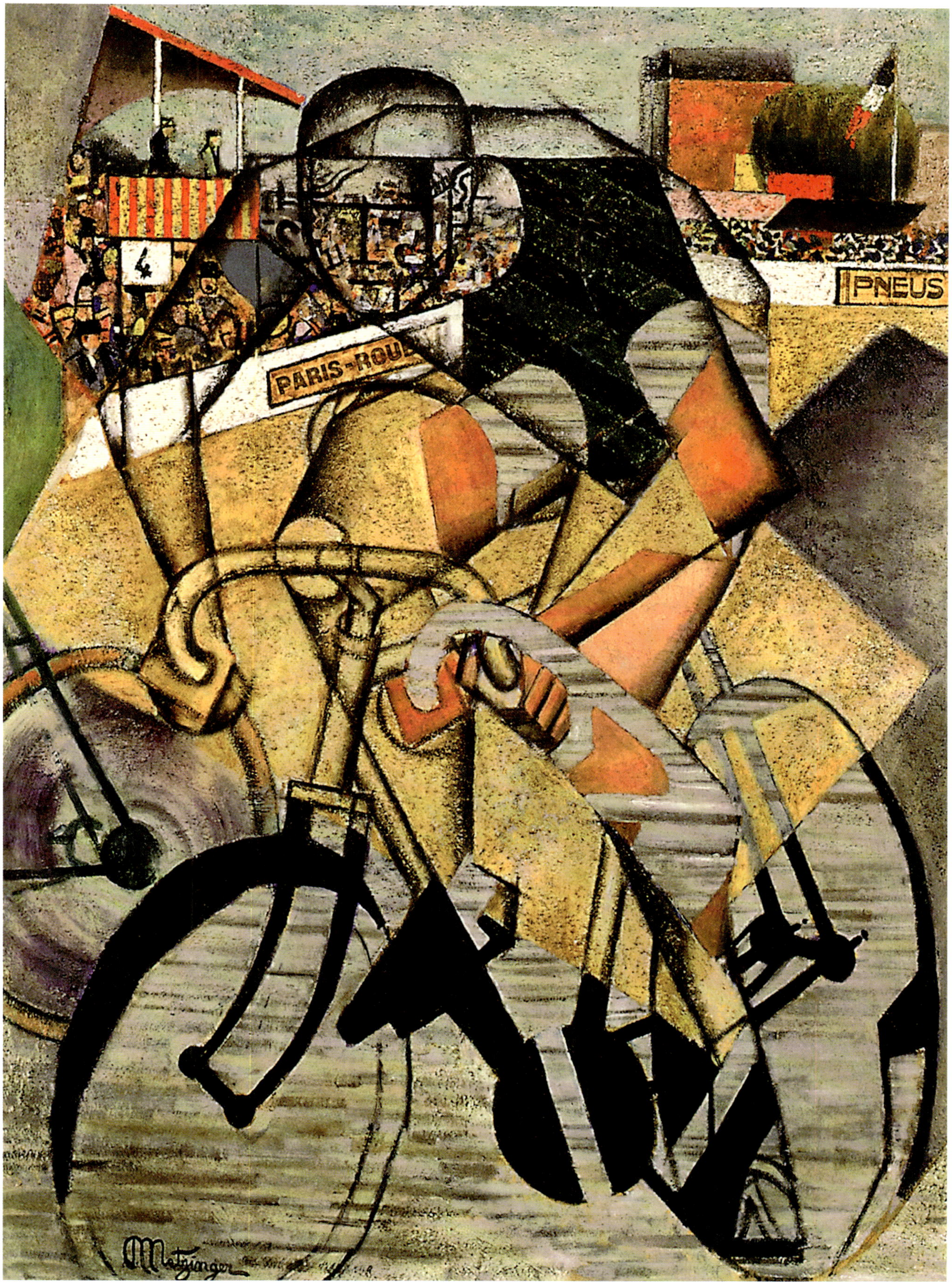
PNEUS
PARIS-ROU
4

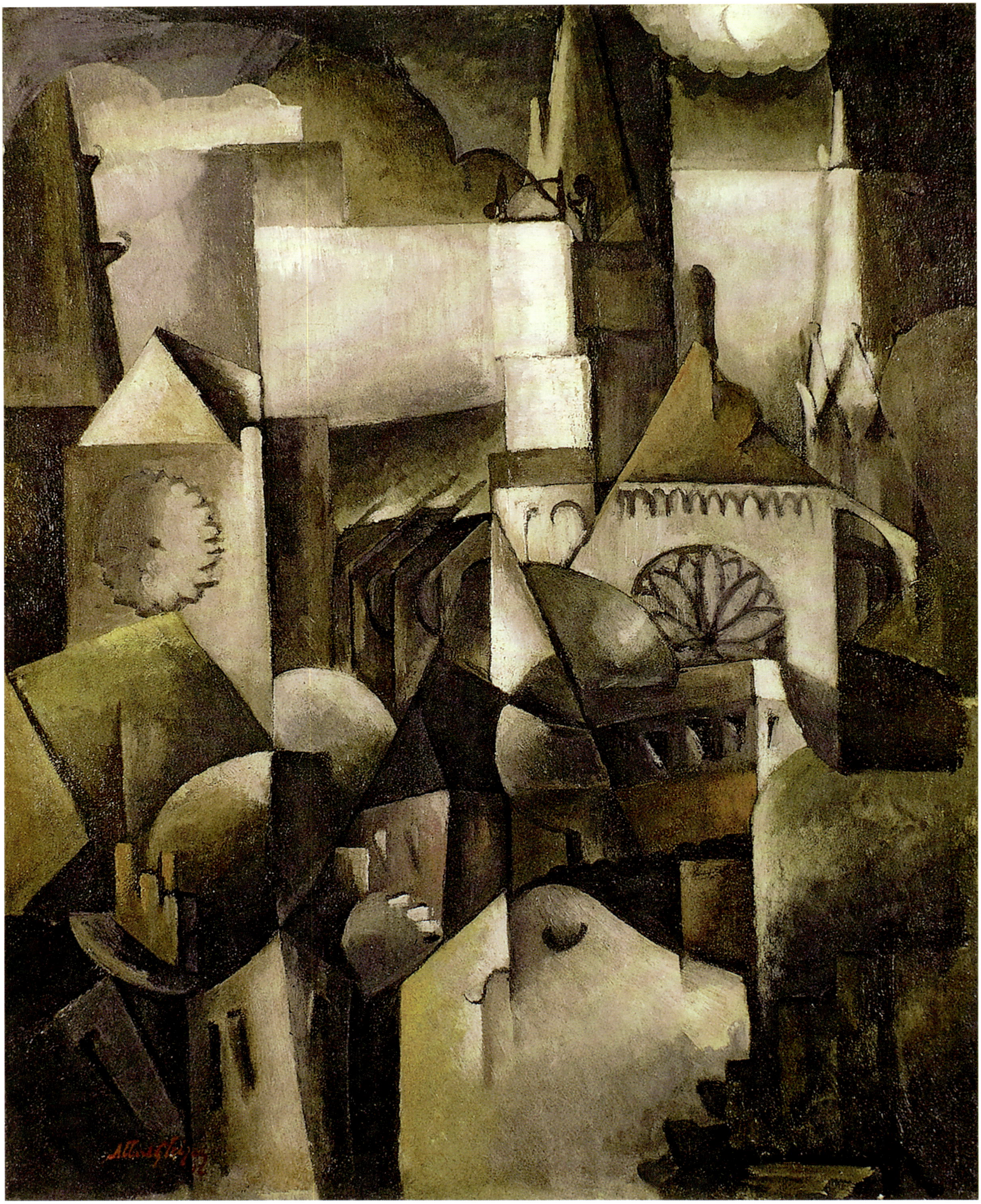

Albert Gleizes

(Paris, 1881 – Saint-Rémy-de-Provence, 1953)

Having learned about drawing through his father's work designing motifs for the textile industry, Albert Gleizes, nephew of the 1875 Prix de Rome winner Léon Comerre, really learned to paint, teaching himself, when he was about twenty years old. As with many artists of this period, his first paintings betray an Impressionistic influence, in particular that of Pissarro or Sisley, but Gleizes's admiration for Cézanne and his continued practice of drawing techniques quickly developed his style. Although landscapes remained for a long time his genre of preference, work on forms, volumes and various points of view testifies to care and particular interest. In 1909, Pierre Jean Jouve's portrait by Henri Le Fauconnier directed him in a decisive way. This painting and Cubism, still barely classified as a unique style for some time after the appearance of Picasso's *Demoiselles d'Avignon*, came to be nourishing sources of power in his work.

In 1912, Gleizes published, along with Jean Metzinger, *Du Cubisme*, a work that definitively established the artist as a leading theorist for the movement. During the years which followed, Gleizes settled down in New York and made several journeys to Barcelona, where he collaborated on Picabia's periodical, *391*. During this period, his paintings, which had been characterised by greys and chestnut browns, monochromic and muted tones, began to show experiments with a variety of tints and the light of colours (*Study for "Hunting"*, p. 186)

After his return to France at the end of the 1920s and into the 1930s, Gleizes developed works that were gigantic in size and worked projects such as the architectural ornamental paintings for Léonce Rosenberg's mansion in 1930 and decorations for a show at the Tuileries in 1938.

This tendency to monumentality was accompanied by the evolution of his style that tended more and more towards large formats. Over the years, geometrical representation in his paintings was transformed into mere representational suggestion, ending in the rotations of energetic curves—reminiscent of the concentric disks of Delaunay—that led the artist to the brink of abstraction. Already in 1931, Gleizes had joined the group Abstraction-Création.

Albert Gleizes,
Chartres Cathedral, 1912.
Oil on canvas, 73.6 x 60.3 cm.
Sprengel Museum Hannover, Hanover.

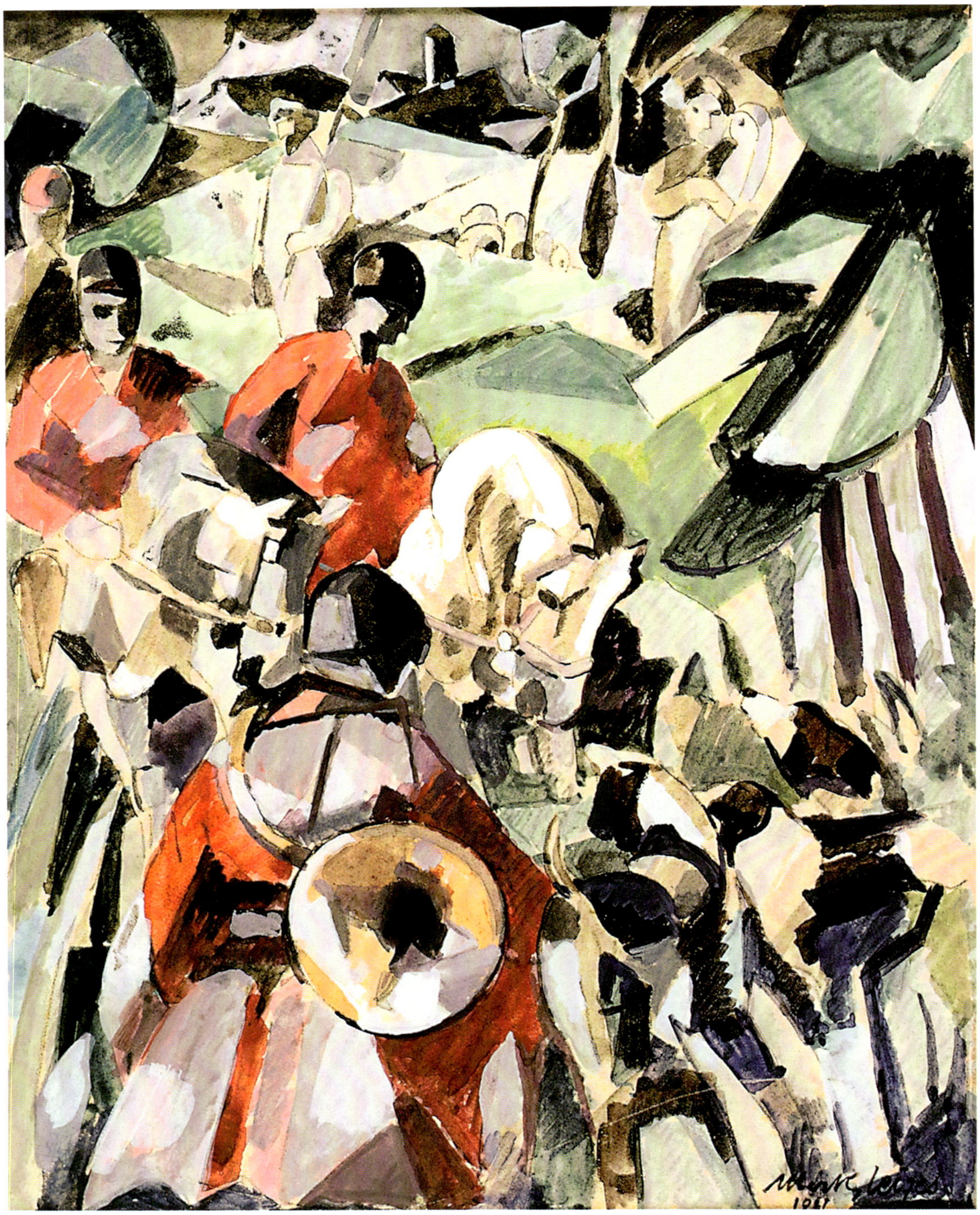

Albert Gleizes,
Study for "Hunting", 1911.
Pencil, watercolour, gouache, ink and wash painting on paper fixed on cardboard, 20.2 x 16.2 cm.
Musée National d'Art Moderne, Centre Georges-Pompidou, Paris.

Albert Gleizes,
Portrait of Jacques Nayral, 1911.
Oil on canvas, 161.9 x 114 cm.
Tate Modern, London.

Gleizes's work became absorbed, at the same time, with a certain religious fervour that he developed by establishing in his villa Moly-Sabata in Sablons an association of artists who shared the ambition of returning to art the notion of sacredness by avoiding the attractions of industrial production, which had, however, originally been a point of origin for his work. Fifty-seven etchings illustrating the *Pensées* of Pascal, which he created three years before his death, bear invaluable testimony to this late-discovered faith and remain impressive samples of the body of work that visionary Guillaume Apollinaire called "the unlimitedness of things".

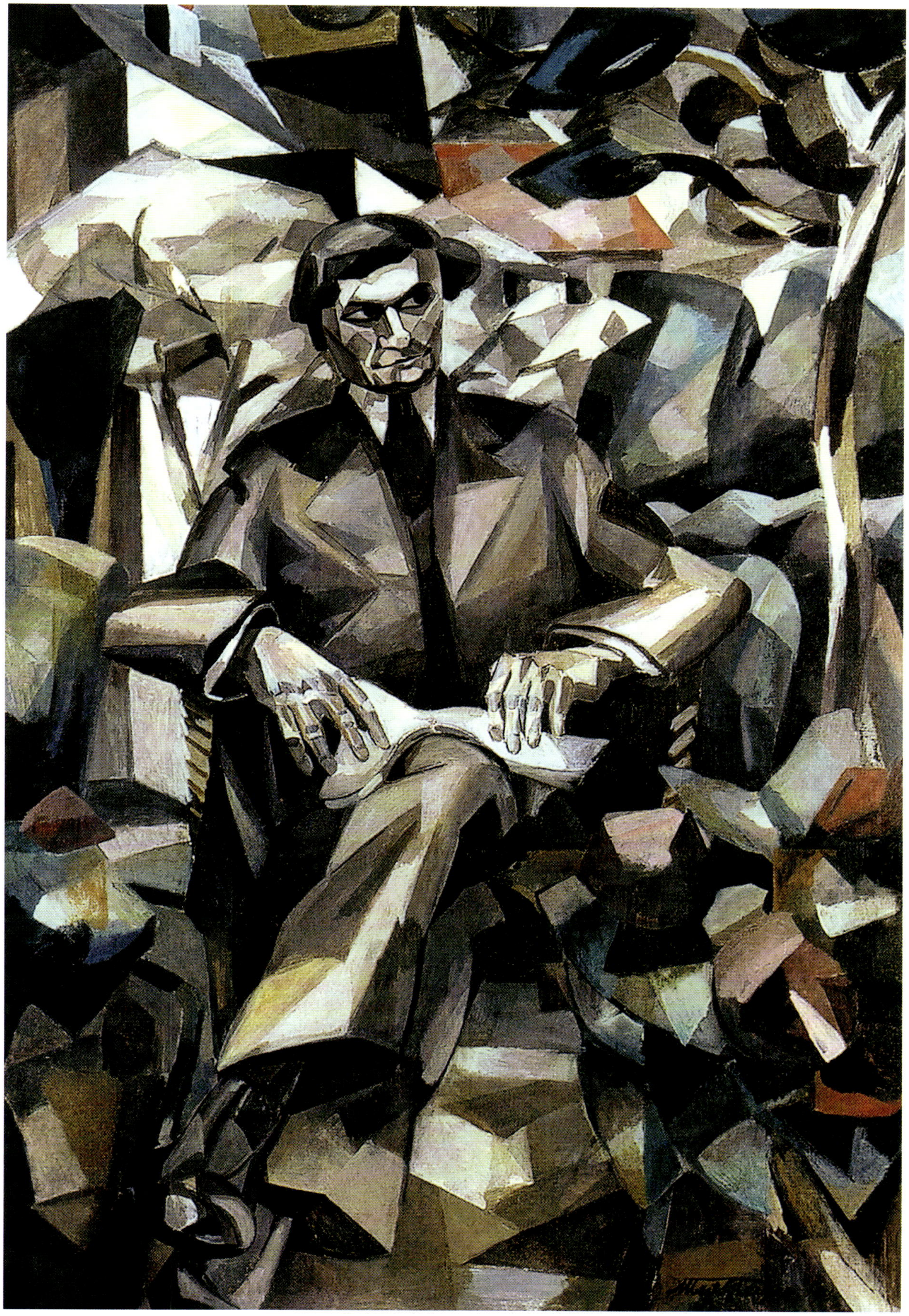

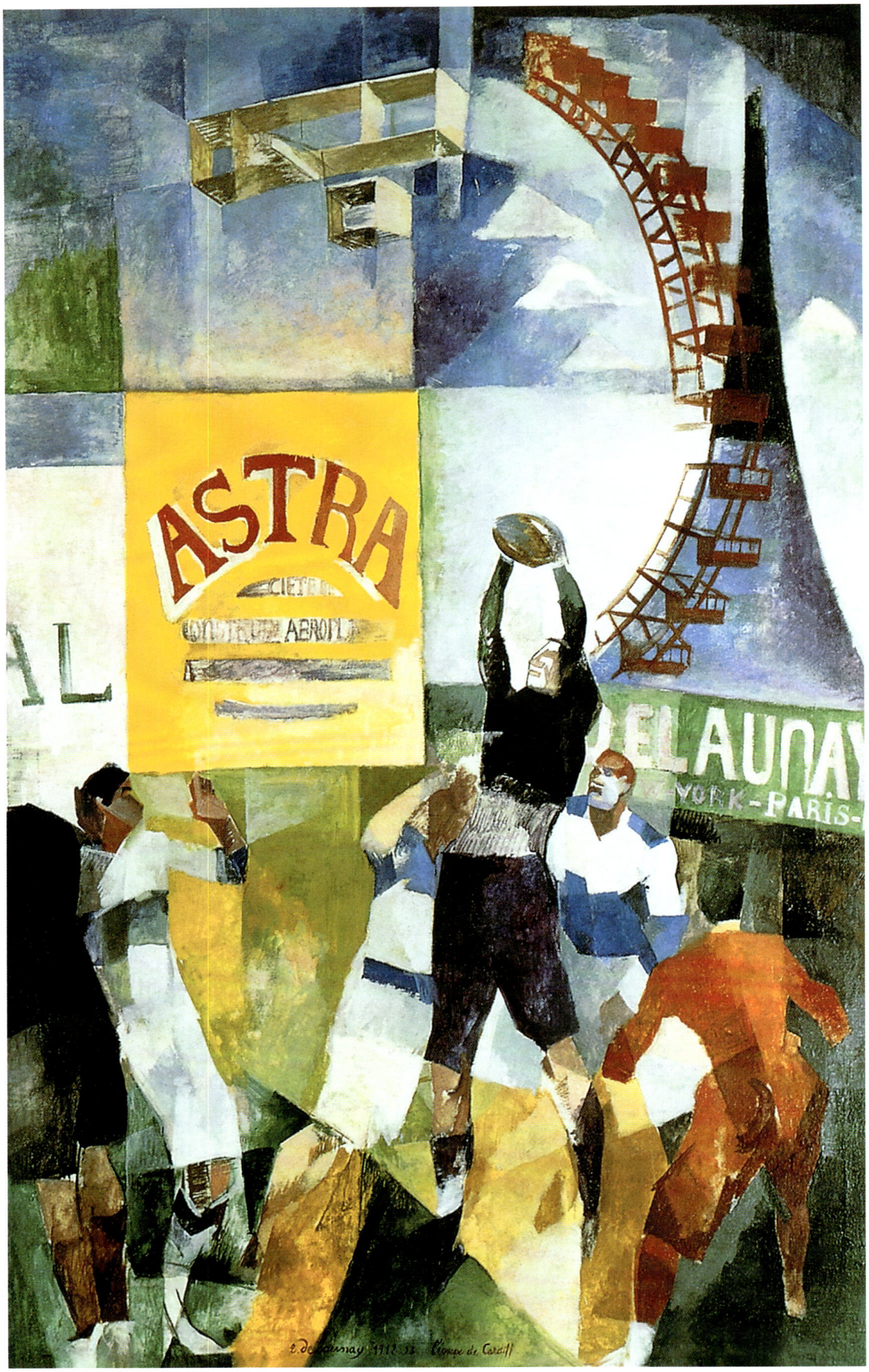
ASTRA
AEROPL
AL
ELAUNAY
YORK-PARIS-

Robert and Sonia Delaunay

(Paris, 1885 – Montpelier, 1941 and Gradiesk, 1885 – Paris, 1979)

The year 1909 marked the meeting of Robert Delaunay and Sonia Terk and the confluence of two lives that were never to part. Both grew in a suffocating bourgeois milieu, from which their artistic expressions allowed them to escape. His parents divorced, Robert Delaunay was educated by his mother's sister. Brought up in St. Petersburg by her maternal uncle, whose name she adopted, Sonia Terk arrived in Paris in 1905, having acquired an artistic education in Germany. At this time, Robert Delaunay had already created his first Post-Impressionist paintings, which blended the influences of Gauguin and the Pont-Aven School together with the pointillism of Seurat.

For some years before their first encounter, the artists evolved parallel to each other, similar to the parallel curves that later became characteristic of their paintings. Robert Delaunay's interest in the work of Seurat inevitably led him to experiment with colours and study the chromatic theories of Chevreul. In 1907, the painter discovered the Cubism of Braque and Picasso, and he began to associate with other artists for inspiration, including Metzinger, Léger and Le Fauconnier.

Registered with the Académie de la Palette, a regional educational authority, upon her arrival in Paris, Sonia Terk presented her first personal exhibition in 1908 at the gallery of Wilhem Uhde, whom she married in order to become a naturalised French citizen. The two artists soon met through their mutual connection with the gallery, and the young lady divorced Uhde to marry Robert Delaunay, whose child she was already carrying. Their union produced little Charles, but also a new artistic interpretation of Cubism, which Apollinaire called "orphism". In this period Robert Delaunay, whose work now betrayed a Cézanian imprint, began his series of prints based on the monuments of Paris (*Eiffel Tower*, p. 19), which marked the dawn of his theories on colour.

Then, having participated in the scandalous exhibition in Room 41 at the Salon des Indépendants of 1911, Robert Delaunay began his series of *Windows* (*Window*, p. 190) and *Circular Disks* (*Circular Forms: Sun and Moon*, p. 191). Less intellectual than that of Gleizes, his artistic approach was essentially operatic, and the rhythmic dynamics of his painting often echo the Futurism that was developing at the same time in Italy. Within this bubbling European mix, where artistic movements multiplied as much as they diversified, Delaunay became acquainted with Expressionism through Klee and Kandinsky and began participating in the exhibitions of the group Der Blaue Reiter.

The work of Sonia Delaunay translates her support of and her active participation in the development of these theories of colour (*Electric Prisms*, p. 45). Driven by the vibrations

Robert Delaunay,
The Cardiff Team (Third Representation), 1913.
Oil on canvas, 326 x 208 cm.
Musée National d'Art Moderne, Centre Georges-Pompidou, Paris.

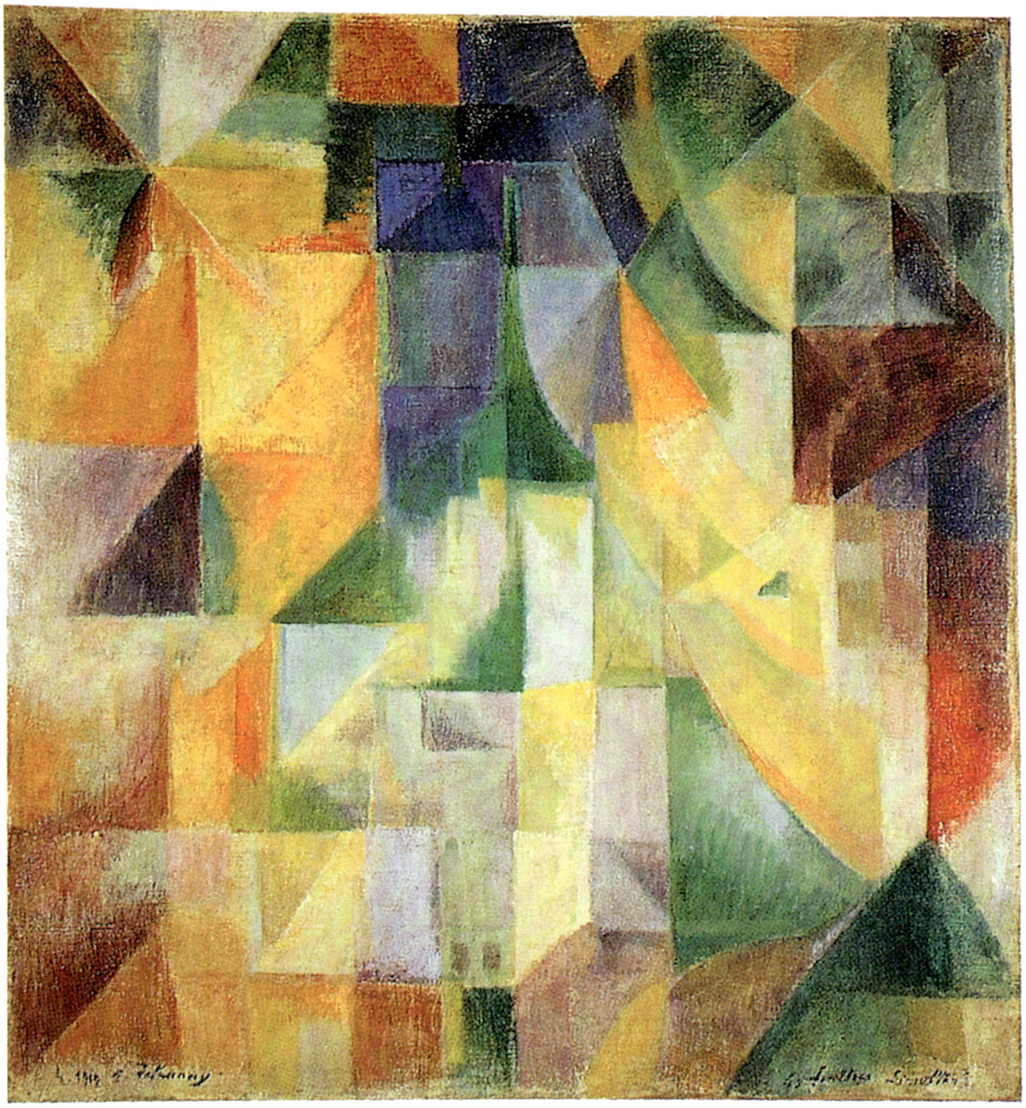

of hues and *Contrastes Simultanés (Simultaneous Contrasts)* (pp. 42-43), the works of the Delaunays evolved towards abstraction in such harmony that it is often difficult to separate and differentiate between their paintings. In a new victory of modernity over classicism, the Delaunays replaced line and shade with the brightness of pure colour, the frank opposition transcending conventional limitations of painting and enabling their compositions to create new forms.

Considering the traditional distinction that separated decorative from fine arts too strict, Sonia Delaunay translated these theories into the decorative arts by creating motifs for objects and fabrics. In 1925, she presented at the International Exposition of Modern Decorative and Industrial Arts beside the dressmaker Jacques Heim, "The Simultaneous Boutique". This aspect of her work, which satisfied her ambition by giving her the opportunity to translate links between paintings and garments, influenced fashion in a

Robert Delaunay,
Window, 1912.
Oil on canvas, 92 x 86 cm.
Morton G. Neumann Collection, Chicago.

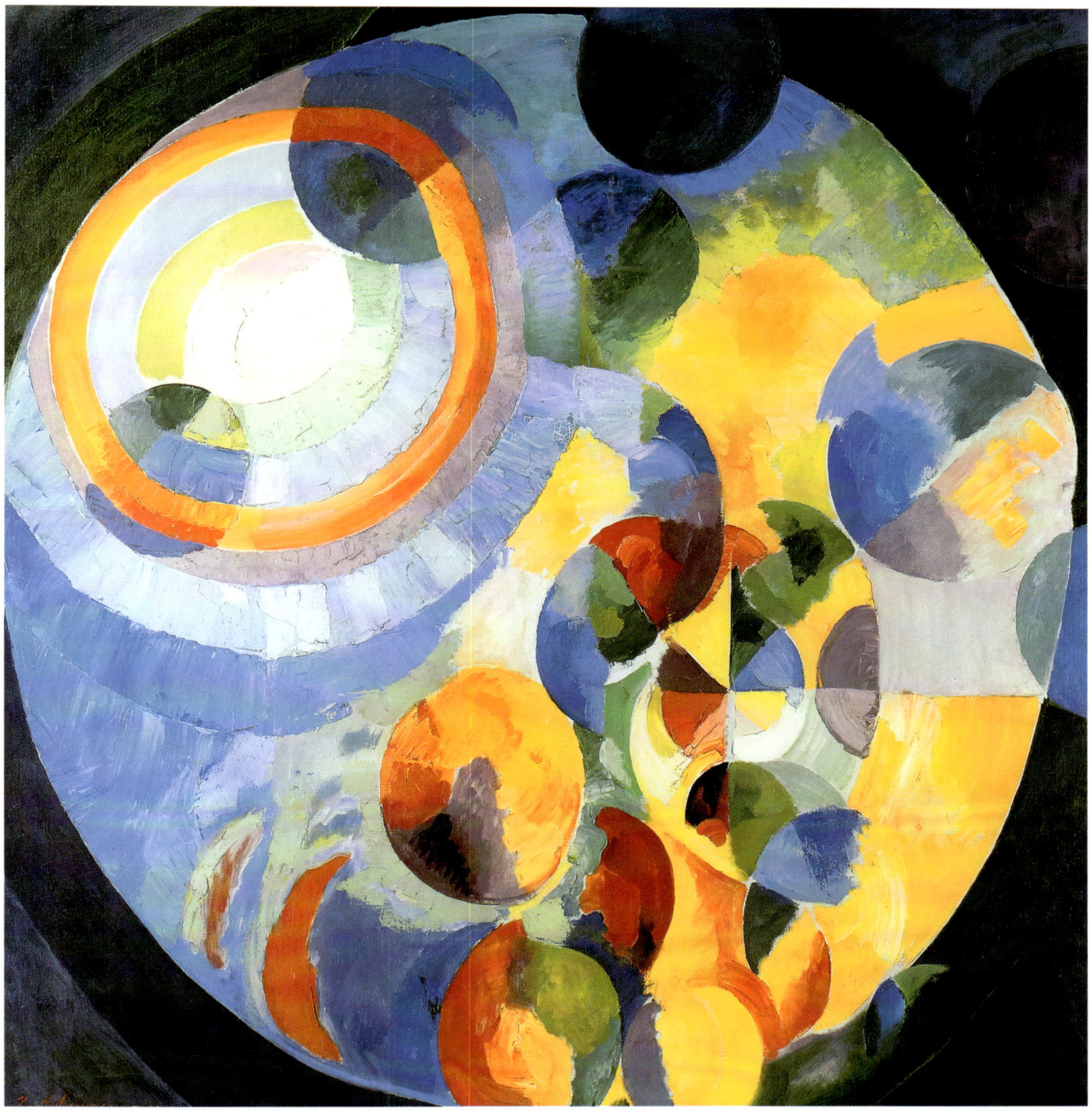

considerable way. In the early 1930s, Sonia Delaunay returned to traditional painting, but, as for a number of artists, the art of the Delaunays always demanded more space to develop. Together, they created wall decorations for a pavilion at the World's Fair of 1937 (a pavilion made of iron rods and open spaces) and transposed the surfaces of their paintings into monumental reliefs using mixed materials: cement, cork, sand, etc. The experiment was repeated the following year.

After the death of Robert Delaunay, Sonia Delaunay continued to exploit this variety of disciplines, painting costumes, set decorations, textiles and canvases, following until the end the path that had led to abstraction that they had drawn together. Nevertheless, through all the many facets of her art, she also answered the call, more personal, to demonstrate that colours can go beyond optical theories to express the essence of multiple aspects of life.

Robert Delaunay,
Circular Forms: Sun and Moon, 1912.
Oil on canvas, 200 x 197 cm.
Kunstmuseum, Zurich.

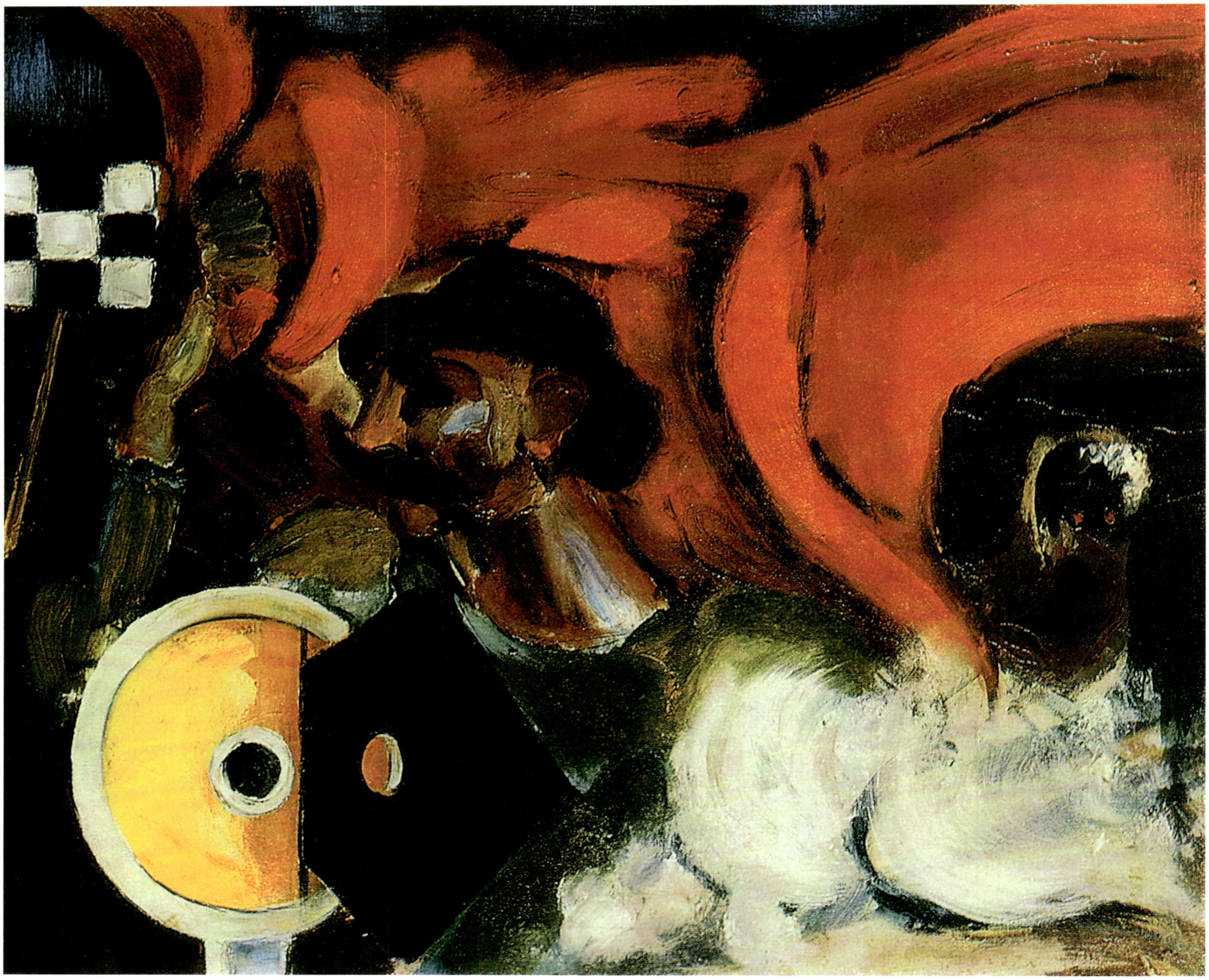

Henri Le Fauconnier

(Hesdin, 1881 – Paris, 1946)

Enrolled first in the Parisian studio of academic John Paul Laurens, then in the Académie Julian, Henri Le Fauconnier presented his works along with those of the Nabis and the Fauves at the Salon des Indépendants in 1905. Translating the influences of these movements, his subjects detached themselves from their support by a thick margin, recalling the contours of Matisse while including corresponding deaf tonalities that illustrated the artist's singularity.

In Brittany, living in Ploumanac'h, Le Fauconnier painted several canvases in this vein, in which, in a form of syncretism, he united Nabism and Fauvism. His rocky landscapes were already drawn along overly simplified lines, but soon the geometric analysis of forms and volumes that he developed led him to attach himself to Cubist research.

His *Portrait of Pierre Jean-Jouve* from 1909 had a notable influence on Gleizes, whom he had befriended while attaching himself to the Abbaye de Créteil group and with whom he collaborated again, along with Metzinger and Léger, in the group in Puteaux. If Le Fauconnier participated in Exhibition Room 41 of the Salon des Indépendants in 1911, his "physical Cubism", as Apollinaire described it, did not go beyond the fragmentary analysis of volumes.

Upon becoming director of the Académie de la Palette, Le Fauconnier separated himself from Gleizes and Metzinger the following year and oriented his art towards the work of Léger before returning to Expressionism, a movement he had already encountered some time beforehand.

His participation in avant-garde exhibitions in Russia (the Golden Fleece Exhibition in 1908 and 1909 and the Jack of Diamonds Exhibition, 1910) had led Le Fauconnier to compose an introduction for the Neue Kunstlervereinigung exhibition that took place in Munich. The personal vision expressed in this work, which describes Cubism leaning towards a more spiritual art—spirituality with which Gleizes experimented towards the end of his life—already marked this progression towards Expressionism.

Moving to the Netherlands in 1914, Le Fauconnier continued on this path by instructing Flemish painters while studying Rembrandt and local Gothic painting. In 1915, he painted *The Signal* (opposite), somewhat anticipating the social expressionism of the post-war period. Then, in the tradition of the old masters, he committed himself to the creation of grand pictorial cycles, in which all Cubist influence disappeared and which no longer had a place his modern world. The artist abandoned Expressionism, as he had Cubism some years before, and, in a final about-face, returned to the realistic painting that had marked his beginnings.

Upon his return to France in 1920, Le Fauconnier no longer participated in the Parisian artistic life that had so influenced him a decade earlier and devoted himself to his art in total indifference to the excitement that surrounded him.

Henri Le Fauconnier,
The Signal, 1915.
Oil on canvas, 80 x 99 cm.
The State Hermitage Museum,
St. Petersburg.

Notes

1. A. Liberman, *The Artist in His Studio*, London, 1969, p. 113.
2. A. Salmon, *La Jeune peinture française*, Paris, 1912, p. 42.
3. D.-H. Kahnweiler, *My Galleries and Painters*, New York, 1971, p. 39.
4. D. Ashton, *Picasso on Art. A Selection of Views*, New York, 1972, p. 163.
5. P. Daix, "Il n'y a pas 'd'art nègre' dans Les Demoiselles d'Avignon", *Gazette des Beaux-Arts*, October 1970, p. 267.
6. A. Malraux, *La Tête d'obsidienne*, Paris, 1974, p. 131.
7. See the works of Daix, Johnson, Steinberg and Rubin in the Selected Bibliography.
8. G. Burgess, "The Wild Men of Paris", *The Architectural Record*, New York, XXVII, May 1910, pp. 400-414.
9. J. W. von Goethe, *Dichtung and Wahrheit*, Book 9.
10. A. Malraux, *op. cit.*, p. 17.
11. J. Gonzáles, "Picasso sculpteur", *Cahiers d'art*, Paris, 1936, vol. 11, p. 189.
12. P. Daix, J. Rosselet, *Le Cubisme de Picasso. Catalogue raisonné de l'œuvre.* 1907-1916, Neuchâtel, 1979, p. 169.
13. *Ibid*, pp. 9, 183-184, 187, 188.
14. L. Steinberg, "Resisting Cézanne: Picasso's Three Women", *Art in America*, November-December 1978, p. 120.
15. E. Fry, *Cubism*, New York, Toronto, 1966, p. 18; W. Rubin, "Cézannism and the Beginnings of Cubism", *Cézanne, The Late Work*, New York, 1977, p. 7.
16. D. Ashton, *op. cit.*, p. 116.
17. D. Vallier, "Braque, la peinture et nous", *Cahiers d'Art*, October 1954, p. 16.
18. P. Daix, J. Rosselet, *op. cit.*, pp. 227f (intr. 8), 233 (intr. 9).
19. J. Golding, *Cubism: A History and an Analysis*, 1907-1914, Boston, Mass., 1968, p. 15.
20. D. Vallier, *op. cit.*, p. 16.
21. S. Fauchereau, *La Révolution cubiste*, Paris, 1982, p. 26.
22. J. Golding, "Cubism", *Concepts of Modern Art*, ed. N. Stangos, London, 1981, p. 55.
23. D. Ashton, *op. cit.*, p. 62.
24. *Ibid.*, pp. 59, 60.
25. R. Penrose, *Picasso: His Life and Work*, London, 1958, p. 160.
26. P. Daix, *La Vie de peintre de Pablo Picasso*, Paris, 1977, pp. 102, 103.
27. G. Chulkov, "Demons and Contemporaneity (Some Ideas on French Painting)", *Apollon*, 1914, Nos. 1, 2, p. 74 (in Russian).
28. J. Flamm, *Matisse on Art*, New York, 1978, p. 134.
29. D. Ashton, *op. cit*, p. 5 (interview with Marius de Zayas, 1923).
30. R. Penrose, "Introduction", *Picasso: Sculpture, Ceramics, Graphic Work* (exhibition catalogue), London, 1967, p. 10.
31. I. Aksenov, *Picasso and His Environs*. Moscow, 1917, p. 18 (in Russian).
32. D. Vallier, *op. cit.*, p. 14.
33. *Ibid.*, p. 16.
34. "Ce n'est pas d'après nature que je travaille, mais devant la nature, avec elle." Cf. E. Tériade, "En causant avec Picasso", *L'Intransigeant*, 15 June 1932, (quoted from D. Ashton, op. cit., p. 18). Another quotation in Ashton's book (p. 19) reads: "Like the Chinese, the Mexicans, I work not after nature, but like her."
35. J. Golding, *Cubism: A History and an Analysis. 1907-1914*. Boston, Mass., 1968, p. 88; E. Fry, *op. cit.*, p. 60 (first published in J. Metzinger, "Note sur la peinture", *Pan*, October-November 1910, pp. 649-651).
36. W. Rubin, E. L. Johnson, R. Castleman, *Picasso in the Collection of the Museum of Modern Art, New York*, 1972, p. 72.
37. R. Rosenblum, "Picasso and the Typography of Cubism", Picasso in Retrospect, *Icon*, 1980, pp. 33-47, 183-188 (notes).
38. E. Fry, "Braque, Cubism and the French Tradition", *Braque: The Papiers Collés*, Washington, 1982, p. 49.
39. F. Garcia Lorca, *On Art*, Moscou, 1971, p. 100 (from the lecture "The Poetic Image of Dons Luis de Góngora", 1926).
40. F. Gilot, C. Lake, *Life with Picasso*, New York, 1965, p. 71.
41. Ya. Tugendhold, "The Shchukin Collection of French Paintings", p. 35; Ya. Tugendhold, *The First Museum of Modern Western Painting (The Former S. I. Shchukin Collection)*, p. 128 (slightly abridged).
42. G. Chulkov, *op. cit.*, 1914, p. 32; Ya. Tugendhold, *op. cit.*, 1923, p. 120.
43. I. Aksenov, *op. cit.*, pp. 24, 26.
44. *Ibid.*, p. 18.
45. *Ibid.*, p. 44.

Bibliography

Aksenov, Innokenty. *Picasso and Environs.* Moscow: Tsentrifuga, 1917.

Ashton, Dore and Pablo Picasso. *Picasso on Art: A Selection of Views.* New York: Da Capo, 1972.

Baumann, Felix Andreas. *Pablo Picasso: Leben und Werk.* Stuttgart: Hatje, 1976.

Barskaya, Anna and Antonina Izerghina. *The Hermitage Collection of French Painting from the Second Half of the 19th to the Early 20th Century.* Moscow: Aurora, 1975.

Burgess, Gelett. "The Wild Men of Paris," *Architectural Record.* New York: May 1910, Vol. 27.

Chulkov, Georgy. "Demons and Modern Life," *Apollon, No.1-2.* St. Petersburg: 1914.

Dagen, Philippe. *Picasso.* New York: Monacelli Press, 2008.

Daix, Pierre. "Il n'y a pas "d'art nègre" dans les Demoiselles d'Avignon," *Gazette des Beaux-Arts.* Paris: October 1970.

—. *La Vie de peintre de Pablo Picasso.* Paris: Seuil, 1977.

— and Joan Rosselet. *Le Cubisme de Picasso. Catalogue Raisonné de l'Oeuvre Peint 1907–1916.* Neuchâtel: Alan Wofsy Fine Arts, 1979.

Fauchereau, Serge. *La Révolution cubiste.* Paris: Denoël, 1982.

Flam, Jack, ed. *Matisse on Art.* New York: Penguin, 1978.

Fry, Edward F. "Braque, Cubism and the French Tradition," *Braque: The Papiers Collés* (catalogue of the exhibition). Washington, D.C.: National Gallery of Art, 1982.

—. *Cubism.* London: Thames & Hudson, 1966.

Gilot, Françoise and Carlton Lake. *Life with Picasso.* New York: McGraw-Hill, 1964.

Goethe, Johann Wolfgang von. *From My Life: Poetry and Truth, Vol. 9.* Princeton: Princeton University, 1994.

Golding, John. "Cubism," *Concepts of Modern Art* (Nikos Stangos, ed.). London: Thames & Hudson, 1981.

—. *Cubism: a History and an Analysis, 1907-1914.* Boston: Boston Book & Art Shop, 1968.

Gonzales, Julio. "Picasso sculpteur," *Cahiers d'Art* (Christian Zervos, ed.). Paris: 1936, Vol. 11.

Kahnweiler, Daniel-Henry. *My Galleries and Painters.* New York: Viking Press, 1971.

Kuznetsova, Irena and Evgenia Georgievskaya. *French Painting from the Pushkin Museum.* Moscow: Aurora, 1980.

Liberman, Alexander. *The Artist in His Studio.* London: Random House, 1969.

Malraux, Andre. *La Tête d'obsidienne.* Paris: Gallimard, 1974.

McCully, Marilyn, ed. *A Picasso Anthology: Documents, Criticism, Reminiscences.* London: Princeton University, 1981.

Metzinger, Jean. "Notes on Painting," *Pan.* October–November 1910.

Penrose, Roland. "Introduction," *Picasso: Sculpture, Ceramics, Graphic Work* (catalogue of the exhibition at the Tate Gallery). London: Arts Council of Great Britain, 1967.

—. *Picasso: His Life and Work.* London: Gollancz, 1958.

— and Elizabeth Cowling. *Visiting Picasso: The Notebooks and Letters of Roland Penrose.* London: Thames & Hudson, 2008.

Rubin, William. "Cezannism and the Beginnings of Cubism," *Cézanne: The Late Work.* New York: Museum of Modern Art, 1977.

Salmon, André. *La Jeune Peinture française.* Paris: Société de Trente, 1912.

Steinberg, Leo. "Resisting Cézanne: Picasso's Three Women," *Art in America, No. 66.* November 1978, pp. 114-33.

Tériade, Efstratios. "En causant avec Picasso," *L'Intransigeant.* Paris: June, 1932.

Teuber, Marianne L. "Formvorstellung und Kubismus oder Pablo Picasso und William James," *Kubismus.* Cologne: Kunsthalle, 1982.

Tinterow, Gary. *Master Drawings by Picasso.* Cambridge: George Braziller, 1981.

Tugendhold, Yakov. "La Collection française de S. I. Chtchoukine," *Apollon, No. 1-2.* 1914.

Tugendhold, Yakov. *The First Museum of New Western Painting (The Shchukin Collection).* Moscow: Petrograd, 1923.

Vallier, Dora. "Braque, la peinture et nous," *Cahiers d'Art 29, No.1.* Paris: 1954.

Index